Kiddie Lit

PUBLISHING FOR THE WORLD
125 Years
THE JOHNS HOPKINS UNIVERSITY PRESS

Kiddie Lit

The Cultural Construction of
Children's Literature in America

Beverly Lyon Clark

The Johns Hopkins University Press
Baltimore and London

© 2003 The Johns Hopkins University Press
All rights reserved. Published 2003
Printed in the United States of America on acid-free paper
Johns Hopkins Paperbacks edition, 2005
9 8 7 6 5 4 3 2

The Johns Hopkins University Press
2715 North Charles Street
Baltimore, Maryland 21218-4363
www.press.jhu.edu

*The Library of Congress has cataloged the hardcover edition of this book
as follows:*

Clark, Beverly Lyon.
   Kiddie lit : the cultural construction of children's literature in
America / Beverly Lyon Clark.
       p.   cm.
Includes bibliographical references and index.
   ISBN 0-8018-6900-5 (acid-free paper)
     1. Children's literature, American—History and criticism—Theory,
etc.   2. Children's literature, English—Appreciation—United States.
3. Children's literature, American—History and criticism.   4. Children—Books and reading—United States.   5. Children in literature.
6. Canon (Literature)   I. Title.
PS490 .C56 2003
810.9′9282 — dc21   2002013939

ISBN 0-8018-8170-6 (pbk.)

A catalog record for this book is available from the British Library.

For Rog, Adam, and Wendy

Contents

Figures

Preface

When I was in graduate school in the 1970s I wouldn't have been caught dead reading children's literature. I remember my astonishment when a friend talked at a party about recently reading Cherry Ames. (Fifteen years later my friend would be elected president of the Children's Literature Association.) It's true that I was writing a chapter on Lewis Carroll for my dissertation. But Carroll was different. One of my graduate advisors, a Victorianist, had published on *Alice's Adventures in Wonderland* in a highly regarded academic journal. And my short chapter on Carroll was simply a stepping-stone to the heart of my thesis, which addressed the uses of a kind of fantasy in contemporary U.S. fiction for adults.

It was nevertheless thanks to the Carroll chapter that I was invited to teach Children's Literature soon after I came to Wheaton College—thanks to that and a commonly held belief, to which I too subscribed, that anyone could teach such a course. What was there to know? Certainly I was not impressed by the scholarship I then started to read. Much of it seemed to focus on bibliotherapy, providing lists of books to help a child deal with the death of a pet or a grandparent, with a science project on dinosaurs, with the stigma of wearing glasses. Most of the books seemed to be annotated bibliographies in paragraph form.

In the early 1980s I was edging into children's literature scholarship by way of Louisa May Alcott. She was a crossover writer, someone whose work could appeal to adults and could be read in adult terms. I could read *Little Women* the same way I read works written for adults; I could try to revalue Alcott the same way feminist critics had been revaluing Kate Chopin and Charlotte Perkins Gilman.

It took me a long time, nevertheless, to appreciate that children's literature as a field deserved the kind of rethinking that feminists had been according works by and about women. One breakthrough for me was reading Jacqueline Rose's *The Case of Peter Pan, or The Impossibility of Children's Fiction* (1984). Here was a work that used the insights of post-Freudian poststructuralism to illuminate children's literature and used children's literature to illuminate our relationship to language, given that both childhood and language are often posited as pure points of origin. Another breakthrough was Perry Nodelman's *Words about Pictures: The Narrative Art of Children's Picture Books* (1988). Suddenly I could see what a distinctive genre the picture book was: this one form of children's literature, at least, offered a new vista for criticism, one requiring attentiveness to the visual and to the interaction between the visual and the verbal. What else, I wondered, could children's literature offer to literary criticism? Then, in 1990, Bernard Mergen, editor of *American Studies International*, invited me to prepare a bibliography of book-length criticism of children's literature. Preparing this bibliography (not fully annotated, though in paragraph form) took a great deal more time than I'd anticipated—of course—and it helped me see some of the varied strands of thinking about children's literature, as practiced by librarians, grade-school teachers, and professors.

That bibliography was the first real step toward this book—the first step toward some understanding of the institutional underpinnings of the field of children's literature, an understanding most fully outlined here in Chapter 3. What surprised me most in my research was how differently children's literature was regarded in the nineteenth century—how highly the nineteenth-century cultural elite regarded such literature, compared to the twentieth-century cultural elite. Although children's literature has continued to garner enthusiasm in the popular press, the more academic gatekeepers all but ignored it in the middle to late twentieth century. In Chapter 1 I examine some of the current ways in which scholars seem to think, or not think, about childhood and children's literature. In the next chapter I examine how, around the turn of the century, what was considered literary shifted from the kind of practice epitomized by Frances Hodgson Burnett to the kind epitomized by Henry James. At a time when women and children were increasingly conflated in the critical imagination, Burnett addressed both. And estimates of her work plummeted. James disdained both, in his criticism at least, though he engaged with women and children more imaginatively and indeed fruitfully in his fiction. Estimates of his work soared. Chapter 3 likewise treats the shift around the turn of the century, but instead of examining the thinking of and response to two paradigmatic authors I examine institutional shifts, in the context of the increasing professionalization of literary study.

In subsequent chapters I turn to case studies of particular authors and continue my pursuit of Alcott and Carroll—and also pursue Mark Twain, L. Frank Baum, J. K. Rowling, and Walt Disney—in order to gauge the trajectories of their critical reputations. Let me stress that I'm not attempting to cover the full field of response to children's literature; rather, I'm attempting to undertake representative soundings of the varied ways in which our culture has constructed children and children's literature. I've chosen authors for whom there are, by and large, long trajectories of published response—and hence the works tend to be novel length and to varying degrees canonical within children's literature, hence also middle class and white. Children's literature has been primarily middle class and white since its inception, though one can find traces of alternative viewpoints in most of the bodies of work I examine. In any case, the case studies I pursue allow me to engage in depth with the nuances of response, both popular and critical, to representative and influential boys' books, girls' books, and fantasies.

In these case studies I turn to reviews and other responses, early and late: my primary materials are not so much the literary texts as the responses to those texts. I am interested in the meanings of childhood and children's literature in American culture—and hence primarily in issues of reception. Since I'm examining published responses, and especially responses by elite literary gatekeepers, my focus is on the responses of adults: I attend more to what adult gatekeepers have thought than to what children have actually read, though the latter issue does surface from time to time. (More generally, I'd argue that all the works I examine continue to be read with interest by many children.) I hope that in mapping responses to, say, *Huckleberry Finn* I will be able to offer new insights into the work itself, but my path to those insights is to scrutinize what critics and others have said, or not said, in the nineteenth century, in the early twentieth century, and in recent decades, to scrutinize the shifts in what is considered suitable for children and for adults, what is noticed or ignored in these varying historical contexts. I want to find out what people thought about the authors and their works and why. For we now think about these figures rather differently from how they were thought of when their works first appeared.

I quote from the reviews and other criticism at some length. In part that's because many twentieth-century critics have seemed unwilling to listen to what nineteenth-century observers said about the audience for, say, Twain and Alcott and what they said about childhood and adulthood. When critics cite differences between nineteenth- and twentieth-century responses, they generally don't pursue them but treat them as anomalous. I pursue these differences through close readings of the reviews and other criticism—to acknowledge their complexity, to probe for their contradictions, to unearth what they say overtly about children and what they imply about juvenility.

In short, I'm not just providing a history of the various critical and popular receptions. I'm also analyzing the responses, reading them symptomatically, if you will. Cultural critics are fond of untangling the interplay among race, class, and gender in literary and other texts. But what if we add age to the mix? How does age complicate the kaleidoscope of difference within the text, one term reinforcing another, substituting for another, pushing another aside, perhaps skewing its import? Analyzing the shifting responses to Alcott and other authors can help us see how socially constructed the current—usually dismissive—views of literary critics are. Recognizing these shifts can help us revalue children's literature, rethink its place in the academy, or accelerate a shift that has already begun, even as we acknowledge that age is not just a simple term of difference but is always complicated by race, class, gender.

I am grateful to Marya De Voto, Monica Edinger, Sue Gannon, Tina Hanlon, Linnea Hendrickson, Deidre Johnson, Bonita Kale, Betsey Shirley, Sanjay Sircar, Sue Standing, Laureen Tedesco, David Watters, and various members of the Children's Literature: Theory and Practice e-mail list, including Michael Joseph, its founder and owner, for leads and stimulating insights. I much appreciate the assistance of Marcia Grimes and Martha Mitchell in tracking down elusive interlibrary loan materials and of Ken Davignon and Dee Jones in reproducing images. I am particularly grateful to Jan Alberghene, Roger Clark, Mike Drout, Shelley Fisher Fishkin, Margaret Higonnet, Uli Knoepflmacher, Roz Ladd, and Mitzi Myers for responding to drafts of chapters. And I want to thank Rog, Adam, and Wendy for constantly pushing me in my thinking about children and children's literature.

Some of the ideas and phrasing in Chapter 1 derive from earlier attempts to chart ways in which we devalue children and childhood, in "Fairy Godmothers or Wicked Stepmothers? The Uneasy Relationship of Feminist Theory and Children's Criticism," *Children's Literature Association Quarterly* 18 (Winter 1993): 171–76; and "On Ignoring the Hidden Laughter in the Rose Garden; or, How Our Anxiety of Immaturity Enables Us to Belittle Students," *Feminist Teacher* 8 (Spring/Summer 1994): 32–27. I have also drawn, in Chapter 3, on a few pages of "Kiddie Lit in Academe," *Profession* (1996): 149–57, and, in Chapter 5, on a few pages of the introduction to *"Little Women" and the Feminist Imagination*, ed. Janice M. Alberghene and Beverly Lyon Clark (copyright 1999, reproduced by permission of Routledge, Inc., part of The Taylor & Francis Group), xv–liv. I am grateful to the editors of the journals, the Children's Literature Association, the Modern Language Association, and the press for permission to reprint those portions. The Beinecke and Houghton Libraries have graciously granted permission to quote from unpublished Alcott letters and nineteenth-century clippings in the Alcottiana collection.

Kiddie Lit

CHAPTER ONE

Kids and Kiddie Lit

Let us all agree to stop using what is, in my view, an unacceptable phrase, namely, "kiddielit" and/or "kidlit." My rationale is as follows: these terms diminish the work we do in the eyes of others; one can use diminutives within a family but they may convey the opposite intent to outsiders.

— KAY VANDERGRIFT

I hate the term too, but my experience has been that it's usually used by people who are genuinely enthusiastic about children's books but somewhat embarrassed about it. More self-deprecating than insulting, if you see what I mean. They mock themselves before you can mock them.

— WENDY E. BETTS

To call children "kids" is bad enough—most of them are surely not the devilish little animal-like goats-in-training that "kid" implies. To call children "kiddies" is even worse: downright condescending, and more than a little supercilious. And to dismissively label as "kiddie lit" the often wonderful and always intriguing writing that I and a number of other people . . . have chosen to devote our professional academic life to is nothing more than insulting.

— PERRY NODELMAN

Nicknames are always unsatisfactory, but they are convenient. Their acceptability has to do with the person who uses them. "Kiddie lit" coming from a respectful colleague is ironical; coming from a skeptical or ignorant colleague, it is pejorative. The name is not the issue, the attitude of the namer is.

— STEPHEN ROXBURGH

We value childhood. But we also dismiss it. We value the image even as we ignore the reality. We love the Gerber babies, the Pillsbury Doughboy, the Michelin-tire kids, to whom we can condescend, preferably in falsetto. Advertisers foreground images of babies even when their product has little to do with children (automobile tires? interior painting? nursing homes?). Every package of toilet paper in my local supermarket features the head of an adorable baby, too young to use the product herself. Presidential hopefuls traverse the United States kissing babies and seize photo ops that capture them hugging their children. Yet the position of the country's children provides little cause for jubilation. There may be recent small gains—fewer teen pregnancies in the past couple of years, a decrease in juvenile homicides. But for many years children in the United States have been overrepresented among those living in poverty, at a rate almost 50 percent higher than the national norm. In 1999, when the U.S. poverty rate was 11.8 percent, 16.3 percent of the nation's children were living in poverty.[1]

In the realm of children's literature, trade publishers happily turn to children's books to bolster their revenues, yet contemporary critics have been slow to take children's literature seriously and treat it canonically. How many lists of the great books of the twentieth century—lists that do not specifically limit themselves to children's books—include such children's classics as *Charlotte's Web* and *Where the Wild Things Are*?[2] The term *kiddie lit* captures our culture's ambivalence toward children and children's literature: dismissive? self-mocking? pejorative? ironical? In subsequent chapters I will map changing attitudes toward children's literature in the last century and a half, changes that allowed *kiddie lit* to emerge as a derogatory term and changes that allow us, now, to revalue, to ironize, it. In this chapter, however, I focus on some of the broader ways in which academics have expressed ambivalence toward childhood in recent decades. A few established mainstream critics, such as James Kincaid and Eve Kosofsky Sedgwick, Margaret Higonnet and U. C. Knoepflmacher, have treated childhood with respect. But many—most of those who do not consciously specialize in children's literature—have been dismissive. Let me give some examples.

In her brilliant *Sensational Designs*, which has remapped the history of American literature, Jane Tompkins wants to redeem from obscurity many of the works she focuses on: *Uncle Tom's Cabin*, *The Wide, Wide World*, and *The Last of the Mohicans*. She wants to redeem them from, in particular, having "come to be thought of as more fit for children than for adults."[3] In the process of choosing works that "offer powerful examples of the way a culture thinks about itself, articulating and proposing solutions for the problems that shape a particular historical moment,"[4] it's hard for a cultural critic to avoid what could be considered—what I would consider—literature for children.[5] Yet Tompkins wants to erase this part of the readership.

In the magnificent, wide-ranging *Heath Anthology of American Literature*, now in its fourth edition, the editors reach out across boundaries buttressed by gender, race, ethnicity, and class—but not age. Even anthologies that aim for the fullest and most diverse coverage avoid that which is associated with children. Or, more precisely, none of the literature that the editors of the *Heath Anthology* include is addressed specifically to children, even if the headnotes for individual authors frequently indicate that the author has written children's stories. When the editors make a token inclusion of an author who is best known for her children's fiction—Louisa May Alcott—they reprint not an excerpt from *Little Women* but one from a "flawed" novel presumably for adults or one of her short stories for adults.

In Carol McPhee and Ann FitzGerald's compilation *Feminist Quotations*, there are more index entries under "Woman/Women as child" than under any similar heading ("Woman/Women as servant," "Woman/Women as redeemer"). The authors of the entries hardly applaud such a comparison, whether the quotation expresses Elizabeth Oakes Smith's outrage, in 1853, that wives and mothers are "coerced like unmanageable children," or Vicki Pollard's, in 1969, that doctors force "women into the role of helpless, stupid, ridiculous little girls."[6]

In *The Political Unconscious*, the astute Marxist critic Fredric Jameson lists "the oppositional voices of black or ethnic cultures, women's and gay literature, 'naive' or marginalized folk art, and the like."[7] Juvenility figures as a metaphoric subtext, set off in quotation marks, naiveté subordinated to the "folk," ontogeny subordinated to phylogeny. Later, when "children's literature" erupts more concretely in his text, its force is again dissipated as metaphor: from the perspective of some utopian future, "our own cultural tradition—the monuments of power societies . . . as well as the stories of fierce market competition and the expressions of commodity lust and of the triumph of the commodity form—will be read as children's books, recapitulating the barely comprehensible memory of ancient dangers."[8]

Finally, in her classic essay in women's studies, "Is Female to Male as Nature Is to Culture?" Sherry B. Ortner challenges the way women have been subordinated through their association with nature. Then, as if eager to deny a kind of guilt by association between women and children, she assumes a "natural" association between children and nature: "Infants are barely human and utterly unsocialized; like animals they are unable to walk upright, they excrete without control, they do not speak. Even slightly older children are clearly not yet fully under the sway of culture."[9] Women shouldn't be degraded by being associated with nature, but it's "natural" for children to be.

This brief sampling of academic evasion and condescension suggests how ready we adults are to dismiss the young, whether it's a case of being a closet juvenilist or of using children as stepping-stones or mere metaphors. I greatly admire the work of these scholars—as I do that of the others whom I consider in this chapter. In fact it's because their work is so good and so influential that their dismissive stance toward children and adolescents is so troubling.

I'm also troubled because I know that I too am guilty of thinking in ways that belittle youth. I'm sometimes tempted, for example, to differentiate between my mostly traditional-age college students, on the one hand, and faculty, administrators, and staff, on the other, by thinking of the latter as "the adults." I've heard colleagues use such language in the context of noting that the students are not yet "mature" enough to do certain things—such as being fully self-governing in the dormitories and sticking to a group decision about acceptable levels of noise at 3 A.M. Yet how many self-styled adults, thrust into a group-living situation where we had not chosen our fellows (or even where we had), would consistently behave in the mature manner we want to consider adult? Those of us who teach young people need to think about what is happening when we claim adulthood for ourselves and not for our students.

We need as well to think about the ways in which our language and culture validate "maturity." As Jacqueline Rose argues in a superb study of the nexus of childhood and language, "Classifying 'otherness' in language as infantile or child-like reduces it to a stage which we have outgrown, even if that stage is imbued with the value of something cherished as well as lost."[10] I want us to think what it means when we use metaphors of immaturity to devalue something. I'm thinking of phrases like "immature response," "childish reaction," "adolescent quarreling," "juvenile behavior," "puerile thinking." I want us to recognize our own "anxiety of immaturity." Not that I want to return to calling women, including traditional-age college students, "girls"; not that I want to call black men, including traditional-age college students, "boys." Given the way our culture currently constructs childhood, we cannot afford to call any adult a child.

Yet I would like to see us revalue the status of childhood. We may never reach a point where the use of the terms *girl* and *boy* would be universally acceptable and even desirable because of a genuine respect for childhood and youth; we may never succeed in making the term *kiddie lit* unequivocally positive. But I would like to see those of us who consider ourselves adults work at imagining children as peers. I'm not asking that we treat children entirely as our equals— I'm not saying that seven-year-olds should have drivers' licenses.[11] Yet if we try to imagine children as peers, we can start to question some of our kitchy-kitchy-koo condescension, some of our temptation to be dismissive by means of the discourse of infantilization. I want here to pose questions, to question our indulgence in age discrimination and point out how it permeates our thinking, intersecting with gender, race, and class, before going on, in subsequent chapters, to explore the significance of these questions for the ways in which we think about children's literature.

In this chapter I'd like to raise questions that touch on the complicated relationship between feminism and childhood. I focus primarily on feminism, partly because it's what has grounded my own thinking about children and children's literature, and in many respects the current wave of feminism has fostered a new receptiveness to children.[12] There are many affinities between feminist theory and theorizing about children. Lissa Paul has pointed to a common ground between women's and children's literature, a shared content of entrapment, a shared language of otherness or deceit.[13] Perry Nodelman has argued that children's literature is a kind of women's writing, a way of finding "an alternative way of describing reality" while still accommodating "social responsibilities."[14] Margaret Higonnet explores the ways in which both women and children have been treated as Other.[15] Certainly most of those who write, edit, buy, and critique children's literature, at least in this century, are women—in striking contrast with the situation of women who have written for adults. As of 2001, only 37 percent of Pulitzer Prizes awarded for fiction had gone to women, and only 8 percent of the Nobel Prizes in literature. Yet women have won 67 percent of the Newbery Medals for outstanding work in children's literature. Given the receptiveness of the field to women, it is not surprising that children's literature has addressed some women's concerns.

The relationship between feminism and childhood is complicated, however, because adulthood is exactly what many feminists want to claim. The cost of doing so is that we grind children under our heels. In 1844 Margaret Fuller complained, "Now there is no woman, only an overgrown child."[16] In 1991 Susan Faludi castigated the desire to return to the nest, what she called cocooning, in part because the latter term "suggests an adult woman who has regressed in her life cycle, returned to a gestational stage. It maps the road back from the feminist journey, which was once aptly defined by a turn-of-the-century writer as 'the attempt of women to grow up.'"[17] If Sandra M. Gilbert and Susan Gubar have argued that women have suffered not so much from a Bloomian "anxiety of influence" as from a more fundamental "anxiety of authorship," a fear of being unable to create, a fear that writing will destroy them,[18] then I would add that women (and other) critics also suffer from an "anxiety of immaturity." They—we—fear that literary creation will be so associated with procreation, and with that which is procreated, that we ourselves might be considered childish. And thus we become anxious to dissociate ourselves from immaturity. Yet as C. S. Lewis notes, "Critics who treat *adult* as a term of approval, instead of as a merely descriptive term, cannot be adult themselves. To be concerned about being grownup, to admire the grownup because it is grownup, to blush at the suspicion of being childish—these things are the marks of childhood and adolescence."[19]

Much of the feminist ambivalence about children is related, I think, to an ambivalence about motherhood. Some feminists have indeed included children in their analyses. In the 1970s a working-class feminist mother such as Tillie Olsen could point out how rare it was for a woman who is a mother also to be a writer.[20] Adrienne Rich, while stressing the recurring question "But what was it like for women?" nevertheless acknowledged the child's "authentic need" and also a common oppression: "In a tribal or even a feudal culture a child of six would have serious obligations; ours have none. But also, the woman at home with children is not believed to be doing serious work; she is just supposed to be acting out of maternal instinct, doing chores a man would never take on, largely uncritical of the meaning of what she does. So child and mother alike are depreciated, because only grown men and women in the paid labor force are supposed to be 'productive.'"[21]

Other feminists, such as Kate Millett, were more specifically resisting male theories and theorists, especially Freud—for whom, with respect to maternity, "it is as if . . . the only self worth worrying about in the mother-child relationship were that of the child."[22] Even now, an oppositional stance toward motherhood persists among liberal feminists, those who favor equal rights, such as Faludi, who in *Backlash* blames media brainwashing for any resurgent interest in motherhood. By the late 1970s a more celebratory stance became possible for cultural feminists such as Nancy Chodorow, who see commonalities among women, whether biologically or socially induced, and often find one in maternal nurturing. The most clear-sighted such theorist, with respect to children, would seem to be Sara Ruddick. In theorizing what she calls maternal thinking, she acknowledges the complexities of mothers' relationships with children, the need for mothers—and fathers—"to assume, at least temporarily, a child's-eye view, in the interest of acting effectively with and on behalf of their children," and the way in which attentive maternal love "lets difference emerge without searching for comforting commonalities, dwells upon the *other*, and lets otherness be."[23]

Most feminists who celebrate motherhood, however, continue to be ambivalent about—or to ignore—children. It is indeed important for feminists to claim subjectivity for mothers, especially if, as E. Ann Kaplan claims, "slippage from talking about the mother to talking from the child's perspective seems endemic" to discussions of motherhood, and especially if "at the very moment when mother-subjects start to gain attention, this subjectivity is displaced into concern with the foetus."[24] Yet "the child's perspective" often undergoes a curious slippage too. For feminist critics characteristically mask their ambivalence about children by eliding two meanings of *child*—as defined by age and as defined by family relationship—so that they can continue talking about themselves and hence ignore real children. Consider the following usage: "I find that while psychoanalytic feminism can add the female child to the male, allowing women to speak as daughters, it has difficulty accounting for the experience and the voice of the adult woman who is a mother."[25] The female child invoked at the beginning of the sentence turns out to be a woman, an adult speaking as a daughter—not a young human. Marianne Hirsch goes on to claim, "I would submit, then, that to a large degree feminist theorizing itself still argues from the position of the child or, to a lesser extent, that of the childless adult woman and continues to represent the mother in the terms originally outlined by Freud"[26]—as if she has in fact been differentiating between the child and the (childless) adult woman. I would submit otherwise: feminist theorizing has rarely recognized, let alone addressed, the position of the child. We are so adult centered that the only child we adults can see is ourselves; we do not recognize what it means to attend to children's perspectives.

Consider Julia Kristeva's musings on motherhood. In the late 1970s, even as she deconstructed gender, she was celebrating the possibilities of dissidence and associating it with "the sudden surge of women and children in discourse."[27] But like other feminists she was more concerned with maternity than with juvenility, with the impact not on the fetus but on the gestating mother of "an identity that splits, turns in on itself and changes without becoming other."[28] This emphasis is largely reiterated in "Stabat Mater," a more concerted theorizing of maternity: even when she allows some space for her own memory of childhood, she is (like other psychoanalytic theorists) more concerned with the adult whom that child will become than with the child as child. As Jane Flax has remarked of such feminist theory as addresses child rearing, "we still write social theory in which everyone is presumed to be an adult"; we tend to include "almost no discussion of children as human beings or mothering as a relationship between persons. The modal 'person' in feminist theory still appears to be a self-sufficient individual adult."[29]

Or consider Janice Radway's musings on a more metaphoric maternity. Radway explores how criticism of the Book-of-the-Month Club, at its inception in the 1920s and since, is implicated in questions of cultural authority, in particular the authority of the autonomous, educated individual. She argues that the discourse of the debates was "deeply gendered."[30] The language of feeding—"forced feeding, pabulum, and indiscriminate consumption," with its "distant echoes of maternal force and infantile regression"—demonized the purveyors of middlebrow culture as maternal and therefore "disgustingly effeminate" (523, 524, 515). Then Radway quickly transfers the effeminacy from purveyors to consumers: the mass audience is conceived as "passively feminine" (524). Only several paragraphs before the end does she seem to recognize that if the purveyor of culture is imaged as maternal, the consumer might be not so much female as juvenile. Only then does Radway decide to question "the necessity of . . . discriminating the child from the man"; she decides to respect "the persistence of childish interests and pleasures within the business of adult life"; she urges "a more dialectical recognition of the fact that the child always haunts us" (526). So when in the same three paragraphs she seeks "a less patriarchal discourse" (526), I can envision a patriarch who is not just husband but also father. But then, abruptly, Radway drops the discourse of juvenility in the final paragraph, returning to that of gender alone. She has been looking, she tells us, at the "necessary connection between rationality, thought, analysis, and gender" (526). Patriarchy reverts to a merely masculine authority when she refers to "a patriarchal society organized by a phallic divide" (526). In short, Radway has had a glimpse of childhood but can't focus on it for long—it disappears from her analysis.

Another strand of literary and cultural theorizing that could acknowledge children is one that explores the parameters of marginality. Yet children are still so thoroughly beyond the pale that feminists who theorize marginality have paid virtually no attention to the position of children. Such critics often address race, gender, class. But rarely age, rarely children. The most expansive lists of social cleavage—such as Susan Stanford Friedman's adumbration of, in addition to gender, "categories like race, ethnicity, religion, class, national origin, sexual preference, abledness, and historical era"[31]—usually fail to include age. Even those that do include age do so only to acknowledge the elderly, ignoring the young. And such failures occur even though, in Friedman's case, the discursive narrative that leads up to her list tells of the divergent views of two generations of academic feminists, with their varying allegiances to theory and activism: the experience that grounds her sense of multiple contexts is profoundly shaped by differences associated with age. Friedman's essay does open some theoretical doors for attention to children. The "categories like" construction acknowledges that her list is not definitive. Significantly, she provides an accessible account of theorizing that attempts to move beyond poststructuralist anti-essentialism to a provisional recognition that the concrete realities of biology, socialization, economics—including, I would stress, age—cannot just be deconstructed but do in fact affect who we are. Still, like almost all other theorists of marginality, feminist and otherwise, Friedman is blind to children. As Mitzi Myers notes, specifically with respect to children's literature, "Even feminist criticism (despite women's historical and biological implication in childhood) looks askance at the child text: it's nobody's baby. Gender has long since been in; generation (except when it has to do with adult sexuality) remains out. Cross-dressing is hot; cross-writing is not."[32]

In general, we tend to assume that what it means to be a child, what it means for an adult to understand a child—never mind what it means to write from or for a child's perspective—is unproblematic. In "Apostrophe, Animation, and Abortion," Barbara Johnson incisively addresses the ramifications of abortion and apostrophe, what it means for a poet who is a mother to address what could be considered a dead child and, more specifically, how gender renders problematic the distinction between addressor and addressee. Yet she concludes by assuming that what it means to be a child is unproblematic: "Whether or not one has ever been a mother, everyone participating in the debate has once been a child. Rhetorical, psychoanalytical, and political structures are profoundly implicated in one another. The difficulty in all three would seem to reside in the attempt to achieve a full elaboration of any discursive position other than that of child."[33] Social critics would not assume that someone who has left the working class still has an uncomplicated appreciation of what it means to be of the working class; similarly with a transsexual's appreciation of what it means to be female, or male; or the appreciation of someone who passes for white of what it means to be black. Yet Johnson can still assume that anyone who was once a child requires no "elaboration" of what it means to be in the "discursive position . . . of child"—not recognizing that, as children's author Avi notes, "it is impossible to be a child once one becomes an adult."[34] Johnson is, like Ortner, like Fuller and Faludi, using children as stepping-stones.

Here I want to enlarge on the stepping-stone phenomenon. The danger of using other marginalized groups as stepping-stones came relentlessly home to me when teaching an American literature course: advocacy of the rights of one group often seems to entail metaphorically castigating another. Consider Fuller's put-down of children as she makes a case for "woman in the nineteenth century." Consider Nathaniel Hawthorne, in *The Scarlet Letter*, where he seems to compensate for creating an uncharacteristically positive portrait of a not entirely submissive woman by, in part, reducing her child wholly to a symbol. Consider Henry David Thoreau, who allies himself, civilly disobedient, with "the fugitive slave, and the Mexican prisoner on parole, and the Indian come to plead the wrongs of his race," even as he metaphorically disavows boys and women: his fellow townsmen try to punish him by putting him in jail, "just as boys, if they cannot come at some person against whom they have a spite, will abuse his dog. I saw that the State was half-witted, that it was timid as a lone woman with her silver spoons."[35]

Women of color have long been aware of the stepping-stone phenomenon. Among African Americans I think of Audre Lorde, Barbara Smith, and Alice Walker, all speaking out against white feminists who were ignoring race—who were using women of color and their labor as stepping-stones—early in the current wave of feminism.[36] It's resistance of this type that led Walker to prefer the term *womanist* to *feminist*, the former embracing willfulness, loving other women, sometimes men, and being "committed to survival and wholeness of entire people, male *and* female."[37]

In fact, the stepping-stone phenomenon appears to be a particular temptation for white members of the middle class, who tend to prize individualism over group effort and hence to image their gain as another's loss. Among other groups this phenomenon seems less common. Many African Americans, for example, seem to have a rather different relationship to juvenility than do many European Americans. On the one hand, it has been important to deny associations of the race with juvenility—with men being called boys. On the other hand, an emphasis on working for the entire race, and for its future, has generally meant more respect for children. Because African Americans have "had to work in concert for survival," the maternal role may be shared by mothers, sisters, aunts, grandmothers, cousins, not to mention fictive kin,[38] and with so much mutual implication in mothering there has been less temptation to devalue children. Black women are unlikely to identify motherhood as "a serious obstacle to our freedom as women," bell hooks argues. "Historically, black women have identified work in the context of family as humanizing labor, work that affirms their identity as women, as human beings showing love and care, the very gestures of humanity white supremacist ideology claimed black people were incapable of expressing."[39] Certainly I have found less evidence of the devaluing of children and childhood in the writings of African-American women than in the work of their white counterparts.[40] Walker, for instance, seeks an egalitarian mode with her daughter: "We are together, my child and I. Mother and child, yes, but *sisters* really, against whatever denies us all that we are."[41]

Another adumbration of the stepping-stone phenomenon is the deployment of stages in developmental theories. For all that we like to think of the United States as a youthful society and often indulge in considerable nostalgia for childhood, we nonetheless disparage what we consider childish and, as Bruce A. Ronda notes, "have insisted on development as the prime motif of identity," have insisted "on a rhetoric of growth."[42] I grant that stage theories can be useful: they can help parents and educators recognize that young people are not necessarily miniature adults but may, for instance, reason and approach abstraction differently. But we need to avoid reifying the stages that theorists have posited. Stage theories become pernicious when entire categories of people seem to be stuck at an early stage. In Lawrence Kohlberg's scheme of moral development, for instance, women tend to be stuck at the third of six stages—leading Carol Gilligan to question why Kohlberg didn't recognize women's "different voice."[43] In Freudian theory, lesbianism is constructed as an adolescent stage, a phase through which one moves to more "mature" relationships[44]—as if one can't be a mature lesbian.

Stage theories are also pernicious because of the way they are inherently dismissive of childhood, the way they image childhood as something other than the ideal, something that needs to be grown out of. As sociologist Barrie Thorne points out, "Conceptualizing children in terms of development and socialization imposes an adult-centered notion of structured becoming upon children's experiences."[45] We see as universal the stages that our age-graded social practices help to create—when, in fact, cultures simply "project onto infants and young children a nature opposite to the qualities prized in adults. Valuing independence, we define children as dependent. . . . The Japanese, who value interdependence, define infants as too autonomous and needing to be tempted into dependence."[46]

If, as Jacqueline Rose points out, we have constructed childhood as "part of a strict developmental sequence at the end of which stands the cohered and rational consciousness of the adult mind," then "children are no threat to our identity because they are, so to speak, 'on their way' (the journey metaphor is a recurrent one). Their difference stands purely as the sign of just how far we have progressed."[47] What would happen if we imaged each "stage" as valuable in its own right? Or what if "we redescribe development as not simply the progressive acquisition of linguistic, and therefore moral, competence," so that "we may be better able to nurture in children the necessary to-and-fro between the inarticulate and the articulate selves; a to-and-fro that might be sustainable throughout life rather than having its last gasp during adolescence, or in mystical states"?[48] How impossible would it be for educators—whose very goal is change, whose foundational assumption is that any given "stage" before the final one is not inherently desirable—to reimagine stages and development? Perhaps the emphasis of some feminist pedagogies on empowering students is a step in the right direction: maybe if the teacher encourages "her women students to say what she does not expect them to say and perhaps would rather not hear,"[49] she would validate not only the students individually but also their "stage" in the life cycle.

One of the attractions—but also dangers—of using metaphors of maturity is that, like stage theory, they image youth as something one grows out of. *Immature* does not seem like a permanent label. At least it does not seem permanent from the perspective of the person doing the labeling. I remember how frustrating it felt, though, to be told that I'd grow out of something—out of adolescent angst perhaps—when at the time it was all there was and I couldn't imagine myself into another place.

Maybe such labeling is particularly pernicious when we do it as a more "polite" way of rendering other distinctions. In the United States we have difficulty finding a language with which to talk about class. So instead we often individualize class characteristics and attribute to people of a class other than our own features of juvenility. Members of the middle class are apt to think of members of the working class, whether they act out aggressions or seem shy, as adolescent. Members of the middle class may also apply to male members of the upper class, the idle rich, a term that doubly inscribes juvenility: *playboy*.

Someone from a different class background simply strikes us as less mature. A friend of mine from a country-club background describes another friend, someone with whom she works, someone whose work she respects, as immature. The second woman is from a working-class background, the only person in her family who has ever gone to college (a state college, rather than the private school attended by the other woman), someone who survived the educational system by playing the role of the quiet "good girl," someone who hasn't had much practice in making "cultured" small talk. Yet is she really less mature—or does maturity have a different meaning for her? She may be socially mobile, no longer exactly working class, yet she probably doesn't think of herself as less mature but might think of others as more, say, artificial. I think too of my aunt. She was loud, wouldn't take anything from anyone, not even her boss at the paper mill. When I was an upwardly mobile adolescent I was embarrassed by what I thought of as her stridency; I thought she was even more adolescent than I was. Yet why should speaking up for one's rights be considered immature?

Or consider the following academic example: in an important ethnographic study of college-student writers, Stephen M. North addresses the experiences of three students in a philosophy class. He doesn't want to make value judgments, saying whose writing is good and whose is not—he claims that "none of these uses of writing for learning is the 'right' one, the most 'appropriate.'"[50] So he finds a covert means of judging, by speaking of the "academic maturity" of the students, relying on William Perry's staging of intellectual and moral development.[51] One student, one of nine children in a family recently arrived in New York from Jamaica, is associated throughout North's study with metaphors of immaturity: from her "innocent approach to philosophy" to her "ingenuous" first paragraph (and likewise her oral report); from her "general naivete" (which would lead one to expect her "to fall into the lower range of Perry's developmental scheme") to the way the course serves for her as "a kind of initiatory rite"; from her seeming to be "the greenest of novices," "an acolyte" when it comes to philosophy, to the discussion of how the problem in one of her writings is that she focuses on "a sort of generalized child."[52] North knows better than to foreground this student's race or class background to explain what he evades calling weakness. Instead he uses youth as a euphemism for weakness: he makes her Other by associating her with childhood. It's a move that allows her to grow out of her less desirable traits (assuming she leaves her class of origin). It's also a move that enables North to underscore that these traits are indeed less desirable, even inappropriate, while thinking he's according the student respect.

I could go on and on with examples of how those of us who are white and middle class continue to use associations with immaturity to disparage or otherwise fail to acknowledge childhood in its own right. I haven't touched on how, say, New Critical strategies for criticizing a work of literature, strategies that privilege complexity, make it difficult to find anything to say about seemingly "simple" works, or how structuralist and poststructuralist approaches succeed in dehumanizing children. Addressing such critics' "terror of Kiddilit," Ursula K. Le Guin explains, "If you want to clear the room of derrideans, mention Beatrix Potter without sneering."[53]

All these ways of belittling and ignoring have a profound impact on the ways in which we think about children's literature. As Perry Nodelman has noted, what criticism of children's literature has been accepted in the academy all too often perpetuates a fatuous vision of childhood and children's literature as a fount of wisdom for adults, "making it a health-giving medicine for adults sick of too much maturity" and implying that "today's children are too stupid to know how to be children."[54] And as Margaret R. Higonnet has said of "the multiple social functions" of children's literature, "First, it preserves a realm of purity, dependence, and ignorance; in turn, it also preserves the system of 'high' literature by fencing out the presocialized and subversive Other, marked by a subliterary verbal code and polluting didacticism; and it inscribes a myth of origins and integrity whose nostalgic appeal has, if anything, intensified in an age dominated by a philosophy of fragmentation and alienation."[55]

Children's literature has low status in literary criticism, even though it would provide a fertile testing ground for investigating the kinds of questions Higonnet raises and for such critical approaches as a reader-response one. Where else would one find a body of literature in which virtually none of those who write it, none of those who edit or publish or market it, and very few of those who buy it, belong to its ostensible audience? Study of children's literature also raises questions about canonicity, commodification, censorship—to mention only three rich cruxes.[56]

My goal in this book is to begin exploring our cultural construction of childhood as it affects children's literature—as it affects how we respond to children's literature, even determining which works we consider to be for children (under which rubric I include both works for children and those for adolescents, collapsing a distinction that has fully taken hold only in the last few decades). For our views of childhood and children's literature are very much constructed, as an attentive reading of nineteenth-century pronouncements makes clear—in that long-gone era when American elite and popular culture had not yet divorced. Children's literature hasn't always been designated *kiddie lit*. I want, in short, to revalue what has been dismissed as kiddie lit.

My project is not that of New Critical literary criticism, exfoliating the wonders of the texts of children's literature. Instead I concentrate on matters of reception—on reception by Americans, specifically by American adults. I seek to understand how children's literature has been received, especially in the U.S. academy but also in more popular venues, and how that reception reveals the construction and deployment of childhood. Reception is notoriously elusive, never easy to gauge. To map some of its contours I look at nineteenth- and twentieth-century reviews and other critical statements, statements in the popular press, polls of favorites, and lists of recommended reading. And I try to plumb for subtexts as I analyze these bits of evidence, to probe for underlying values and expectations. With one exception, the works I've chosen have long and often quirky trajectories: each chapter, except the last, begins in the nineteenth century and ends in the twentieth, tracing one of the many paths that reveal changing receptions and perceptions. My aim here is not to be comprehensive but to offer suggestive case studies, in-depth analyses that, in concert, reveal the complexity of changing attitudes toward children and children's literature.

First, in Chapter 2, I look at two key turn-of-the-century figures, whose opposed trajectories and whose divergent rhetorical deployments of childhood provide a glimpse of how attitudes toward childhood were changing at a pivotal moment. Chapter 3 steps back from individual trajectories to look at some of the changing institutional frameworks associated with literature—the shift in the arbiters of elite culture from genteel editors to professional scholars, the increasing bifurcation of high and low culture. The next four chapters offer case studies tracing the vagaries of reputation for authors associated with three key genres of children's literature: the boys' book, the girls' book, and (in two chapters) fantasy. The final chapter offers some reflections on other recent developments in the construction of childhood in the twentieth century.

CHAPTER TWO

What Fauntleroy Knew

The positioning of children and childhood in the American imagination has changed over the last two centuries. Children and childhood were less segregated from adults and adulthood in the nineteenth century, before the split between high culture and low, before literary authority shifted from genteel editors to the professoriate, as I detail in Chapter 3. Respected nineteenth-century critics were less likely to engage in maneuvers like those outlined in Chapter 1, more likely to acknowledge "that the novel in our civilization now always addresses a mixed company, and that the vast majority of the company are ladies, and that very many, if not most, of these ladies are young girls" with "vivid, responsive intelligences, which are none the less brilliant and admirable because they are innocent."[1] Those are the words of William Dean Howells, the most influential editor and critic of the late nineteenth century.

In this chapter, in my first assay of the nineteenth-century critical climate in the United States, I turn to the work of two key figures, and the responses to their work, to illustrate some of the ways in which child and adult audiences were bifurcating by the end of the century. I track the critical trajectories of the two writers as I do for other figures in later chapters, but here I also trace the writers' very different rhetorical deployments of childhood at a key moment in the cultural positioning of the child—to uncover the secrets that the authors and their works can reveal.

Frances Hodgson Burnett, born in England in 1849, later emigrating to the United States, benefited from the conjuncture of audiences in the nineteenth century, writing "serious" literature for adults, popular literature for adults, and, overlapping with the last, literature for children. By the beginning of the twentieth century, however, she was no longer treated as an important writer. Henry James, born six years earlier in the United States, later emigrating to England, marks the turn-of-the-century shift in sensibility in an opposing way: ever the serious writer, he campaigned to create a preserve for serious writing uncontaminated by popularity or juvenility.

Before 1885, when she published *Little Lord Fauntleroy*, Burnett enjoyed notable critical acclaim. In 1877, when she published *That Lass o' Lowrie's*, the *New York Herald* proclaimed, "There is no living writer (man or woman) who has Mrs Burnett's dramatic power in telling a story."[2] The *Atlantic* praised her "deep insight into human suffering and aspiration" and predicted that she would take a place "among the few eminent women novelists whom we distinguish from good masculine novelists only that we may pay them an added reverence."[3] Burnett reveled in finding herself at the back of the February *Scribner's* "in a line with Bret Harte and Edward Everett Hale, authors of 'three remarkable serials by American writers!'"[4] As an obituarist noted almost fifty years later, "Everybody read [*That Lass o' Lowrie's*], and a great future was predicted for the author."[5]

Her next several novels received high praise as well. The editor and poet Richard Henry Stoddard claimed in 1881, "She impresses me as understanding her suffering and sinning characters as fully as Dickens ever understood his—as having a more genuine affection for them, and as never at any time caricaturing them."[6] Alfred, Lord Tennyson, claimed that a passage in *Through One Administration* (1883) was "the finest piece of English he had ever seen."[7] An essayist in the *Century* in 1883 called Burnett one "of the seven writers who hold the front rank to-day in general estimation," along with Henry James and William Dean Howells.[8] That same year, a writer for the London *Quarterly Review* declared Burnett's *Louisiana* (1880) "one of the most charming sketches which any imaginative writer has produced for years past . . . —a book which Nathaniel Hawthorne might have been proud to call his own."[9]

In July 1886 the *Critic* listed Burnett as one of a hundred (actually 107)

"American authors perhaps worthiest of being read by their fellow-countrymen of the present day," one of only eleven women so named.[10] Five months later, in a review of *Little Lord Fauntleroy*, Louisa May Alcott rejoiced that Burnett, one of "our best and brightest," had written a book for children or, more precisely, for both children and adults, a book that would "do the old as much good as the young."[11] In 1893 the readers of the *Critic* voted *Little Lord Fauntleroy* one of the forty "greatest" books "yet produced in America, or by Americans": it ranked thirty-third, behind *Little Women* but ahead of *Tom Sawyer*, *Huckleberry Finn*, and anything by Henry James, none of whose works appeared on the list.[12]

Yet the publication of this same *Little Lord Fauntleroy*, as a serialized story in *St. Nicholas* in 1885, in book form in 1886, and finally as a dramatization in 1888, was a watershed for Burnett. The book was a runaway best-seller, one of the three best-selling titles in the United States in 1886.[13] In 1893 it was second only to *Ben-Hur* as the book most likely to be held by American public libraries.[14] In 1898 it was one of only two American children's books chosen most often—one of the top seventeen—in a readers' choice poll conducted by the British *Pall Mall Gazette*.[15] As Jerry Griswold points out, *Fauntleroy* spoke, in the United States, to a post–Civil War need for myths of domestic harmony, myths that would legitimate American genealogy: if prevailing cultural myths before the war created an America that was a child rebelling against a father, "the new myth of national identity had to be based on the conviction that if the nation was to endure, it was necessary to reassert order and continuity rather than flounder in a state of perpetual revolution."[16] If the American Cedric Errol is the legitimate heir to his grandfather, the Earl of Dorincourt, and hence is Little Lord Fauntleroy, then America is legitimate heir to Britain.

The huge success of this attempt to address children as a significant part of her audience encouraged Burnett to focus more on writing for children. It also catapulted her into the thick of popular culture in a way that her earlier fiction, popular though it was, did not. Her enthusiastic admirers ranged from nine-year-old Helen Keller ("I do love Lord Fauntleroy," she wrote in a fan letter) to British Prime Minister William Gladstone (who made a point of being introduced to Burnett and of telling her that Fauntleroy "charmed him").[17] Then-canonical American man of letters Oliver Wendell Holmes addressed Burnett as a writer "who knows the human heart," adding, "You should be very happy, for what mother ever had such a darling child as your dear little Lord Fauntleroy?"[18] Similarly canonical James Russell Lowell wrote to Burnett's publisher, "I should be glad to have the author know how much pleasure the book gave me.

I feel so grateful to her."[19] Mark Twain embroidered a slipper for the actress who starred in the American dramatic version; Lewis Carroll gently teased his favorite child actress about coveting the role.[20] As a critic wrote in 1918, *Fauntleroy* "caused a public delirium of joy."[21]

This was a delirium that Burnett both encouraged and deprecated. She proudly claimed that illustrator Reginald Birch based his drawing of Fauntleroy on her son Vivian but also strenuously denied that her boys, even if they sometimes sported Fauntleroy curls and lace, were foppish.[22] She happily endorsed playing cards and candy, and there were Fauntleroy toys and writing paper, a chocolate Fauntleroy, Fauntleroy perfume—not to mention the popularity of his trademark velvet suit with sash and lace collar and cuffs. Fauntleroy was an early merchandising phenomenon.

For decades after the appearance of *Fauntleroy*, Burnett continued to be praised in the popular press. In 1888 a reviewer of Burnett's dramatization of the novel noted, "Mrs Burnett shows herself a true poet though her Pegasus may be a rocking-horse."[23] As late as 1924 the *New York Times* obituarist described her as "one of the foremost of novelists," "the world-famed creator of 'Little Lord Fauntleroy,'" someone noted for "the literary timbre of her works," with a style at once simple and witty.[24] The obituarist in the London *Times* concluded, "It is chiefly, almost solely, by this idyll of child life that Mrs. Hodgson Burnett's name is known to the multitude of readers and theatre-goers. The story has a quality all its own. In her other books and plays Mrs. Burnett was less successfully Dickensian, sentimental, naïve. *Little Lord Fauntleroy* had for millions of readers and theatre-goers the compelling attraction of the laughter that is akin to tears."[25]

Yet at this time when "serious" and "popular" literature were beginning to separate, the popular success of *Fauntleroy* pushed someone who had previously been able to combine critical acclaim and a modicum of popular success into the second camp. Critics in elite venues were becoming less enthusiastic about Burnett's work, even though nineteenth-century custodians of high culture, including Holmes and Lowell, had commended *Fauntleroy*.

Burnett herself seems to have shifted in her goals during the final decades of the nineteenth century. Early in her career she wrote to an editor that she was "trying to please the critics" with her novel *Haworth's* (1879); by the late 1890s she was saying that she never read her critics.[26] Certainly she wouldn't have wanted to dwell long on the last review devoted to her work in the *Atlantic Monthly*: in 1896, her writing in *A Lady of Quality* (1896) was described as violent, her style as anachronistic, and the reviewer, finding it hard to be patient

Vivian Burnett (*above*). Reginald Birch's Fauntleroy (*opposite page*).
Vivian Burnett, *The Romantick Lady (Frances Hodgson Burnett): The Life Story of an Imag-*
ination (Scribner's, 1927); Reginald Birch, *Little Lord Fauntleroy* (Scribner's, 1886)

with "the sophistry of such a novel," concluded, "There are many striking scenes in the book and a great deal of brave language, but the artificiality of the morality of the tale eats into its literary virtue, and one feels that he has had an unpleasant time of it for nothing."[27] Seven years later, in what is apparently the last review of children's literature to appear in the *Atlantic*, H. W. Boynton played with the common reviewer's formula that a book was suitable for both young and old by referring briefly to *Fauntleroy* as "fit for the enjoyment of the sentimental and the humorless of any age."[28]

Enthusiasm in less elite venues was waning too. As early as 1897 a reviewer in the *New York Times* noted that "Mrs. Burnett's methods . . . have developed a singular crudity since the days of 'Louisiana' and 'That Lass o' Lowrie's.'"[29] Fourteen years later, in a sympathetic account of *The Secret Garden*, a *New York Times* reviewer nevertheless castigated *Fauntleroy* for its "sloppiness of sentimentality," its "goody-goodiness and . . . artificiality."[30] The American Library Association may have included *Fauntleroy* in its 1904 *A.L.A. Catalog* of books recommended for public libraries, but not in its 1926 edition. Indeed, in the 1920s Burnett was called the "high priestess of the omnipotent cult of the second-rate," someone whose "mesmerized sycophants proclaim her pot-boilers to be masterpieces."[31] Boynton described a late novel as "the apotheosis of Burnettian slush."[32]

Overall, dismissive twentieth-century critics in the *Atlantic* and elsewhere were reacting to Burnett's championing of romance in a critical climate more receptive to "realism,"[33] to her popularity in general, and to her popularity with women and children, at a time when what would soon be called highbrow was defining itself as opposed to the effeminate and the juvenile. Twentieth-century critics were also reacting to associations with what they would construe, after George Santayana coined the term in 1911, as the "genteel tradition" (with which they would often associate the feminine). For many, the figure of Fauntleroy epitomized genteel and feminine culture.

What Fauntleroy had provided in the late nineteenth century was, first of all, a figure that spoke to both adults and children, a figure that maintained the conjuncture of child and adult audiences, even if older readers were likely to justify their interest by stressing what younger readers would learn from Fauntleroy.[34] A contemporary reviewer who announced that "Cedric is a creation of which Mrs. Burnett may justly be proud" might well add, "He made nobles and ancestors real to American children and taught English children the value of truth, honesty, and friendship, even when offered by an illiterate groceryman and a wild, rough street Arab."[35] The writer also admitted the appeal of Fauntleroy's story to adults—how eagerly "fathers and mothers waited their turn to touch the magazine" in which the story first appeared, waiting for "the favored first reader" to relinquish it.[36] This was, furthermore, a time when genteel readers expected all fiction to provide models for emulation. To be considered suitable for children, a work might be held to such a standard with some stringency, but all literature was expected to nourish our aspirations for the ideal.

As for the ideals that Fauntleroy embodied, he provided—to both elite critics and general readers—a brilliant, albeit contradictory, synthesis of competing ideals of masculinity, including those of the Christian gentleman, the self-made man, the masculine primitive, and the newly emerging social-economic elite.[37] It's worthwhile dwelling briefly on Burnett's portrayal of these four ideals, for her synthesis accounts, I think, for some of the immense power of her creation with her contemporaries.

The values of the Christian gentleman—self-control, courtesy, sincerity, and above all service to others—had dominated middle-class culture in the early nineteenth century and continued to hold sway in such cultural institutions as publishing and education, but elsewhere during the late nineteenth century they were in decline (caricatured, for instance, in Mark Twain's Sid Sawyer). The genteel would be increasingly associated with the feminine and would be further castigated as a result of this association. In fact, it would be so strongly associated with the feminine that what often speaks most powerfully to twentieth-century critics—eager to disavow genteel ideals—is the femininity of the nineteenth-century cultural elite.[38] Some of the most astute recent critics writing on Fauntleroy emphasize his embodiment of femininity[39]—which is true enough. But at this time when gentility had been claimed by the middle classes yet still had filiations with the aristocracy, and the genteel ideals for youth and age were indistinguishable, gender traits cannot be isolated from those associated with class and age.[40]

Contrasting with the ideal of the Christian gentleman is that of the self-made man, who valued industry, frugality, initiative, and getting ahead. Industry could be compatible with the norms for gentility, particularly if industry were in the service of moral goodness, improving "each shining hour," like "the little busy bee" in Isaac Watts's popular verse. One should undertake "labor *and* self-denial," as the founder and longtime editor of the *Nation*, E. L. Godkin, stressed.[41] Frugality could perhaps be compatible too. But taking individual initiative in order to advance oneself was not. As George H. Calvert noted in *The Gentleman*, a book popular enough to go into at least three editions between 1863 and 1866, "The habit of acquisitive eagerness, of buying as cheap and selling as dear as possible, eats into the marrow of manliness; and overreaching and crafty trafficking are as incompatible with gentlemanhood as perjury is with piety."[42] The favorite term of opprobrium among the genteel—expressing that which is to be avoided—is "vulgarity," a term that could often be applied to the self-made man.

The norms associated with the third ideal, that of the masculine primitive, include valuing the instinctual, physical strength, and personal force. These could be reasonably compatible with the norms for the self-made man, though the masculine primitive attended more to the physical man than to the economic one. The norms were much less compatible with those for the Christian gentleman, for whom cultured civility was decidedly superior to brute force or instinct. As for favorite terms of opprobrium, both the self-made man and the masculine primitive would be anxious to dissociate themselves from the feminine—and were inclined to consider both the genteel cultural elite and the economic elite sissies.

Members of the social-economic elite were concerned with material display, with fashion and conspicuous consumption, and aped the hereditary privileges of the European aristocracy. These values are at odds with those of the self-made man, who valued frugality over fashion and believed in democratic equality. They are likewise at odds with those of the Christian gentleman, who valued inner worth over outer display and who considered himself democratic: birth was presumably not a bar to the gentility of inner worth—one simply needed somehow to be educated in its values, whether "through home influences" or "through schools or colleges," to quote Godkin again.[43]

I should stress that the four strands of masculinity I've sketched here are ideal types, constellations of values circulating in nineteenth-century American culture. No real person could embody a single ideal, however much he tried—there was too much slippage among the four strands of values. Late-nineteenth-century masculinity was unstable, contested, contradictory. And hence anyone who seemed to reconcile these varied strands—if I may pursue a kind of post-structuralist analysis of historical discourses—would allay considerable cultural anxiety. Burnett succeeded in doing just that in *Fauntleroy*.

To a society that now looks upon Christian gentility as quaint, the genteel values may seem most salient in the figure of Fauntleroy. Certainly Cedric values service: when granted boons by the agent of his newfound grandfather, he wants nothing more than to provide shelter and clothing for the needy apple woman whom he has befriended and to set up Dick the bootblack in his own business. In keeping with genteel ideals, young Cedric exhibits manly self-control (uncomplainingly bearing himself "with excellent courage" when deprived of the presence of his mother, for instance)[44] and an innate courtesy and sincerity as well. He likewise bridges masculine and feminine, youth and age, this boy who is "a mixture of maturity and childishness" (75).

He also exhibits some physical prowess, winning a race with other boys in New York and, in England, rapidly becoming a fine horseman: in his efforts at riding he simultaneously exhibits the fearlessness ("Not much afraid, is he?") of the masculine primitive and the industrious determination ("I never see one stick on more determiner" [149]) of the self-made man. And as an American boy who lives frugally with his widowed mother but then suddenly becomes heir to wealth and title in England, he embodies other components of the various strands of masculinity as well. He may be "dressed in gal's clo'es" (195), as Dick, the book's clearest embodiment of the self-made man, forgivingly acknowledges.[45] Yet Cedric certainly gets rich quick, even if he is more likely to take initiative to help others than to help himself. And this self-proclaimed democrat acquires the hereditary privileges of the British aristocracy without having to ape them: the Van Dyck–style lace and knee breeches in which his mother has always dressed him seem to manifest not conspicuous consumption but inner worth, a prefiguration of his later status. As Anne Scott MacLeod has aptly noted, "*Little Lord Fauntleroy* combined the attractions of class society with a flattering view of the democratic personality and thus appealed greatly to Americans who wanted to believe themselves better than their less successful countrymen, as good as any aristocrat, and equal to anything."[46]

In short, Burnett forged a synthesis that seemed to resolve the contradictions among competing ideals, at this time of rapid industrialization, when the norms for masculinity were undergoing contested change. For this important cultural work she was repaid with considerable critical esteem and the immense popularity of her best-selling book (and the play based on it) and of the figure she had created, a figure whose narrative plausibility masks the incompatibility of the ideals he embodies.

And, of course, the way that Fauntleroy went on to figure in the popular imagination, the use of his material trappings, rang other changes on the constellations of values associated with masculinity. Boys were dressed as Fauntleroy as a way of presumably signaling their Christian gentility while in fact signaling wealth and conspicuous consumption—thus did consumer values overlay those of Christian gentility. And late-nineteenth-century boys eager to be promoted from knee breeches to trousers—as a way of signifying their access to maturity—would later remember the promotion as a disavowal not so much of youth as of gentility and of the femininity with which that gentility was increasingly associated.

Castigating Burnett in the twentieth century was a way of castigating things Victorian, of demonstrating that both criticism and the critics themselves had outgrown the lace and knee breeches of yesteryear. By the 1920s, the Fauntleroy phenomenon was generating considerable critical distaste. Robert Lee White dates the decline in popular enthusiasm to Thomas Beer's 1923 biography of Stephen Crane, which recounts Crane's giving to boys "tricked out" like Fauntleroy the money to cut their hair, and Crane's claim that "no kid except a sick little girl would like Lord Fauntleroy"—though I could also point to dismissals such as the already-cited 1911 review of *The Secret Garden*.[47] Certainly Burnett's death in 1924 called forth a spate of pieces in the *New York Times* that, if not wholly disparaging, were quick to relegate *Fauntleroy* to the past, to things Victorian.[48] Burnett's sister showed some of the prevailing unease when, the year after Burnett's death, she stressed that Burnett's son Vivian, model for Fauntleroy, "became a young American"—and she went on to quote from one of his mother's letters relating his trek through subzero weather to report a story: "Isn't that plucky for a boy who has grown up surrounded by every luxury and pleasure in life, who wore velvet and lace collars and had all he asked for?"[49]

White goes on to cite Fred Lewis Pattee's dismissal of Fauntleroy in the 1929 *Dictionary of American Biography* as an "insufferable mollycoddle" and James Hart's discussion in 1950 of how Fauntleroy "plagued little boys" of Des Moines and Detroit who were forced to wear Fauntleroy's "fussy costume."[50] In 1924 Irving Cobb proclaimed in a fictionalized memoir (in the chapter "Little Short Pantsleroy"), "*Little Lord Fauntleroy* infected thousands of the worthy matrons of America with a catching lunacy, which raged like a sedge fire and left enduring scars upon the seared memories of its chief sufferers—their sons, notably between the ages of seven and eleven."[51] And in 1927 John Nicholas Beffel, happily reporting on what he called "the Fauntleroy pestilence," claimed,

> In Davenport, Iowa, in the year of the Burnett play's opening, an eight year old burned down his father's barn because he was compelled to dress up in Fauntleroy fashion. In Madison, Wisconsin, a kid with brick colored curls battled in vain to be severed from them. After he had been inserted forcibly into velvet jacket and pants, he walked up to a policeman in front of the principal hotel there and deliberately kicked the bluecoat in the shins to call attention to his plight. In Worcester, Massachusetts, another victim of the plague traded off an expensive Fauntleroy suit to passing gypsies for some old clothes bearing patches which the local sufferer considered admirable.[52]

F. J. Harvey Darton, an influential historian of children's literature, lamented in 1932 that "the odious little prig in the lace collar is not dead yet."[53] As Francis Molson has noted, more attention seemed to be paid in the mid twentieth century to the "plague" or curse of Little Lord Fauntleroy than to anything else about Burnett—whether the blight was said to have afflicted small boys in general, actors who took on the role and were then stereotyped, or Reginald Birch, the original illustrator.[54] Burnett's "reputation as the author of *Little Lord Fauntleroy*," Marghanita Laski stated in 1951, "has far outshadowed any other she might deservedly have had."[55]

In John Rowe Townsend's words, "Instead of adding to its author's reputation, as it should," *Fauntleroy* "hangs albatross-wise round her neck."[56] It should have added luster to Burnett's reputation; as Laski states, it is "the best version of the Cinderella story in modern idiom."[57] The character of Fauntleroy does not deserve the dismissal he has often received, unread, in the twentieth century. Mark Spilka notes that *Fauntleroy* may have "essentialized certain assumptions of the genteel tradition about women and children which were then in jeopardy," but it also portrayed its hero not as a sissy but as "'strong' . . . as well as tender," as "fearless," as able to withstand pain, as someone with athletic drive and a "manly concern for others."[58]

It's curious that Fauntleroy was the target of so much vitriol. His sartorial style did not originate with Burnett or with Reginald Birch.[59] It's a throwback to the seventeenth century, as memorialized in the paintings of Anthony Van Dyck and again, a century later, in those of Thomas Gainsborough and others. At the beginning of the twentieth century, the most famous painting perhaps in the Western world (vying for that honor with *Mona Lisa*)—the one that in 1921 fetched the largest sum ever paid—was Gainsborough's *Blue Boy*.[60] Enthusiasm for *The Blue Boy* may well have been fanned by Fauntleroy, yet the public would have known that the painting came first. I have found no opprobrium attaching to *The Blue Boy*, however, in the popular press.[61] A work by a long-dead Master, no matter how foppish the style of the subject, was above reproach.

As the figure of Fauntleroy was becoming an object of scorn, Burnett's books for children were disappearing from lists of recommended reading. In 1922, in the *Bookman*'s list of "One Hundred Story Books for Children," only Burnett's *Lost Prince* appears, not *Fauntleroy* nor, for that matter, *The Secret Garden* or *A Little Princess*.[62] In four midcentury lists of recommended reading that I use as touchstones—the 1934 *What Shall the Children Read?* by the children's author Laura E. Richards; the 1947 *Children's Classics*, by the librarian Alice M. Jordan; the 1958 *Parent's Guide to Children's Reading*, sponsored by the National Book Committee; and the 1960 edition of *Good Reading*, sponsored by the College English Association—Burnett is not even mentioned.[63]

She had also lost popularity with general readers, especially by the 1920s. In a 1923 listing of the hundred books most circulated in American public libraries, many of them works of children's literature, only Burnett's adult novel *The Shuttle* appears, in a last-place tie.[64] In a 1936 listing of the 254 authors whose books were most circulated in Chicago-area libraries, many of them again children's literature, Burnett's name is fifty-seventh.[65] In surveys of children's reading in the 1920s and 1930s, Burnett and her work consistently rank below Louisa

Thomas Gainsborough's *Blue Boy* (1770)
Courtesy of the Huntington Library, Art Collections, and Botanical Gardens,
San Marino, California

May Alcott and Mark Twain: more precisely, Burnett ranks seventh, fifteenth, twelfth, and fifteenth, to put incommensurate surveys in chronological order.[66] And the highest finish for *Fauntleroy*, on these surveys, is twenty-eighth. Nowadays it's the rare undergraduate who has even heard of Fauntleroy (I'm lucky if one student in fifty raises a hand when I ask), and in my two decades of surveying students about their two or three favorite children's books, no one has ever mentioned *Fauntleroy*. A far cry all this from *Fauntleroy*'s second-place position in libraries in 1893 or its place as the third most-circulated book among fourth graders in New York City school libraries in 1913.[67]

That other children's classic by Burnett, *The Secret Garden* (1911), the one that critics would now rate more highly, was slow in gaining popularity. It may have been positively reviewed in the *New York Times*, praised for its author's "thorough understanding of the heart of childhood," "loving pleasure in the beauty of the out-of-doors," "skill in the management of simple materials," and "charm of style,"[68] but it didn't take the country by storm. *The Secret Garden* does not appear in Frank Luther Mott's listings of best- and better-sellers in *Golden Multitudes*. It wasn't even mentioned in Burnett's obituaries in the London *Times* or the *New York Times*, or in eulogies published in the leading children's magazine, *St. Nicholas*; nor was it named in Fred Lewis Pattee's entry on Burnett in the *Dictionary of American Biography* of 1929, though he mentions twelve of her other novels and claims that "she is at her best in her stories for juveniles."[69] And the only juvenile title by Burnett that appears in the *A.L.A. Catalog* of 1926, a list of ten thousand books recommended for library purchase, is *Sara Crewe*, an early version of *A Little Princess*.[70] Even in 1953 the pioneering children's book editor Louise Seaman Bechtel called *The Secret Garden* sub-literature, a landmark perhaps, but such a book is "not necessarily a rightful inheritance, however popular."[71]

Two latter-day book-length compilations of the favorite childhood reading of famous people are suggestive of the different trajectories of *Fauntleroy* and *The Secret Garden*—the rocketing then plummeting popularity of *Fauntleroy*, the slow but steady growth of a following for *The Secret Garden*. In the 1971 *Attacks of Taste*, a relatively highbrow list of famous people (including W. H. Auden, R. Buckminster Fuller, Margaret Mead; mostly male) mentions Burnett only once, and that one reference is to *Fauntleroy*. The novelist Robert Nathan situates his interest in such a "sentimental" book "in a very different age" from the present one, "the world before 1914."[72] The 1980 *Books I Read When I Was Young* includes statements from people famous in both highbrow and popular culture:

the editors invited contributions from figures named by schoolchildren as heroes. No one here mentions *Fauntleroy* as important in his or her childhood. But *The Secret Garden* is cited ten times—even more frequently than *Little Women*—by figures ranging from Anne Baxter to Joan Rivers, from Dick Van Patten to Charlotte Zolotow.[73]

If the 1924 obituary in the *New York Times* failed to mention *The Secret Garden* and called *Little Lord Fauntleroy* "the crowning achievement" of Burnett's career,[74] by 1961 a feature essay in the *New York Times Book Review* could name *The Secret Garden* "the best of Mrs. Burnett's books," thanks to its depth and its "dash of acidity."[75] Indeed, if critics and most adult readers were ignoring *The Secret Garden* in the 1920s and 1930s, the children polled in the four surveys cited earlier were not. In each of the surveys that specified individual titles, *The Secret Garden* outpolled *Fauntleroy*. It was starting to catch on. Another sign of grassroots popularity is that since 1949 there have been four film versions of *The Secret Garden*, three of them since 1987, and at least four musical adaptations, including an award-winning Broadway production in 1991–93.[76] By 1989 one edition of the book, that illustrated by Tasha Tudor, had sold more than four million copies.[77] During a sample six-week period in 1994, *The Secret Garden* was the third-best-selling chapter-book for children, behind books first published in 1993 and 1994, just ahead of *Charlotte's Web*.[78] It presumably continues to sell three hundred to four hundred thousand copies a year.[79] *The Secret Garden* has had a kind of secret, subterranean life comparable to that of *Little Women*, though perhaps its survival has been even more subterranean. When I compare notes on childhood reading with female friends and colleagues, *The Secret Garden* is usually the title that is mentioned as a breathless afterthought, the secret love. Marghanita Laski is not the only one to consider it "the most satisfying children's book I know," and Anne Scott MacLeod rightly asserts that "the Burnett book that passed from child to child, now as then, is not *Fauntleroy* but *The Secret Garden*."[80] I can't claim, as Alison Lurie does, that *The Secret Garden* is the most popular book in my college-level course,[81] but it comes close. *The Secret Garden* may even appeal more to girls today than does *Little Women*.

Why was *The Secret Garden* for so long such a well-kept secret? Its relative invisibility, early in the twentieth century, may reflect the success of Henry James and other critics in squelching the young and the feminine. For it was associated with both. And unlike *Little Women* it was first published at a time when gatekeeping critics were repudiating the young and the feminine; it didn't have a preexisting following to maintain at least some visibility. The increasing unease with *Fauntleroy* served to tarnish Burnett's reputation as well. Yet to the extent that *The Secret Garden* reached its target audience, it struck a chord.

Burnett's portrayals of childhood are often astute. If in *Fauntleroy* she speaks to an adult image of childhood (Cedric is not as sissy as he is sometimes imaged, but he is idealized), in *The Secret Garden* she conveys more complex portrayals of children, at least in Mary and Colin if not the idealized Pan figure, the laboring-class Dickon. As Laski notes, "I do not know of any children's book other than *The Secret Garden* that frankly poses this problem of the introspective unlikeable child in terms that children can understand and then offers an acceptable solution."[82] The spoiled and orphaned Mary works out that she is lonely by learning of the loneliness of a robin, without its parents, and then realizing that she too is lonely: "She had not known before that this was one of the things which made her feel sour and cross. She seemed to find it out when the robin looked at her and she looked at the robin."[83] And upon hearing of the death ten years earlier of her uncle's wife, this girl who had never been required to think of other people is reminded of "a French fairy story she had once read called 'Riquet à la Houppe.' It had been about a poor hunchback and a beautiful princess and it had made her suddenly sorry for Mr. Archibald Craven."[84] The portrayal of "the garden as a metaphor for the female body and place where female roles can be learned and rehearsed" may also make a "subliminal sexual appeal" to "prepubertal girls."[85]

It is of course true, as Jerry Phillips argues, that Burnett relies on class and imperial privilege to elevate the British child.[86] It is also true that Mary recedes in importance as the book progresses and Colin gains center stage. Heather Murray notes that Mary becomes less active, more of a spectator, until finally "she is named no longer—present but not present, ghostlike, a marking absence. When Colin and his father walk back to the house, we do not know: does Mary walk behind them? does she go back to the garden? or is she standing in some intermediate place, between the manor and the garden?"[87]

Still, the image that stayed with me, from my own childhood reading, was not of Mary or Colin but of the garden. Phyllis Bixler Koppes has unpacked many layers of meaning, the way Burnett has drawn on fairy-tale, mythic, and pastoral traditions.[88] I would not have been able as a child to spell out the layers of symbolic resonance, the way the garden draws upon—or can be read as drawing upon—the Edenic and the pagan, the Platonic and the georgic, the psychoanalytic and the colonial unconscious, maybe not even "Mistress Mary" and versions of "Cinderella." Nor was I a child particularly fond of growing things. But the garden and its secrets spoke to me. Unlocking the secrets hidden from Cedric Errol and Mary Lennox enables these child characters—and the reader —to make new family connections, fostering growth. And this increasing maturity does not entail putting away childish things, cutting off connections with what has gone before, but entails expanding one's sense of wonder and connection—as it would not for Henry James, for whom childhood and maturity were opposed, the presence of the one requiring the absence of the other.

In 1883 in the *Pall Mall Gazette*, James anonymously savaged Burnett's first play: "The play would be infantine if infants ever expressed themselves in falsetto."[89] He could think of no worse insult. Between her writing for children and her writing for women—not to mention her popularity and marketability—Burnett was all that James was rebelling against.[90] And sometimes quite explicitly. He visited her with some frequency in London in the early 1890s, and they continued to be on reasonably cordial terms, she more cordial than he. She wrote of him to her son in the 1890s, "He is a man who is so a gentleman and fine and kind in every instinct."[91] It is tempting to read between the lines of graciousness and persiflage in James's letters to her—when he addressed her as "Noblest of Neighbours, and Most Heavenly of Women!"—to find more than a mild irony, as he deftly evaded invitations when they were neighbors in Sussex.[92] In the 1883 review of her play he had said of the British production, "It would be unfair to criticise it seriously, it is so very primitive an attempt at dramatic writing."[93] In a letter two years earlier he had written of the American production that it "made one blush for the human mind."[94] In 1892 he referred to Burnett, after attending another play, as "a fatally deluded little woman"—the delusion was presumably with respect to the quality of the play—and later he called her the Mrs. E.D.E.N. Southworth of the current age.[95] The comparison was not a compliment.

In the early twentieth century, no one with critical stature was prepared to find value in *Fauntleroy* or even to notice *The Secret Garden*. In high culture, anything considered effete or feminine had to be squelched: not even silencing the feminine, as Burnett herself does in *The Secret Garden* when she increasingly relegates Mary to the periphery, spoke loudly enough to be heard.

In 1883, a critic in the London *Quarterly Review* claimed that Burnett had "given the world the best American novels of the present day."[96] The reviewer was explicitly comparing her work, pre-*Fauntleroy*, with that of Henry James, to his "Daisy Miller" and *The Portrait of a Lady*, lamenting the "philosophic instruction and dawdling sentimentality" of the James stories.[97] This judgment may not have been widely echoed at the time—though the *Century* essayist's placement of both Burnett and James in the "front rank" in 1883, cited earlier, suggests that it wasn't entirely anomalous. The British reviewer may have been writing partly out of nationalistic pique, in response to William Dean Howells's then-extravagant claim that James was superior to Charles Dickens and William Makepeace Thackeray. But the appearance of such a comment in a prestigious journal underscores that, in the 1870s and early 1880s, the critical standings of Burnett and James were more or less comparable. James may have been the one publishing work in the prestigious *Atlantic*, but both were promising young writers. Their reputations would soon diverge, Burnett successfully addressing a popular audience of adults and children, and James, failing to achieve great popularity, focusing more and more on an elite audience, one that would increasingly acknowledge him as the Master.

As Felicity A. Hughes has demonstrated, James played a key role at the turn of the century in the separating out of literature for children and literature for adults.[98] Yet even while he was making fine discriminations about the audience for fiction, in order to segregate literature for children and create an audience for his own works, he turned, in the late 1890s, to central child characters in his fiction. What he did, in effect, was to use children and childhood as stepping-stones for his own "mature" views, both in his adumbrations of the art of criticism and in his practice of the art of fiction—this author whose place in the canon of American literature was assured even before his death in 1916.

The judgment of the *New York Times* in 1916 was that James was "one of the most masterful writers of his generation," and subsequent judgments have by and large rated him even more highly.[99] True, he has had his detractors. In 1930 Vernon Louis Parrington, an influential early Americanist, claimed, "The spirit of Henry James marks the last refinement of the genteel tradition, the completest embodiment of its vague cultural aspirations."[100] James was not, in short, immune from the kind of critical disparagement—Parrington used the term *genteel* five times in his brief discussions of James—that so quickly attached itself to Burnett. Yet as Richard A. Hocks has claimed more recently, James's "massive corpus, or rather some part of it, comes in for a drubbing at regular intervals, though such attacks are always followed by a resurgence of new scholarship that obliterates the attack."[101] Whether the critical winds favor realism, modernism, or postmodernism, critics always find a good deal to say about James. For Cynthia Ozick, James is the one "great avatar . . . of modernism" who becomes, "as the years accumulate, . . . more and more compellingly, our contemporary, our urgency."[102] Critics may focus on different works at different times—do his final novels mark a decline of realism or a major phase for modernism?—but James continues to attract their attention.

He is one of only six authors to whom a full chapter is devoted in each of three landmark literary histories of the twentieth century: *The Cambridge History of American Literature* (1917–21), the *Literary History of the United States* (1948), and the *Columbia Literary History of the United States* (1988). Burnett is barely mentioned in any of them. He is likewise accorded a chapter in the influential *Eight American Authors: A Review of Research and Criticism* (1963). In that chapter, Robert E. Spiller suggests that James "has been the subject of perhaps more critical essays than any other American novelist."[103] Since 1963 James has been one of the five American novelists attracting the most attention in scholarly books, articles, and dissertations, racking up 1,672 citations, at last count, in the Modern Language Association's CD-ROM bibliography, outpacing Burnett by a ratio of twenty-eight to one.

James's practice of the novel has, furthermore, profoundly influenced twentieth-century writers, and his theorizing about the art of the novel has had, if anything, an even more pronounced influence on both writers and critics. A 1916 obituarist in the London *Morning Post* may have found the fiction "too often mannered and obscure" but called James "the greatest theorist on the novelist's art who ever wrote in English."[104] James's ideas about "the art of fiction"— to quote the title of one of his influential essays, a title that many contemporaries would have considered an oxymoron—set the terms for Anglo-American discussion of fiction in the early twentieth century and beyond. As noted recently in the influential *Johns Hopkins Guide to Literary Theory and Criticism*, his criticism also created "a new consumer, a new reader for fiction, one who might be convinced of the seriousness of prose fiction as an art form and be attuned to the technical strategies of its presentation."[105]

James's works were never wildly popular. Michael Anesko has demonstrated that they sold well enough for James to support himself, yet none appears in an 1893 listing of the 172 most circulated works of fiction in U.S. libraries or in a 1923 listing of 100 such works.[106] Nor did any sell enough copies to appear on Frank Luther Mott's lists of best- and better-sellers in the United States before 1945.[107] Although James figures on an 1886 listing of the worthiest American authors, an honor roll created by the editors of the *Critic*, his work is entirely omitted from a listing of "best American books" created by the readers of the same journal seven years later.[108]

Henry James frequently characterized the audience for literature that sold—literature by such a writer as Burnett—as childish. And I turn here to scrutiny of James's rhetorical deployment of childhood, in his nonfiction and fiction. I do so in part because his thinking was profoundly influential. His protestations and tropes, his condemnations and swerves, also register shifts that were occurring more broadly throughout the culture at the turn of the century.

In reviews and essays that he wrote throughout his career, James consistently used metaphors of juvenility—"puerile," "infantine," "jejune"—to disparage. "Heaven defend us from the puerile!" he exclaims in an early review,[109] an expostulation that functioned as a motto throughout his career, not least in his 1883 review of Burnett's play. He chafed against a public that seemed to him to be dominated by women and children. In 1866 he complains that the novel he is reviewing seems "written for children; a work below the apprehension of the average man and woman, or, at the very most, on a level with it, and in no particular above it"—a work therefore "stupid" and "dull."[110] In 1880 he notes that the novel in English "is almost always addressed to young unmarried ladies, or at least always assumes them to be a large part of the novelist's public. . . . Half of life is a sealed book to young unmarried ladies, and how can a novel be worth anything that deals only with half of life?"[111] In 1901 he regrets "the 'innocence' of literature," "the allowances that we understand works of imagination and of criticism . . . make to the 'young.'"[112]

Often James conflates women and children, as in his 1880 reference to "young unmarried ladies"—though in that essay he goes on to disassemble the conflation, in part, by characterizing the audience for the novel as "virgins and boys." But although he eventually laments that "great fortunes, if not great reputations, are made, we learn, by writing for schoolboys,"[113] boys do not figure greatly in his schemes of disparagement.

In fact, James very much admired the work of a nineteenth-century writer now considered one of the quintessential writers for boys. (The reference to "virgins and boys" echoes the title of a collection by this other writer, *Virginibus puerisque*.) In *Partial Portraits* James includes essays on such figures as Ralph Waldo Emerson, George Eliot, Guy de Maupassant, Ivan Turgenev—and Robert Louis Stevenson. This last essay, first published in 1887, hints at some of the ways in which James would soon borrow from Stevenson (or at least borrow from his own thinking about Stevenson), whether he praises the way *Treasure Island* (1883) not only "embodies a boy's vision" but also, uniquely, functions as "a study of young feelings" (as James's *What Maisie Knew*, with a shift in gender, would go on to do) or gently chastises Stevenson for providing too explicit an explanation of Dr. Jekyll's transformations (as James's *Turn of the Screw*, in hinting at the ghostly, would not).[114]

More crucially, the essay on Stevenson reveals the contours of James's own disparagement of youth—in this, the piece that most required him to confront juvenility in works he wanted to praise. What James finds most striking—the "real originality"—is the way Stevenson joins a brilliant style with a "love of youth," "the feeling for happy turns" with "the feeling of one's teens" (144, 145). From James's perspective, "turns" and "teens" are all but incompatible, hence making Stevenson's accomplishment truly extraordinary. More precisely, Stevenson's "rare" accomplishment "is the singular maturity of the expression that he has given to young sentiments: he judges them, measures them, sees them from the outside, as well as entertains them. He describes credulity with all the resources of experience, and represents a crude state with infinite ripeness"— even at times "lifts the subject into the general air: the execution is so serious that the idea (the idea of a boy's romantic adventures), becomes a matter of universal relations" (145–46). Which, of course, no mere juvenile fiction could be.

James underscores this perceived incongruity between attention to youth and attention to style, to artistry, throughout the essay, as he struggles to accommodate Stevenson's accomplishments to his own hierarchies of taste. Sometimes James excuses Stevenson's focus by way of the latter's intensity, an intensity that "amounts to a passion, and a passion, in the age in which we live, strikes us on the whole as a sufficient philosophy" (144). Sometimes James imagines that Stevenson must be defensive, while admitting that he does not in fact seem to be: almost "everything he has written is a direct apology for boyhood; or rather (for it must be confessed that Mr. Stevenson's tone is seldom apologetic), a direct rhapsody on the age of heterogeneous pockets" (145). Sometimes James simply suggests that it is a "happy occasion" when Stevenson presents "the strange, the improbable," not just as they "shine from afar in the credulous eye of youth" but "as they present themselves to a maturer vision" (164)—as in *The Strange Case of Dr. Jekyll and Mr. Hyde* (1886). Sometimes James half—or wholly—denies that Stevenson's juvenile fictions are indeed for boys. *Treasure Island*, for instance, "is a 'boy's book' in the sense that it embodies a boy's vision of the extraordinary, but it is unique in this, and calculated to fascinate the weary mind of experience, that what we see in it is not only the ideal fable but, as part and parcel of that, as it were, the young reader himself and his state of mind: we seem to read it over his shoulder, with an arm around his neck" (168). As for *Kidnapped* (1886), James tries to dismiss as only hypothetical any claim that this masterpiece is for boys: "There would have been a kind of perverse humility in his keeping up the fiction that a production so literary as *Kidnapped* is addressed to immature minds, and, though it was originally given to the world, I believe, in a 'boy's paper,' the story embraces every occasion that it meets to satisfy the higher criticism" (171–72). So of course it can't really be addressed to boys. Or girls. (There's no explaining my own childhood fondness for this book.)

The other key distillation of James's critical thinking about children and childhood appears, not inappropriately, in "The Future of the Novel" (1899)—not inappropriately because, in the popular imagination, thoughts of the future often lead to thoughts of children. In his discussion here of the audience for fiction, James often, again, lumps together women and children—a grouping whose heterogeneity is obscured, in part, by the Victorian elasticity of the term *girl*, which could refer not only to young children and adolescents but to unmarried women in their twenties. Indeed, James acknowledges as much when he complains "that the larger part of the great multitude that sustains the teller and the publisher of tales is constituted by boys and girls; by girls in especial, if we apply the term to the later stages of the life of the innumerable women who, under modern arrangements, increasingly fail to marry."[115] He decries "the vulgarization of literature"—specifically, the salience of "the reader irreflective and uncritical," which is to say "ladies and children" (338). In his criticism James is thus dismissive of children, yet in this essay he also hopes—conflating the age of the individual with the age of a genre—that "the future of the novel" might be redeemed by "the satiety of the very readers for whom the sacrifices have hitherto been supposed to be made"—by the women whose "position and outlook" were even then changing and also, implicitly, by children (343).

James's age metaphors in the essay reinforce these meanings. He calls, as usual, for a "mature" criticism (341). Yet the object of his attention, the novel, is curiously gendered and aged—or perhaps not so curiously. The novel is here variously feminine and a child's toy. One should not be obliged to "like" a particular work of literature, just as one should not be obliged to fall "in love" with a particular woman (339). The novel is also, or perhaps only to those who mistreat it, a "plaything that has helped create for [man] the illusion of leisure"

(343). The novel has perhaps taken on the attributes of its undesirable audience. Or perhaps, as object, it is Other to man the creator—like women, like children and their playthings. Or perhaps by taking on the attributes of the marginal beings with which it is associated it can in fact be redeemed.

If the novel is to be associated with that which is Other, perhaps it's not completely surprising that even as James was disparaging children in his criticism, he was turning to children to redeem his fiction. And, in the process, he portrayed them with considerable insight.[116] Almost a decade after Burnett turned to children, James did too—though to child characters in his fiction, not to the child audience.[117]

Five years after writing his essay extolling Stevenson, James published "The Pupil" (1892), a story that focused on a child, though his access to the child is still, as it would be in *The Turn of the Screw* (1898), through the consciousness of an adult, specifically the child's tutor. James is not yet ready to write directly through the consciousness of a child. And the child in "The Pupil," initially eleven years old, eventually fifteen, has to possess preternatural cleverness and delicacy—has to have "a small loftiness," "an element of reflection," that is "absolutely anomalous in a juvenile nature"[118]—to make him worthy of attention. This child who appears at times "elderly," at times "infantine," as living in the ambiguous "morning twilight of childhood" (306, 307, 326), is above all a Jamesian figure of reticence and tact. Still, in turning to childhood James is conscious of the models of children's literature, conscious here of writing against what he conceives as the boy's book. The climax is "too sudden and too violent; the thing was a good deal less like a boy's book" (344). And it is less like a boy's book, further, in its final collapse of joy.

The references to children's literature are a more organic part of *What Maisie Knew* (1897), a text that is largely filtered through a child's consciousness—indeed, it's the text in which James most fully deploys the child and his play with childhood. I therefore devote close attention to it here.

If the apartments of the wealthy American lover of Maisie's father are like the Arabian Nights, that's because they seem so to Maisie. And if Maisie, initially six, then some years older, is highly sensitive and intelligent, she's not preternaturally so—though no sooner do I write this sentence than I come across an uncannily divergent verbal echo in the early criticism: "What Maisie knew . . . may seem to have been learned by a preternaturally precocious child, so that her actuality has not, perhaps, the relief desired by her author."[119] Yet to a twenty-first-century reader who has made a habit of listening closely to children and who is familiar with the talk of children in families that are not biological nuclear ones, Maisie's insights are striking but not impossible.

In contrast with "The Pupil," too, it's not so much the narrator who confounds the child character's age and gender, treating Maisie as a "man of the world," but another character, her stepfather, Sir Claude: he calls her variously "old boy," "old man," "old chap," "old girl," "dear old woman," "dear old man," even "Maisie boy." He eventually notes, "I'm always talking to you in the most extraordinary way, ain't I? One would think you were about sixty and that I—I don't know what anyone would think *I* am. Unless a beastly cad!"[120] One recent critic refers to this passage as projecting "a grossly premature senility."[121] Another is closer to the mark when she sees a kind of "delicate homosexuality" in the camaraderie between Maisie and Sir Claude.[122] I see James's phrases and passages as confounding categories of age and youth, likewise male and female. Maisie breaks out of preexisting categories, for James.[123] If the confounding of categories is subtler than in *Fauntleroy*, James's project nonetheless echoes Burnett's. One of the ironies of the two authors' inverse mirroring is that the twentieth-century disparagement of things genteel demolished Fauntleroy but did not destroy James, whose favored characters, the Ralph Touchetts and Lambert Strethers, perhaps even Sir Claude, are genteel enough to strike many readers as a bit effeminate and indeed yearn to be of service, though they lack the missionary zeal that impelled Fauntleroy. James may not be attempting a synthesis of competing discourses—though Sir Claude does indeed embody some of the conflicting strands of masculinity—but he succeeds in capturing some of the shifting views of childhood as they were in turn inflected by gender.

In treating Maisie seriously, in having Sir Claude treat her seriously, James has had to prise her out of the pigeonhole to which he has elsewhere tried to confine children. Despite his own weaknesses, Sir Claude is the only one of Maisie's four parents and stepparents who takes her seriously: in keeping with the leveling tendencies of his motley terms for her, he speaks to her as an equal. At the same time, in his efforts not to expose her to his affair with her stepmother, not to mix her up in a business for which she has indeed been a pretext, he treats her protectively as a child. But he does so in a way that takes her seriously as an individual in her own right, not just as the pretext that she has been for other parental figures. And so it is he, finally, who lauds her for making the only possible right choice at the end.[124] Should she give up her sometime caretaker Mrs. Wix, someone else who has cared for her largely in her own right, and someone who so strenuously objects to the proposed joint and adulterous guardianship of Sir Claude and Mrs. Beale, the second wife of Maisie's father (Sir Claude being the second husband of Maisie's mother), that she refuses to be a party to it? Maisie is willing to give up Mrs. Wix, but only if Sir Claude will give up Mrs. Beale. Which he finds, weak and irresolute as he is in so many things, he cannot do. Maisie ends by going off alone with Mrs. Wix. Thus does she keep "the torch of virtue alive in an air tending infinitely to smother it," as James notes in his 1909 preface to the volume (preface, 8). Thus does she lend credence to Sir Claude's earlier claim that "her character's the most extraordinary thing in all the world" (*Maisie*, 98).

James takes Maisie seriously too—in a way that he does not the abstract infant of his criticism. He does so despite his own critical distaste, early in his career, for "stories about precocious little girls," who are "in themselves disagreeable and unprofitable objects of study," as he put it in an 1865 review of Louisa May Alcott's *Moods*.[125] And does so despite his complaint in 1881 that making "the young unmarried American female" central, as he had himself been doing in such fiction as *The Portrait of a Lady*, "is of necessity a limitation."[126] Yet in *Maisie* he sought that limitation once again. For James the novelist, as he would eventually note, "the finer, the shyer, the more anxious small vibrations," including Maisie's, are not negligible (preface, 13), even if, for James the critic, the possibility of producing such small vibrations in real-life Maisies is. As Barbara Everett argues, Maisie is different from the children in James's short stories, such as the boy in "The Pupil," not just by being the presiding consciousness but by being heroic, someone whom James treats with moral respect, "a saluted equal."[127]

A gauge of the seriousness with which James treats Maisie is his attentiveness to her psyche. Anticipating twentieth-century research into the cognition of children, James brilliantly renders some of the ways a child might half-know adult affairs, her mind collecting "images and echoes to which meanings were attachable—images and echoes kept for her in the childish dusk, the dim closet, the high drawers, like games she wasn't yet big enough to play" (*Maisie*, 23). When Maisie is told that staying with her father and Miss Overmore (still her titular governess, soon to become Mrs. Beale, her stepmother) is acceptable, because the latter is her governess—Maisie's presence keeping the couple "perfectly proper"—but going to her mother, who has "picked up" a gentleman, is unacceptable, Maisie wonders aloud "that if she should go to her mother perhaps the gentleman might become her tutor." "The proposition was complicated enough to make Miss Overmore stare" (*Maisie*, 40–41).

Or consider the way Maisie reasons out the age relationships among her parents and stepparents:

> For Sir Claude then Mrs Beale [Beale Farange's second wife] was 'young,' just as for Mrs Wix Sir Claude was: that was one of the merits for which Mrs Wix most commended him. What therefore was Maisie herself, and, in another relation to the matter, what therefore was mamma? It took her some time to puzzle out with the aid of an experiment or two that it wouldn't do to talk about mamma's youth. She even went so far one day, in the presence of that lady's thick colour and marked lines, as to wonder if it would occur to any one but herself to do so. Yet if she wasn't young then she was old and this threw an odd light on her having a husband of a different generation. Mr Farange [Maisie's father] was still older—that Maisie perfectly knew; and it brought her in due course to the perception of how much more, since Mrs Beale was younger than Sir Claude, papa must be older than Mrs Beale. Such discoveries were disconcerting and even a trifle confounding: these persons, it appeared, were not of the age they ought to be. This was somehow particularly the case with mamma. (*Maisie*, 66–67)

Thus does Maisie try to reason out the confused relationships among the adults who impinge on her, in terms that are meaningful to her. Yet the age terms she reasons with intersect in suggestive ways, for the adult reader, with the sexual terms she does not yet have access to, this child whose innocence is "so saturated with knowledge," whose mind has "fewer names than conceptions" (*Maisie*, 132, 145). At the same time, Maisie's reasoning foregrounds the key distinguishing feature of this novel devoted to her, the axis of complexity here for James: that of age.

James also sensitively renders other features of Maisie's childhood. Consider how Maisie learns something of why adults find her innocent questions hilarious, by play-acting with her doll Lisette: "Little by little . . . she understood more, for it befell that she was enlightened by Lisette's questions, which reproduced the effect of her own upon those for whom she sat in the very darkness of Lisette. Was she not herself convulsed by such innocence? . . . Well, she discovered a little, but never discovered all" (*Maisie*, 37). James likewise has some fun with the way a young child might construe a metaphor, and also how she might acquire language, in reflecting on an encounter between Miss Overmore ("papa's companion") and Mrs. Wix (an emissary from Maisie's mother): "As for Mrs Wix, papa's companion supplied Maisie in later converse with the right word for the attitude of this personage: Mrs Wix 'stood up' to her in a manner that the child herself felt at the time to be astonishing. This occurred indeed after Miss Overmore had so far raised her interdict [against Mrs. Wix] as to make a move to the dining-room, where, in the absence of any suggestion of sitting down, it was scarcely more than natural that even poor Mrs Wix should stand up" (*Maisie*, 43).

James may be gently laughing at Maisie here, winking at the adult reader over her literalness, but by and large he respects her. Maisie, unlike her parents, is sensitive to others and their needs, tactfully silent when she knows that speaking would hurt: in the words of M. A. Williams, she is someone whose "fearless originality fosters a subtlety of perception and a deep concern for human needs," someone who "dramatizes the transforming power of a free and wondering engagement with reality, an engagement that reveals a wealth of creative possibilities."[128] She is someone whose moral awareness James treats with delicacy, tact—and seriousness.

Yet if on some level James takes childhood seriously, it's really what he calls "the death of her childhood" (preface, 10) that interests him. He focuses on Maisie's access to knowledge and knowing—that which, in his thinking, defines childhood through its very lack. It's not so much childhood that he takes seriously as its loss. And ultimately James takes Maisie seriously only in order to use her.

He uses her to mirror her society, to reflect it and to reflect on it: he refracts his commentary on the mores of the sexually enterprising through this young child's consciousness. Muriel Shine suggests that Maisie lacks "psychological authenticity" since "she is completely devoid of anger or resentment" over her treatment by adults.[129] To focus his treatment of her cognitive and moral consciousness, James has stripped Maisie of emotions. Literary child abuse, if you will. Or to put it more psychoanalytically, "the daughter is not only to be exploited, but to derive pleasure from her exploitation."[130] Of course James doesn't treat his adult characters much differently. It's largely a matter of degree. As Sara Blair tellingly argues, "the female body" becomes "the cultural space in which the work of James's mastery is undertaken."[131] Yet of all the characters whose consciousnesses are central in his work, Maisie is probably the one whose emotions are most stripped, the one whose necessary and necessarily powerful and inchoate feelings of loss and rejection are barely hinted at.

Another way in which James's treatment of Maisie would seem to differ from his treatment of adult characters, certainly in degree if not in kind, is his use of her to polish his developing technique. She enables him to burnish the technique of having a central consciousness refract mere facts: he experiments with "her so limited consciousness," making it "the very field of my picture while at the same time guarding with care the integrity of the objects presented," then watches the results as his theme refuses "to remain humble, even (or perhaps all the more resentfully) when fondly selected for its conscious and hopeless humility" (preface, 8)—a humility all the more marked because his subject is both child and female. He expatiates on the delicious difficulty thus: "Small children have many more perceptions than they have terms to translate them; their vision is at any moment much richer, their apprehension even constantly stronger, than their prompt, their at all producible, vocabulary" (preface, 9). Though of course they don't offer the same scope as a Lambert Strether in *The Ambassadors* (1903), of whom James said, "I rejoiced in the promise of a hero so mature, who would give me thereby the more to bite into—since it's only into thickened motive and accumulated character, I think, that the painter of life bites more than a little."[132] James uses Maisie, in short, as a stepping-stone to his late great novels.

Some contemporary critics appreciated James's accomplishment in *What Maisie Knew*, its "supreme delicacy" (*delicacy* is a frequent term in favorable reviews), James's success "in analysing and purifying the baser passions of our nature by passing them through the pure mind of a little child," the book's portrait of "the elemental fineness of girl-nature."[133] But some reviewers found James's treatment of Maisie, in this "hopelessly sordid and vulgar story,"[134] objectionable. More, it seems, because of his hinting at "unlovely and squalid" affairs, "repellent to taste and feeling, to law and gospel,"[135] more because of Maisie's proximity to adult sexuality than because of James's use of her for his own purposes of aesthetic development—though it can be difficult to disentangle the two objections.[136] The reviewer for the British *Spectator* notes, "The elaborate ingenuity with which this wretched little child is hemmed round with undesirable relatives in our opinion entirely robs the figure of its intended pathos."[137] The American *Literary World* reviewer laments that James "exhibits not one ray of pity or dismay at this spectacle of a child with the pure current of its life thus poisoned at its source."[138] And the *Critic* reviewer captures much of the ambivalence of the contemporary response: "The skill and tenderness with which Mr. James has handled this unheard-of plot go far toward winning his pardon for the atrocity of having devised it."[139] As James himself describes the critical response, "I was punctually to have had read to me the lesson that the 'mixing-up' of a child with anything unpleasant confessed itself an aggravation of the unpleasantness, and . . . nothing could well be more disgusting than to attribute to

Maisie so intimate an 'acquaintance' with the gross immoralities surrounding her" (preface, 12).

Whatever the response to the individual merits of the novel, for a significant number of critics, early and late, *Maisie* has come to represent important shifts in James's work. When exactly does what has since been called James's late phase, his major phase, begin? Some find *Maisie* pivotal, referring perhaps to "a body of readers who had been faithful to Mr. James until the days—say—of *What Maisie Knew* (1897), but who since then have found themselves plunged into constantly deeper bewilderment."[140] Edmund Wilson cites Ford Madox Ford as having noted that with *Maisie* "the style first becomes a little gamey."[141] Marius Bewley even avers that "*What Maisie Knew* seems to me by far the greatest novel of the later James."[142] James himself, at the time of writing, considered it "probably what I have done, in the way of meeting the artistic problem, of best."[143]

More recently Ruth Bernard Yeazell zeroes in on the key feature of the late works: "At least as early as *What Maisie Knew* James had exploited not merely his protagonist's distance from the facts but her power innocently to imagine them otherwise."[144] Barbara Everett has argued at greater length that "Maisie is the first and most simply original of the novelist's late protagonists," that in this novel of the 1890s he succeeds in bringing together depth of feeling, moral idealism, and social truth.[145] Alfred Habegger has urged that "*What Maisie Knew* remains James's most living novel," with "a power to move, shock, and stir that is missing from the more studied—and, yes, better-rounded—novels of the so-called major phase."[146]

Maisie also becomes pivotal from another perspective, in connection with a shift in critical consciousness. Frances Hodgson Burnett's work has lent itself only imperfectly to the kind of formalist analysis popular in mid-twentieth-century criticism but rather better to the kind of analysis I attempted in discussing the discourses of masculinity in *Little Lord Fauntleroy*. Some of the forces that have led to a renewed interest in Burnett's work in the past couple of decades, as poststructuralist criticism has come to the fore, criticism less focused on formal qualities than was the New Criticism, have also led to a renewed interest in *Maisie*. This newer criticism, as Lynn Wardley puts it, "departs from a model of Henry James as the worldly intellectual on whom nothing is lost to construct a Henry James whose consciousness, and that of his protagonists, is structured by the cognitive rules and suppositions of an historically specific discourse."[147] Richard Hocks suggests that the novels that have gained critical attention in this climate, constituting almost a new Jamesian canon, are a kind of "problem novel," often "works that used to be thought of as experiments with greater or lesser success, but always as interesting attempts that merely prepared the way to the great achievements of the 'major phase.'"[148] *Maisie* is one of these works.

Yet despite this recent attentiveness to Maisie, and despite the enormousness of the James industry, she and James's other fictional children have received little attention as children. As John Carlos Rowe astutely reasons,

> James's representation of these bourgeois children is perhaps his most profound indictment of the bourgeoisie's lack of a proper historical consciousness, its failure to develop those means through which it might transform and renew itself. And yet we hardly notice how the children in Henry James's fiction are as orphaned, abandoned, and abused as the fictional children of Mark Twain. . . . It is a neglect or repression that we cannot attribute to James but may well be a consequence of our own reading habits as bourgeois readers, intent as we are on separating the serious business of adult relations from the trivial work our children must perform every day.[149]

Yet perhaps Rowe is being too kind to James. James's latter-day readers have simply been all too well schooled in the view of childhood for which James himself was an early advocate.

Maisie also represents, implicitly, an important shift at the turn of the century in the relationship between childhood and serious fiction. And the much greater quantity of criticism on James than on Burnett, then and now, makes it feasible to sketch, through the critical response to *Maisie*, an increasing dissociation between childhood and serious fiction. Some early critics mark the shift by lambasting James for turning to such trivia as a child's perceptions, effectively turning his own critical prejudices against him. W. C. Brownell, writing in the *Atlantic* in 1905, admits to a preference for fiction about "figures already on their august pedestals" and notes that "a writer interested in the *Antigone* and imbued with the spirit of its succession, would naturally and instinctively be less absorbed in what Maisie knew—to mention what is certainly a very remarkable, but what is also, by the very perfection of its execution, shown to be a fantastic book, except on the supposition that whatever is, is important."[150] *Fantastic* is not, for Brownell, a term of praise. H. G. Wells implies a similar attitude in 1915, when his lightly fictionalized mouthpiece describes the "eviscerated people" in James's remarkable stories as "concentrated on suspicion, on a gift, on possessing a 'piece' of old furniture, on what a little girl may or may not have noted in an emotional situation. These people cleared for artistic treatment never make lusty love, never go to angry war, never shout at an election or perspire at poker."[151] Little girls are simply of no significance. Even Edmund Wilson, two decades later, though convinced that *What Maisie Knew* is "among James's masterpieces," notes that in the 1890s "the Jamesian central observer, through whose intelligence the story is usually relayed to us, has undergone a strange diminution. The observer is no longer a complete and interesting person more or less actively involved in the events, but a small child."[152]

Early critics often used the dissociation of childhood from the serious as a metaphor for putting James in his place, a metaphor all the more telling because of James's own insistence, in his criticism, on the importance of maturity. The *Atlantic*'s Brownell, for instance—referring to Sir Walter Scott's comments on the importance of "the education of the heart" and on how the writer must "have some very young ideas" in his head if he does not foster it in his fiction—inquires, "Is it possible that Mr. James's controlling idea is a 'young one'?"[153] Two decades later Van Wyck Brooks would discern in the "formidable projections" of James's "geometrical intellect" "the confused reveries of an invalid child."[154] Max Beerbohm's 1915 parody "The Mote in the Middle Distance" is both a commentary on Maisie (her insignificance? her impossibility?) and a reductio ad absurdum of James's method: it embodies the preternatural consciousness of a child peering—no, not peering—at the foot of his bed very early one morning, his young sister, in the adjacent bed, commenting, "'Of course, my dear, you *do* see. There they are, and you know I know you know we wouldn't either of us, dip a finger into them. . . . One doesn't,' she added, 'violate the shrine—pick the pearl from the shell!' . . . Something, perhaps, of the bigotry of the convert was already discernible in the way that, averting his eyes, he said, 'One doesn't even peer.'"[155] The shell whose pearl tempts the boy's gaze is his Christmas stocking.

In his fiction, in short, James embraces children, using them in his middle years to clarify his own vision.[156] As Everett argues, not only does the child protagonist of *What Maisie Knew* usher in James's late phase, "a new irrealism," but subsequent adult protagonists too are importantly childlike, albeit with "a more mature innocence," making weakness heroic when they convert inability into principled refusal.[157] For what Maisie knows remains a mystery and is ultimately less important than what she refuses to do.

The fact that she knows, though, marks the death of her childhood, her crossing of what was for James the great divide that separates child from adult. The secrets hidden from Maisie and from Mary Lennox may not be altogether different: there's a veiled eroticism evoked by the rebirths, the "us is nesting," of the secret gardeners. Yet probing these secrets yields vastly different results for the two authors. Knowledge for James meant severance and separation, not the reassertion and celebration of connection that it meant for Burnett. In *Fauntleroy* as in *The Secret Garden*, the revelation of secrets and the rhetorical deployment of childhood enabled one to bridge gaps in age, class, gender, nationality. For James, however, knowledge meant Maisie's separation from parents and stepparents as well as from childhood. James used Maisie to quash childhood and family connection. More sensitive than Maisie's parents and stepparents, James nonetheless, like them, ultimately abuses childhood.

And in doing so he anticipates virtually all the recent stances of appropriation and dismissal that I sketched in Chapter 1. Like Susan Faludi, James uses a child—in his case, Maisie—as a stepping-stone. He stages her development not just as Lawrence Kohlberg might do, psychologically, but also theatrically, making her a spectacle. Like Fredric Jameson, he appropriates the metaphors of childhood in his criticism—only to ignore their implications when, as with Janice Radway, they might muddy his analysis. Like Jane Tompkins, he is a closet juvenilist, particularly in his critical discussions of Stevenson. Like Barbara Johnson, he treats the position of child as unproblematic in his criticism, if not always in his fiction. James anticipates and creates our own uses and abuses of childhood.

Burnett traveled in her lifetime from the Old World to the New, from Manchester, England, to Tennessee and Washington and Long Island (with excursions back to Sussex). James's transatlantic crossing was the reverse. Born in New York, he spent his mature years in London and Rye, severing many connections with his own childhood, with the idea of childhood, and with that New World where civilization remained, in his view, in its childhood. Much as the physical trajectories of Burnett and James were opposed, so too were the trajectories of their critical reputations, as Burnett's reputation declined and James's rose. Yet there are subtle affiliations between the two authors. James found a home in the civilized Old World of his ancestors, rejuvenating it even as he cultivated his affinity with its gentility—though that's not the word he would have used. He attempted to grapple with competing strands of masculinity. James effectively became Fauntleroy. Yet, unlike Fauntleroy, James succeeded in staking a claim as the Master and creating a lasting reputation in the academy—whose workings I address in the next chapter—by repudiating juvenility.

Kiddie Lit in the Academy

The nineteenth century was a time "when majors wrote for minors," to invoke the title of a 1952 essay by Henry Steele Commager. A time, Commager said, when "almost every major writer . . . wrote for children as well as adults, and . . . for over a century the line between juvenile and adult literature was all but invisible." Some of Commager's details may now seem quaint: he could assume that contemporary young people would not be given Fitzgerald or Hemingway, and he could ask, with respect to Emerson, "What boys or girls have failed to read him by the time they have finished high school?"[1] But his main point still holds. As Jerry Griswold has pointed out, the best-sellers between 1865 and 1914 were as likely to be *Heidi* as *Madame Bovary*, *Alice's Adventures in Wonderland* as *Our Mutual Friend*.[2] They were in fact more likely to be *Little Women* than *The Portrait of a Lady*, more likely to be *Treasure Island* than *Moby-Dick*—more likely to be Burnett's *Little Lord Fauntleroy* than James's *What Maisie Knew*.[3]

To glimpse the status of children's literature in the nineteenth century, consider the most popular American magazine for children. Begun in 1827, the *Youth's Companion* achieved a circulation that in 1885 outstripped that of all other U.S. magazines, for children or adults.[4] In skimming Lovell Thompson's anthology of highlights from the magazine, I find contributions by almost all the authors considered preeminent during the nineteenth century: Washington Irving, William Cullen Bryant, Ralph Waldo Emerson, Henry Wadsworth Longfellow, John Greenleaf Whittier, Oliver Wendell Holmes, Harriet Beecher Stowe. Not to mention other nineteenth-century writers and also writers from the twentieth century, such as Richard Henry Dana, William Dean Howells, Catharine Maria Sedgwick, Louisa May Alcott, Emily Dickinson, Hamlin Garland, Mark Twain, Bret Harte, Sarah Orne Jewett, Edith Wharton, Jack London, Willa Cather, Susan Glaspell, Robinson Jeffers, Robert Frost, Stephen Crane. And that's just a partial list.[5]

Or consider that a general magazine, the kind we would now consider a magazine for adults, could absorb a magazine primarily targeting juveniles. In 1870 *Scribner's Monthly, An Illustrated Magazine for the People* absorbed the *Riverside Magazine for Young People*.[6] It's hard to imagine a modern equivalent—the *New Republic* absorbing *Jack and Jill?* The *New Yorker* absorbing *Ladybug?*

The leading "adult" journals of the day—among them, the *Atlantic Monthly*, the *Nation, Harper's New Monthly Magazine, Scribner's Monthly*, the *Critic, Literary World*—were attentive to children. Even in the 1890s the editor of *Harper's* claimed to print nothing "that could not be read aloud in the family circle."[7] During the last four decades of the nineteenth century these journals devoted considerable space to reviews of children's literature. As Richard L. Darling concludes in a study of review writing during the decade and a half following the Civil War, "At no other time have such fine critics, such gifted authors, such discerning minds, devoted so much intelligent energy to a critical examination of children's books. What critic with the stature of William Dean Howells has reviewed children's books in the twentieth century?"[8]

The position of children's literature now, at the start of the twenty-first century, is very different. Neither *Harper's* nor the *Atlantic* reviews children's literature. And even as I draft and revise this chapter, the *New York Times Book Review*, which Mary Harris Veeder calls the "one journalistic venue where expansive coverage of children's books is featured," has gone from a weekly page devoted to children's literature, supplemented by semiannual special sections, to a biweekly, to a monthly page.[9] Nor do the Jacques Derridas or Henry Louis Gateses or Stephen Greenblatts of criticism theorize about literature for children. The reasons for this lack of attention include those addressed in Chapter 1: our cultural anxiety of immaturity, our unwillingness to take children seriously. But there are also institutional reasons, reasons that are implicated in the anxiety of immaturity but go beyond it.

To pinpoint some of these reasons why children's literature now has only a precarious purchase in the U.S. academy, why so many academics consider it unworthy of serious attention, I explore here the institutionalization of children's literature in the United States in the twentieth century.[10] A key player in my narrative is the discipline that, to its detriment, came to be most closely associated with children's literature, one having such low status among literary critics that it is often not even considered a discipline.

"We are told that women—and unmarried women at that—do three-fourths of the novel-reading in the world; and that, consequently, novels must be so fashioned as to please and attract the feminine mind, and especially the junior feminine." So declaims Julian Hawthorne in 1888, in his essay "Man-Books,"[11] echoing his better-known father, who had famously complained in 1855 that his own novels had had to compete with those by "a d——d mob of scribbling women," and also echoing the younger Hawthorne's acerbic contemporary H. H. Boyesen, who indicted the nineteenth-century audience as an "Iron Madonna who strangles in her fond embrace the American novelist." Julian anticipates "that the great American novelist, when he comes, will give us a man-book"; meanwhile he finds only one or two "man-books" in nineteenth-century American literature—W. S. Mayo's *Kaloolah* and perhaps Herman Melville's *Moby-Dick*.[12]

Certainly mid-nineteenth-century reviewers of novels tended to assume a general readership that was young and feminine, as Nina Baym has documented in an illuminating study. Children and youths are assumed to be part of the audience for novels—for fiction that is not yet segregated into children's stories and adults' books. In 1843 a writer for the *Ladies' Repository* worries that novels "are devoured by thousands, nay millions, of men, women, and children"; in 1847 a writer for the *Christian Examiner* laments the seductive power of such literature over "the strong-hearted youth of New England."[13] Even in the intellectual *North American Review*, in 1846, a writer is concerned about "the multitudes of men, so-called, besides women and children," who feed on mere husks (57). To give just a few more examples of the assumption that young people will of course read what is published as fiction: in 1847 a writer in *Sartain's Union Magazine* excoriates fiction that isn't "a safe companion for youthful and excitable minds" (191); in 1859 a writer in the popular *New York Ledger* fears that the portrayal of vice as enticing would "make silly girls and sillier boys in love with handsome, dashing villainy" (179); and in 1843 a writer in the *North American Review* frets that such a portrayal of vice "conducts many a youth to a wretched life, a lonely grave, or, perhaps, to the pirate's doom" (178). Ah yes, all those youths becoming pirates. Those who are not prophesying doom similarly assume a youthful readership, as when, in 1853, an editor of the popular *Godey's Lady's Book* casually notes that cheap literature can have a beneficial effect "by fostering a love of purer recreation than the young would otherwise cultivate" (49). Many reviewers would agree with one who said, in 1850, "A great book is one that interests all classes of the community."[14]

Even the manly Mayo and Melville—to revert to Julian Hawthorne's counterexamples—are not immune from the voracious appetites of juveniles. Mayo's maturity, likewise his masculinity, is effectively dismantled when Hawthorne goes on to say that he gave a reprint of *Kaloolah* "to our boys, and never thought to look into it ourselves. Perhaps even the boys themselves failed to appreciate it. It seems to me that the American boy of to-day is a good deal like a girl in trousers."[15] A peculiar way of putting it: this epitome of the man-book is really for boys—certainly "we" didn't want to look at it again—except that the boys don't noticeably care for it, because they're really girls. The real audience of nineteenth-century fiction is, whatever its biological age and sex, young and feminine. And a nineteenth-century call for the man-book, for the great American novel that will defy the "junior feminine," turns out to be a plea for children's literature after all.

As for Melville, reviewers frequently assumed that his work, especially his early sea adventures, was suitable for children—suitable for everyone around the fireside or kerosene lamp; it was in fact read aloud in many families, including Longfellow's.[16] An enthusiastic reviewer of *Typee* exclaims, in 1846, "What will our juvenile readers say to a *real* Robinson Crusoe, with a *real* man Friday?"[17] A year later a reviewer for the *Columbian Magazine* muses, "Typee has been read, we suppose, by every man, woman and child in the Union who undertakes to keep pace at all with the march of the current literature."[18] A recurring refrain in these reviews is that Melville's books can "win the attention of a child" and also "stir the profoundest depths of manhood"; that in these books "the little child" might "find entertainment, and genius salute the author as the rising sun"; even that such "pure, manly English" as Melville's is precisely the language "a child can always understand," the childlike and manly not just juxtaposed but equated.[19] When Melville died in 1891, his reputation in eclipse, a writer in the *Boston Post* may have been dubious about the answer to his question, "Do boys between the ages of ten and seventy read his books now?"—but not, it appears, about the age of a suitable audience.[20] And rarely, especially at midcentury, is an association with juvenility disparaging. In 1856 a British reviewer may indeed consign *The Piazza Tales* to "a very young public," but it takes a twentieth-century critic to feel dismay that in 1849 a reviewer treats *Redburn* as "an interesting book for juvenile readers" or that in 1889 an extract from *Moby-Dick* appeared in the *Harper's Fifth Reader*, a school textbook.[21] For most nineteenth-century observers it was a matter of course that Melville was not just for adults.

Evidence of such a mingled audience for literature appears in other nineteenth-century writings as well. The first of Erastus Beadle's dime novels announces, in 1860, the hope of reaching "all classes, old and young, male and female."[22] The historian Barbara Sicherman, in examining the letters and other writings of a middle-class family of the late nineteenth century, is struck by the "intense preoccupation with books, including children's books, well into adulthood," and notes that six of the ten best-selling books in the United States in 1875–95 were children's books.[23]

Or consider this comment, published in 1895:

> The distinction between books for the young and books for the old is a somewhat arbitrary one, and many have discovered for themselves and their children that instead of one poor corner of literature being fenced off for the lamb, planted with tender grass which is quickly devoured, and with many medicinal but disagreeable herbs which are nibbled at when the grass is gone, the whole wide pasture land is their native home, and the grass more tender where fresh streams flow than it possibly can be in the paddock, however carefully planted and watched.[24]

It's significant that these words were written late in the century. Children had become a lucrative market by then, their literature increasingly separated from that for adults: the author is trying to mend the split. Also significant is that the author is Horace Scudder. At the time he published these words he was editing the *Atlantic Monthly*, the most prestigious of the nineteenth-century literary magazines, the "journalistic equivalent," as a latter-day scholar has stated, "of a Phi Beta Kappa key."[25]

Before becoming the editor-in-chief of the *Atlantic* in 1890, Scudder had devoted much of his career to bringing literature to children: he was the author of the many Bodley stories and other tales, the advocate of Hans Christian Andersen, the editor of the *Riverside Magazine for Young People*, an anthologist of nursery classics, a proponent of assigning classic literary texts in the schools, and the editor of the Riverside Literature Series for Young People. Scudder thus embodies the stunning confluence of the worlds of editing, publishing, and writing in the nineteenth century—including the confluence of the book worlds of children and adults.

But back to the Riverside Literature Series for Young People. The purpose of this series, consisting of what a recent scholar has described as "the first educational paperbacks,"[26] was to make classic texts, especially American classics, available to the schools. Through his choices for the series, and through his essays and speeches, Scudder had a profound impact on both the American curriculum and the nineteenth-century canon of American literature. More precisely, he had an effect on the canon partly because of his effect on the curriculum. By bringing together students and texts he was able to combine "philanthropic national citizenship and connoisseurship," the conjunction of which defined the "high realism" that was then in critical favor.[27] The emergence of a relatively well defined canon occurred in tandem with the expansion of the U.S. educational system. As Jerry Griswold has noted of the early nineteenth century, addressing such texts as McGuffey's readers, "the American schoolroom was . . . the place where canons were made."[28] Canonical works are precisely those that a culture wishes to preserve by passing them on to its young. Canonical works are always, in some sense, literature for children.

Scudder was also a pivotal conceptualizer of the nature of childhood—and of children as an audience for literature. The *Atlantic* was a crucial vehicle for his ideas on childhood and education. As editor, he frequently published other authors' essays on this topic; his views were also reflected in the scores of reviews, signed and unsigned, that he contributed to the magazine in the final decades of the nineteenth century—so many that, as a eulogist noted, he "contributed more pages to the Atlantic than any other writer."[29] Moreover, Scudder's views on childhood and education were intimately related to his sense of mission for the *Atlantic,* and for literature more generally. He wanted to educate, to elevate, "to keep the magazine at the front of American literature," as he noted in his diary upon being named editor, and to serve "God in this cause of high, pure literature."[30] His use of the word *pure* is not accidental: for Scudder, the best literature always had a high moral purpose. The goals of the best literature for adults were congruent, for him and for other nineteenth-century arbiters of culture, with the goals of the best literature for children: the best literature for adults was in fact the best literature for children.

Scudder's views of childhood and children's literature are perhaps best captured in the collection of essays he called *Childhood in Literature and Art*, a study of children in literature and of literature for children, the book from which I've quoted the passage about not fencing off children's literature from the rest of the pasture. These essays were first delivered as Lowell Institute lectures in 1882, then published in the *Atlantic* in 1885, and finally gathered in a book in 1895. Scudder's insights are usually astute, even if some now seem a bit dated.

He is too intent, for instance, on persuading his readers that his Romantic view of childhood innocence is the one true view, that seeing childhood as "joyous, innocent," and as satisfying "the eye that looks for beauty and delicacy" is the mark of great literature.[31] Such a view may be attractive, even seductive, yet it is hardly the only one. A post-Freudian would consider it, shall we say, naive. As Alexander V. G. Allen noted in the *Atlantic* the year after Scudder's death, *Childhood in Literature and Art* might be considered "deficient when judged by the later methods of psychological research."[32] Yet Allen went on to state that the book nonetheless "has this distinctive value that it keeps in the open, avoiding the morbid and the recondite, adhering solely to the objective estimate, the conscious rather than the subconscious life, true always to its title, childhood as revealed in those two most powerful modes of presentation, literature and art. It is therefore a book for the few. Those with the highest opportunity for cultured reflection will most deeply appreciate its beauty and worth." Thus does Allen come to terms—aided by the non sequitur connecting sunny consciousness and elite status—with Scudder's "confinement of his abilities to the visual angle of childhood."[33] Rather than being more naive than Freud, Scudder is more elite ("for the few"), even elitist. Allen calls upon a declining genteel ideal even as he reveals some uneasiness with the appreciation of childhood that was its frequent concomitant, an uneasiness underscored by the inconsequentiality of his sudden "therefore." He would not, perhaps, wholeheartedly subscribe to Scudder's comment in a letter of the 1870s inviting Representative James A. Garfield to remember "the Fletcher of Saltoun saying which our college orators used to quote so regularly—I care not etc. so men's minds are affected for good or evil by the bent which their feelings take when they are children, by the associations which they form with images then presented to them."[34] By 1903 Scudder's appreciation of childhood seemed passé.

Yet many of Scudder's insights in *Childhood in Literature and Art* are not. Despite some tendency to idealize childhood, he has a keen eye for condescension, for literature in which the topic of childhood is a pretext for reflections that are not necessarily accessible to a child—for childhood colonized as a pastoral ideal.

His comment that Longfellow in, say, "The Children's Hour," was not so much writing for children as about them is right on the mark: "This poem, perfect as it is in a father's apprehension, yields only a subtle and half-understood fragrance to a child."[35] More than one generation of schoolteachers has failed to attend to such an insight, has chosen that poem as a text for children to memorize. The result for me, at least, is that Longfellow's iambs and anapests will always be a schoolchild singsong. It is a poem I have not felt a desire to look at since my unfortunate encounter with it in elementary school.

Scudder may have been unusual among prominent nineteenth-century men of letters—among whom one would necessarily number the editors of the *Atlantic*—for the strength of his advocacy of children and children's literature. But he was not unusual in being such an advocate. All three men who edited the *Atlantic* between 1871 and 1898—William Dean Howells, Thomas Bailey Aldrich, and Scudder—also published significant children's literature. They were likewise, Howells and Scudder especially, advocates of literature for children. Poet, journalist, and man-about-town, Aldrich wrote the autobiographical *Story of a Bad Boy* (1869) early in his career, and this work of what is now considered children's literature is what he is best remembered for. Howells similarly addressed a child audience in his autobiographical *A Boy's Town* (1890) and in *The Flight of Pony Baker* (1902). Thanks to his editing of the *Atlantic*, his subsequent critical essays in *Harper's*, his friendships with Mark Twain and Henry James, and his own fiction, Howells is often considered the dean of American letters in the late nineteenth and early twentieth centuries. Elected the first president of the American Academy of Arts and Letters, he was, in his prime, the preeminent arbiter of literature. As H. L. Mencken claimed, with characteristic irreverence, turn-of-the-century critics "could no more bring themselves to question" Howells's work "than they could question Lincoln's Gettysburg speech, or Paul Elmer More, or their own virginity."[36] Yet despite his cultural stature—or, more precisely, because of it, given that he so well embodied nineteenth-century norms and attitudes—Howells was receptive to children's literature and to children as an audience. He was fully conscious that the *Atlantic*, when he edited it, was read by young and old: he was anxious when making editorial decisions to "print nothing which a father may not read to his daughter," anxious not to burn "the cheek of the young person."[37] He wrote enthusiastic reviews of books that are now considered children's literature. And he wrote for children too.

Under the leadership of these three men, the *Atlantic* was receptive both to reviews of children's literature and to general discussions of it. Books that we might now call boys' books received extended commentary: such a book could afford pleasure, in Howells's words, "to the boys themselves, and to every man that happens to have been a boy."[38] In 1870 Howells finds the publication of Aldrich's *Story of a Bad Boy* a significant event in American literature, one with enormous potential for "the work which has so long hovered in the mental atmosphere a pathetic ante-natal phantom; pleading to be born into the world—the American novel, namely."[39] In 1876 he calls Twain's *Adventures of Tom Sawyer* "incomparably the best picture of life in that region [of the country] as yet known to fiction."[40] In 1877 he declares Charles Dudley Warner's *Being a Boy* "a beautiful and amiable book, which must become dear to its readers, young or old, as a friend becomes dear. It has a personality, sweet and charming; and the lover of Mr. Warner's humor will find it here in a thousand furtive turns and twinkles."[41] Even "popular" books for children by Oliver Optic or Martha Finley (whose Elsie Dinsmore has become a byword for sentimental piety) would be accorded a sentence or two. During the nineteenth century the *Atlantic* regularly reviewed children's literature; after 1898 it reviewed very little.

As for more general discussions of literature for children, in the 1880s Aldrich included a spate of such essays in the *Atlantic*. Most were by Scudder. In addition to the historical studies later reprinted in *Childhood in Literature and Art*, Scudder wrote about the relationship between literature and the education of children: he urged the use of full works of classic literature in the schools, instead of the McGuffey-style anthology of snippets, thus anticipating the whole-language movement of a century later—except that he emphasized classic literature. And by classic literature he meant either, for the early grades, the "genuine literature" afforded by traditional fairy tales and those by Hans Christian Andersen or, for older children, classic "adult" works of American literature by such figures as Longfellow, Bryant, Emerson, and Whittier. Scudder looked with dismay on the then-current "disposition to separate the reading of the young from the reading of the mature."[42] So too, though somewhat more ambivalently, did the essayist Agnes Repplier, a frequent contributor to the *Atlantic*; her piece "What Children Read," in the January 1887 issue, celebrates the nourishment children have imbibed from reading Shakespeare and Sir Walter Scott, and from reading tales for children of the previous century by Maria Edgeworth, whose child characters, unlike those of contemporary writers such as Alcott, knew their place. Repplier's nostalgic claims for an author who was probably one of her own childhood favorites simultaneously merge the interests of child and adult (Repplier as child, Repplier as adult) and, in her praise of the becoming reticence of Edgeworth's child characters, hint at the desirability of keeping children in their place, separate from adults.

Despite occasional expressions of ambivalence, the view that children's reading should overlap with adults' reading is frequently urged in the *Atlantic* and elsewhere toward the close of the nineteenth century, at a time when the two readerships were, in fact, diverging. In 1897 Charles Dudley Warner proclaims in the *Critic*, "I would give a child no literature I did not like myself."[43] In the same year, in *Outlook*, Hamilton W. Mabie urges the value of books that "are quite as interesting to mature as to young readers" and admits Greek and other myths because they too have spoken to adults in "the childhood of the race."[44] By 1900 Everett T. Tomlinson's acknowledgment of "the 'masterpiece only' theory" of childhood reading and his agreement that, "as has been said, no book can be called of value for a child which is without interest to his elders" suggest the currency of such ideas.[45] Yet, more than the earlier writers, Tomlinson is also willing to admit the possibility of a separate literature for children, a field where "much yet remains to be done."[46]

It's perhaps not accidental that by 1900, when the *Atlantic* published Tomlinson's essay, the magazine was being edited by Bliss Perry. Perry came to the *Atlantic* in 1899 from Princeton and left it, a decade later, for Harvard. Howells may have been offered academic positions and granted honorary degrees, Scudder too, but Perry was a full-fledged member of the emerging professoriate. In the 1890s Scudder published a number of scholarly essays by professors in the *Atlantic*—on Greek literature, *Faust*, Chaucer—but he was not himself affiliated with a university.

Perry, the once and future professor, lamented that Houghton Mifflin, the publisher of the *Atlantic*, valued Kate Douglas Wiggin's *Rebecca of Sunnybrook Farm* over Sarah Orne Jewett's *Country of the Pointed Firs*—the latter more highly rated by "professors of literature"—simply because the former outsold the latter.[47] Heaven forbid that one could find literary value in a classic addressed to children. And, lacking Scudder's insight, Perry would declare Longfellow's reputation safe since Longfellow had become "the children's poet": "The sweet voices that recite with delicious solemnity *The Children's Hour* might tell us more about Longfellow than we professional critics—with our meticulous pedantry, our scrutiny of 'sources,' our ears so trained to detect overtones that we lose the melody—shall ever learn."[48] Those poor children. There's no doubt that Perry found the balancing act between culture and commerce difficult, as the custodians of high culture were shifting to the academy and the *Atlantic* readership was becoming more geographically and socially dispersed: in a history of the magazine, Ellery Sedgwick suggests that "Perry's *Atlantic* was one of the last public forums in America for discussion of major works and figures of Western humanism outside an academic context," including such figures as Chaucer, Dante, Voltaire, Austen, Wordsworth, Zola.[49] But it's also true that, for Perry, children and childhood would no longer be enlisted in the active service of culture. Perry found Scudder's devotion to public service admirable but was ultimately bemused that Scudder's "imagination envisaged every hour of hack work as a permanent contribution to the development of American culture and character."[50] For Perry and for other arbiters of culture in the early twentieth century, children and childhood were either havens for a culture no longer vital (Longfellow) or tokens of what was undesirable in commerce (Wiggin).

By the 1920s, Paul Lauter has suggested, the arbiters of American literature were no longer literary clubs and magazines but the professoriate, almost all white males.[51] Richard H. Brodhead might demur that the key cultural arbiters at this time were not yet the professoriate but rather nonacademic critics.[52] In fact, there was considerable slippage between the two groups: three of the four editors of the scholarly *Cambridge History of American Literature* (1917–21) shifted, like Bliss Perry earlier in the century, between academic positions and positions in literary journalism, as editors of such journals as the *Nation* and the *Saturday Review of Literature*. But all these cultural arbiters, academic and nonacademic, were white males who were college educated and hence influenced by the professoriate, whether or not they were themselves members. Under their tutelage, the canonical authors of American literature were shifting from Longfellow, Lowell, and Stowe to Melville, Twain, Thoreau, and James. Elizabeth Renker argues that American literature created itself as a profession by shedding femininity and appropriating the language of science, a change fueled by two world wars. It "achieved institutional maturity" by shedding juvenility as well, as Renker acknowledges only implicitly, metaphorically.[53] Not for nothing was a 1915 manifesto of early-twentieth-century criticism by Van Wyck Brooks—a book whose most memorable contribution was the coining of *highbrow* and *lowbrow*, thereby providing terms for discussing and indeed fostering such separations as that between children's and adults' literature—titled *America's Coming-of-Age*. If nineteenth-century America was pervaded by the metaphor of America as child, then the nation's emergence as a world power in the twentieth century was marked by a desire to put away childish things.[54]

Or at least the desire to put away childish things was urgent for the white male critics. Among African Americans there was instead a concern to uplift the race. As such scholars as Dianne Johnson-Feelings have documented, many of the figures active in the Harlem Renaissance—including Langston Hughes, Arna Bontemps, Jessie Fauset, Nella Larsen—wrote for children. Or perhaps, like many nineteenth-century writers, they wrote for children and adults: Marian Wright Edelman maintains that *The Brownies' Book*, a children's magazine founded by W. E. B. Du Bois and others in 1920, "really *wasn't* a children's magazine. It was a magazine for parents and children to read together, to learn from together, and to spark their thoughts and dreams and desire for more knowledge."[55]

In any case, all the authors whose currency rose during the canon ferment of the early twentieth century, all those who made it into the canonical mainstream, were white men. Most of them—in particular, Melville, Thoreau, and James—did not explicitly write for children.[56]

Milestones in the professionalization of English include the proliferation of graduate study in the last quarter of the nineteenth century, spearheaded by the Johns Hopkins University (founded in 1876), and the establishment of the Modern Language Association (MLA) in 1883 and its publication of *PMLA* (*Publications of the Modern Language Association*), beginning in 1884.[57] In skimming the contents of *PMLA* since its inception, I find little before 1966—and only a trickle of pieces thereafter—on children's literature. In the earliest decades, when philology and folklore vied with source study for preeminence and when the journal published minutes of conference presentations, one finds discussion of a talk addressing the European (of course) sources of Uncle Remus or discussion of the balladic nature of cowboy songs of the Mexican border. The respondents to the talk about Uncle Remus may refer to versions of tales that they heard in childhood, but they use their childhoods only to authenticate their authority—to claim "a pure point of origin in relation to language"[58]—and they go on to discuss whether the tales came from France by way of Haiti and how much Joel Chandler Harris might have fabricated his versions. Certainly there is no indication that any of these scholars conceived of the subject under discussion as children's literature. Similarly, in 1915 Ronald S. Crane concludes a seventy-page disquisition on the history of Guy of Warwick with a paragraph that finally admits children to the pages of *PMLA*; he laments that by the eighteenth cen-

THE CHILDREN'S LONGFELLOW

Illustrated

HOUGHTON MIFFLIN COMPANY

BOSTON & NEW YORK

1908

Bliss Perry would approve.
Above, Rome Richardson, *The Children's Longfellow* (Houghton Mifflin, 1908). *Opposite page*, from *The Children's Hour* by Henry Wadsworth Longfellow, Illustrations by Glenna Lang (reprinted by permission of David R. Godine, Publisher, Inc., Copyright © 1993 by Henry Wadsworth Longfellow, Illustrations by Glenna Lang).

HENRY WADSWORTH LONGFELLOW

The Children's Hour

ILLUSTRATIONS BY GLENNA LANG

tury, when scholarly interest in the tale was quickening, the lay audience was comprised only of children: "To such uses had come a story once read and admired by all Englishmen!"[59]

The midcentury editorial practices of *American Literature*, a journal established in 1929 and published in association with the American Literature Group of the MLA, are likewise telling. *American Literature* was slightly more receptive to children's literature than was *PMLA*. In the 1930s, 1940s, and 1950s it published an article on Twain's *Prince and the Pauper* (an essay that did not suggest the book could be considered children's literature, though that is how most scholars now classify it), reprinted a lost Alcott story for children, and published a dismissive note on Hawthorne's mythological tales retold for children. Melville, Poe, and Twain all receive significant attention in more than seventy essays published in the journal during these years; Emerson, Hawthorne, and James receive more than forty each; even such a forgettable figure as Paul Hamilton Hayne receives significant attention in nine essays. But I can find only three essays, the three mentioned above, that could be said to attend to children's literature.

Another window on the twentieth-century development of the field of American literature and its relationship to that of children's literature is provided by three important literary histories, cooperative compendia of scholarship, each devoting more than a thousand pages to American literary history. The four-volume *Cambridge History of American Literature* appeared in 1917–21; the three-volume *Literary History of the United States*, an explicit reworking of the terrain covered by the *Cambridge History*, in 1948; the single-volume *Columbia Literary History of the United States*, an explicit reworking of the terrain covered by the first two compendia, in 1988.[60]

The *Cambridge History* appeared at a time when American literature was undergoing reconceptualization, when the canon was shifting: the collection devotes single chapters both to authors in the process of being demoted within the canon (Longfellow, Whittier, Lowell) and to authors being elevated (Thoreau, Twain). This was also a time when American literature was still trying to find a foothold in academia, a time when a key debate within English departments was on the value of a belletristic appreciation of literature versus a more scientific, philological inquiry. The latter approach lent itself to study of older texts, texts that were hundreds or thousands of years old—medieval and classical texts—and hence was not conducive to the study of American literature in English. American literature did not yet have an assured position within the academy, a situation that the publication of *The Cambridge History of American Literature* helped to remedy.

Within the field of American literature itself there were divisions between a historical focus on literature as an expression of national life and an aesthetic focus on individual works of art. By midcentury the aesthetic focus—with its tendency to limit itself to a restricted range of masterpieces—would dominate. But in the early decades of the twentieth century, the historical focus still held considerable sway in the academy and in the *Cambridge History*. As the editors announce in their preface to the first volume, the *Cambridge History* is "a survey of the life of the American people as expressed in their writings rather than a history of *belles-lettres* alone."[61] The emphasis on the relationship between literature and national life is further signaled by the way the editors divide literature into periods—relying on political events, especially wars, rather than aesthetic movements per se. It is also signaled by a willingness to discuss works that aesthetic purists might not, strictly speaking, consider literature, "such as travels, oratory, memoirs, which have lain somewhat out of the main tradition of literary history but which may be, as they are in the United States, highly significant of the national temper" (1:xi). Thus there are chapters devoted to historians, to orators, to magazine writers, to journalists, to educational and philosophical writers. And to writers of children's literature. The chapter "Books for Children" is striking both because it exists in this scholarly history, even as the discourse was professionalizing, and because it provides insight into how the academy—specifically, the chapter author, Algernon Tassin of Columbia University—viewed and categorized children's literature.

One significant feature of Tassin's insights is the ease with which he classifies certain nineteenth-century novels as children's literature, novels that have in recent decades been resurrected as important women's literature, which is to say literature for adults. Tassin may somewhat self-consciously note that Harriet Beecher Stowe's *Uncle Tom's Cabin* "is now almost exclusively a juvenile" (2:401)—his phrasing signals that it wasn't always so considered—yet he never indicates that Susan Warner's *Wide, Wide World* was ever anything other than juvenile literature. What Tassin marks, in effect, is the passage of these works, earlier or later, out of the canons of adult culture, leaving works of such power, for lack of anywhere else to go, in the nursery.

Other revealing insights emerge in the comments on Alcott and Twain. Tassin acknowledges the "abiding charm" of *Little Women* and grants it "the most assured position" (2:402)—among books for children, presumably. Even more assured than the position of Twain's work? Perhaps. Or maybe Twain's work belongs in yet another category. In Tassin's account, *Tom Sawyer* and *Huckleberry Finn*, equally, "immediately took the foremost place as stories of the American boy, and in a surprisingly short while became world classics" (2:405). He then temporizes, "They are not explicitly treated as boy's stories throughout, and in each are description and social observation beyond the appreciation of young readers; yet they have doubtless never failed with boy as with man to reap the highest triumph possible to fiction, the reader's recognition of his own psychology and temperament" (2:405–6). The fact is that children's literature almost always has to address adults as well as children: who is writing it, after all, and publishing it and most often buying it? But Tassin seems uncomfortable about treating *Tom Sawyer* and *Huckleberry Finn* as children's literature. So he temporizes—not yet indulging in the soon-to-be-popular maneuver of segregating the two works (witness, arguably, the Twain chapter of the *Cambridge History*), not yet categorizing *Tom Sawyer* for boys, *Huckleberry Finn* for men.

Finally, Tassin's comments reveal how the premises of the *Cambridge History* open the door to inclusion of children's literature. He chauvinistically argues that "more conscientious, intelligent work has been done in American writing for children than has been the case elsewhere"; he adds, "American literature for children has reached a comparative eminence which it shows in no other department" (2:407, 409). More importantly, he claims that "one can get more of American life from the juvenile than from adult fiction of the period" (2:406). One might therefore conclude that the most characteristically American achievement of American literature is its literature for children, that no other literature so distills the "national temper" that the editors of the *Cambridge History* wanted to capture.

The editors of the 1948 *Literary History of the United States*, however, try to close the door to any such thinking. As they proclaim in their prefatory "Address to the Reader," the *Literary History* diverges from the earlier emphasis on the "national significance" of various American writers by giving greater attention to "the timeless values in our writing," to attend to "the Poes, the Hawthornes, and all writers who were primarily artists, and whose merits often did not depend upon the peculiar circumstances of American history."[62] The editors go on to stress that although their volumes will examine "the varied and extensive experience of a national culture on its way, . . . the objective of the history will be to record and explain the great men and women who have made this culture speak to the imagination" (1:xvi). Literature, for them, "is any writing in which aesthetic, emotional, or intellectual values are made articulate by excellent expression" (1:xvi).

Despite this conscious shift in emphasis from the *Cambridge History*, the *Literary History* does not entirely jettison works that served nonaesthetic purposes: there are chapters on early reports and chronicles, essays, history, oratory. Simply because it was a history, the volumes had to be more inclusive than were other contemporary academic studies. But the chronicles and essays did presumably have to meet some standard of "excellent expression"—a standard that children's literature, apparently, could not meet. It receives no chapter of its own, and one is hard pressed to find the few sentences that do refer to it—usually disparagingly—in the fourteen hundred pages of text.

The fullest discussion of children's literature appears in the chapter "Humor," in which two pages are devoted to "humorous childhood stories" (2:746)—though these are not discussed as children's literature, nor would all the stories necessarily be considered children's literature, then or now. Aldrich's *Story of a Bad Boy* gets a paragraph, likewise Stephen Crane's *Whilomville Stories*, and Booth Tarkington's stories get several. The critic concludes his discussion by saying of Tarkington's heroes, "Like all great humorous creations they reconcile us to other men by reminding us that we are all comical—and on the whole decent—boys" (1:747–48). Something that Jo March's humorous dinner party could not, by definition, do.

More dismissively, the chapter on Hawthorne devotes part of a sentence to the works for children: "By writing he earned his bread, even composing stories for boys and girls" (1:418). But what other attitude might one expect from a critic who disparages certain symbols in drafts of *The Marble Faun* as jejune and the story of *The Blithedale Romance* as naive, and who celebrates Hawthorne's eventual emancipation from a "naïve view of the art of writing" requiring that fiction be an "illustration of moral precepts" (1:440)? For this critic, anything associated with childhood, as he reveals through his underlying pattern of metaphor, exists only to be outgrown.

A chapter on the European reception of nineteenth-century American literature, transatlantic crossings, concludes by referring to the "vast freight of popular literature, of which this brief survey has taken no account—the stories of Louisa Alcott, Frank Stockton, Thomas Bailey Aldrich, Susan Warner, Elizabeth Phelps, E. P. Roe, Marion Crawford, many others. It bore, amid the flood of sentimental romance, the more distinctive art of the regionalists . . ." (1:635). Children's literature is here reduced to a few figures—Alcott, Stockton, Aldrich, possibly Warner, possibly Phelps—and thereby coupled with "the flood of sentimental romance." It's equated with popular literature and dispatched from the mainland, from the bedrock of American literature. Alcott, as we shall see, spent virtually all her life in the United States, a choice that she defines in *Little Women* as independently American, a choice very unlike those made by James and the expatriate writers of the 1920s or even by Twain in the 1890s. These authors who physically left North America remain firmly on American bedrock when it comes to defining American literature; the author who stayed home is metaphorically shunted abroad—here and in one of the two other mentions of Alcott in the fourteen hundred pages of the *Literary History*.

Also intriguing is a chapter on Longfellow, Lowell, and Holmes, the first two demoted from a chapter apiece in the *Cambridge History* to this joint chapter with Holmes. These three writers were not addressing children as an isolated audience, but children were indeed part of their broad nineteenth-century readership. Odell Shepard, the author of the chapter, implies as much when he states that Longfellow's seventy-fifth birthday, in 1882, "was celebrated in every schoolhouse in the United States" (1:595). These poets, who early in the twentieth century were squeezed out of the upper echelons of the canon, were in fact often called the schoolroom or fireside poets: both metaphoric venues invite the presence of children. And the presence of children, to twentieth-century critical eyes, connotes inferiority. Shepard is overt about such a connotation in his discussion of Lowell: "Another source of Lowell's failure may have been that incorrigible youthfulness which he, like many of his countrymen, seems to have mistaken for a virtue. 'I continue as juvenile as ever,' he wrote to his daughter at the age of sixty-nine. 'I was passing a Home for Incurable Children the other day, and said to my companion, "I shall go there one of these days"'" (1:604). Shepard perceptively acknowledges the nineteenth-century willingness to embrace childhood and children but clearly disapproves of it.

Elsewhere in the chapter, Shepard, like other contributors to the *Literary History*, acknowledges another strand of thinking about American literature, one that, as Tassin pointed out, has made room for children's literature: namely, consideration of what makes American literature American. The editors of the volume stress their intention to deemphasize the "national significance" of the writers they discuss. Yet the intention was not uniformly acted upon; the authors of some chapters continue to laud certain figures for being very American.[63] Shepard, however, recognizes—and plays with—the dangers of the trope of Americanness: "The perennial question with regard to Longfellow's 'Americanism' is not so difficult as it has been made to seem. Surely the best proof that a man belongs to his people is given when they accept him as their representative and beloved voice. By this test Longfellow is the most American poet that America has ever had. He is so much of our kind that a close reading of him helps our understanding of ourselves, not always in a flattering way."[64] Shepard adds, "Yet after all it is not a poet's main business to represent his time and his country, to have witty or profound ideas, or even to hold sound opinions" (1:595). Artistry, "conscientious and deliberate," takes precedence. At times Longfellow did indeed achieve "a grand simplicity of style which seems the perfectly natural expression of his own essential goodness, his serenity, and his peace of heart"—"especially in old age" (1:596). Artistry that makes our "national culture . . . speak to the imagination" (1:xvi), to reiterate the words of the *Literary History*'s editors, would thus seem not to be associated with youth. It requires age, "maturity." Not for nothing did Shepard devote much of his scholarly career to exhuming Bronson Alcott, father of the author who, by the beginning of the twentieth century, came to be considered—and dismissed, at least by the professoriate—as the quintessential writer for children.

More than many of his contemporaries, Shepard recognized that seeking what is American in American literature, seeking what is truly representative, may be at cross-purposes with seeking what is artistically excellent, however defined. Key critics in the following decade would ignore this insight as they published volumes such as *The American Adam* or *The American Novel and Its Tradition*: they would find their exemplars of excellence to be quintessentially American—not recognizing how they were collapsing "American" and "excellent." Hawthorne, Melville, and Twain came to embody the individual's struggle with an oppressive and destructive society, often through escape to an unsettled wilderness, in critical narratives that Nina Baym has called "melodramas of beset manhood."[65] For the master myth created by the critics is decidedly masculine: women are associated with the society that needs to be escaped and often with the wilderness that needs to be tamed, not with the individual that does the escaping and taming. Hence an author portraying a woman who attempts such an escape is violating woman's true nature; an author portraying characters who do not attempt such escapes is writing, at best, minor literature. Children's literature, too, is excluded by this master myth of the 1950s, unless a work portrays an adolescent male rebelling against the status quo—becoming a melodrama of beset adolescence, if you will—but then the work would no longer be considered children's literature. Stories that are marketed as children's literature, like other stories of socialization, of acculturation to American society, are not quintessentially American.

Forty years after the *Literary History*, the eclectic *Columbia Literary History of the United States* consciously turns from an emphasis on so-called timeless aesthetic standards and claims to celebrate "diversity, complexity, and contradiction by making them structural principles."[66] It positions itself as part of "the current effort to reconstruct the history of the literature of the United States in ways that do not exclude certain writers because of biases involving gender, race, or ethnic and cultural background" (xii). It jettisons the emphasis on "excellent expression" proclaimed by its 1948 predecessor and celebrates its own inclusion of such genres as "the diary, the journal, scientific writing, journalism, autobiography, and even film" (xix). In fact, though, inclusion of these genres is not unique to the *Columbia Literary History:* the 1948 *Literary History* had referred to—and in most cases included extended discussions of—all those genres. And despite its vaunted inclusiveness, the 1988 volume devotes none of its sixty-six chapters to children's literature. Nor is there significant discussion of children's literature anywhere in its twelve hundred pages. In her chapter "The Rise of the Woman Author," Nina Baym astutely acknowledges that, before the Civil War, authors of domestic fiction were conscious of addressing the young as well as the old; she goes on to state that "one should not neglect to mention" tractlike works "nor the development of a thriving literature for children, much of it written by women," and she devotes almost three paragraphs to Alcott (303). And Jack Salzman devotes several pages to Horatio Alger, Frank Merriwell, and Elsie Dinsmore in his "Literature for the Populace." But the other references to children's literature are incidental or oblique.

At times these references are framed in terms of tapping "the potentially lucrative market for children's literature" or exploiting "the popularity of children's books" (416, 635). Only market incentives can justify such a turn in Hawthorne and Twain. More often, references to literature that has been addressed to or claimed by children do not frame it as children's literature. Admittedly, failing to mention that Laurence Yep's *Dragonwings* (1975) was published as a novel for the young may be a way of granting Yep full stature in the emerging pantheon of Asian-American authors. Citing only *The Prince and the Pauper* as Twain's contribution to children's literature, however—not *Huckleberry Finn*, nor even *Tom Sawyer*—is a way of keeping children's literature in its place. If a book is really good—which, as one of the "more superficial examples" of Twain's "narratives of time-travel," *The Prince and the Pauper* is not—it must be for adults.

Beyond these asides, consider the figures that the volume excludes. The only reference to Frances Hodgson Burnett in the *Columbia Literary History* is a brief mention of her dramatic work. There's no reference at all to Jacob Abbott or Peter Parley, to Frank Stockton or Mary Mapes Dodge, to the magazines *St. Nicholas* or the *Youth's Companion*, to L. Frank Baum or Kate Douglas Wiggin or Laura Ingalls Wilder or Maurice Sendak, no reference to works for children by E. B. White or Thomas Bailey Aldrich. Even the 1948 *Literary History* had not altogether excluded references to Abbott or Parley, to the *Youth's Companion* or Wiggin. By 1988 children's literature was, if anything, even more invisible in the academy than it had been in 1948.

Not everyone was ignoring children's literature. Academic literary critics may have done so, but we critics hardly constitute the universe. I'd like to turn here to the discipline I alluded to earlier, the one that literary critics often do not even consider a discipline, the one that effectively assumed the guardianship of children's literature.

In the 1870s, when Caroline M. Hewins created her first list of titles recommended for children, children's literature started becoming the province of librarians. During much of the nineteenth century, few social or circulating or even public libraries allowed children to borrow books or even to enter the library ("Children and Dogs Not Allowed"), but by the end of the century most U.S. public libraries were catering to children, sometimes with separate children's rooms and specially trained librarians. By the middle of the twentieth century more than half of the books borrowed from public libraries each year were lent to juveniles.[67] As early as 1877 Minerva L. Sanders—perhaps the first librarian to allow children under twelve to use public library books—set aside a corner of the Pawtucket, Rhode Island, library for children, providing small chairs for them. By 1878 Hewins, in Hartford, Connecticut, was publishing a list of titles recommended for children; her *Books for the Young* (1882) was the first venture of the Publishing Section of the American Library Association (ALA). In 1890 Mary Bean opened a separate children's room in the Brookline, Massachusetts, library. In 1898 the Pratt Library School in Brooklyn added a training course for children's librarians. In 1901 Anne Carroll Moore chaired the first meeting of the Section for Children's Librarians of the ALA, and in 1906 she became the first head of the children's department of the New York Public Library.

Standard histories of the public library may feature the names of men—Justin Winsor, Melvil Dewey, William Frederick Poole—but all the leaders among children's librarians seem to have been women,[68] sometimes to the dismay of latter-day historians. "The romantic air of enthusiastic tenderness so prominent even today in any discussion of children in the library," writes Dee Garrison, "is in sharp contrast to the more normal tendency of librarians to indulge in searching self-criticism in every other phase of library work. The incongruity becomes more understandable when it is remembered that the children's section of the library was created and shaped by women librarians. Here, as in no other area, library women were free to express, unchallenged, their self-image."[69] Given that it was somewhat more acceptable for a middle-class woman to enter the workplace if she worked with children, the attention to literature for children may have facilitated the entry of women into the field, even as their entry fostered a climate conducive to the nurturing of children's literature—at the same time that the arbiters of literature for adults increasingly were men.[70]

Librarians have provided a haven for children's literature and have also played a vital role in shaping it. In the 1920s through the 1950s, a single librarian, the Superintendent of Work with Children for the New York Public Library, exerted considerable influence on the development of children's literature. Thanks to her position in the New York Public Library (1906–41), her leadership in the ALA (she was the first chair of the Children's Services Section), her annual lists of recommended books (1918–41), and her columns in the *Bookman* and then in the *New York Herald Tribune* Sunday supplement, Anne Carroll Moore assumed a position that has been called "olympian" and "magisterial." "Hers was the authoritative voice in the world of children's books"; her office, "the center of the children's book world in New York City."[71] As Leonard Marcus notes, "Such was her reputation nationally that inclusion on the list [the annual list of recommended new books] all but assured a book a respectable sale; omission might just as easily mean oblivion. Editors, authors, and illustrators routinely stopped by to visit with Miss Moore and seek her counsel on their works in progress."[72] Authors and illustrators such as the award-winning Marcia Brown and Hendrik van Loon even dedicated books to her.[73]

Moore gave copiously of her advice to parents and booksellers, to fellow librarians, to publishers and editors. "I hope you are not undertaking the edition of Grimm and Andersen of which you wrote before Christmas," Moore wrote in 1936 to an editor at Little, Brown; "I liked neither the plan for the selection nor the artist chosen to illustrate the tales."[74] And the editors listened. In 1913 George Dutton of E. P. Dutton and Company wrote to Moore, "It was largely at your suggestion that we have gone ahead with" a series addressing "child life in foreign countries."[75] In 1956 Moore wrote to an editor at Holt, "I believe that Mr. Courlander's material could be made into an interesting and valuable collection"—and his *Terrapin's Pot of Sense* was published the next year, illustrated by the artist whom Moore recommended.[76] In 1938, dismayed by the liberties that the books based on the Disney film had taken with the Grimms' "Snow White," Moore pressured Coward-McCann to get the award-winning Wanda Gág to translate and illustrate the tale. Gág did so. She decided not to dedicate her book to Moore after her editor urged that there be "no hint that the book was a result of pressure from librarians."[77] Two weeks later the editor wrote of bringing the illustrations to Moore and "trotting after her as she rushed from department to department all over the library showing them."[78] In 1939 the ALA named Gág's *Snow White and the Seven Dwarfs* a Caldecott Honor Book.

As an editor for Coward-McCann said to Moore in 1929, "Lay us down a law and we'll try to follow you."[79] And lay down the law Moore did. The editor Grace Hogarth recalls being summoned to the infamous Room 105 of the New York Public Library in the 1930s—the idea of declining the request seems not to have occurred to her—and then being asked, with respect to the picture book on her first juvenile list, "Why . . . have you, representing the Oxford University Press, published this trash?"[80] A few years later, in 1938, the publisher Bill Scott sought an appointment with Moore and brought his first five juvenile books, which included work by Esphyr Slobodkina, Clement Hurd, and Margaret Wise Brown, all of whom would go on to have illustrious careers (Hurd and Brown later created the early-childhood classic *Goodnight Moon*). "Mr. Scott," Moore asked, "do you want to know what I think of these books?" He responded affirmatively. "Truck, Mr. Scott! They are truck!"[81]

As her response to the work of Slobodkina, Hurd, and Brown suggests, Moore's judgment was hardly infallible. She also advised E. B. White not to publish *Stuart Little*, his first children's book, fearing it might "become an embarrassment rather than the source of continuing pleasure and rewarding return any book from his pen should command."[82] She didn't like *Charlotte's Web* either.

Needless to say, editors and authors were not always fond of Moore. As a librarian who had worked for her noted, mildly, in an encomium, "Now and then an irate author descended upon us."[83] The editor Susan Hirschman recalls Louise Seaman Bechtel, the first children's book editor at Macmillan (starting in

1919), saying forty years after the fact, "That goddamned Anne Carroll Moore! She didn't like that book [Lewis Hine's *Men at Work*] and she didn't buy it for the New York Public Library and . . ."[84] Yet Moore—and her colleagues—played an important role in making children's literature a haven for the imaginative, for creating a climate in which award-winning books could also be strong sellers. Hirschman also recalls, "As much as we all complained about the library market when we had it, those librarians were people who had standards and criteria and who had been educated and trained in book selection. What's happening now is that there aren't many standards except 'big is better' and 'shiny and glitzy is good'" (293). Barbara Bader sees Moore and her colleagues as underscoring "that making books for children was important work, that making beautiful books was almost a duty."[85] Certainly Moore stressed the aesthetic importance of children's literature, downplayed the urge "to inform, instruct, or improve," and emphasized the need "to awaken, enlighten, and enlarge the minds and hearts of children"—"to rouse the spirit of curiosity, to send the reader on a voyage of exploration and discovery."[86]

Of course, Anne Carroll Moore was not the sole mover in shaping children's literature at this time. Other librarians were active as well, in interaction with publishers, booksellers, and educators. Kay E. Vandergrift refers to a 1927–28 report of an ALA committee on children's books that lists "the decisions of publishers in response to what were apparently requests from the committee to reprint specific books along with notices of new editions being considered by publishers." In summing up the response of publishers to a series of questions or requests, the report states, "The publishers deeply appreciate the devotion of children's librarians to the cause of children's literature, and desire to cooperate with them and forward in every way practicable and possible the suggestions librarians offer for the betterment of the spiritual and physical makeup of children's books."[87]

Indeed, individuals often enacted the crisscrossing of various roles within their own careers; many leaders in the field worked in more than one area during the course of their lives. To mention only a few examples, Bechtel had been a teacher before becoming Macmillan's children's book editor and then went on to reviewing; her colleague at Doubleday, May Massee, had been a teacher, librarian, and book-review editor; and the current grande dame of children's publishing, Margaret McElderry, worked as a librarian under Moore. In 1974 McElderry noted of the relationship between editors and librarians of children's literature, after commenting on the streams of "editors, authors, illustrators, re-

viewers, educators, and librarians" who came to Moore's office, "Such a relationship has never existed to any degree between adult editors and librarians. It continues to be a particular strength of the children's publishing and literary world."[88]

The interrelations are reminiscent of the way in which Horace Scudder, for
one, connected various realms in the nineteenth century. With one significant
exception: Scudder was also the editor of the leading literary journal of his day,
and hence he succeeded in connecting the literary world of children to that of
adults. Soon after the Atlantic Monthly Press published the children's book
Jane, Joseph, and John, in 1918, Moore decided to ask (very timidly, she claims)
over a Boston telephone, "'Does "Jane, Joseph and John" mean that The Atlantic Monthly Press is going to undertake the publication of children's books?'
'Oh, no, nothing of the kind,' came the reply in cheerful but positive tones. It
was not the editor who spoke, he was then in Europe. If anything very unusual
and original for children were to come in, it might be considered for publication, but there were no 'plans.'"[89] Some such plans were nevertheless announced
in 1919. But not in consultation with Moore. It was no longer possible to play
the role of Scudder, or even of his "good friend" Mary Mapes Dodge, who edited *St. Nicholas* and collaborated with him.[90] The boundaries separating editing,
publishing, education, and library work for children were startlingly fluid in the
early twentieth century, but the boundary between literature for children and
literature for adults was much less so. As a reviewer for the *Dial* noted as early
as 1901, "The great masters of English fiction did not think that writing tales to
tell to their juniors was in any way beneath their dignity a generation ago; today there seems to be a great gulf fixed."[91]

In any case, a key enactment of the twentieth-century crisscrossing of roles
in the children's book world is that Frederick Melcher, a bookseller and also the
editor of *Publishers Weekly*, came up with the idea for the Newbery Medal, to be
awarded by the librarians of the ALA. The ALA started awarding the Newbery
Medal, for the outstanding contribution to American children's literature during the previous year, in 1922; the Caldecott Medal, for outstanding illustrations
in children's books, in 1938. Both awards continue to be enormously influential,
especially given the numbers of children's books purchased by libraries. In the
years immediately following the 1965 Elementary and Secondary Education
Act, 80 to 90 percent of children's book sales were apparently to libraries, and
even now, after cuts in library funding, 50 to 60 percent continue to be.[92] If a library buys no other children's books in a given year, it buys the Newbery and
Caldecott winners. I've heard, from a prominent reviewer and a prominent ed-

itor, that winning one of the medals can lead to total sales of sixty to a hundred thousand copies—and comes close to ensuring a permanent place on a publisher's backlist.[93]

One way in which award-givers have shaped the field is by being responsive to women writers: 67 percent of the Newbery winners have been women, a percentage at least twice as high as that for any comparable award for "adult-stream"—mainstream—literature. The award-givers have been less responsive to issues of race. As Donnarae MacCann notes, pointing to the award of the Newbery Medal to *The Voyages of Doctor Dolittle* even as Du Bois's pioneering children's journal *The Brownies' Book* ceased publishing because of insufficient circulation, "The increasing institutionalization of children's literature . . . helped extend the lifespan of the white supremacy myth."[94] Yet, I would argue, librarians—perhaps more attuned to the impact of books on individual readers—have been quicker to respond to representations of race than have literary critics. I look at the creation of the Coretta Scott King Award in 1970, at the New York Public Library's periodic bibliographies *The Black Experience in Children's Literature*, beginning in 1974, and at a number of edited volumes produced in the 1970s, 1980s, and beyond.[95]

Academic critics, however, have not particularly noticed any of these activities by librarians. The many reasons why twentieth-century literary critics have looked down on children's literature—even critics attuned to other kinds of marginalization—include an urge to dissociate America and American literature from youthfulness and an insistence on cultural independence from the parent country. They include an urge to achieve "institutional maturity," as Renker puts it.[96] Also suspect are the popularity and profitability of much children's literature. Yet another reason for critical condescension is that children's literature is associated with librarians, a group that the professoriate generally treats more as handmaidens than as fellow scholars and teachers. I use the term *handmaidens* advisedly: even if the leadership has often been predominantly male, most librarians and library staff members are women. Although it wasn't until 1852 that the Boston Public Library hired a woman clerk, by 1891 female librarians outnumbered their male colleagues at the annual ALA convention. By 1910, 78.5 percent of U.S. library workers were female; by 1920, almost 90 percent. [97]

What librarians publish as part of their professional work, their research, is apt to be collections of interviews with or essays by authors (underscoring that authors are people too) or else bibliographies, including bibliographies of books that can help a child deal with divorce or with the death of a grandparent or with being disabled. I suspect it would be hard to find a field more heavily "bibli-ographied" than children's literature. But neither such collections nor bibli-ographies carry great prestige with literary critics.[98]

Nor do librarians. Except on the occasional acknowledgments page of a criti-cal tome (in tandem with the now notorious expressions of gratitude to the scholar's wife), the work of librarians is usually ignored by academic critics. And the attitudes of such critics toward librarians and toward children's literature complexly intertwine. The devaluing of one can lead by contagion to the de-valuing of the other. The stereotypical lady librarian can become the scapegoat responsible for the sad estate of whatever a critic wants to rescue from oblivion, as subsequent chapters will reveal. More often, the work of librarians is simply as easy to ignore as is children's literature. Attitudes toward children's literature are never simple; they're always complexly connected to attitudes associated with gender or class or, in this case, a particular profession.

Consider that the MLA, in preparing its CD-ROM and print bibliographies, has not, until very recently, routinely screened most of the children's literature journals that have strong associations with librarianship or education. The MLA decisions were not necessarily targeted at excluding children's literature, per-haps just at drawing disciplinary boundaries. Yet, since the boundaries separat-ing literary criticism, education, and librarianship are particularly permeable for children's literature, this last has been only imperfectly represented in the MLA bibliography, the standard bibliography in literary criticism. The MLA has nev-ertheless seemed rather more willing to cross other disciplinary boundaries. Among the more than four thousand journals it has screened to locate articles on language and literature are *Asian Music, American Anthropologist, Child Devel-opment*, and *Infant Behavior and Development*. Not that it has completely ignored children's literature: for a number of years it has screened *Children's Literature*, the *Children's Literature Association Quarterly, The Lion and the Unicorn*, the *Eng-lish Journal*, and (as of 1995) *Canadian Children's Literature*. But until 1998 it did not screen *Bookbird, Journal of Youth Services in Libraries, Horn Book Magazine, School Library Journal, Language Arts, New Advocate, Five Owls, Voice of Youth Ad-vocates, Junior Bookshelf*, or even the prestigious British journal *Signal*—to cite ten journals that publish work of interest to scholars of children's literature.[99]

On a lesser note, but probably a much too representative one, the "major" re-search university where I went to graduate school subscribes or has subscribed to more than thirty thousand periodicals. In my early research for this chapter, I initially found that, of the above-mentioned journals important to scholars of children's literature, the library had subscribed only to the *English Journal* and *Children's Literature*. It canceled the subscription to the annual *Children's Literature* in 1985. After checking its more recent holdings, I can modify my report somewhat: the research library did acquire the 1991 issue of the annual, and in 1995 it started subscribing to *The Lion and the Unicorn*. It may be that academic prejudices are loosening a little. Perhaps the current positioning of children's literature in the academy is best captured by a reader of an early draft of this chapter, who noted that the academy is currently living an unresolved paradox: "On the one hand, there is a burgeoning interest in children's literature and an increasing number of sophisticated critics in that field, yet, on the other hand, the prejudice against the field has hardly abated at all."

In the nineteenth century, then, the American arbiters of elite culture were receptive to children's literature, considered it important, took it seriously. Even the most elite such arbiters, the editors of the *Atlantic*, devoted considerable space to reviewing and discussing children's literature. As the cultural arbiters professionalized in the early twentieth century, however—as gatekeeping shifted from literary journals to the academy—children's literature simply dropped off the cultural radar screen. Academics ignored it. The stewardship of children's literature passed into the hands of librarians—but academics tended to ignore the work of librarians too.

Now, at the turn of a new century, the positioning of children's literature seems to be entering a new phase. Thanks to literary criticism that has questioned the received canon, thanks to feminist and other criticism that has explored and celebrated the hitherto marginal, the academy may be becoming more willing to take children's literature seriously again.

Maybe, for instance, the profession can rethink the achievements of Louisa May Alcott, who in the twentieth century was dismissed for being an author of children's literature, however quintessentially. Maybe it can also rethink the achievements of Mark Twain, whose great American novel is also, importantly, a classic work for children. Maybe it can rethink the achievements of fantasy writers such as L. Frank Baum, whose work was dismissed even by many of the custodians of children's literature. These are issues I will engage in the next chapters, as I turn from a focus on cultural institutions in the United States to case studies of three genres of children's literature.

CHAPTER FOUR

The Case of the Boys' Book

Whitewashing Huck

If *The Adventures of Tom Sawyer* is a "boys' book," *Adventures of Huckleberry Finn* is, rather, "a book which boys enjoy" but "does not fall into the category of juvenile fiction."[1] Thus does T. S. Eliot, in 1950, formulate a key difference between the two currently most popular books by Mark Twain, a formulation that has resonated with Twain critics ever since. A standard critical line has been that Twain was not fond of children's literature and wasn't trying to write it—and therefore did not write it—when he was creating such a masterpiece as *Huckleberry Finn*.

Yet before 1950, American critics and reviewers did not always differentiate between *Tom Sawyer* and *Huckleberry Finn* by assigning the former to children's literature and the latter to literature for adults—if indeed they differentiated between the two books. In the nineteenth century both were considered boys' books, suitable for boys of all ages. Tracing responses to Twain's work since it appeared confirms how differently nineteenth- and twentieth-century critics have defined and responded to children's literature and starts to demonstrate that the shift in response has not happened in any simple or lockstep fashion. Gender and genre, among other things, have a significant impact on reception.

Mapping the trajectory of response to Twain offers a unique perspective on differences in thinking about children and children's literature, by providing a case study of how American critics have defined the audience for, and have themselves responded to, the boys' book (then sometimes called the boy's book, now sometimes called the boy book). Discussions of Twain in the past century and a quarter do, however, show one major continuity: whether as a gauge of value or as a source of discourse, they constantly invoke childhood.

Before I turn to the responses of academic and other elite critics, though, I might note that a willingness to invoke childhood, coupled with a tendency to overlook some of the fine discriminations of T. S. Eliot and other twentieth-century critics, is certainly apparent in popular thinking about Twain, as evidenced in newspapers, magazines, and advertising. Take the latter-day critics' sharp differentiation between *Tom Sawyer* and *Huckleberry Finn*. In the popular imagination the two books are often conjoined, as their frequent incarnations in cartoons and advertising attest: two boys on a raft, or two boys and a man. Even when writing in a venue more elite than popular, in the *Atlantic* in 1901, Charles Johnston refers to "the immortal trio" of Tom, Huck, and Jim: "the Tom Sawyer trio, in those sunlit days on the great river, with the raft floating along, and the boys telling tales, or puffing at their corncob pipes, or going in swimming, is, and will probably long remain, the high-water mark of humor and imaginative creation for the New World,—the most genuinely American thing ever written."[2] *Tom Sawyer* and *Huckleberry Finn* are so thoroughly confounded in Johnston's imagination—as even now in the popular imagination—that he conflates the two books, placing Tom on the raft with Huck and Jim as they float down the Mississippi.

Conflated or not, both books were highly popular in the twentieth century. They appear on Frank Luther Mott's lists of best-selling books before 1945, with *Tom Sawyer* forging "far ahead" of *Huckleberry Finn* after the turn of the century; John C. Gerber estimates that, as of 1985, world sales of *Huckleberry Finn* had probably exceeded twenty million.[3] A 1923 poll suggests that *Tom Sawyer* was the fourth most circulated work of fiction in U.S. libraries; *Huckleberry Finn* tied for fourteenth.[4] In a 1934 tally based in St. Louis, the Missouri-born Twain was "the most widely read American author"; in a tally published in 1936 and drawing on Chicago-area libraries, Twain came in ninth.[5]

Twain's works also fare well in polls of younger readers. In the largest and probably most reliable early-twentieth-century nationwide tally of schoolchil-

All aboard the raft, in the 1931 Paramount film version of *Huckleberry Finn*: Huck, Jim—and Tom
The Story of the Paramount Picture "Huckleberry Finn": Taken from Mark Twain's Immortal Classic of Childhood (Lubin Press, ca. 1931), p. [15])

dren's favorite reading, a survey of books read and liked by 36,750 children in 1924–25 (children largely of what we would now call middle-school age), *Tom Sawyer* came in first; *Huckleberry Finn*, ninth.[6] Twain's works may not appear in the report of a 1913 survey of New York City schoolchildren in the first through eighth grades, but in surveys of boys, especially boys aged ten or older, *Tom Sawyer* and *Huckleberry Finn* rank variously third and fourteenth (in 1907); fourth and fifth (1909); second and seventh (1917); fourth and sixth (1920); second and ninth (1927); first and fourth (1927); eighth and fifth, fourth and twentieth, fifth and fourth (at increasing age levels, 1931); first and third (1937); and second and sixth (1949).[7] And famous people ranging from Pat Boone to Bill Bradley, from Bill Cosby to George McGovern, from Barry Lopez to Judith Krantz, list *Huckleberry Finn* or *Tom Sawyer* or both as childhood favorites.[8]

Moreover, the images of Tom and Huck, indeed the image of Twain himself, appear everywhere in the media—in advertising for a cemetery in Los Angeles or for a dry-cleaning establishment in North Carolina and of course at various sites in Disney World.[9] When my son was ten years old, he wondered, after noting the portrayal of Twain in reruns of *Star Trek: The Next Generation,* "But how can he be dead? The actor looked just like him." Mark Twain lives. It's hard to grow up in the United States without knowing what he looked like. And Twain continues to be the property of children as well as adults.

Twain himself notoriously vacillated about the intended audience for what are now sometimes called his boy books. In June 1875, while drafting *Tom Sawyer,* he wrote to William Dean Howells that the manuscript "is likely to follow its own drift, & so is as likely to drift into manhood as anywhere."[10] Howells responded with enthusiasm, urging that this could be Twain's "chief work" and not to "waste it on a *boy*" (3 July 1875; 1:90)—though it's unclear whether he meant not to limit the novel's scope to Tom's childhood or not to limit its audience to children. Twain replied that it was "*not* a boy's book, at all. It will only be read by adults. It is only written for adults" (5 July 1875; 1:91). After reading the manuscript, however, Howells persuaded Twain that he would hit the right "key" if he treated the story "explicitly *as* a boy's story," adding, "Grown-ups will enjoy it just as much if you do" (21 November 1875; 1:110).[11] Twain agreed, toning down the satire and strong language, as he noted two months later, "since the book is to be for boys & girls," since it is "professedly & confessedly a boy's & girl's book" (18 January 1876; 1:122). He went on to say, in his preface to *Tom Sawyer,* "Although my book is intended mainly for the entertainment of boys and girls, I hope it will not be shunned by men and women on that account, for part of my plan has been to try to pleasantly remind adults of what they once were themselves, and of how they felt and thought and talked, and what queer enterprises they sometimes engaged in."[12]

A few months later Twain described *Huckleberry Finn,* which he was then embarking on, as "another boys' book" (9 August 1876; 1:144). And perhaps his paying so little attention to the adolescent Huck's sexuality may result not so much from Twain's prudishness, as has been claimed,[13] as from a sense of the decorum of literature for children: what nineteenth-century reviewers most decried in books whose audience included children, what struck critics for elite magazines such as the *Atlantic* as a boundary marker between literature for children and that for adults, was the presence of "love-making," which is to say courtship. By evading adult sexuality, Twain could write another book for boys—while not excluding adults.

Many mid-twentieth-century critics, eager to distance *Tom Sawyer* from *Huckleberry Finn,* have tried to explain away (as perhaps "only a manner of speaking") Twain's early statement that *Tom Sawyer* was for adults and that *Huck-leberry Finn* (it "had been begun as journeywork") was a boys' book.[14] Recent critics who have wanted to claim not just *Huckleberry Finn* but also *Tom Sawyer* for adults have stressed Twain's assertion, when writing *Tom Sawyer*, that it was "*not* a boy's book," dismissing the comments in the preface as perhaps "a marketing gambit" and pointing to a later comment in one of his notebooks: "I have never written a book for boys; I write for grown-ups who have *been* boys."[15] But as Albert E. Stone, Jr., judiciously remarks, Twain "constantly rewrote the past to fit the moods and needs of the present; hence these vacillations must be accepted at face value. They indicate merely that Twain was of two minds about the readers for whom he finally published *The Adventures of Tom Sawyer* in 1876."[16] They also reflect the extent to which the two audiences were not yet fully discrete.

The intermingling of these audiences in Twain's thinking is highlighted by the history of the last two Tom Sawyer stories that he published. *Tom Sawyer Abroad* first appeared in a magazine that we now see as targeting children, *St. Nicholas* (1893–94); *Tom Sawyer, Detective* first appeared in *Harper's Monthly* (1896), whose primary audience we consider to be adults. And as if to underscore the congruence of their audiences, both sequels were reprinted in a single volume in 1896. Imagine a modern author publishing a story in *Ladybug* in 1999, one in the *New Yorker* in May 2001, and reprinting both in a single book in December 2001.

As I noted in Chapter 3, nineteenth-century observers did not make the sharp differentiations between literature for children and literature for adults that we do now. Writing for an audience of boys and girls—or, better yet, writing for boys of all ages—did not necessarily diminish a writer's stature. And the audience for all fiction was still conceived of as encompassing both young and old.

As I turn to the responses of nineteenth-century critics, it's worth pointing out that reviewers and other critics were as attentive to *Tom Sawyer* and *The Prince and the Pauper*, both of which are now generally classified as children's literature, as they were to *Huckleberry Finn*. The number of reviews garnered by the three books was roughly comparable. In *Mark Twain: The Contemporary Reviews*, Louis J. Budd lists thirty-seven reviews for *Tom Sawyer*, thirty for *The Prince and the Pauper*, and thirty-five for *Huckleberry Finn*.[17] In other nineteenth-century criticism, *Tom Sawyer* and *Huckleberry Finn* were usually discussed in tandem, and it's fair to say that they received equal attention. *The Prince and the Pauper* seems to have received about as much. The distribution of scholarly attention during the final decades of the twentieth century, however, as gauged by entries in the MLA CD-ROM bibliography, has been very different. *Huckleberry Finn* received more than five times as much attention as *Tom Sawyer.* And *Tom Sawyer* received more than six times as much as *The Prince and the Pauper.* That marked imbalance was simply not the case in the nineteenth century.

Most of the early responses to *The Adventures of Tom Sawyer* (1876) assume children will comprise part of the audience. Some reviewers, including writers for the *Saturday Review,* the *Scotsman,* and the *New York Times,* simply describe *Tom Sawyer* as a book for children, especially boys. The *New York Times* reviewer may conclude with a parenthetical aside—"if the book really is intended for boys and girls"[18]—but not in order to celebrate how the book speaks to a mature understanding, as a modern reader might expect. Instead the reviewer finds *Tom Sawyer* a little too sensational, too sanguinary: if the book is for children, it should be more circumspect. The reviewer has earlier stated, "We are rather inclined to treat books intended for boys and girls, written by men of accredited talent and reputation, in a serious manner" (56–57). What it means here to treat children's books seriously is to treat them as serious matters for children—to gauge how edifying they are. It is also to treat them with the same kind of respect and attention accorded to books for adults, at a time when most commentators looked to all literature for moral as well as aesthetic value. As William Dean Howells urged in another context, "Morality penetrates all things, it is the soul of all things," and no novelist should write "without feeling bound to distinguish so clearly that no reader of his may be misled, between what is right and what is wrong, what is noble and what is base, what is health and what is perdition, in the actions and the characters he portrays."[19] In any case, most reviewers who treat *Tom Sawyer* as a book for children are positive, though a few, like the *New York Times* reviewer, express misgivings that follow from their conception of audience: the book may be a bit sensational, the language a bit vulgar and slangy, the author too willing to endorse lying.

Other reviewers—including those for the *Academy,* the London *Times,* and the *San Francisco Sunday Chronicle*—follow Twain's lead in his preface and treat the book as being aimed at both children and adults. Often these are the reviews that wax most enthusiastic, whether to hint that a book that speaks to adults is better than a book that speaks to children alone or simply to register the reviewer's own adult pleasure in the volume. Moncure Conway says, "The book will no doubt be a great favourite with boys, for whom it must in good part have been intended; but next to boys we should say that it might be most prized by philosophers and poets."[20]

Five years later Twain published *The Prince and the Pauper*, his full-length work that later commentators have been most willing to relegate to children's literature; certainly it appeared on lists of recommended reading for children well into the middle of the twentieth century.[21] Its nineteenth-century reception was similar to that for *Tom Sawyer*, though enthusiasm was somewhat more likely to correlate with the critic's nationality (some British writers smarted under Twain's criticism of royalty) than with his or her sense of the age of the intended audience. Those who address age tend to be enthusiastic and tend to consider the book suitable for young and old, for "young people of all ages," as the title page announces.[22] The 1881 reviewer for the *Critic* even suggests, contrary to more recent views, that *The Prince and the Pauper* "is far less distinctly juvenile than was *Tom Sawyer*," thanks to its "gentle humor and a poetic quality which appeal to that remnant of childhood which in the happiest lives survives even into old age."[23] The qualities that now strike readers as rendering the book juvenile—its relatively linear plotting, its kindly portrayals of characters (their virtue suitably rewarded), its foregrounding of what Howells elsewhere called "the more smiling aspects of life"[24]—are what made it serious and significant literature in the nineteenth century. Contemporary readers variously referred to it as "a book which has other and higher merits than can possibly belong to the most artistic expression of mere humor," as Twain's "masterpiece in fineness," as ranking "far above any of the author's previous productions," as marking Twain's emergence as a "true literary artist."[25] Twain himself referred to it, not entirely tongue in cheek, as "grave & stately work . . . considered by the world to be above my proper level."[26] In short, as Arthur Lawrence Vogelback declared in 1942, *The Prince and the Pauper* was "the first work on which critics generally agreed that Mark Twain displayed notable abilities as a serious writer and literary artist."[27]

As for *Adventures of Huckleberry Finn* (1885), it's a truism among Twain critics that the early response was mixed—by which they mean that nineteenth-century reviewers variously praised and condemned the book. But this early response was also mixed in its assessment of the targeted audience.

Almost all the reviewers and other nineteenth-century critics who allude to the intended audience assume that it includes children. If a reviewer is enthusiastic about the book, then both children and adults are likely to be mentioned.[28] Occasionally a critic makes an explicit connection between the worth of the book and the range in age of the audience: in 1898 the British writer Sir Walter Besant states, "The first quality that I claim for this book . . . is that it does appeal to all ages and every age." Such a claim is important, he adds, because "I lay it down as one of the distinctive characteristics of a good story that it pleases— or rather, seizes—every period of life; that the child, and his elder brother, and his father, and his grandfather, may read it with like enjoyment."[29]

If the reviewers of *Huckleberry Finn* focus on children alone as the audience, then they usually express misgivings. A writer for the *Cleveland Leader and Herald* notes that the book is "hardly suitable for a Sunday school"—at a time when Sunday schools were increasingly the domain of children, as indeed they are in *Huckleberry Finn* itself.[30] Latter-day Twain critics are fond of reporting that Louisa May Alcott declared, "If Mr. Clemens cannot think of something better to tell our pure-minded lads and lasses, he had best stop writing for them."[31] Yet I have found it difficult to locate a legitimate source for Alcott's comment: the earliest citation I have tracked down is *The Mauve Decade* (1926) by the literary gossip Thomas Beer.[32] The breezy style and gossipy nature of the book do not inspire confidence in its accuracy. Still, the alleged comment is so perfect for the purposes of Twain enthusiasts—for underscoring Twain's early persecution by those associated with the elite milieu of Concord and for contrasting him with the writer now seen as the quintessential nineteenth-century writer for children—that they might almost have invented it. Perhaps they did.

And, of course, *Huckleberry Finn* was notoriously banned from the Concord Public Library—as "rough, coarse and inelegant, dealing with a series of experiences not elevating"[33]—precisely because its suitability for children was at issue. Twentieth-century critics have focused on the ensuing phrase in the much-cited report of the *Boston Transcript*: "the whole book being more suited to the slums than to intelligent, respectable people." The class difference asserted here intriguingly echoes a literary cleavage between the genteel ideals of the old *Atlantic* and the new realism that Howells, for one, was increasingly championing. Latter-day critics intent on distancing themselves from the genteel tradition have focused on the class prejudice, a prejudice that was certainly and significantly there. Yet most nineteenth-century critics were acutely aware not just of class but of age, aware that the age of the audience was a key issue in the banning, whether they lament that "every boy and girl in Concord will make a point to get that book and read it" or exult that the banning will induce "every smart boy and girl in the town to buy it and read it on the sly."[34]

It's also striking that these early critics do not sharply distinguish *Tom Sawyer* from *Huckleberry Finn*. Louis J. Budd, the one other recent critic who seems to have been struck by the then-congruent reputations of the two books, notes that, before perhaps the 1920s, even those who judge *Huckleberry Finn* as the better book do not see it as "of a much brighter magnitude, just better."[35] The early commentators may note in passing that *Huckleberry Finn* is a sequel or companion to *Tom Sawyer*, may excoriate the improprieties in both books, may admit that the vulgarity in *Huckleberry Finn* isn't any worse than that in *Tom Sawyer*, may even suggest that *Huckleberry Finn* marks a literary advance over *Tom Sawyer*. And Brander Matthews, an early champion of Twain and later a professor at Columbia, may claim that *Huckleberry Finn* does "not quite reach these two highest points of *Tom Sawyer*"—the comic whitewashing scene, the thrilling encounter with "Indian Joe" (Matthews's euphemistic phrasing) in the cave—but "we incline to the opinion that the general level of the later story is perhaps higher than that of the earlier."[36] Yet Matthews and other contemporaries of Twain do not see *Huckleberry Finn* as immeasurably better, as Twain's unique masterpiece. *Huckleberry Finn* is "perhaps higher" but not yet the great American novel, and both it and *Tom Sawyer* were still generally read as books for boys.

There was also a tendency for Twain's contemporaries to think more highly of *The Prince and the Pauper* than do most later critics. A writer singles it out in 1897 for special praise as "the most dramatic and the most feelingly written" of Twain's works.[37] In 1909 a textbook author concludes that "it is not impossible that future critics may come to regard *The Prince and the Pauper* (1882) and *The Personal Recollections of Joan of Arc* (1896), two serious and dignified pieces of writing, as Mr. Clemens's best work."[38] In general, the Prince and his Pauper offended genteel American critics less than did the more raucous Tom and Huck. The book also seemed more tightly constructed, less episodic than *Tom Sawyer* and *Huckleberry Finn*. But this was also a time when a children's book such as *The Prince and the Pauper* could achieve stature among critics. A writer for the *Atlantic* in the 1940s could be bemused that in the previous century Twain was considered a humorist and a writer for children and hence, he implies, dismissed,[39] yet in the nineteenth century being considered a writer for children was not grounds for dismissal. Writing books that adults considered suitable for children meant writing in accord with genteel ideals; such writing was thus accorded more prestige, at the time, than certain "realistic" or "humorous" works. Hence a book that we might now categorize as for children, such as *The Prince and the Pauper*, could indeed have a higher standing with many in the cultural elite than a book that we might now categorize as for adults, such as *Huckleberry Finn*. In sharply differentiating between serious literature and children's literature, modern critics find it difficult to recognize the power of what the nineteenth century considered serious—and hence for children.

In any case, *Huckleberry Finn* had its champions among early reviewers and other critics, but the book was not usually praised for being truly accessible only to an elite and adult few—a common strategy among twentieth-century critics who have wanted to make sure the book isn't considered children's literature, even if in the next breath they celebrate Twain's democratic Americanism. Nor was *Huckleberry Finn* usually praised as the great American novel. Consider the statements of the one nineteenth-century critic who might seem to extol *Huckleberry Finn* above all other novels: in 1891 the British scholar Andrew Lang called *Huckleberry Finn* "the great American novel," in fact, a masterpiece—as a number of more recent critics are fond of noting. Yet it's worthwhile to examine his comments in greater detail than most recent critics have done. They do not acknowledge, for instance, that Lang calls *Tom Sawyer* a masterpiece too, that he regrets that both books are "masterpieces which a fallacious appearance has confounded with boys' books and facetiae" because, apparently, Twain's "natural and cultivated tendency to extravagance and caricature is only to be checked by the working on the profound and candid seriousness of boyhood."[40] Lang's attitudes here are complex. He considers "boys' books" inferior yet associates boyhood with a "profound and candid seriousness." He reveals, in short, an increasing ambivalence about literature for children—this scholar who had himself written for children and is now best remembered for his color-coded collections of fairy tales.[41] And although Lang considers *Huckleberry Finn* far better than *Tom Sawyer*, he still yokes the two together, considering both masterpieces.

At the time of Lang's comments—more generally, in the final decades of the nineteenth century and early decades of the twentieth—the status of children's literature was becoming unstable. In a small minority of other early responses to Twain I can find traces of such instability. I'd like to look more closely at three of these: one appeared in the *San Francisco Chronicle* in 1885, one in the *Library Journal* in 1907, one in the *Atlantic* in 1903. I should stress that I have chosen these pieces not because they are representative of the majority of published opinion on Twain—my principle for choosing most of the reviews and other criticism I have so far cited in this chapter. The pieces to which I now turn are suggestive rather than representative: they reveal the shifts in attitudes toward cultural Others that were starting to emerge in the United States. All three pieces register an increasing condescension toward children's literature, a condescension that was inconsistent and at times contradictory. Taken together, they hint at the instability and permeability of categories of age and gender as thinking about American literature—and its canon—was shifting.

The *San Francisco Chronicle* had printed an enthusiastic review of *Huckleberry Finn* on March 15, 1885; after the Concord banning, it printed a fierce defense, on March 29. The issue of the banning, in other nineteenth-century criticism too, but especially here, brings the issue of suitability for children into sharp focus. The writer of the defense fully recognizes that the purpose of the banning was to protect juveniles. He or she asserts, "The managers of this library evidently look on this book as written for boys, whereas we venture to say that upon nine boys out of ten much of the humor, as well as the pathos, would be lost."[42] After citing jokes and instances of sarcasm that a boy would be unlikely to understand, the writer even concludes, unlike almost every other contemporary observer, that "this is not a boy's book." The banning, in short, raises the question of age parameters, and to squelch the library banning, at least in part, this writer seeks to place *Huckleberry Finn* in an adults-only compartment—to make it safe for adults by barring children from its readership. But having eliminated boys from the intended audience, the writer still needs a moral touchstone. If age can't provide one, then gender will: regarding charges of vulgarity and grossness in *Huckleberry Finn*, "there is not a line in it which cannot be read by a pure-minded woman." The banning of the book leads to a substitution of gender for age, an acknowledgment of females as well as males, a need to turn to women once boys have been banished.

Subsequent responses to *Huckleberry Finn* sometimes invoke femininity as well, but often to startlingly different effect. In 1907 a male librarian named E. L. Pearson, writing in the *Library Journal*, caricatures the lady librarian who excommunicates Tom and Huck from behind "the little dimity curtains of Extreme Respectability" to make her preserve safe for Little Lord Fauntleroy—in order, himself, to press the claims of *Tom Sawyer* and *Huckleberry Finn* as boys' books.[43] Anecdotal evidence suggests that Twain's two books did indeed find only precarious purchase in some public libraries. There was the Concord banning in 1885, removal from a recommended reading list in Denver in 1902, and removal of the two books from the children's rooms of the Brooklyn Public Library in 1905—to cite only substantiated cases, not someone's broad generalization about *Huckleberry Finn*'s being banned "everywhere."[44] Also suggestive is

Huck still seen as shocking lady librarians in 1958
Saturday Review, 22 March 1958, 37; courtesy of the de Grummond Children's
Literature Collection, the University of Southern Mississippi, Hattiesburg

that in an 1893 poll of the most-circulated novels in American libraries, *Tom Sawyer* ranked only sixty-ninth and *Huckleberry Finn* ninetieth—lower than six works by Charles Dickens and four by Louisa May Alcott.[45] This rather modest popularity, surprising in books that are now so well known and that were indeed the subject of considerable written commentary in the nineteenth century, may well reflect limited availability in public libraries.[46]

Yet a contemporary account of the 1902 Denver incident in *Harper's Weekly* not only claims that "no books have been more warmly applauded" than *Tom Sawyer* and *Huckleberry Finn*, and that "none have been so widely accepted as among the very best books for the young," but adds, "'We have no better bait for boys who don't read,' is the universal verdict of the librarians."[47] Women librarians did not universally excommunicate Tom and Huck. Indeed, Twain appeared on what were probably the two most influential lists of books recommended for children around the turn of the century, lists compiled by women librarians. In 1882, three years before *Huckleberry Finn* was published, Caroline Hewins included *Tom Sawyer* in *Books for the Young: A Guide for Parents and Children*.[48] In 1909 Marion E. Potter, assisted by Bertha Tannehill and Emma L. Teich, included *Tom Sawyer, Huckleberry Finn*, and *The Prince and the Pauper* in the first edition of the *Children's Catalog: A Guide to the Best Reading for Young People Based on Twenty-Four Selected Library Lists*. And *Tom Sawyer* and *Huckleberry Finn* have continued to appear on other twentieth-century lists—the *Bookman's* 1922 "One Hundred Story Books for Children," the American Library Association's 1933 *The Right Book for the Right Child*, Laura E. Richards's 1939 *What Shall the Children Read?*, Alice M. Jordan's 1947 *Children's Classics*, and the College English Association's 1960 *Good Reading*. Among the twentieth-century book lists for young people that I've been able to locate, the only notable one on which Twain is absent is compiled by a man: a list in a 1907 article in the *Ladies' Home Journal* by Hamilton Mabie.[49]

In any case, what's significant about Pearson's essay in the *Library Journal* is the extent to which he castigates females to reclaim the books for boys. As with the reviewer for the *San Francisco Chronicle*, age and gender are the counters one plays with to expostulate against library banning, but here the alignment is precisely the opposite: instead of allying himself with women to banish boys, Pearson reclaims the books for boys by castigating and caricaturing women.[50]

Four years earlier H. W. Boynton had played with the boundaries of children's literature to still different effect, in a general review of books, "For the Young," in 1903, apparently the last collation of reviews of children's literature to appear in the *Atlantic*. Boynton states, "A boy . . . will devour tales like Tom Sawyer or Huckleberry Finn, though he cannot understand their real merit as studies of boy-character."[51] Boynton goes on to say unequivocally, "The adult intelligence is necessary to understand them." He thus polices the border between literature for children and that for adults—and, still coupling *Tom Sawyer* and *Huckleberry Finn*, prefers to put them not in the first but in the second category. More curiously still, between the two quoted sentences he inserts this one: "As narratives of delightfully meaningless depravity they have been excluded, not unreasonably, from more than one public library." Like the writer for the *San Francisco Chronicle*, Boynton excludes children from the intended audience—but this time from the audience for both books—even as he seems to endorse the bannings.

In short, the end of the nineteenth century and beginning of the twentieth witnessed an increasing tendency to separate children's literature from literature for adults—traces of which tendency are discernible in discussions of Twain's work. Yet the separation does not occur consistently. Both age and gender are undergoing destabilizing pressures, leading, in different observers, to opposing alignments. *Huckleberry Finn* could be claimed for men and women, excluding children, as a way of making a place for it in public libraries; *Huckleberry Finn* and *Tom Sawyer* could be claimed for men and boys, excluding women, as a way of making a place for both in the juvenile collections of public libraries; both books could be claimed for adults and for that very reason excluded from public libraries.

Most critics and essayists, into the first decade or two of the twentieth century, continued to yoke together *Tom Sawyer* and *Huckleberry Finn*. And I return now to citing representative, as well as particularly influential, criticism and essays, this time from the early twentieth century.

Even in 1918 and 1921, in volumes 2 and 3 of *The Cambridge History of American Literature*—one of the landmark literary histories to which I devote attention in Chapter 3—*Tom Sawyer* and *Huckleberry Finn* are still tenuously yoked. In 1918, in the chapter "Books for Children," Algernon Tassin notes that both books "immediately took the foremost place as stories of the American boy, and in a surprisingly short while became world classics. They are not explicitly treated as boy's stories throughout, and in each are description and social observation beyond the appreciation of young readers; yet they have doubtless never failed with boy as with man to reap the highest triumph possible to fiction, the reader's recognition of his own psychology and temperament."[52] In the chapter devoted to Twain, published three years later in the third volume, Stuart P. Sherman declares, "*Huckleberry Finn* exceeds even *Tom Sawyer* almost as clearly as *Tom Sawyer* exceeds *The Prince and the Pauper*."[53] That claim has since been read as high praise for *Huckleberry Finn*, but its strength depends on how much *Tom Sawyer* exceeds *The Prince and the Pauper* (and in turn on how one regards *The Prince and the Pauper*). In fact Sherman does not sharply differentiate the two Mississippi books: he refers to *Tom Sawyer* as Twain's "first masterpiece" and *Huckleberry Finn* as "his second masterpiece of Mississippi fiction."[54]

By the 1920s most critics agreed to classify *Tom Sawyer* as children's literature in order to separate it from *Huckleberry Finn* and extol the true greatness of the latter.[55] By then most literary critics considered children's literature inferior to adults': as Bernard DeVoto said of *The Prince and the Pauper* in the following decade, "In existing as a child's book, it has little validity for adults."[56] "For *Huckleberry Finn* to soar majestically as a classic," in Louis Budd's words, "it first had to be divorced from *Tom Sawyer*. Most crucially, it had to live down its rumored past as a children's book."[57]

In 1921, in *The American Novel*, Carl Van Doren sees *Huckleberry Finn* as vying with *The Scarlet Letter* as "the greatest American novel"—as, he says, what critical "choice ordinarily narrows down at last to."[58] Critical discomfort with childish things has grown sufficiently, and critical worship of *Huckleberry Finn* is still sufficiently restrained, that Van Doren can say that if Twain had portrayed "the life of the river satirically on the largest scale, instead of in such dimensions as fit Huck's boyish limitations of knowledge, he might possibly have made a better book."[59] In 1923, William Lyon Phelps, who earlier called both *Tom Sawyer* and *Huckleberry Finn* masterpieces, now associates *Huckleberry Finn* with *The Scarlet Letter* and claims, "Of all the novels written by Americans, these two stand out conspicuously above the rest."[60] In 1932, DeVoto more grandly claims that Huck's journey is immortal, that *Huckleberry Finn* "is American life formed into great fiction."[61] And in 1935, as Twain critics are fond of repeating, Ernest Hemingway declares, "All modern American literature comes from one book by Mark Twain called *Huckleberry Finn*."[62]

Van Wyck Brooks, against whose 1920 psychoanalytic study DeVoto was reacting, provides the most pyrotechnic display of misgivings about juvenility and Twain. In *The Ordeal of Mark Twain*, Brooks is willing to call *Huckleberry Finn* "Twain's unique masterpiece," to declare its "supremacy among all Mark Twain's writings." But he also endorses Arnold Bennett's judgment that although *Huckleberry Finn* and *Tom Sawyer* are "episodically magnificent, as complete works of art they are of quite inferior quality," calling this judgment "the view that prevails to-day."[63] Brooks does not yet fully relegate *Tom Sawyer* to the juveniles, at least no more than the rest of Twain's work; two decades later, however, he would admit that he "had failed to write the most important chapter, in which I should have praised 'Huckleberry Finn.'"[64] But in his 1920 study, Brooks's constant derogatory use of metaphors of juvenility—referring to Twain's "arrested development," his "naïve passion," his "childlike self-magnification," his "childish incuriosity," his "reckless juvenility," his "spendthrift adolescence," his "infantility," "immaturity," "puerilities"—certainly widens the gap between children and adults.[65]

Part of Brooks's strategy in *The Ordeal* is to associate the genteel values of the previous century with juvenility. He castigates Twain's wife by highlighting the juvenile associations of the nineteenth-century fireside: "her instinctive notion of literature was of something that is read at the fireside, out loud, under the lamp, a family institution, vaguely associated with the Bible and a father tempering the wind of King James's English to the sensitive ears and blushing cheek of the youngest daughter. Her taste, to use the harsh but accurate word, was infantile" (154–55). Yet it's not just gentility that is childish, for Brooks, but also the emerging business ethic of self-made men: "Who does not see in the extraordinary number of books about boys and boyhood written by American authors the surest sign of the prevalence of that arrested moral development which is the result of the business life, the universal repression in the American population of all those impulses that conflict with commercial success?" (216). Nevertheless, Brooks occasionally finds positive value in juvenility. He argues that Huck's very childlikeness freed Twain's creativity: "Anything that little vagabond said might be safely trusted to pass the censor, just because he was a little vagabond, just because, as an irresponsible boy, he could not, in the eyes of the mighty ones of this world, know anything in any case about life, about morals or civilization" (238). Brooks sometimes registers his passion with gendered language (Twain being, of course, emasculated), but his volume is more fully permeated by the discourse of juvenility. If Twain could write "con amore," according to Brooks, only about and for children, Brooks can write passionately only through childhood. In marking Twain's passage into the canon, Brooks underscores the centrality of constructions of childhood in criticism of Twain.

Also central to Twain criticism at this time, less metaphorically and more overtly central, was its construction of Twain's work as American. The 1920s and 1930s witnessed the rise of the study of American literature, and, as I've noted in Chapter 3, within the emerging field there were debates between those who wanted to focus on literature as an expression of national life and those who wanted to focus on the aesthetic expression of individual works. *Huckleberry Finn* lends itself to both approaches.

With respect to the first, a recurring refrain in criticism of the 1920s and 1930s and beyond is "how thoroughly American" Twain is, how he is "the incarnate spirit of America," "was almost indissolubly attached to America, and America to him," how "his life was an epitome of the national history of his period."[66] Even Fred Lewis Pattee, skeptically quoting biographer Albert Bigelow Paine's statement that Twain is "the man most characteristically American in every thought and word and action of his life," grants the premise underlying Paine's claim: "If so, then is he tremendously worth studying."[67] We are in the presence of a powerful paradigm, a paradigm that has taken on a life of its own, when DeVoto claims, "It is only because the world [Huck] passes through is real and only because it is American that his journey escapes into universals and is immortal."[68] Only because it is American that it is universal? In any case, *Huckleberry Finn*'s setting, on the river that runs through the heart of the country, and its panoramic satire of American society, make it American, even more American than *Tom Sawyer*, and hence a stronger candidate for the great American novel.

At the same time, Twain's use of language—his use of dialect and the poetry of his prose—gives scope to those who seek greatness in aesthetic expression. In DeVoto's words, "The successful use of an American vernacular as the sole prose medium of a masterpiece is a triumph in technique."[69] When, a few years later, T. S. Eliot rhapsodizes over Twain's portrayal of the Mississippi River as that which reminds us "of the power and terror of Nature, and the isolation and feebleness of Man," indeed that which "makes the book a great book,"[70] he provides a Modernist lens through which to read *Huckleberry Finn*, a lens that would lead us to appreciate symbols and poetic imagery for evoking emotion. Here too *Huckleberry Finn* excels *Tom Sawyer*.

To return to my tracking of Twain's reputation, other sources register shifts in Twain's critical esteem more broadly, shifts in what an educated public or, eventually, literary experts deem important or canonical literature. I might stress that what I'm pursuing here is not popularity with the general public but esteem. And to do so I backtrack a little chronologically to cast my net beyond Twain criticism per se. In an 1893 readers' poll of the "best American books," sponsored by the *Critic*, neither *Tom Sawyer* nor *Huckleberry Finn* appeared in the top forty; Twain's *Innocents Abroad* came in twentieth, after works by Oliver Wendell Holmes, James Russell Lowell, Washington Irving, and others.[71] In a 1902 poll of ten critics and writers, requesting each to name the ten most characteristically American books, *Huckleberry Finn* is listed twice, though other Twain works are also cited; Lowell's *Biglow Papers*, by comparison, is named by seven experts; *The Scarlet Letter*, by five.[72] In 1926, when high school and college teachers were asked which were America's masterpieces, books deserving "a permanent place in this section of the world's literature," *Huckleberry Finn* came in third, after Poe's *Tales* and *The Scarlet Letter*; *Tom Sawyer* came in twenty-third.[73] In 1927 *Huckleberry Finn* was one of ten works authored by Americans that were included in a *Saturday Review* "American canon"—though it was still "that immortal book of boys."[74] Or perhaps, in a throwback to nineteenth-century norms, *Huckleberry Finn* was chosen precisely because it is for boys and hence among "the books which have most influenced Americans" (191): Longfellow was chosen over Whitman in part because the former "is admirably adapted to youth" (191–93). In a 1949 poll of twenty-six specialists in American literature, *Moby-Dick* and *The Portrait of a Lady* managed to edge past

Huckleberry Finn in listings of the twenty best American books, but Twain's work was fifth.[75]

By 1950 the stature of *Huckleberry Finn* had become secure, a stature signaled—and in part created—by Lionel Trilling's and T. S. Eliot's introductions to editions of the work, in 1948 and 1950, both introductions much reprinted since. Eliot asserts that *Huckleberry Finn* is "the only one of Mark Twain's various books which can be called a masterpiece"; Trilling, that it is not just Twain's "masterpiece" but "one of the world's great books and one of the central documents of American culture."[76] In 1948, too, the *Literary History of the United States* proclaimed *Huckleberry Finn* "unquestionably one of the masterpieces of American and world literature."[77]

Twain's position solidified in part because of the increasing attention paid to American literature, both inside and outside the academy. Perhaps this increase in attention was due in part to America's rise to world power at the close of World War II, accompanied by a need for cultural assertion during the Cold War. Certainly *Huckleberry Finn*'s place in American culture solidified during this time, which Jane Smiley calls the Propaganda Era, an expression that elides Cold War propagandism with critical propagandizing by the likes of Trilling and Eliot.[78]

Certainly, too, this was a time when the most acclaimed fiction tended to explore such matters as alienation from society and to focus on quests for identity in what Kenneth S. Lynn calls runaway novels: themes that *Huckleberry Finn* readily accommodated—and fueled.[79] The contemporary novel that most fully embodied such themes was J. D. Salinger's *Catcher in the Rye* (1951): this story of a prep-school boy on the lam in New York went through eight printings within a month and a half, creating what Terry Teachout calls "one of the gaudiest literary success stories of the postwar era."[80] By the end of the 1950s, once some of the youthful enthusiasts of the early 1950s had become academics perhaps, *Catcher* was receiving a good deal of attention from literary critics, and Salinger seemed, as George Steiner asserted with misgivings, "firmly enthroned in the critical pantheon."[81] The 1960s witnessed five book-length collections of critical essays on Salinger and two special issues of important journals.[82] Thanks in part to the synergy between Twain's and Salinger's novels—the old and the new exemplars—prevailing critical paradigms for American literature stressed the relationship between innocence and experience, what it meant to be an American Adam in the New World wilderness, at odds with society. As William Van

O'Connor stated at the time, validating the claims of maturity though not of *Huckleberry Finn*, "Innocence, that strange word in American life, helps to account for Twain's place, and the place of *Huckleberry Finn*, in the hierarchy of American literature."[83]

Since then, unlike Twain's, Salinger's reputation has declined. *Catcher* is now taught less often in high schools than it once was: in 1981 a writer for *Esquire* was claiming it as the second "most frequently taught novel in public schools," but in 1988, according to a more fully documented national survey, it was not among the ten titles most frequently assigned in U.S. high schools.[84] And in terms of critical reputation, Salinger may have been the subject of several scholarly collections of essays in the 1990s but, as Teachout noted in 1987, "it has been a long time . . . since anyone worth listening to thought Salinger a first-rate writer, long enough that most of us have forgotten just how seriously he used to be taken by some of our best critics."[85] Salinger has also come to be seen more and more as a writer for children, more specifically for the young adult niche of the children's book market—a niche that *Catcher* helped create. As James R. Kincaid has memorably put it, *Catcher* "has collapsed into the world of Snoopy, E.T., and Bill Cosby: fatuous, sentimental, childish."[86]

Huckleberry Finn, however, has not followed. It is probably the most frequently taught novel in U.S. high schools, possibly in U.S. colleges as well. In a 1984 poll of what high school students should read, *Huckleberry Finn* placed third, after Shakespeare and American founding documents; in a 1988 poll of what students actually read in high school English classes, *Huckleberry Finn* was second only to Shakespeare's plays among book-length works, read in 70 percent of the public high schools surveyed.[87] Of course, popularity as a high school text does not unequivocally preserve a book from juvenility. As for scholarly interest, there might not have been quite as much attention to Twain's work as a whole in the last four decades, according to listings in the MLA CD-ROM bibliography, as there has been to Faulkner's, Melville's, or Hawthorne's. But with respect to individual novels, only *Moby-Dick* has been more written about since 1963 than *Huckleberry Finn*—801 listings compared to 642. And in nonscholarly venues, Twain receives more attention than any other nineteenth-century American author.[88] Now, in the new millennium, few would contest Jonathan Arac's assertion that *The Scarlet Letter, Moby-Dick*, and *Huckleberry Finn* are the three American novels that "monopolize curricular and critical attention," thanks to a process that he calls hypercanonization.[89]

And what of the work itself? *Huckleberry Finn* continues to be imbricated with conceptions of childhood. Critics who have sought to elevate *Huckleberry Finn* have made large claims for Twain's style and have found unifying patterns in the work. Some find a pattern of Huck maturing; others stress the continuity between beginning and end, perhaps emphasizing patterns of play.[90] At issue is whether the ending—when Tom joins up with Huck and Jim and plays at helping Jim escape from captivity on the Phelps farm by putting him through adventure-fiction tortures out of storybooks (Tom knowing full well that Jim is now legally free)—is out of key with Huck's increasing sense of social responsibility and human connectedness with Jim or is simply a return to the playful genre and tone of the opening chapters.[91] At issue, in short, is whether Huck grows up or remains a child.

In terms of genre, the issue is whether Huck's story is a bildungsroman, a story of maturation, or a boy book.[92] Critics trace the history of the boy book from Thomas Bailey Aldrich's *Story of a Bad Boy* through *Tom Sawyer*, Charles Dudley Warner's *Being a Boy*, and Howells's *A Boy's Town*. Key features of such books are that they imply middle-class norms, that they relate the boy to nature, adumbrating a pastoral idyll characterized by presexual innocence, and retreat from adult experience.[93] They tend not to have linear plots but rather to be episodic: they do not depict the maturing of a boy so much as the state of boyhood. It's a genre with which *Huckleberry Finn* shares some elements, certainly a genre within whose broad outlines the book was read in the nineteenth century.

Latter-day critics who read *Huckleberry Finn* in this tradition, such as Edwin H. Cady, can thus excuse the much criticized conclusion of *Huckleberry Finn*—when Jim is no longer treated with dignity—by describing it as simply a return to the boy-book elements of the opening chapters, to the book's proper bathos and anticlimax: "no man could have his dignity genuinely threatened by a comic phantasmagoria."[94] Though to head off the dangers of this reinscription of the boyish, Cady carefully limits what he means by the boy book: "a book written not so much for the entertainment of boys as for the purpose of exploring and defining the experience—and its significance—of the American boy."[95] *Huckleberry Finn* is not, for Cady, children's literature. Adult-oriented critics forget that, as Aidan Chambers notes, "children are quite as capable of entering into the adult view of themselves as adults are of re-entering childhood, if the fiction enables them to do so."[96] They also forget that children's literature is always written for both children and adults; to be published it needs to please at least some adults. That adults may read a children's book differently does not mean the book is not for children.

In these debates over the ending, the status of *Huckleberry Finn* continues to be peculiarly bound up with its associations with childhood. But such associations also come into play in the process of canonization, in the jockeying for a position in the canon. For the most canonical books, as nineteenth-century critics such as Horace Scudder were quick to recognize, are those taught to young people. We venerate and preserve such works by giving them to the young.

Critics endorsing the canonization of *Huckleberry Finn* have emphasized the seriousness of its themes—an undertaking not unconnected to its relationship with children's literature, which twentieth-century critics have usually wanted to construe as frivolous. As Justin Kaplan puts it, serious critics now avoid the process of "lollypopping," of reducing Twain to humorist and, in effect, children's author: "Americans of Mark Twain's time and somewhat after tended to cherish him as a nostalgic recorder of boyhood high-jinks, a genial, harmless entertainer. As soon as the smiles faded from their faces they trivialized his genius and irony, his dark vision of humanity, and his moral passion."[97] Now critics stress the recurrence of death in *Huckleberry Finn*, the vexed relationship between the individual and society, the struggle with conscience. As Dixon Wecter noted in 1948, using a metaphor frequently invoked by other critics, "The odyssey of Huck's voyage through the South reveals aspects of life darker than the occasional melodrama of *Tom Sawyer*."[98] Darker indeed. This metaphor resonates curiously with another critical controversy that emerged in the 1950s.

For many modern readers the issue is not that Huck is dark but that he remains too white. In 1907 William Lyon Phelps had praised *Huckleberry Finn* for lacking the "red-hot indignation" that had marred *Uncle Tom's Cabin*: "Mark Twain gives us both points of view; he shows us the beautiful side of slavery—for it had a wonderfully beautiful, patriarchal side—and he also shows us the horror of it."[99] In 1932 DeVoto could still refer to "the childlike race of slaves."[100] It's in reaction to such perspectives—the "beautiful" side of slavery, the "childlike" race—that the current rift has developed.

An influential early essay was Ralph Ellison's "Change the Joke and Slip the Yoke" (1958).[101] He and other critics have pointed to such issues as Twain's use of blackface minstrel stereotyping (and his predilection for declaiming scenes that feature such stereotyping on his lecture tours); the inconsistent foregrounding of Jim's dignity and manhood; the extraordinary premise of Jim's willingness to head south to escape from slavery; the tonal dissonance of the book's ending, especially the changes in the portrayal of Jim; the frequency with which the word *nigger* appears; whether Huck learns to respect blacks as a whole or only one individual; and whether, in key interchanges, Twain is satirizing or reinforcing—effectively whitewashing—the racism of the status quo.

Behind the critical commentary, fueling it, is again the issue of banning books. In 1957 the *New York Times* reported the removal of an edition of *Huckleberry Finn* from the New York City list of approved textbooks for elementary and junior high school students. Since then the book has been contested in Pennsylvania, Washington, Florida, Virginia, Texas, and elsewhere, making it the ninth most frequently challenged book between 1965 and 1982, the sixth most challenged between 1982 and 1996, the third most challenged in 1995–96; it dropped out of the top eight in 1998–99. At issue in part is the book's status as a classic. Peaches Henry points to the conjunction of the book's full emergence as a classic and the 1954 Supreme Court decision outlawing segregation in public schools: the relationship between Jim and Huck plays out the issues of integration, whether one sees the two as overcoming the prejudices fostered by segregation or as reinscribing them.[102] In any case, the urge to teach *Huckleberry Finn* became strong and remains so. As in Scudder's day, the classic status of an American text is peculiarly related to its being taught to young people.

For, again, as for Scudder, what American youth need to be taught, especially it seems in eleventh grade, is literature that is characteristically American. And this is a category that, according to the literary establishment, Twain's work seems to fit exceptionally well. As Arac points out, *Huckleberry Finn* is not a work that directly addresses national concerns but is a hypercanonical literary narrative that readers aggressively allegorize to make it of national significance.[103] Even though Twain was essentially an expatriate in the 1890s, his Americanness has never been doubted. For various critics he has been "distinctively American," "purely and wholly American," "typically American," "through and through American"—to quote some adumbrations I haven't previously cited.[104] If *Huckleberry Finn* is the representative American text, then the need to assess its portrayal of American race relations is all the more acute—precisely because of its impact on those who are learning what it means to be American.

Once again, the controversies over *Huckleberry Finn*—where to draw the line between those who may read it and those who may not—pivot on its relationship to young people. Even the most outspoken recent opponent of the book, John H. Wallace, is opposed specifically to its use in junior and senior high school, not to its use in college courses.[105] Scholars who defend the book talk of its style and lyricism and humor; when they address race, they tend to generalize about Twain's ironic treatment of the status quo, perhaps also the extent to which he derived Huck's voice from oral African-American sources, making his stance ultimately antiracist. Scholars who are more ambivalent about the book are more likely to acknowledge the child audience and are concerned whether all readers will be able to grasp the irony of Twain's treatment. Not all of these critics would agree with Julius Lester, who has stated in an impassioned plea, "While I am opposed to book banning, I know that my children's education will be enhanced by not reading *Huckleberry Finn*."[106] But they usually situate their objections to *Huckleberry Finn* in a context that includes young people, whether they query its "suitability for public schools" or for "young black readers" or suggest that it requires "a reading audience of some maturity and perceptive insight."[107]

Critics who defend the book usually ignore age. Or they make contradictory claims—in one breath proclaiming the novel's worth by saying it is not really a boys' book; in the next, proclaiming its eminent suitability as a class text for children. Or age markers creep back in, metaphorically, as a way of evading attention to class and race: a white teacher concerned that black students need "to transcend their initial emotional response" to the frequent appearance of *nigger* in the text may attribute their difficulties "to their lack of maturity as both students and individuals."[108] By and large, Huck's defenders are rarely willing to accept the claim that the book might be a boys' book. They do an uneasy dance around the issue of whether the target audience includes children, though a leading proponent of teaching the book in schools, Shelley Fisher Fishkin, has recently declared, "Ultimately this is a book for children—for it teaches them what they need to know to make it to adulthood whole. It can teach them to challenge their parents and teachers and to question society's laws. It can make them ask impertinent questions of their history books and knock local heroes off their pedestals. It can encourage them to suspect organized religion and to doubt the truth of most of what they've been taught."[109]

If race is now the pivot for mediating between adult and child readers, the book itself mediates between child and adult by way of racial projection. In both *Tom Sawyer* and *Huckleberry Finn*, Twain turned to projection onto a nonwhite adult male to broker the widening gap between childhood and adulthood. In *Tom Sawyer*, Injun Joe functions as a scapegoat for negative features of adult masculinity: the potentially murderous competition for wealth becomes, in him, quite literally cutthroat. At the same time, he enacts the adventure stories that Tom likes to playact with his friends—if the game does not include a real pirate then a real Indian will do, or rather a half-breed, half projection. Killing off

Injun Joe in the cave where Tom himself has so nearly died, Twain deflects from Tom the worst excesses of those who, like Tom, seek to get rich quick. Nevertheless Tom and Huck happily inherit Injun Joe's ill-gained treasure. Like self-made men they get rich quick—they achieve the trappings of middle-class maturity through the agency of an adult male whose direct ministrations they do not have to suffer. In *Huckleberry Finn*, Jim enables Huck's maturing, if indeed Huck matures, though in a tamer fashion. Jim functions as both a friend and a father, often alternating between the two. He is able to function as both in large measure because he is African American: in Toni Morrison's words, "Huck's desire for a father who is adviser and trustworthy companion is universal, but he also needs something more: a father whom, unlike his own, he can control. No white man can serve all three functions. If the runaway Huck discovered on the island had been a white convict with protective paternal instincts, none of this would work, for there could be no guarantee of control and no games-playing nonsense concerning his release at the end. Only a black male slave can deliver all Huck desires."[110] A nonwhite man enables a white boy's growth, at the expense this time not of the man's life but of his manhood.

A key crux, among these age-related issues, is that of Jim's manhood. Black men have a long history of being stereotyped as boys, of being called boys. Even those whites who have stressed positive features of boyhood—simplicity, innocence—usually do so condescendingly. And most European Americans in the nineteenth century did not stress positive features in their thinking about African Americans. Nineteenth- and early-twentieth-century social thinkers tended to see some races as more advanced than others, often categorizing blacks, as in the DeVoto passage cited earlier, as infantile. Given this history it has been vital for adult blacks to dissociate themselves from juvenility. Yet, paradoxically, many do so by turning to the needs of children.[111] Many do so by, in effect, seriously treating *Huckleberry Finn* as children's literature.

Steven Mailloux has noted the peculiar disjunctions between the book's 1880s context, a time of heightened attention to the "Negro Problem," a time when Twain himself went on a reading tour with an outspoken commentator on the problem, and the dearth, the virtual nonexistence, of attention to race in nineteenth-century responses to *Huckleberry Finn*. Instead, the book was implicated in an ongoing cultural conversation about bad boys, inside literature and out. That focus contrasts in turn with the prominence of race in more recent discussions of *Huckleberry Finn*.[112] The disjunction is less stark—the underlying continuity of the cultural conversations about *Huckleberry Finn* becomes clearer—once we acknowledge the centrality of children and of constructions of childhood to both debates. Criticism of Twain continues, in short, to recur to childhood.

Mark Twain's critical currency rose in the early twentieth century as literary criticism professionalized, cresting in midcentury as the position of American literature solidified in the U.S. academy, but this gain was at the expense of those of his books that were increasingly defined as children's literature. The most curious split is between *Tom Sawyer* and *Huckleberry Finn*, both considered to be for young and old in the nineteenth century. To distance themselves from nineteenth-century critics and their genteel ideals, many twentieth-century critics resorted to gendered language: no longer were they the sissies and mama's boys, the Sid Sawyers, of yesteryear. But gender alone, as some turn-of-the-century criticism falteringly reveals, was not fully adequate for making fine discriminations regarding Twain. So twentieth-century critics turned to age. And by assigning one book to the category of literature for children and the other to that of literature for adults, critics were able to subordinate *Tom Sawyer* and elevate *Huckleberry Finn*. *Huckleberry Finn* has not always been considered the great American novel. Its greatness has had to be constructed—and was constructed at the expense of *Tom Sawyer* and, I would argue, at the expense of a fundamental respect for childhood and children's literature.

At the same time, even now, the segregation of child and adult audiences is not absolute. For if a work is to be canonical it must be taught to the young, must be, in some sense, literature for children. *Huckleberry Finn*, I would argue, no less than *Tom Sawyer* or *The Prince and the Pauper*, is for children. And critics who have defended the teaching of *Huckleberry Finn* to the young have unwittingly agreed. Issues of race and class—does *Huckleberry Finn* subvert or whitewash racism?—further intersect with age in recent critical discussions of Twain's work, and also with gender. But to gauge more fully the difference that gender makes in the construction of children's literature in the United States, I turn next to a woman writer identified with girls' books: Louisa May Alcott.

CHAPTER FIVE

The Case of the Girls' Book

Jo's Girls

In 1862, the editor of the *Atlantic Monthly* told Louisa May Alcott, "Stick to your teaching; you can't write." She responded, "I won't teach; and I can write, and I'll prove it."[1] Which she soon did. The *Atlantic* had already published two of her stories, under a previous editor, and the captious James T. Fields would go on to publish two more, and also a poem in 1863. Alcott would eventually become a best-selling author, the financial mainstay of her extended family. By 1880, according to the *New York Times*, she was "generally regarded as the most popular and successful literary woman in America."[2]

In another sense, though, Alcott did indeed fail to prove that she could "write" and did indeed stick to her teaching. For after 1868, when she published the first part of *Little Women*, she devoted herself mostly to literature primarily targeting children, to *An Old-Fashioned Girl*, *Little Men*, *Eight Cousins*, *Rose in Bloom*, *Jo's Boys*—not to literature for the *Atlantic*. By the elite literary standards that the *Atlantic* represented, she was no longer, in a sense, writing. And although her children's literature was less didactic than most contemporary works for children, a pedagogical purpose was never far from her sights. She was, in short, teaching, as the *Atlantic* editor had advised.

Alcott figured little in the elite literary culture that was growing up around the *Atlantic*. She did not publish in the magazine after 1863, though some of her subsequent work was reviewed in its pages. In a letter to a later editor, Thomas Bailey Aldrich, she mentions that her publisher "once told me that you 'hated' me because my little works sold well."[3] Aldrich himself reportedly regaled the Radical Club with a flippant verse in which he situated Alcott's "Rose in Bloom on a silk divan" amid "fumes of sandalwood," sipping wine with her Arab lover—in a harem, in short.[4] So much for the homely pieties with which Rose and other Alcott characters became associated. The trajectory of Alcott's reputation over the last century and a half has been very different from Twain's. The quintessential writer of girls' books has figured very differently in the American critical imagination from the quintessential writer for boys. But Alcott did figure, very much, elsewhere.

Whatever elite critics have made of her work, Alcott has been prominent in the popular imagination. Consider the 1990s: in 1994 the release of a major motion picture version of *Little Women*; in 1995 the touting of a previously unpublished Alcott thriller, *A Long Fatal Love Chase*; in 1996 the announcement—on the front page of the *New York Times*—of the "discovery" of Alcott's first novel, *The Inheritance*. In her review of the film of *Little Women* for the *New York Times*, Janet Maslin declared the book "the gold standard for girlhood across America."[5] Stephen King, reviewing *A Long Fatal Love Chase* for the *New York Times Book Review*, found the tale quite good, though ultimately not as good as *Little Women*.[6] In popular venues from newspapers to consumer culture, from polls of favorite books to lists of recommended reading, Alcott has continued to have wide currency.

Consider her imprint on consumer culture. T-shirts and book bags, samplers and sachet dolls, not to mention puzzles, magnets, note cards, posters, diaries, and reproductions of Alcott's mood pillow, are all available in the Orchard House ("Home of the Alcotts") gift shop. At least five doll companies offer dolls based on *Little Women*, including Madame Alexander, the queen of American doll-makers, who claims to have designed more than 125 sets of *Little Women* dolls. In Madame Alexander's Hundredth Anniversary Collection catalogue, one of nine dolls pictured is Meg March—Meg, presumably, because she was a party girl: her "feminine party-dress, trimmed with pearl, applique and delicate ribbon roses, is perfect for the ball. Hair bows of ribbon and pearl, and taffeta slippers make her the perfect Little Woman."

As Barbara Sicherman points out, middle-class women ranging from M. Carey Thomas and Jane Addams to Simone de Beauvoir remembered finding validation, in Alcott's work, of their ambitions for independence and achievement.[7] That number includes many women writers, ranging from Gertrude Stein to Ursula Le Guin to Sonia Sanchez.[8] Immigrants too, such as Elizabeth G. Stern and Juris Jurjevics and Leo Lerman, have devoured the book, in their case to learn how to become more American, which is to say more American middle class—more a part of the American family, if you will, rather than less.[9] The iconoclastic Camille Paglia may liken the novel to a horror movie, but the response of Miss Manners is more representative: *Little Women*, she remarked, is "where I learned that although it's very nice to have two clean gloves, it's even more important to have a little ink on your fingers."[10]

The novel was enormously popular virtually from the appearance of its first volume in October 1868. I say "virtually" because, although the early sales of *Little Women* were brisk, they were modest compared to early sales of Alcott's subsequent publications. Within a month of issuing part 1 of *Little Women*, Roberts Brothers had printed three thousand copies—a goodly number. But within a month of issuing part 2, in April 1869, it needed seven thousand copies of the new volume; within a month of issuing *An Old-Fashioned Girl* in 1870, thirty thousand copies; within a month of issuing *Little Men* in 1871, forty thousand.[11] *Little Women* went on to become Alcott's biggest seller: in 1947 Frank Luther Mott named it one of the twenty-one best-sellers in U.S. history.[12]

I also say "virtually" because the early reviews of the first volume (part 1), though positive, did not predict the huge success the book would go on to have. More attention was paid to part 2, published the next year (the two parts are now usually published in a single volume), including a review in *Harper's Monthly*. Still more periodicals reviewed *An Old-Fashioned Girl* in 1870 and *Little Men* in 1871—including, respectively, the *Atlantic* and *Scribner's*. In its review of *Little Men*, three years after the appearance of *Little Women*, the *New York Times* referred to Alcott as someone "whose name has already become a household word among little people."[13] In 1875 a reviewer in the *Independent* referred to *Little Women* as a "perfect success": Alcott "will be remembered by it when we are all in our graves and unborn generations will laugh over its tempting pages."[14] In the same year a writer for *Harper's*, in the essay "Concord Books," noted that Alcott "took the public heart by storm six years ago" and is now "established as a prime favorite with old and young. . . . Not Miss Burney, not Mrs. Stowe, not Bret Harte, after the appearance of the *Heathen Chinee*, ever received the adulation that has been poured out at Miss Alcott's feet by a host of enthusiastic juveniles. And the seniors are not much more moderate."[15] Mark Twain was one of innumerable parents who read Alcott's work aloud to their families.[16] In 1895 Frank Preston Stearns recalled, "Grave merchants and lawyers meeting on their way down town in the morning said to each other, 'Have you read "Little Women"'; and laughed as they said it. The clerks in my office read it, so also did the civil engineer, and the boy in the elevator. It was the rage in '69 as 'Pinafore' was in '78."[17]

Why did *Little Women* become such a rage? Appearing eight years before *The Adventures of Tom Sawyer*, it marked a departure from previous moralizing in children's literature, the kind in which all the naughty boys were "eaten by bears, or tossed by mad bulls, because they did not go to a particular sabbath-school," and "all the good infants who did go" were of course "rewarded by every kind of bliss, from gilded gingerbread to escorts of angels, when they departed this life, with psalms or sermons on their lisping tongues," to quote *Little Women* itself[18]—though to a latter-day reader the book may still seem somewhat preachy. It can be seen as inaugurating a new genre for children, as it melded some aspects of the sentimental novel popular in the 1860s—the emphasis on sisterliness, perhaps the importance of motherhood—with the domestic fiction long a staple of literature for children. It was perhaps the first American book explicitly directed to girls as an audience, at a time when children's literature was only starting to undergo gender segregation (and even so, its contemporary enthusiasts included men and boys). *Little Women* also provided a taste of the intelligentsia's Concord for the American middle class, a concrete, even spirited taste. As Van Wyck Brooks later suggested, Alcott "invested the Concord scheme of life with the gaiety and romance of a Robin Hood ballad"; or as an anonymous reviewer in the *New Yorker* noted in 1958, defending the importance of literature for children, Alcott "may be the most widely read transcendentalist today."[19]

But perhaps the most frequently invoked explanation for Alcott's success is, to quote several anonymous nineteenth-century observers, "the thorough reality of her characters," her "power of intense realization and portraiture," "her thorough genuineness and steady adherence to the real."[20] Mary Cantwell updates such claims when she declares, in a recent *New York Times* editorial, "To me, *Little Women* was fact. But, then, that's the way it is with all great novels. Their reality erases the reader's."[21] Barbara Sicherman and Margery Fisher point specifically to Alcott's ear for language, her vivid dramatization of scenes, and her mastery of techniques of characterization.[22]

Enthusiasm for Alcott's realism has had its dangers, however: it could readily lead to dismissal of her work as artless, a mere transcription of fact. A writer for the *New York Times Saturday Review of Books and Art* condescendingly stated in 1902, "She had no need to imagine, to think of consistence, to rectify and enlarge, to cull anecdotes from the records of children with nothing but childish tasks to occupy their minds. She had only to unveil the mirror of her heart."[23] Certainly most reviews of Ednah Cheney's 1889 hagiography, published the year after Alcott's death, concluded that Alcott's life was better than her art. It has been hard in fact for many reviewers and other critics to recognize the life in her art. Few reviewers were as astute as one writing for *Scribner's* in 1871: with respect to Alcott's "absolute fidelity to real life," the reviewer asserts, "she is entitled to greater praise as an artist than has been bestowed upon her; ultimately she will be recognized as the very best painter, *en genre*, of the American domestic life in the middle classes; the very faithfulness, the aliveness—there *ought* to be that word—of her pictures prevents their having full justice done them at once."[24]

When Alcott died, in 1888, a notice of her funeral appeared on the front page of the *New York Times*. In 1893 she was second only to Charles Dickens as the novelist whose works were most circulated in U.S. public libraries.[25] In 1918 *The Cambridge History of American Literature* referred to Alcott's work, in a chapter on "Books for Children," as "the notable success of the period" and as still having "the most assured position" among nineteenth-century books for children.[26]

As for other signs of her popularity, in 1871 the two most popular books in the New York Mercantile Library, the largest U.S. lending library, were *Little Women* and *An Old-Fashioned Girl*; in 1896 the first book listed as "among the books most in demand" in Wisconsin Traveling Libraries was *An Old-Fashioned Girl*.[27] In an 1893 poll of librarians, and again in a 1922 poll of librarians and educators, *Little Women* headed the list of those considered children's favorites.[28] When, in 1913, a Scranton minister asked his fifteen hundred Sunday School pupils to recommend convalescent reading, *Little Women* headed the list, outpolling the second-place item by six to one.[29] In a 1927 poll reported in the *New York Times*, high school students were asked, "What book has interested you most?" Their top choice—to the consternation of the headline writer—was not the Bible but *Little Women*.[30] Other early-twentieth-century surveys of children's reading place Alcott's work at or near the top—first in a 1927 survey of readers of *Youth's Companion*, third (or actually second, according to my recalibration) in a national survey of schoolchildren in 1924–25.[31] Even polls of general or adults' reading are likely to place Alcott high—ninth, or perhaps fourth.[32] In 1912 the Cleveland public library needed 325 copies of *Little Women* to satisfy the demand; the New York City branch libraries, more than a thousand.[33]

In part this popularity reflects a certain institutionalizing of Alcott, especially in schools and libraries. Certainly her work appears frequently on lists of recommended children's books: the influential 1882 *Books for the Young* by librarian Caroline Hewins, an 1890 essay in *The Parent's Review* by the British reviewer Edward Salmon, a 1912 list in the *Crisis* by Harlem Renaissance novelist Jessie Fauset, the 1939 *What Shall the Children Read?* by children's author Laura E. Richards, the influential 1958 *Parent's Guide to Children's Reading* by Nancy Larrick, and the 1990 edition of Betsy Hearne's *Choosing Books for Children*. It's characteristic that in the first edition, in 1909, of the *Children's Catalog: A Guide to the Best Reading for Young People Based on Twenty-Four Selected Library Lists*, a volume that catalogued three thousand books, Alcott is accorded twenty-three entries—compared to three for Twain, twelve for Dickens, and three for Lewis Carroll.

But it wasn't just adult, institutional efforts that enabled Alcott's work to live on. It may have been from an adult perspective that she earned her nineteenth-century sobriquet "the children's friend." Children would not themselves refer to her that way. But another theme that emerges in accounts of Alcott's work is that of love: children, especially girls, have simply loved her books. I'll cite just three examples. In 1888 fiction writer Harriet Prescott Spofford referred to Alcott as "the writer better loved by the children of America than Shakespere himself."[34] In 1933 the American Library Association recommended six of Alcott's works in *The Right Book for the Right Child* and called *Little Women* "the best-loved of all home stories."[35] In 1938 Katharine Anthony's biography of Alcott appeared serially in the *Woman's Home Companion* under the title *The Most Beloved American Writer* (with illustrations by, who else, Norman Rockwell).

Yet love wasn't a popular concept with the literary establishment or with what had by then become the critical establishment. It was renamed "sentimentality" and condemned. *Little Women* was consigned, often unread, to sweet inanity. Madelon Bedell points to the way *Little Women* provided a kind of counter to the modern girl of the 1920s in an F. Scott Fitzgerald story, where the March girls are considered "inane females."[36] Lavinia Russ writes of being told by Ernest Hemingway, "'You're so full of young sweetness and light you ought to be carrying *Little Women*.' (He had never read it.)"[37]

But despite such highbrow indifference, Alcott lived on. In 1941 she was the representative author in a New York Public Library listing of eleven "Women

Who Helped Mold America," though the blurb under her picture in the *New York Times Magazine* is defensive: "The progressively trained youth of today may class 'Little Men' and 'Little Women' as A No. 1 sissies, but if it hadn't been for Louisa May Alcott's books there might be no progressive education."[38] When in a 1958 musical version of *Little Women* for television Beth failed to die, the producer and sponsor received a deluge of letters, and the sponsor's advertising agency produced a survey showing that 98 percent of the American public "remembered" that in the novel Beth died.[39] A decade later, in 1968, *Little Women* was still one of the two most circulated books in the New York City Public Library.[40] Even in 1996 the New York City branch libraries had more than four hundred copies of the book, as well as more than a hundred video and sound recordings.

A final sign of Alcott's prominence in the popular imagination in the first half of the twentieth century is that in 1928 and again in 1935 the *New York Times* published brief stories that mentioned both Alcott and Hawthorne, one story on the preservation of a house in which both had lived, another on a cobbler who claimed to have shod all the Concord notables of the previous century. The headline of the second story, "Cobbler, 86, Recalls Emerson, Hawthorne," omits Alcott—as indeed I would have expected (even though the cobbler seems to have been more forthcoming on the subject of Alcott), given the cultural importance accorded to Hawthorne in the nineteenth and twentieth centuries. His reputation was at its most precarious, however, during the early decades of the twentieth century, at that time when an old canon was being dislodged and a new one was emerging.[41] So perhaps I shouldn't have been startled that the main headline for the 1928 story names only Alcott: "To Preserve Alcott Home"—the home being not Orchard House, the one now most associated with her, but Hillside, later called Wayside, and now more associated with Hawthorne.[42] Alcott apparently trumped Hawthorne in 1928. I'm not insisting that a shift in Alcott's stature, relative to Hawthorne's, occurred in the 1930s or thereabouts. But I believe there was some lessening of interest in Alcott among the gatekeepers of the popular media at that time, after a brief surge of interest during the 1932 centenary of Alcott's birth and following the 1933 release of the film of *Little Women* starring Katharine Hepburn as Jo.

Fitzgerald and Hemingway weren't the only ones to condemn Alcott, unread. But even those of us who make claims for Alcott's continuing cultural importance—and she has remained important to generations of girls—can be surprised by the stature she seems to have had early in the century, her looming presence in the popular imagination.

In the American *critical* imagination Alcott's place has been much less assured, as will become clear when I sketch her positioning in the nineteenth century, the early- to mid-twentieth-century critical response, and finally a late-twentieth-century critical revival.

Alcott may not have moved in the most elite and exclusive literary circles in the nineteenth century, but she was nevertheless highly regarded. Emblematic of her positioning is her relationship to two lists published in the *Critic*, a leading New York literary journal, late in the century. On June 3, 1893, the editors published a listing of works that, according to readers' votes, constituted the "best" American books, works that readers effectively considered canonical. Emerson's *Essays* comes first, followed by *The Scarlet Letter. Little Women* is twenty-fifth, one of only two books in the top forty that would now generally be considered juvenile literature. (*Little Lord Fauntleroy* comes in thirty-third; neither *Tom Sawyer* nor *Huckleberry Finn* appears on the list.) In short, the relatively elite readers of the *Critic* had not fully sifted children's literature out of the canon. The editors themselves, however, were further along in this process—and were less willing to countenance Alcott. In an earlier listing, on July 24, 1886, of a hundred (actually 107) American authors "worthiest of being read," they named Emerson and Hawthorne, of course, and also Burnett and Twain, even James and the then relatively forgotten Melville. They did not, however, include Alcott. Her work may be good for children, as reviews in the *Critic* repeatedly iterated, but it did not count, for professional critics, as great literature: "Good wine needs no bush, and Miss Alcott needs no reviewer," notes an 1882 reviewer in the *Critic*; eight years later, after her death, a reviewer writes, "Miss Alcott wrote no book equal to her powers, no book of enduring literary worth; and this was because she wrote for bread, and with a rapidity too great for the best work."[43] To put it another way, Alcott's work might be canonical from the perspective of the amateur critics who read the *Critic* but not from the viewpoint of the professional ones who edited it.

Or consider the leading U.S. literary journal in the second half of the nineteenth century, a journal that at that time reviewed not only literature for adults but also children's literature. Alcott herself considered the *Atlantic* the most prestigious place to publish: in 1858, when she was twenty-six, she noted in her journal, "I even think of trying the 'Atlantic.' There's ambition for you!"[44] A year later, one of her stories was indeed accepted by the *Atlantic;* in the next few years, four stories and a poem met "the Atlantic test," as she called it.[45] Yet prestige was one thing, money another—and earning money to support her impecunious family took priority over mere critical approbation. As she noted in her journal when editor James Russell Lowell accepted the first of her *Atlantic* stories, "Hurrah! My story was accepted; and Lowell asked if it was not a translation from the German, it was so unlike most tales. I felt much set up, and my fifty dollars will be very happy money. People seem to think it a great thing to get into the 'Atlantic;' but I've not been pegging away all these years in vain, and may yet have books and publishers and a fortune of my own."[46] As Richard H. Brodhead argues, it is striking that in the pivotal 1860s, when high and low culture were in the process of separating, Alcott still had access to all levels—to the high culture being cultivated by the *Atlantic;* to the low culture being created by such story-papers as *Frank Leslie's Illustrated Newspaper,* whose readership still overlapped with that for domestic fiction; and to an older strand of culture that affirmed a "domestic-tutelary model of writing."[47] Alcott could choose her market depending on her needs; for her, prestige was fine, but money more important still. And after 1863 she did not publish in the *Atlantic*—though the journal did go on to review five of her works.

In the late nineteenth century, when colleges were just beginning to teach American literature and university presses had barely begun to publish scholarship, the most prestigious magazines took children's literature—including Alcott's—seriously enough to review it. *Harper's Monthly* reviewed fifteen of Alcott's works; the *Critic,* whose existence overlapped with Alcott's by only seven years, reviewed eight; the *Nation,* nine; *Literary World,* twenty. And in 1889 in the pages of *Cosmopolitan* (admittedly not an elite journal) one could hear sentiments like the following: "About twenty years ago a million or more men, women and children enjoyed the most delightful literary surprise which native wit had devised within the century"—namely, *Little Women.*[48]

One of the reasons why Alcott was accorded critical esteem in the nineteenth century is that literature for children and for adults was, as I've been arguing throughout this book, less segregated than it is now. Alcott may have written *Little Women* with the idea of targeting girls, yet, as Sheryl A. Englund points out, the first editions of parts 1 and 2 of *Little Women* were standard-sized books with dark cloth bindings, "packaged scarcely differently from adult novels."[49] The editors of *Godey's Lady's Book* asserted in 1870, "Meg, Jo, Beth, and Amy are friends in every nursery and school-room; and even in the parlor and office they are not unknown."[50] In 1882 Caroline Hewins recommended not only *Little Women* and *Little Men* as "books for the young" but also Alcott's *Hospital Sketches*, a collection now generally classified as for adults. In 1885, in contrast, the Indianapolis Public Library classified all of Alcott's books as adult fiction.[51] Only in 1904 do I find something that fully resembles more recent sortings: in the 1904 *A.L.A. Catalog* of eight thousand volumes recommended for popular libraries, the eleven Alcott entries are sorted as they might have been at the end of the twentieth century, with *Hospital Sketches* and *Work* listed as adult fiction and other titles as juveniles.[52] Nineteenth-century experts simply didn't agree on how to separate Alcott's oeuvre into juvenile and adult categories; rather, the categories bled into each other.

Nevertheless, the most prestigious of the nineteenth-century U.S. magazines, the ones with the greatest claims to high culture—such as the *Atlantic* and *Harper's* and the *Nation*—did review children's literature, but they were sometimes uneasy about doing so. Their reviewers were less likely to rejoice that Alcott's work interested both "children and those of older growth," as a reviewer for *Godey's Lady's Book* commented in 1874.[53] They were less likely to assume, as did a reviewer in the *National Anti-Slavery Standard* in 1869, that works we might now consider literature for adults, such as the stories in *Hospital Sketches*, would "afford much additional pleasure to the numerous readers of *Little Women*, into whose hands the book will be sure to go."[54] Instead, elite reviewers sometimes attempted to police a boundary between literature for children and literature for adults—at least they did so for Alcott, a policing they rarely attempted for Twain.

The most frequently invoked boundary marker was the absence or presence of romance. In 1881 in the *Atlantic*, for instance, Horace Scudder does not "altogether find satisfaction in the suppressed love-making of these young people" in Alcott's *Jack and Jill*.[55] As late as 1911 a writer for the *Atlantic* found "an inexcusable amount of love-making" in both *Under the Lilacs* and *Jack and Jill*.[56] Even Lyman Abbott, who in an 1871 review for *Harper's* would happily suggest that children would read *Little Men* with interest while their parents would read it with profit, could note the marriages in part 2 of *Little Women* and remark that it "is a rather mature book for the little women, but a capital one for their elders."[57] Alcott directly challenged such a perspective in the opening paragraph of part 2 of *Little Women*: "if any of the elders think there is too much 'lovering' in the story, as I fear they may (I'm not afraid the young folks will make that objection), I can only say with Mrs. March, 'What *can* you expect when I have four gay girls in the house and a dashing young neighbor over the way?'" (*LW*, 293). Elite critics were likely to feel some discomfort with children's literature that overstepped their sense of propriety, and indeed with children's literature itself, unless the literature seemed to be primarily for boys.

At times the discomfort felt by an *Atlantic* reviewer could engender a Jamesian circumlocution, a backhanded disavowal of the absence of "adventure and sensation": "If we said that Miss Alcott, as a writer for young people just getting to be young ladies and gentlemen, deserved the great good luck that has attended her books, we should be using an unprofessional frankness and putting in print something we might be sorry for after the story of the 'Old-fashioned Girl' had grown colder in our minds."[58] With less circumlocution, Henry James himself, hoping to put children in their place—the better to create a fictional niche for adults only—castigated Alcott for being "vastly popular with infant readers," for catering to their views "at the expense of their pastors and masters," for not writing the charming kind of tale that Lyman Abbott's father, Jacob, had written for a previous generation, with the aunts "all wise and wonderful," the nephews and nieces never "under the necessity of teaching [the adults] their place"—a view that echoes those of socially conservative reviewers in the *Catholic World*.[59] And this view is in turn echoed by a critic for an unidentified newspaper responding to James's review, in a clipping in the Alcott files at the rare-books library at Harvard: her books "are vastly amusing and entertaining to the adult mind, and so they are coming to be to the childish, especially to the girlish, but after all it is questionable whether this premature study of character has not a very oldening and sickly effect."[60] Her books would appear to be more suitable for adults than for children.

The most critical, most dismissive of the journals reviewing Alcott was the *Nation*, which published not only James's review of *Eight Cousins*, cited above, but a review of *An Old-Fashioned Girl* that famously predicted that Alcott's work would fail to please "more generations than one," a review of *Work* that found it "totally devoid of imagination" and hence "nothing as a work of art," and a review of Ednah Cheney's biographical collation that takes off from criticism of Alcott's slang and grammatical lapses to indict her for establishing "a mental tone which is more or less destructive both of a delicate aesthetic feeling and of a careful scientific mode of thought."[61] But the reviewers for the *Atlantic* also were uneasy about Alcott's work. They were far more receptive to boys' books than to ones considered suitable for girls. After all, the two men who edited the journal between 1871 and 1890—William Dean Howells and Thomas Bailey Aldrich—themselves wrote classic boys' books. Howells likewise wrote long positive reviews of Aldrich's *Story of a Bad Boy,* Twain's *Adventures of Tom Sawyer,* and Charles Dudley Warner's *Being a Boy* for the magazine. The *Atlantic* was less receptive to Alcott. Its reviews of her work were shorter, and it reviewed only five of them (none while the captious Fields was editor). The first review, as if in response to the popularity of *Little Women,* which the *Atlantic* hadn't reviewed, was that of *An Old-Fashioned Girl* in 1870, quoted above. After the initial circumlocution, the reviewer complains about "some poor writing and some bad grammar" but finds the "little book" pleasing, "almost inexplicably pleasing," given its "plain material." The reviewer of *Jack and Jill,* in 1881, also seems puzzled, though the befuddlement is more rhetorical. After objecting to "the suppressed love-making," Horace Scudder faults Alcott for a self-consciousness that impairs the book's simplicity and concludes, "We are no doubt unreasonable readers; we object to the blood-and-thunder literature, and when in place of it we have the milk-and-sugar we object again. What do we want?"[62]

The *Atlantic* reserves its greatest enthusiasm for *A Modern Mephistopheles*—a "remarkable" book, "instinct with ability." Although uneasy with the heightened "figurative and hyperbolical atmosphere," the reviewer admits "that there is signal force of some sort in this peculiar production." The language has "a sculpturesque effect," its paragraphs often seemingly "set to solemn rhythm."[63] Of course, this book was not presumably for children, nor was it necessarily drawing on a genre that had made its primary appeal to females. It was also published anonymously. The reviewer thought it could only be by Nathaniel Hawthorne's son Julian. The *Atlantic* was most enthusiastic, in short, when neither the book's genre nor its author's name was identified as feminine and when the book was not specifically addressing children. In a review not of Alcott's work but of Cheney's book about her life, an *Atlantic* writer acknowledges that there is "much that is both winning and repelling in her stories" and then laments that "great possibilities were lost in Miss Alcott's career."[64] Clearly these possibilities were not activated when a woman wrote for children.

Furthermore, if a work was addressed largely to girls—and Alcott consciously set out, in *Little Women,* to write for girls, in response to her editor's request—it was likely to be considered, by the cultural elite, as having a less broad appeal, as being less serious.[65] Yet gender and age intertwined complexly in the nineteenth century in determinations of literary value. The market for children's books (including those for adolescents)—to the extent that children's books comprised a market distinct from that for adults—was less overtly gender segregated than it subsequently became. Alcott's work had considerable crossover appeal—remember those lawyers and merchants, that civil engineer and that elevator boy, whom Frank Preston Stearns records as having thrilled to *Little Women.* I might also note an 1880 comment in the *New York Times:* "There is a tenderness, a sweetness, a peculiar gentleness about Miss Alcott's works which we really think no one else has. There runs no vein of over-sentimentalism in her books, for, with a rare insight into a boy's nature, she rather likes to describe him as having strong masculine traits."[66]

In consciously writing for girls, Alcott was not necessarily excluding adults or boys, at this time when the ideals of masculinity were not yet completely dominated by those of the self-made man or the masculine primitive. What strikes the latter-day reader about many reviews of Alcott's work is the assumption not only that both old and young will enjoy it but that both males and females will— remember the *Atlantic* reviewer's easy reference, in the circumlocutory sentence, to "young people just getting to be young ladies and gentlemen." By the turn of the century the winds had shifted enough that Teddy Roosevelt could feel self-conscious about having enjoyed girls' books: "At the cost of being deemed effeminate, I will add that . . . I worshiped 'Little Men' and 'Little Women' and 'An Old-Fashioned Girl.'"[67] Nevertheless, this eventual Rough Rider worshiped Alcott's books when he was a child. In 1912, when a theatrical production of *Little Women* was sweeping the country, the first authorized dramatization, a New Jersey newspaper reported that a Buffalo bartender declared, through his tears, "This piece is d——d fine."[68] The norms had shifted enough for it to be newsworthy that such a tough customer was moved by the story. But the play still had crossover appeal. In more recent decades, the men who admit to having liked *Little Women* are apt to be immigrants such as Juris Jurjevics or Leo Lerman, for whom—like Jo's neighbor Laurie, who "can't help watching" (*LW,* 65) the Marches when they forget to pull the curtain—the book offered a window on a middle-class family.

Value judgments were complicated by issues of class too. Another strand of criticism running through the nineteenth-century reviews is a concern over Alcott's language, her use of slang, her occasional grammatical lapses—in these works by someone who was admittedly a fast and somewhat careless writer. But language was also one of the few markers of class in a nation that thought of itself as democratic and virtually classless. It wasn't just the elite *Atlantic* and various British journals that faulted Alcott for her language. So did that high-toned women's journal *Godey's Lady's Book:* its editors disparage the frequent use of *ain't* for *isn't*, which gives Alcott's work a *"faux air* of vulgarity," even as they lament, with respect to characters in *An Old-Fashioned Girl,* "a dash of vulgarity as well as hardness in their lives that makes us fear that Miss Alcott has been unfortunate in her experience of Boston life."[69] Alcott was also faulted for her language by Thomas Wentworth Higginson, a member of the intellectual elite and frequent champion of women writers, now best remembered perhaps for his patronage of Emily Dickinson. In the 1888 edition of his *Short Studies of American Authors,* Higginson does devote one of eight chapters to Alcott—in the company of Hawthorne, Poe, Thoreau, Howells, and James (also Helen Hunt Jackson and Edwin Percy Whipple). Yet he concludes, with respect to Alcott, that "the instinct of art she never had. It is difficult to imagine her as pondering a situation deeply, still less as concerning herself about phrase or diction. . . . Morally and socially Miss Alcott may well be a model to all young writers; but if they are moved by a profound passion for the art of writing,—if they wish to reach an audience remoter than that of to-day,—if they wish to do something that shall add to the lasting treasure of the great literature on which they have fed,—they must look beyond her to greater and more permanent models."[70] Once again she is denied artistry, in this case at least partly because of her use of language.

The best response to criticism of Alcott's language—criticism of her slang if not her artlessness—appeared in *Scribner's* in 1876, in a review of *Eight Cousins.* The reviewer notes that Alcott is often accused of "a certain literary crudeness," yet she "is unquestionably one of the few women who can make not merely small children but even college Sophomores talk with something of the raciness of real life."[71] The reviewer goes on to note that condemnation has been especially loud in England: "One would think that a child a hundred years old might be entitled to some voice in arranging his own vocabulary; but the theory seems still to prevail in some quarters, that all new Americanisms, however indispensable, are slang, and all new Anglicisms, however uncouth, are classic." Certainly some such argument—the need to create an American vernacular for fiction—contributed to establishing Twain as a classically American author, among the cultural elite, a few decades later. Not so for Alcott, despite this critic's efforts to stress her vernacular Americanness.

In short, the more a journal (or a critic) was oriented to the concerns of adults, especially males, of a certain class standing and with a certain pretension to cultural elitism, the more likely it (or he or she) was to sneer politely at Alcott. And the less likely it was to take children's literature—the genre with which Alcott's name became increasingly synonymous—seriously.

After the turn of the century, elite American critics were even less likely to treat children's literature and literature by women—and hence Alcott's work—seriously. As Nina Baym argues, by the end of the nineteenth century Alcott and Harriet Beecher Stowe were the only women who had survived a canonical winnowing process; by the early twentieth century, they too had dropped out of the canon of important literature.[72]

Alcott's work may be represented in editor-novelist-critic Charles Dudley Warner's thirty-volume *Library of the World's Best Literature*, published in 1896, and in a 1901 imitation, Harry Thurston Peck's *International Library of Masterpieces*.[73] But her writing is excluded from the fifty-volume *Harvard Classics*, published in 1910—"the five-foot shelf of books"—even though its editor acknowledges the needs of young people by appending "Selections from the Five-Foot Shelf of Books for Boys and Girls from Twelve to Eighteen Years of Age." And in 1952 Alcott certainly didn't appear in Robert Maynard Hutchins's fifty-four-volume *Great Books of the Western World* (nor is she mentioned in the preface, when Hutchins excuses his omission of some American writers).[74]

In a literary history published in 1900, Harvard professor Barrett Wendell could compare *Little Women* to Jacob Abbott's earlier Rollo books and say dismissively that its "personages display that rude self-assertion which has generally tainted the lower middle class of English-speaking countries."[75] Wendell is still operating from a nineteenth-century perspective in which Alcott is not genteel enough—she hasn't yet become too genteel for the academy. So he still mentions her and other authors of children's literature. By the 1950s one would not find references to Alcott in major works of criticism, what would soon be considered classic works, such as R. W. B. Lewis's *American Adam* or Richard Chase's *American Novel and Its Tradition*, or in histories such as Robert E. Spiller's *Cycle of American Literature* (no references to Jacob Abbott either).

At a time when Twain's literary reputation was stabilizing and rising, in the early to mid twentieth century, Alcott's was declining. In the final decades of the nineteenth century and the early decades of the twentieth, almost all the hundreds of books and articles addressing Alcott appeared in popular venues. Occasionally pieces appeared in highbrow journals such as the *New Republic* or the *Atlantic*, but not in the journals emerging within academia, journals that would be considered scholarly. No Alcott criticism was published in scholarly journals of literary criticism until the 1940s.[76]

Let me track Alcott's scholarly reputation in the twentieth century in greater detail by comparing the quantity of criticism devoted to Alcott with that devoted to her father, Bronson, a minor Transcendentalist to whom followers of Emerson have paid some attention. During the twentieth century, scholarship attending to just about every literary figure increased a great deal: Bronson Alcott, for instance, went from three entries in the scholarly MLA bibliography in the 1930s to twenty-one in the 1980s. A Bronson-to-Louisa ratio enables one to gauge whether interest in Louisa outpaces the general trend.

Between 1921 and 1941 the annual bibliography published by the MLA lists eight items under Bronson's name—and none under Louisa's. Between 1942 and 1979 there is a rough parity between the two. Between 1980 and 1999 Louisa outpaced Bronson five to one. According to indexes provided in *Dissertation Abstracts International*, before 1982 Ph.D. dissertations devoting substantial attention to Bronson outnumbered those devoting comparable attention to Louisa by more than two to one. Since then the valence has reversed, with dissertations in which Louisa figures importantly outnumbering those in which Bronson does by more than three to one.[77]

Or consider the kinds of attention that the *New York Times Book Review* has devoted to Bronson and Louisa. The *Book Review* is the section of the *Times* with the strongest ties to the cultural elite in academia, given that it often reviews books published by university presses and many of its reviewers are academics. Situated between high academic culture and popular culture (it also prints the *New York Times* best-seller lists), the *Book Review* functions as both a bellwether of intellectual opinion and a shaper of it: researchers suggest that 75 percent of the American intellectual elite reads the *New York Times Book Review*.[78] In any case, a review of a book primarily devoted to Bronson, an account of his communal-living experiment at Fruitlands, appeared on the front page of the *Book Review* in 1915.[79] Not until 1965 is a piece focused on Louisa accorded front-page treatment, and then it's a reprint of an essay that had appeared in the London *Sunday Times Magazine:*[80] an American cultural gatekeeper could acknowledge the importance of Louisa only after a British one had given its imprimatur. A number of items variously on Bronson and Louisa had appeared in the middle sections of the *Book Review* during the intervening years; the most emblematic is a 1950 review of Madeleine Stern's *Louisa May Alcott*, still the standard biography. This brief review by a Dartmouth professor, entitled "A Boy's Spirit under Her Bib," focuses more on Bronson than on Louisa, even relating incidents that Stern had not.[81] It's pretty clear whose spirit, from the perspective of the Ivy League elite, truly animated Louisa.

Alcott's two indexed appearances in one of my touchstone literary histories, the 1948 *Literary History of the United States*—other than in the volume devoted to bibliographical materials—are both in the context of catalogues of the reception of American writers abroad. One is in a discussion of a list of American books translated into Swedish: "a curious selection from new and half-forgotten authors, with Louisa May Alcott rubbing elbows with Dashiell Hammett."[82] These references contrast with twelve index entries for Bronson. A more curious omission, and one that testifies perhaps to a disjunction between popular and academic tastes, is in the third, posthumous volume of Vernon Louis Parrington's classic *Main Currents in American Thought*, published in 1930: "Alcott, Louisa M." does indeed appear in the index, but Parrington's reference to "the grotesque vaporings of Alcott" is actually to Bronson. Whoever compiled the posthumous index seems to have been more attuned to popular or perhaps feminine tastes than to academic ones. Edward Wagenknecht ingenuously noted in 1952, after suggesting that *Little Women* might be "the most beloved American book" after *Tom Sawyer*, "It needs—and is susceptible of—little analysis; critics have, therefore, generally neglected it."[83] They were not, however, neglecting *Tom Sawyer*.

Alcott's work never attracted the vituperation that *Little Lord Fauntleroy* did: if Laurie's modeling of Christian gentility in *Little Women* struck some readers as insufficiently masculine, he was not roundly denounced as an insufferable mollycoddle. Still, doubts about Alcott's accomplishments have been sufficiently widespread that they even appear in discussions of children's literature: the librarian Alice M. Jordan cannot fail to mention *Little Women* in her 1947 account of "children's classics," but she notes that the book endures "in spite of its sentimentality and doubtful English."[84] Only a maverick outside the academy, the radio personality and critic-at-large Clifton Fadiman, was willing in the 1950s to declare *Little Women* one of ten works in English most likely to be "universally alive" in five hundred years.[85]

On the few occasions when Alcott is discussed in elite venues in the mid twentieth century, she is often dismissed because of her associations with children. Such an attitude appears with particular clarity in a 1938 review by Odell Shepard, who was, not coincidentally, Bronson's biographer. Shepard claims that Louisa "never emerged from adolescence"—"she never grew up."[86] In fact, "living almost always among intellectuals, she preserved to the age of fifty-six that contempt for ideas which is normal among boys and girls of fifteen. . . . She seems to have felt, moreover, that love, marriage, and child-bearing were interruptions of serious business—although she never quite made out what the serious business of life really is, unless it be earning a livelihood." Which of course it couldn't be, for a woman. Certainly it wasn't for the improvident Bronson. And what is the serious business of life? If it's not love and marriage and work, perhaps it's war, for Shepard goes on to indict Alcott for referring to the war between France and Prussia as a "silly little war": "these words show the bounce and swagger of a mind that has never really faced life's darker mysteries." One reason for her popularity, Shepard concludes, is "that the American public is itself immature in thought and mood."

Perhaps the fullest expression of midcentury critical dismay with Alcott—though at times hedged and oblique—appears in a review in the London *Times Literary Supplement* in 1957.[87] The anonymous reviewer, only minimally concerned with the edition of *Little Men* that is his or her pretext, is someone who can describe Mrs. Jo and Professor Bhaer as "conducting a rare collection of little horrors up the steep paths of virtue": "How can [Alcott] go on reporting the conversations and plays of these egregious infants, as if they were so important?" And the reviewer is someone who laments the emasculation of children's novels in the previous forty years. Having therewith vented some spleen, he or she declares that *Little Women*, "it is fair to say, is beyond the reach of criticism. When a book like this is so loved and cherished—and not merely by the unintelligent—any critic who feels he should discuss Miss Alcott's sentimentality and priggishness will be shown the door." The reviewer nonetheless devotes considerable attention to the failings of the March family books—and with, I hate to admit, some insight. Finally, though, he or she makes a summary judgment, seemingly more even-handed than the opening sentences, thanks to convenient catchwords of midcentury criticism— *sentimental, classic, universal*—and claims that Alcott's books "are not sentimental rubbish, but they are not classics either, in the sense that they have a relevance outside their time and place, a universal message to communicate." By the standards of midcentury criticism, Alcott's continuing popularity doesn't count as even a hint of "universality."

Nor does Alcott fare well with critics whose focus has been on finding quintessentially American works—the pursuit of which seems to have dominated midcentury criticism, as Nina Baym has eloquently demonstrated.[88] Forget that

Alcott was never an expatriate—never spent the better part of a decade or more outside the United States, as did James and Twain. Forget that she provided a window on the American middle-class family. A story about a boy and a man rafting down the Mississippi could be quintessentially American, but not one about a family of women guarding the home front during the Civil War. If American works are about the individual in opposition to family and society, the individual testing himself in the wilderness, as midcentury critics were fond of claiming, then *Little Women* does so only in rather subtle ways.

Let me pursue the Americanness of *Little Women* a bit more—make more of a case, if you will, for the novel's candidacy for canonical status. Although set during the Civil War, *Little Women* engages very little with the fighting. The war provides an excuse to remove the father from the March family (he's at the front as a chaplain); Marmee tells of encountering a man who has sacrificed his sons to the war; the girls knit quantities of blue socks, presumably in support of the Union effort. But perhaps the most important ways in which *Little Women* responds to the Civil War are thematically and imagistically. As Ann Douglas has noted, *Little Women* is "about a house conflicted but not divided, a family that offered an analogy and possibly a corrective to America."[89]

Little Women also engages very little with Abolitionism, though Alcott and her family were staunch Abolitionists. As Janice M. Alberghene has pointed out, the racial subtexts of the book are deeply submerged. The rescue of Amy from icy waters, by Laurie and Jo, is effectively a reworking of Alcott's own rescue from the Boston Frog Pond by a black boy.[90] A gesture of cross-racial harmony is thus translated into a trope for the dangers of sibling jealousy. As for the "merry little quadroon" who joins the school begun by Jo and her professor at the end of part 2 of *Little Women*, he is a figure for the limits of the school's inclusiveness—and has conveniently disappeared by the time of the sequel, *Little Men*. Conveniently because, even in *Little Women*, "some people predicted that his admission would ruin the school" (*LW*, 597), as indeed happened when Bronson Alcott admitted an African American to his Temple School. And a story about a nineteenth-century school for whites that admitted a student of color would have had to be a different story from the one that Alcott wanted to write. Or sell.

Blacks nevertheless figure imagistically earlier in the text of *Little Women*. Amy's experiences at school, in Mr. Davis's classroom, humorously recapitulate the Civil War. Mr. Davis has banished gum "after a long and stormy war" and has "made a bonfire of . . . confiscated novels and newspapers" in his efforts to keep order among fifty "rebellious girls" (*LW*, 85). As for the pickled limes that Amy surreptitiously brings to school, they have been declared "a contraband article." During the Civil War, only three years earlier, fugitive slaves had often been referred to as contrabands. So much for the dignity of escaped slaves.

In addition to playing with Civil War themes, *Little Women* is a national narrative in other respects as well.[91] The "Camp Laurence" chapter, in which the March girls and their neighbor Laurie entertain British visitors, proclaims the book's American qualities while playfully reenacting the War of Independence. A British young lady condescends to Meg when Meg admits to working as a governess: "'Oh, indeed!' said Miss Kate; but she might as well have said, 'Dear me, how dreadful!' for her tone implied it, and something in her face made Meg color, and wish she had not been so frank" (*LW*, 166). Laurie's tutor, Mr. Brooke, whom Meg will eventually marry, quickly asserts, "Young ladies in America love independence as much as their ancestors did, and are admired and respected for supporting themselves" (*LW*, 166). Laurie and the March girls, inspired by "the spirit of '76," happily defeat the British visitors at croquet.

Later, too, themes of American independence underlie the book's meanings, subtly modifying them. Amy is associated with European influences: "For, in spite of her American birth and breeding, she possessed that reverence for titles which haunts the best of us,—that unacknowledged loyalty to the early faith in kings which . . . still has something to do with the love the young country bears the old,—like that of a big son for an imperious little mother, who held him while she could, and let him go with a farewell scolding when he rebelled" (*LW*, 363–64). As the March girl most susceptible to the charms of titles—least likely to rebel, as it were—Amy is the sister who will go to Europe. Jo proceeds on a visit with Amy to their Aunt March, self-conscious about her tendency "to burst out with some particularly blunt speech or revolutionary sentiment" before her aunt (*LW*, 367). Then in the context of discussing a charity fair to benefit the freedmen, Jo declares—"with her nose in the air, and a revolutionary aspect"—"I don't like favors; they oppress and make me feel like a slave; I'd rather do everything for myself, and be perfectly independent" (*LW*, 368). Thus does she deprive "herself of several years of pleasure" and receive "a timely lesson in the art of holding her tongue" (*LW*, 368). For Amy is the one chosen as a companion for a European tour. The result is negative, socially, for Jo, but the American context that Alcott provides makes Jo's actions positively rebellious. At the same time, the invocation of slavery and freedmen conflates the Revolutionary and Civil Wars. This translation from Revolutionary to Civil War—from a war often imaged as

child breaking free of parent to one imaged as brother striving with brother—
underscores the sibling rivalry between Jo and Amy, perhaps also the need to
overcome such rivalries. But in the process, race is again submerged in order to
gain a victory for middle-class womanhood. Only someone who had never herself been a slave could say that social obligations "make me feel like a slave."

Some of the revolutionary potential of the metaphor of independence is de-
fused when it is later applied to Meg's adjustments to domesticity. She has lost
her girlish republican "independence" upon the arrival of "the first heir to the
throne," becoming a "slave" to her son, imagistically an "enemy"—but the "revolution of some kind [that] was going on" is an internal one (*LW,* 477, 486, 489).
Meg tears herself away from over-involvement in her children, learns to interest herself once again in her husband and his concerns, not to pursue independent ones of her own.

Entranced by the thought of rafting down the Mississippi River or harpoon-
ing whales in the South Seas, and how quintessential these experiences must be,
mid-twentieth-century critics did not notice that *Little Women* is very much an
American book.

Despite highbrow dismissals and scholarly silence, critical activity with respect
to Alcott revived in the 1940s, then waned, then waxed again in the 1960s and
1970s, subsequently accelerating. Not that *Little Women* has now definitively
made it into the canon, but it's certainly not as invisible in the academy as it was
during much of the twentieth century.

In 1943 Leona Rostenberg published her discovery that Alcott had written
thrillers under the name A. M. Barnard.[92] Rostenberg's colleague Madeleine B.
Stern embarked on her still unflagging career of writing about or reprinting Alcott in books and academic journals.[93] Their efforts had some effect on the critical climate. So did Brigid Brophy's front-page essay in the *New York Times Book
Review* in 1965. Brophy tackles the charge of sentimentality head on: "the dreadful books are masterpieces," she admits, drying her eyes, but she makes that admission "with some bad temper and hundreds of reservations."[94] The directness
with which Brophy addresses sentimentality is one reason for her impact. Another is where she published it.

The recent increase in scholarly attention to children's literature has had
some impact on Alcott's reputation too. The educators and librarians who functioned as the guardians of children's literature early in the twentieth century had
been attending to Alcott all along: the *Elementary English Review,* begun in 1924,

devoted its November 1932 issue to Alcott. Alcott also figures importantly in the field of children's literature that has emerged within literary criticism during the last couple decades of the twentieth century. The scholarly journals that cater to this emerging field have been receptive to Alcott since their early years: *The Lion and the Unicorn* published an essay on Alcott during its first year, in 1977; *Children's Literature in Education*, in 1978 and again in 1980; *Children's Literature*, in 1981 and frequently thereafter.

The late-twentieth-century feminist movement has had an impact as well, an enormous impact, and I'm going to sketch its dalliance with Alcott in some detail. The early-1970s emphasis on equal rights, what has been called liberal feminism, would hardly have been anathema to Alcott, who was vocal in her support of working women and women's suffrage. Yet liberal-feminist themes are not particularly salient in *Little Women*—at least not to a late-twentieth-century reader. Jo makes some attempts at being independent, as I've already noted. As the sister who whistles, runs, talks slang, and carelessly spills coffee on her best dress, she is the one who least conforms to prevailing norms for femininity. She also earns money for her family through her writing. So her eventual marriage to Professor Bhaer, and her willingness to give up her published writing (at least until the last book in the Little Women series, *Jo's Boys*, published in 1886), can seem to be a capitulation to prevailing norms—especially if one feels that an individual work must have a unified effect, that whatever happens early is subordinate to the ending. Such a capitulation may seem even less forgivable since Alcott herself did not indulge in it, for she never married and never stopped writing.

Certainly not all feminists have forgiven Alcott. Some of the first academic journals to publish work on Alcott may have been feminist journals such as *Women's Studies*.[95] Yet in 1972 Patricia Meyer Spacks was simply dismissive of Alcott's little women: "The book is not one an adult is likely to reread with pleasure."[96] In 1978 Nina Baym viewed the publication of *Little Women* and the Elsie Dinsmore books as a watershed marking "the decline of woman's fiction, . . . because they represent the transformation of woman's fiction into girl's fiction."[97] In 1979 Sandra M. Gilbert and Susan Gubar lamented Jo's "learning to write moral homilies for children instead of ambitious gothic thrillers"—which thrillers would have been "assuredly major," they declare, unlike literature for children.[98]

A feminist approach particularly hospitable to study of Alcott emerged in the late 1970s: what has been called cultural feminism, focusing on women's traditions, women's connections with other women. In discussing "communities of women," for instance, Nina Auerbach gives *Little Women* equal billing with Jane

Austen's *Pride and Prejudice* (1813), a work that had retained at least a foothold in the U.S. academy during the difficult middle decades of the twentieth century.[99] In some respects *Little Women* even comes out better, in Auerbach's analysis, since Alcott's women are more truly supportive of one another than are Austen's.

Another impetus for renewed attention to *Little Women* was the reprinting of forgotten works, especially Alcott's pseudonymous thrillers. The appearance of *Behind a Mask* (1975), *Plots and Counterplots* (1976), and other collections has encouraged critics to read *Little Women* in yet another way, to find the raging sensations beneath the surface of this book (which Alcott herself was tempted to dismiss as "moral pap" for the young), as Judith Fetterley, for one, has done.[100]

By the 1980s feminist engagement with poststructuralism—and with what is sometimes called French feminism—led to a willingness to value not just some presumed unified effect of a work of literature, with special emphasis on its ending, but also its contradictions. A work becomes powerful if it captures key cultural conflicts and does not fully resolve them: a disjunction between overt and covert messages can be valued as a source of power. A central, powerful contradiction in *Little Women* has to do with the position of women. In particular, whom should Jo marry? Or should she marry?

In two much-cited 1869 letters, Alcott complains that "publishers are very *perwerse* & wont let authors have their way so my little women must grow up & be married off in a very stupid style" and "'Jo' should have remained a literary spinster but so many enthusiastic young ladies wrote to me clamorously demanding that she should marry Laurie, *or* somebody, that I didnt dare refuse & out of perversity went & made a funny match for her."[101] Laurie, the charming boy next door, has always been the most popular choice with the reading public for Jo's husband. Scholars have devoted considerable energy to the issue as well, whether they condemn Professor Bhaer, Jo's eventual choice, as too much a father figure or praise him for his feminine qualities, whether they condemn Laurie's wealth, which would have made Jo's life too easy, or praise him for having supported Jo's writing. Whichever arguments one finds persuasive, the impassioned attention that Jo's choice receives is a testament to the power of *Little Women*—"the lack of satisfying closure helping to keep the story alive, something to ponder, return to, reread, perhaps with the hope of a different resolution," as Barbara Sicherman observes.[102] And perhaps, through its divergence from the happily-ever-after ending with the handsome young prince, the choice of Professor Bhaer even leaves unresolved the question of whether a woman has to marry. By providing a "perverse" choice, Alcott leaves cultural conundrums—what makes a good spouse? what is suitable work for a woman? should a woman, in fact, marry?—invitingly open.

Which is also a way of saying that responses to Alcott often enact, even now, a central feminist debate between a liberal-feminist ideal of autonomy and a cultural-feminist ideal of connectedness. Does Jo provide a model of independence, even if she ultimately capitulates to marriage and stops writing? Or does she embody a sense of connectedness with a community of women? And does she then negate that community or expand it when she undertakes the education of both boys and girls in the sequel *Little Men*? Does she submit to prevailing cultural norms or contest them? Or perhaps negotiate among competing norms or even deconstruct them? Does the intensity with which the competing ideals are evoked illuminate key cultural conflicts in both the nineteenth and twentieth centuries—and therefore in itself account for the book's impact on popular and feminist imaginations?

One final useful development in feminist criticism is an increasing emphasis on recognizing differences among women, starting with those associated with race, class, and sexual orientation and going on to include perhaps age. Girls are females too. And children's literature is literature. Just as "The Yellow-Wallpaper" has been a touchstone for feminist criticism of American literature for adults (from its rediscovery in the 1970s, to its canonization, to recent work questioning its racial subtext),[103] the touchstone for feminist interest in children's literature is *Little Women*. If *Signs* and *New Literary History* have started publishing essays on children's literature—and *American Literature* has again published some—you can almost be certain that the essays address Alcott. In *New Literary History*, for example, a case study of response to *Little Women* fleshes out Catharine R. Stimpson's theoretical discussion of canons, one that makes room for affective response—a reply, if you will, to the midcentury debate over Alcott as "beloved" or, more negatively, "sentimental."[104]

Dismissiveness, condescension, and marginalization of Alcott and other authors of children's literature are now less common than in the 1970s. The roster of mainstream feminist critics who have accorded *Little Women* serious attention includes Ann Douglas, Elaine Showalter, Nina Auerbach, Judith Fetterley, Carolyn Heilbrun, and Catharine Stimpson. The number of Ph.D. dissertations focusing on Alcott has gone from zero in the 1960s to twenty-two in the 1980s to thirty-three in just the first half of the 1990s. Twelve book-length scholarly studies of Alcott have appeared since 1980.

Significant Alcott scholarship has also appeared in conjunction with new editions of Alcott's work. Not only is there the work of excavation and its concomitant editorial decisions (the original 1868 text of *Little Women* or the expurgated 1880 one?), but the accompanying introductions or afterwords are often significant contributions to scholarship—more so in the case of *Little Women* than for any other novel I know of. Many scholars—including Auerbach, Douglas, Showalter, Madelon Bedell, and Valerie Alderson—have written introductions or afterwords that go well beyond the standard brief appreciation and salient biographical facts. Such suturing of popular culture and serious scholarship, as scholars try to reach a general public, is an emblem of how *Little Women* currently exists at the interface of the two. Scholars are attending to Alcott because she has been so popular—often because she was so important to them in their own childhoods.

Alcott's work now appears in such important textbook anthologies as the *Heath Anthology of American Literature* and the *Norton Anthology of Literature by Women*. Still, in these academic contexts she has generally been represented—as is still usually the case when her work is addressed in mainstream scholarly books and periodicals—by her "flawed" works for adults rather than her better known, and often simply better, works for children. Mainstream American critics of Alcott continue to indulge in a move characteristic of many adults when they "rediscover" a work of children's literature, especially if that work is targeted at adolescents: if it speaks to adults, then it can't really be for children. Given, further, the relative lack of critical attention to the more realistic modes of children's literature, it may be that much easier for adult-oriented critics to appropriate domestic fiction like Alcott's for themselves, leaving the children with fantasy and fairy tales. In the second edition of the *Norton Anthology of Literature by Women* (1996), however, the excerpt from Alcott's *Work* has been replaced with chapters from *Little Women*. The publisher's brochure proclaims that these chapters "introduce a genre new to the anthology: children's writing."

Yet despite these encouraging developments, and despite the 1994 film of *Little Women*, the appearance of *A Long Fatal Love Chase* on best-seller lists in 1995, and the televising of an adaptation of *The Inheritance* in 1997, I can't help wondering whether scholarly attention to Alcott might be a sign of her decline in the popular imagination. Anecdotal evidence suggests that she does not have the same riveting appeal for young women now in their teens and twenties as she had for their predecessors, that fewer young women now would say, with Anna Quindlen, "*Little Women* changed my life."[105] And given the difficulty of extracting and compiling information about sales for works no longer covered by copyright, anecdotal evidence is about the best we have to go on. Certainly in my own "Children's Literature" course, *Little Women* has slipped from second or third place in annual informal surveys of favorites in the early 1980s to ninth or tenth place in the 1990s and beyond—when it manages to make it into the top ten. It's tempting to speculate that the increasing efforts to institutionalize Alcott, to hail the importance of her work as literature, may be an attempt, however unconsciously, to compensate for some erosion of her power to speak to young people. If she is starting to disappear from popular memory, scholars may need to work all the harder to memorialize her.

Alcott, then, consciously wrote a book for girls, in 1868, and thereby found her publishing niche, but it was difficult thereafter for her to be considered anything other than the "children's friend." Still, during the nineteenth century her work was read and appreciated by adults as well as children, by males as well as females. If *Little Women* was especially appreciated by young people, it was not at all confined to the nursery. As children's literature became increasingly segregated from literature for adults, however, Alcott was increasingly identified with the former and lost favor with the critical establishment—an identification and loss that some boys' books, at least, seemed to elude. Alcott's general popularity didn't seem to flag until perhaps the 1930s or 1940s, and even so continued to be strong among middle-class girls, at least until the last decade or so.

Now, thanks to the current women's movement and the publication of Alcott's lost thrillers, her work is receiving serious attention from U.S. literary critics. At times this reengagement with Alcott by the literary elite has been uneven. At times it takes the form of attempts to rescue a token work from the children's ghetto, leaving the ghetto intact. Certainly the careers of *Tom Sawyer* and *Huckleberry Finn* suggest that the literary establishment is adept at gerrymandering the literary landscape to ghettoize some works as juvenile while rescuing others from such opprobrium. Yet I'm hopeful that the faltering first efforts to take *Little Women* seriously represent a real step toward reconstruction and revision, of both Alcott and children's literature.

CHAPTER SIX

The Case of American Fantasy

There's No Place Like Oz

Before 1900, the United States produced no *Alice's Adventures in Wonderland*, no *Water-Babies*, no *At the Back of the North Wind*. There was no American fantasy literature to speak of—no juvenile literature creating worlds that break the rules of everyday physical existence. Or at least so goes a recurring refrain among literary historians. In 1976 Selma G. Lanes suggested that "a deeply held faith in the fairy-tale aspects of the American dream" meant that, "in most home-grown American fairy tales, no magic is ever more powerful than the overriding reality of the American life experience."[1]

Yet revisionists have recently contested such claims. Gillian Avery, in the fullest published history of American children's literature, traces a fantasy tradition that begins in 1838 with James Kirke Paulding's *A Christmas Gift from Fairyland*. Mark I. West refutes the naysayers with his collection *Before Oz: Juvenile Fantasy Stories from Nineteenth-Century America*, in which he reprints stories by Louisa May Alcott, Horace Scudder, Julian Hawthorne, Thomas Bailey Aldrich, Charles Carryl, and many other writers.[2]

Still, it's true that the history of fantasy literature in the United States differs from that in Britain. The enduring American children's classics of the nineteenth century, the works that have been treasured by generations of children and adults, are *Tom Sawyer, Little Women,* and other novels participating in realistic traditions, whether their focus is on accommodating domesticity or escaping it. Whatever fantasy literature was being written did not figure in the national imagination as contributing to a Golden Age of children's literature.

Furthermore, this fantasy literature was relatively unlikely to participate in what is sometimes called the high fantasy tradition, with its worlds of wondrous deeds, created by such British writers as George MacDonald, William Morris, C. S. Lewis, and J. R. R. Tolkien. Critics writing about fantasy are likely to have rather different concepts of the genre, depending on what they take as the quintessential fantasy. For Eric S. Rabkin, Lewis Carroll's Alice books define the genre, and the defining characteristic is the contravening of the ground rules of the narrative's world.[3] For Brian Attebery, Tolkien's *Lord of the Rings* is definitive, and he sees the genre as requiring some violation of natural law, as structurally comedic, and as evoking wonder.[4] Those who define fantasy in the latter way (Attebery excepted) have not usually found much fantasy in the United States in the nineteenth and early twentieth centuries. American fantasy has simply not been highly visible to certain followers of fantasy literature.

But there's also another factor that complicates the visibility and trajectory of American fantasy: the contours of the relationship between literature for children and literature for adults, and the nature of their bifurcation around the turn of the century, differed in the United States and England. Felicity A. Hughes has written about the difficulties that have been created in twentieth-century thinking about fantasy and about children's literature (and literary theory more generally) by the bifurcation between "serious" and other literature—especially fantasy.[5] She makes a compelling case for the ways in which authors attempting fantasy have been pushed toward children's literature and authors of children's literature have been pushed toward fantasy—at least her case is compelling with respect to the British traditions on which she draws. In the United States, however, the intermingling of traditions led to a different positioning for fantasy: the turn-of-the-century split between literature for children and literature for adults was just as marked, but fantasy hasn't figured as strongly in either tradition. More precisely, it hasn't figured as strongly among the highbrow custodians of either tradition. So when fantasy does appear, it is not taken seriously by either the custodians of high culture for adults or the custodians of children's literature. Though such a claim is complicated by Americans' appreciation for British fantasy.

To explore the American love/hate relationship with fantasy, in this larger study of the reception of children's literature in the American academy, I turn in this chapter and the next to three cases: here, to the reception of what has come to be considered the preeminent American exemplar of fantasy for children; in the next chapter, to the reception of the preeminent exemplar of nineteenth-century British fantasy, together with a recent upstart. In these chapters, as elsewhere, I'm seeking to provide not a broad survey of a particular genre, in this case fantasy, but rather a close study of the reception of two or three highly suggestive cases, to see how such study illuminates our shifting constructions of childhood and children's literature.

If 1900 is often used as a turning point in the history of American fantasy, that's because this is the year when *The Wonderful Wizard of Oz* (subsequently entitled *The Wizard of Oz*) was published. It's a truism among Oz enthusiasts, echoed by many literary historians, that *Oz* was the first American work of fantasy. In the words of literary critic Edward Wagenknecht in 1929, *The Wizard of Oz* embodied "the first distinctive attempt to construct a fairyland out of American materials."[6] According to a writer for the *New York Times Book Review* in 1956, *Oz* was "the first enduring and truly indigenous American fairy tale."[7]

For even as he drew on European folk materials, L. Frank Baum became, as John Goldthwaite puts it, "the Edison of narrative fantasy, finding ways of lighting it up and making it talk that no one had ever thought of before."[8] Baum brought technology to fantasy, the wizard achieving his effects technologically—much as Disney's *Beauty and the Beast* is Americanized, Belle's father changed from a merchant to an inventor. *Oz* overcomes what has been described as a national lack of interest in fantasy, at least in the country's early centuries, by focusing on a devotion to material things, "new scenery, new artifacts, new wealth."[9]

Oz is also an American response to Lewis Carroll's *Alice's Adventures in Wonderland* (1865). In the same year that Baum published *The Wonderful Wizard of Oz* he also published *A New Wonderland*. He had been much struck by the portrayal of Alice; the secret of her success, Baum wrote, was "that she was a real child, and any normal child could sympathize with her all through her adventures."[10] He wanted to do something similar with his protagonist in *Oz*.

Critics have frequently noted the connection with Carroll. An early reviewer states that *Oz* "is penned with the wild extravagance of fancy that is noticeable in that children's classic, *Alice in Wonderland*"; another concludes a 1904 review of *The Marvelous Land of Oz* by comparing Baum's protagonist Tip to "Alice of undying memory."[11] Filmmakers too have underscored the connection. In the 1939 MGM film—about which I'll have more to say later—Aunt Em complains about "all this jabberwocking about when there's work to be done": the *jabbering* of everyday language becomes Carrollian *jabberwocking*, hinting at a place beyond the looking glass where one can have adventures and slay one's worst monsters.

Baum enthusiasts like to claim that *Oz* was the "fastest selling children's book in America" or even "the runaway all-time children's best seller."[12] Shirley Jackson may have suggested in 1959 that she "cannot actually think of more than a dozen children who know their way around the Land of Oz," yet in 1957 Martin Gardner referred to a survey of teenagers (conducted in 1956, the year the MGM film first appeared on television) in which they cited the Oz books most, among the books they liked best when young; he also reported that Milwaukee children had worn out 135 library copies of *Oz* in eight years.[13] According to one estimate, more than ten million copies of *Oz* were in print by 1978.[14]

Yet it's notoriously difficult to estimate the sales of books in the public domain. And even while they're still under copyright, which protected *Oz* until 1956, one can get wildly different reports of sales. According to Frank Joslyn Baum and Russell P. MacFall, between 1903 and 1956 *Oz* sold 4,195,667 copies.[15] A writer for the *New York Times*, however, reports sales of only 237,896 copies by 1954.[16] It's simply not clear whether *Oz* has sold as many copies as *Wonderland*, *Little Women*, or *Tom Sawyer*. As of midcentury these latter three were on Frank Luther Mott's list of the 21 all-time best-sellers in the United States; *Oz* was not.[17] In fact, *Oz* did not appear on Mott's longer list, the 325 best-sellers whose sales have equaled 1 percent of the population in their year of publication. Yet Mott is not entirely consistent: at one point he states that *Oz* "was the most popular juvenile of the turn of the century," but elsewhere he indicates that its sales were exceeded by *Mrs. Wiggs of the Cabbage Patch* (1901), *The Call of the Wild* (1903), *Anne of Green Gables* (1908), and *A Girl of the Limberlost* (1909), works that are now usually considered juvenile literature.[18]

In the fullest survey of the reading habits of early-twentieth-century children, the results published in the 1926 *Winnetka Graded Book List*, Baum finished well down in the pack: *The Wizard of Oz* ranked 142d, far behind the front-running *Tom Sawyer*, *Heidi*, and *Little Women*, far behind *Wonderland* at 18th and *Little Lord Fauntleroy* at 28th.[19] At the same time, just the inclusion of *Oz* indicates that the researchers thought it met a minimal test of quality; a mimeographed supplement reveals that the compilers omitted some popular works that failed to meet that test, including *Pollyanna*, *The Bobbsey Twins*, and *A Girl of the Limber-lost*.[20] In a study of the reading interests of twenty-four thousand children in the late primary grades, published in 1958, *Oz* ranks thirty-third, behind *Tom Sawyer* and *The Secret Garden*, ahead of *Huckleberry Finn*, *Fauntleroy*, and *Little Women*, well ahead of *Wonderland*.[21] More recently, and on a much smaller scale, in informal surveys in my "Children's Literature" course, *The Wizard of Oz* has ranked twentieth in popularity: it has been named one of the two or three favorite childhood books by 3 percent of the undergraduates polled during the last two decades, behind *Wonderland* but ahead of *Tom Sawyer*. In short, *Oz* has been popular, but I'd hesitate to call it the best-selling or most popular juvenile in the United States.

The early response to *Oz* was positive. The *New York Times* reviewer enthusiastically described it as "ingeniously woven out of commonplace material" and as rising "far above the average children's book of today, high as is the present standard."[22] The *Dial* reviewer found it "really notable among the innumerable publications of the young, making an appeal which is fairly irresistible to a certain standard of taste."[23] In a review of the second Oz book, the *New York Times* reviewer referred to the Scarecrow and the Tin Woodman as "friends of all babies" and as having "disported themselves with rare grace through the pages of Mr. Baum's previous volume."[24] At the time of his death in 1919, Baum was considered worthy of a brief obituary notice in the *New York Times*.[25]

Despite his popularity with reviewers and the general public, Baum has not been particularly popular with the literary establishment. If in *The Cambridge History of American Literature* (1917–21), the literary history most receptive to children's literature among the three histories I tracked in Chapter 3, Alcott is barely mentioned, Baum is not mentioned at all. And there's certainly no mention in the 1948 *Literary History of the United States* or the 1988 *Columbia Literary History of the United States*. The custodians of high culture seem to have attended to Baum's work even less than they have to the work of other children's authors.

Among experts in children's literature too, Baum's purchase was precarious during the first half of the century. Another truism among Oz enthusiasts is that *The Wizard of Oz* was despised by children's librarians. Martin Gardner claimed in 1962, "To this day there are thousands of children's librarians around the nation—kindly, bespectacled, gray-minded ladies—who will tell you with pride that they do not permit a single Oz book to sully their shelves."[26] The one schol-

arly collection of essays on *Oz*, a collection that reprints Gardner's essay, highlights this thinking by devoting one of three groupings of essays to "Librarians
and Oz."

Early histories and textbooks of children's literature do indeed ignore *Oz*.
Baum aficionados point to the first editions of Cornelia L. Meigs's *Critical History of Children's Literature* (1953) and May Hill Arbuthnot's *Children and Books*
(1947).[27] They could also point to F. J. Harvey Darton's *Children's Books in England* (1932), which attends to American literature as well as British, but not to
Baum. And when Baum is mentioned in other histories and textbooks he is often
disparaged. In *Children's Literature in the Elementary School*, a textbook first published in 1961 and reprinted frequently since, Charlotte S. Huck finds *Oz*
"somewhat pedestrian when compared with other books of its kind" because of
a "lack of wonder and awe."[28]

As for its positioning in public libraries, *Oz* was excluded from a Kansas City
library in the 1920s, from the children's rooms of the New York Public Library
in the 1920s (by Anne Carroll Moore), and from the open stacks of the Detroit
Library in the 1950s (by Ralph Ulveling); in 1959 the state librarian of Florida
encouraged public libraries to withdraw *Oz* from circulation[29]—to cite documented cases of exclusion. Nor does Baum figure much, in the first half of the
century, on lists of recommended reading or of widely circulating library books.
None of his works appears in a 1907 *Ladies' Home Journal* list of "books for
young people" or in a 1922 *Bookman* list of "One Hundred Story Books for Children."[30] Nor are any mentioned in Laura E. Richards's 1939 *What Shall the Children Read?* or in the College English Association's 1960 *Good Reading* or in the
list appended to Alice M. Jordan's 1947 *Children's Classics* (nor, for that matter,
are any of Frances Hodgson Burnett's works included in these lists). Baum's
works are absent from various lists of books recommended by the American Library Association: the 1904 *A.L.A. Catalog: Eight Thousand Volumes for a Popular
Library, with Notes*, the 1926 *A.L.A. Catalog: An Annotated Basic List of Ten Thousand Books*, the 1933 *The Right Book for the Right Child*, the 1945 *Buying List of
Books for Small Libraries*, and the 1960 *Basic Book Collection for Elementary Grades*
(Burnett is absent from the last three as well). No books by Baum appear on lists
of most-circulated books in U.S. libraries in 1923 or 1933–34,[31] possibly reflecting librarians' reluctance to stock Baum. In an essay in the *Library Journal* in
1932, substitute titles are proffered for "unrecommended juveniles," the "unrecommended" including books featuring Tom Swift, Tarzan, Elsie Dinsmore—and Oz.[32]

Nevertheless, three of Baum's works are listed in the 1909 *Children's Catalog: A Guide to the Best Reading for Young People Based on Twenty-Four Selected Library Lists*.[33] And in Nancy Larrick's *Parent's Guide to Children's Reading* (1958), sponsored by the National Book Committee, *Oz* is mentioned in the same breath as *Little Women* and *Tom Sawyer*, as "high on any list of favorites," specifically what parents remember as favorites in their own childhoods.[34] Baum's work wasn't excluded from all libraries or by all librarians. In recent years *Oz* is mentioned almost as a matter of course whenever classic works of children's literature are named. The one exception I've come across is the Children's Literature Association's list of canonical children's literature, memorialized in three *Touchstones* volumes published in 1985–89—though when the membership of the association was polled in 1976 on the "ten best American children's books," *Oz* was included, eighth on the list.[35] Jim Trelease includes *Oz* in his *Read-Aloud Handbook* (1985)—and omits *Wonderland*. Betsy Hearne's *Choosing Books for Children* (1990) includes *Oz* in a listing of forty classics that still live, along with *Little Women*, *Tom Sawyer*, *Huckleberry Finn*, *The Secret Garden*, and *Wonderland*. Alison Lurie lists it in 1990, along with *Tom Sawyer*, *Little Women*, and *Wonderland*, as among the "sacred texts of childhood."[36]

In short, *Oz* has been excluded from the children's collections of a number of libraries yet has not been universally banned. As Lois Belfield Watt aptly notes, librarians have been divided, the Oz books removed from children's rooms in Detroit and Washington but defended and circulated by librarians in Chicago and Milwaukee.[37]

Just as interesting to me as Baum's low profile among literati in the early years— among both the custodians of children's literature and the custodians of high culture—is the energy devoted by latter-day critics of *Oz* to librarian bashing. In 1957, for instance, Bernard M. Golumb speaks out, in the *Library Journal*, against "the profession-wide disdain for the Oz books."[38] In 1964 in *Library Occurrent*, Richard Paul Smyers questions whether a book in print for sixty-four years should be dismissed as trash; he goes on to point out that in the course of ten months, a single copy of *Oz* in a South Bend bookmobile was checked out fifteen times.[39] In 1971 C. Warren Hollister complains, in his defense of *Oz*, that librarians and critics focus too much on theme, characterization, plot, and style in judging children's books, and not enough on what he calls three-dimensionality, by which he means not the dimensionality of the characters but "the magical tugging of the child-reader through the page into the story—into the other world."[40]

The urge to bash librarians, the "common knowledge" among Ozmapolitans that librarians hate *Oz*, that, in Michael Patrick Hearn's words, Baum "was not always warmly received by the ladies,"[41] has taken on something of a life of its own. Sometimes the "common knowledge" exists in uneasy contrast with a contrary anecdote. Osmond Beckwith describes his pre-1950 encounter with *Oz* thus: "In my own childhood I had known Baum only from his *Ozma of Oz*, a book I seem to remember having found in our school library: odd if true, for schools consistently denied shelf space to Oz as to most ephemeral or 'fad' books which children read to the exclusion of anything else."[42]

Few Ozophiles are as strident on the issue as Gardner, who castigates librarians as belonging to a profession that attracts "a prosaic, matter-of-fact mind. An individual with a soaring imagination is not likely to be happy shuffling file cards and carrying on a librarian's routine chores."[43] But many Baum critics participate, to varying degrees, in the impulse to scapegoat the lady librarian. In this they resemble the critics of American literature early in the century, as I've discussed in Chapter 3—though to opposite effect. If women can't be blamed for catering too much to popularity and not attending enough to literary excellence, then they can be blamed for the reverse—for encouraging "literary," hence "emasculated," children's books.[44] It's true that not all libraries stocked Baum's work, but women librarians were no more likely to censor books than were their male colleagues: "Women were predominant in the profession, but they were more than proportionately represented as advocates of freedom."[45] The urge to blame lady librarians is symptomatic of a cultural anxiety about childhood and children's literature, an anxiety that set in about the turn of the century, once an interest in children and children's literature could be branded as genteel, hence feminine, and then dismissed.

His librarian bashing aside, Gardner provides useful insights into why Baum didn't find great favor among specialists in children's literature. For one thing, the custodians of American children's literature were wary of fantasy. "Fantasy is not for everybody," Gardner contentiously puts it. "I know of no studies by professional psychologists on this matter, but I hazard the guess that an eight-year-old's liking for fantasy reflects the strength of this imagination. . . . I suspect also that it is from the ranks of such children, when grown, that come our most creative individuals."[46] I've already noted that the nineteenth-century children's books that have taken hold in the American national consciousness tend to participate in realistic traditions. In Roger Sale's words (though he means in his formulation to include rather than exclude Baum), American children's literature "is not realistic literature for the most part, but it tends to include or to accommodate the real with an ease, even an optimism, that is generally not found in European children's books."[47] Such a tendency was reinforced by John Dewey's turn-of-the-century preference for stories that do not encourage children to escape from reality and by Lucy Sprague Mitchell's advocacy of realistic tales in the 1920s and 1930s, as embodied in the Here and Now storybooks. U.S. children's literature has been much more receptive to the family story and to bad-boy books than to fantasy.

Baum wasn't particularly aiming to write elite literature for children, though he did serialize one of his fantasy fictions in the most prestigious children's magazine of the day, *St. Nicholas.* Mostly Baum was aiming for sales and popularity, at a time when popularity and quality were increasingly seen as divergent. He placed his books not with respected East Coast publishers—even though he received invitations from such firms as Harper, Scribner's, and Appleton's—but with more marginal Midwestern ones.[48] The crux of the matter seems to be, as Gardner rightly observes, that the Oz books were a series and were published by a Chicago firm that specialized in series books, at a time when hack-written series produced by such "fiction factories" as the Stratemeyer Syndicate were starting to flood the market.

Admittedly, books for children often come in series. Carroll's *Through the Looking-Glass* was a sequel to *Alice's Adventures in Wonderland.* Alcott followed the first volume of *Little Women* with a second one, then with *Little Men* and eventually *Jo's Boys;* even her *Old-Fashioned Girl* was often seen, during the nineteenth century, as part of the Little Women series, though it included none of the same characters. And Twain's *Huckleberry Finn* could be read as constituting part of a Tom Sawyer series, which would go on to include *Tom Sawyer Abroad* and *Tom Sawyer, Detective.* But the early decades of the twentieth century witnessed a new phenomenon: mass-marketed series for children, formula fiction, most written under pseudonyms, and many produced via a fiction factory. A presiding entrepreneur such as Edward Stratemeyer would come up with a two- to three-page outline and farm it out to hack writers, who could produce a book in a couple of weeks.[49] Librarians and other critics of children's literature were wary, to say the least, of such volumes. And often they expressed themselves with a stridency about this "mile-a-minute fiction"—known to "debauch and vitiate" and to do "incalculable" harm[50]—that adult readers nowadays, who have happily survived their own binges on Nancy Drew or Tom Swift or the Hardy Boys, find puzzling. Baum's standing with the arbiters of children's literature was hardly helped by the fact that his Oz books were produced by publishers of such series—or that he himself would go on to write, under pseudonyms, the Sam Steele series, the Boy Fortune Hunters series, the Aunt Jane's Nieces series.

In fact, at a time when serious practitioners of literature for adults were practicing art for art's sake (it helped if, like Henry James, they could fall back on some family wealth), and when respected practitioners of literature for children could lay claim to practicing art for children's sake, Baum's career history could be seen—despite his claims of catering to the desires of children, or rather because of his responsiveness to the children's market—as impelling him to practice art for money's sake. He'd had a checkered career, as poultry breeder, theatrical impresario, variety-store owner, newspaper editor, traveling salesman, editor of a trade journal for store-window trimmers. He was often impelled from one career to the next by the failure of what he'd invested in: the burning down of his opera house, the financial failure of his store or newspaper. He eventually lit on writing for children, and his second attempt, the 1899 *Father Goose, His Book*, proved highly successful—becoming "the best-selling American picture book of its day," according to Michael Patrick Hearn.[51] This success determined the main contours of his subsequent career, though even then he would make detours from the fantasy fiction that his readers clamored for, sometimes attempting to mount musical extravaganzas or motion pictures based on the fiction (at times successfully, though often not); sometimes writing very different fictions under pseudonyms: adventure stories for adults, a series of adventure stories for adolescent boys, and various series for girls, including the ten very successful volumes of the Aunt Jane's Nieces series by "Edith Van Dyne."

It's not just Baum's checkered career history that could taint him as seeking lucre. Cultural critics are fond of pointing to the conjunction of Baum's interest in window trimming and the Oz books (he published *The Art of Decorating Dry Goods Windows* the same year that he published *Oz*), the extent to which Baum's world is permeated by consumerism, by the desire for objects that are only images.[52] What is the Wizard of Oz, after all, but a fraudulent advertiser, promising miracles to would-be consumers but unable, finally, to come through with the goods, at least for Dorothy? The amiability with which Baum finally treats the Wizard, in the original *Oz* book, suggests that he is not particularly critical of such hucksterism. The extent to which the Wizard is a stand-in for the author may even hint that writing is hucksterism too. As Susan Wolstenholme has astutely reasoned, it's not just Baum's trade journal that "blurred the boundary lines separating writing, theatre, and merchandising": for Baum, writing simply was "both showmanship and salesmanship."[53] Wolstenholme also notes that Baum was prescient of twentieth-century cultural trends—with his interest in film, including the trick photography required for what would now be called special effects; his positioning himself in Hollywood when it was still a small town; his ideas for creating a theme park in California; his idea of creating a musical based on Snow White.[54] Born a few decades later, he could have been Walt Disney.

It's hard to tell, with respect to Baum's writing career, where the showmanship stops. Michael Patrick Hearn and Michael O. Riley have stressed that Baum started his second Oz book, *The Marvelous Land of Oz* (1904), with the intention of turning it into a musical comedy. The final gender transformation of the main character echoes the theatrical pantomime tradition associated with the Principal Boy, who is really—is ultimately revealed as—a woman; the army of beautiful girls was a budding chorus line; and the prominence given to the Tin Woodman and the Scarecrow probably reflects the phenomenal success of vaudevillians David Montgomery and Fred Stone in those roles in the earlier production of *The Wizard of Oz*.[55] Baum hoped to replicate the success of that musical extravaganza, which had been produced in Chicago in 1902 and on Broadway in 1903.[56] Baum's publishers consciously promoted not just *The Marvelous Land of Oz* but also the play *The Woggle-Bug*, creating Woggle-Bug buttons, a card game, and a contest. Baum likewise wrote a promotional comic-page series for a Sunday newspaper, *Queer Visitors from the Marvelous Land of Oz* (eventually revised and published in book form as *The Visitors from Oz*, in 1960) and a brief volume called *The Woggle-Bug Book*.

One can well wonder which is the "real" commodity here—or the real work of art, if you will, that the rest is promoting. Surely not the playing cards or the newspaper comic pages, even if the latter did in fact comprise "original" writing. The play, it would seem. (It flopped.) Though actually all items are selling one another, thus anticipating modern merchandising tie-ins and, more generally, the interpenetration of entertainment and advertising—an interpenetration manifested in recent years in Saturday morning cartoons that are spin-offs of tangible merchandise (the Strawberry Shortcake phenomenon) or of Disney films, and in the decisions of action-film producers to create scripts that foreground what is marketable as toys.

In his attention to the marketplace Baum may not have been much worse than Twain, an author whom Baum seems consciously to have copied, going on the road in 1908 with a slide, film, and lecture show and dressing in a white suit, Twain's trademark. Twain, after all, chose non-elite publishers, pursuing the subscription method of publication since he figured to make more money that way; he went on speaking tours to raise funds; he invested disastrously in the Paige typesetting machine as he dabbled in publishing as well as writing. But Twain was also a close friend of the dean of American letters, William Dean Howells, and was being published in the *Atlantic*. Baum came later. He never published in the *Atlantic*. He wrote at a time when prestige was increasingly divorced from the overt pursuit of profit, and when children's literature was increasingly divorced from that for adults and had become, by definition, non-elite.

It may be true, as Gardner suggests, that fantasy is a somewhat specialized taste. I'm struck, in accounts of favorite childhood reading, by how many people cite both *Oz* and *Wonderland*, or otherwise suggest an interest focused on fantasy. Allen Tate, Tennessee Williams, and Judith Krantz, for instance, mention both Carroll and Baum as childhood favorites.[57] Andre Norton, for whom the Oz books were her "greatest love," went on to write fantasy and science fiction herself.[58] So did Ray Bradbury: "By the time I was 9, . . . I lived, most of the time, in Emerald City. Mr. Baum taught me how to begin to dream, to fantasize, to have fun with images in my mind."[59]

And yet there continues to be some discomfort with *Oz* among adult readers. Although some British commentators have been positive,[60] others are distinctly cool. John Goldthwaite states that Oz "is a place I think you really must discover in childhood to love."[61] Mary F. Thwaite reports that *Oz* "won much fame at home and abroad, more so than it deserves."[62] In her pathbreaking history of American children's literature, Gillian Avery acknowledges that the book has become "part of American folklore" but adds that "of all American classics this is the most difficult for a foreigner to appraise."[63] She is particularly discomforted by the easy optimism, the blandness, the lack of stylistic subtlety, the avoidance of promising themes raised in the opening pages set in Kansas.[64] In a contribution to the 1995 *Children's Literature: An Illustrated History*, Avery and her coauthors note the "quite remarkable neglect" of *Oz* "by the critical establishment" but also assert, "It is generally agreed to be no more than workmanlike in its prose, and pedestrian—not to say utilitarian—in its invention."[65]

There seems as well to be a curious gender politics at play in Baum's following. Like *Wonderland* and other works of fantasy, *Oz* has happily attracted a host of

allegorical readings: the most popular seem to be psychoanalytic, psychothera-
peutic, and political, the book a parable on Populism, the film a commentary on
the New Deal.[66] Yet no one seems to have claimed, as a result of this crossing of
disciplinary boundaries, that *Oz* is the exclusive domain of adults. For *Wonderland*, perched between elite culture for adults and elite culture for children, the
line of fracture in the critical imagination is articulated by age, as I will show in
Chapter 7; for *Oz*, perched between elite and non-elite culture, whether for
children or adults, the line of fracture seems to be articulated by gender.

Anecdotal evidence suggests that, among young people, the Oz books are
more popular with girls than with boys. Baum himself thought that his audience
was primarily girls.[67] When asked whether *Oz* is especially popular with young
girls, Martin Gardner responded, "I'm afraid it is."[68]

Yet when boys do take to Oz they seem more likely to become lifelong devotees. In Edward Wagenknecht's words, "Most of the great Baum devotees of mature years that I happen to know are not women but men."[69] There has emerged
a cultish, somewhat beleaguered, mostly male fan community for the Oz books,
as distinct from—though not necessarily exclusive of—the movie. The fans of
Oz seem more beleaguered than, say, *Secret Garden* followers, who do not seem
to feel persecuted but simply delighted to find fellow aficionados; *The Secret
Garden* may have suffered fewer overt attacks by librarians, but it was just as absent from midcentury lists of recommended reading. Perhaps the strongest evidence of Baum's following is in the pages of the *Baum Bugle*, published since
1957 by the International Wizard of Oz Club, initially a mimeographed fanzine,
now, in the words of a leading Baum scholar, "a reputable semi-scholarly
journal."[70]

Another sign of devotion is the innumerable continuations of Baum's Oz sto-
ries, both official and unofficial. Baum himself wrote fourteen Oz books (or
more, if one counts his Little Wizard series for young children); his publishers,
Reilly and Britton, later Reilly and Lee, officially published twenty-six more, by
various authors, in the fifty years following Baum's death. Since 1972 the Oz
Club has published six new volumes, several by "official" writers for Reilly and
Lee (are these then "official" volumes?), and distributed four graphic novels.
Then there are the two versions of a book written by Baum's son, only one of
which was published—since he wasn't being published by his father's publisher,
and Reilly and Lee sued; a previously unpublished book by one of Baum's illustrators, later an "official" writer for the series; and a book by Baum's great grand-
son. Not to mention scores of novels by other fans, some published, some exist-

ing in typescript or privately printed, and the stories published in the annuals *Oziana* and *Oz-story*.[71]

This devotion often strikes young. Jack Snow offered to become Baum's successor as Royal Historian of Oz when he was twelve, though it was twenty-seven years before Snow published his first Oz book.[72] Justin Schiller founded the International Wizard of Oz Club when he was fourteen (or twelve, according to some accounts). Michael Patrick Hearn completed the first edition of *The Annotated Wizard of Oz* when he was twenty-one, publishing it when he was twenty-three.[73] Like other phenomena that have spawned fanzines, *Oz* has encouraged a kind of reader participation, not just the consuming of the product and associated merchandise but the creating of products as well. Baum himself stressed the extent to which he drew on ideas from child fans, noting for instance how the germ of *The Lost Princess of Oz* (1917) was a question from an eleven-year-old, who wondered what would happen if Ozma were lost or stolen.[74] Carroll and Alcott also admitted to drawing on the ideas of their child friends, but in Baum's case the involvement of children seems to have empowered young people to write, quite directly—to continue the Oz saga for themselves.[75]

These Oz books can be described as simulacra, as Richard Flynn has portrayed them, drawing upon Jean Baudrillard's concept of copies of copies with no original.[76] Oz himself is an imitation of a wizard, faking his magical effects, the book about him a kind of imitation of *Wonderland*. The sequels are imitations of the "original" book or of one another. The MGM film is an imitation of the book, with some subsequent books drawing more on the film than on the text versions. And for most people, encountering the movie version first, the book is in effect a simulacrum of the film.

Or more precisely, unlike *Wonderland*, *Oz* has given rise not so much to imitations, to creations of new Ozes, as to continuations, further explorations of Baum's Oz. This urge to create continuations is a popular-culture phenomenon manifested also in the Baker Street Irregulars and the Trekkie fanzines. It may be in part that Arthur Conan Doyle, Gene Roddenberry, and Baum created memorable characters.[77] Even more important, though, would seem to be the creation of an alternate world, the pea-soup fog of London, the brightly lit and colorful Oz. It helps too if it's a world that the originator has increasingly elaborated in a series of works. If Carroll's work is particularly memorable for its word and logic play (hard to imitate well?), Baum's is memorable for its world. And I think that's what Warren Hollister was getting at with his concept of three-dimensionality, the tugging of the reader "into the other world." In the words of twelve-year-old Katy Lau, "For me the lure of Oz is that it's a whole world inside books and it seems so real! . . . When I read the Oz books it's very easy to get lost in its magnificent world!"[78] What's at stake is not so much identifying with particular characters but identifying, if you will, with an entire universe.

In any case, the hardcore fans, the adults who can't get enough of Baum, are mostly men. There may be an occasional exception, such as Ruth Plumly Thompson, author of nineteen of the official Oz books.[79] Yet the women literary critics who have written of Baum's work, and they are relatively few, have tended to be more measured in their enthusiasm than adult men. And sometimes this gender politics plays itself out intriguingly within commentaries. In a 1977 review of Oziana in the *Los Angeles Times*, Ray Bradbury provides a particularly rich gendering of Ozomania. He frames his account by positing a road trip across the United States: he imagines stopping at libraries along Route 66 in the 1930s and ends, of course, with the metaphor of the yellow brick road. He starts with some relatively gentle librarian bashing, as he notes that "librarians, plus certain citified intellectuals, were certain-sure from 1901 on up to, well, at least the '50s, that L. Frank Baum couldn't write his way out of Munchkin Country or across that Deadly Desert."[80] Baum is now carried in most libraries, he adds. Bradbury closes by suggesting that we can now "survive the Tweedledum snobs and the Caterpillar librarians and, in the hands of children, make the journey without fading, melting, vanishing or dying, ever." He is, of course, contrasting the gatekeepers' attitude toward Oz with their attitude toward Wonderland.

Bradbury's argument in the middle sections of his review hinges on love: Baum's love for what he was writing, the film-makers' love for what they were doing when they filmed *Oz* in 1939, the readers' love for the characters of *Oz*. "We do not really love Alice or any of the creatures she meets," Bradbury writes, "when she steps through the Looking Glass or pops down the Rabbit Hole." "We love *Alice in Wonderland*, the book. We do *not* love its people"—unlike the "amiable frauds" populating Oz. "Alice moved in intellectual collisions and came forth not one wit wiser than when she fell in"—unlike Dorothy. We leave Looking-glass world shouting, "Good Riddance"; "As we storm-fly out of Oz we look back at it as home and can hardly wait to return."

Curiouser and curiouser. Bradbury values love over logic, that which has been stereotypically associated with the feminine over that which has been associated with the masculine, though the framing of his comments hints at approval of being on the road, usually a masculine prerogative in our literary culture. Bradbury's framing, furthermore, reverses the way Baum's *Oz* is framed by "home." Bradbury's resituating of Oz as home powerfully comments on a recurring crux in Baum studies and revalues its traditional gendering. The movie, in particular, reinforced the message that there's no place like home (in the book, Dorothy says only once, in passing, "There is no place like home")[81] even while acknowledging the yearning for somewhere over the rainbow. But in both book and film, home and away are in tension. Is it good to be home in Kansas? Or is Dorothy's true home in Oz—where, indeed, she returns and stays in subsequent books in the Oz series? Is Dorothy's return to Kansas a token of maturity or a regression to childhood dependency? Does she give up her flight of independence to return to domestic drudgery? Bradbury prefers Oz, as I think most readers do, even when they think the piety of returning home is suitable for readers who are younger than they are. And by calling Oz home, Bradbury simultaneously regenders the masculinity of the quest and enlarges the scope of home.

But that's not all. In the midst of his essay appears the following: "Baum was, at heart, a little-old-maid librarian crammed with honey-muffins and warm tea. Lewis Carroll sipped his tea cold, digested ciphers and burped logic gone a teensy bit awry. Carroll would have got you out of bed at five in the morning to recite logarithms. Baum would have leaped in your bed and done you in with a pillow fight."[82] Baum, in short, is now a librarian, and a female one at that: librarians too have been revalued, positively—lovable Baum one of them after all. On the other hand, I'm not sure that it's Baum the old-maid librarian who is leaping into Bradbury's bed at the end of the passage. Or maybe she is, honey muffins, after all. Bradbury engages in gender play, crisscrossing stereotypes, revealing Baum as a man for all genders—and illuminating the gender crossing of responses to Baum. He wrote of a girl, whom many men are willing to accompany or perhaps identify with, but in order to do that they must exorcise the feminine, the stock figure of the lady librarian, even as book and film exorcise a Wicked Witch. Susan Wolstenholme posits that the Oz books "proposed 'childhood' as an androgynous alternative to masculinity and femininity."[83] And there's truth in that. But for many of the men who became Ozophiles, the gendering of their immersion in Oz has remained deeply buried.

What seems clear is that, like *Little Women*, *Oz* can appeal both to those who want to escape the confines of domesticity and to those who crave domestic security. Some critics tracing Dorothy's trajectory argue that she is independent and liberated and pursues a quest that parallels those in canonical American literature—"The search for Aunt Em is no less exciting, no less heroic, and no less dangerous than the escape from Aunt Sally."[84] Yet Dorothy's return to the safety and domesticity of home is something about which many women have felt some ambivalence, especially as that return is emphasized in the 1939 movie version, the adventures in Oz rationalized as a mere dream.[85]

As these various commentaries I have cited suggest, *Oz* is receiving increasing attention from literary and cultural critics. Articles on Baum may not have appeared in as many prestigious venues as have those on Carroll, yet they have appeared in such journals as *Representations* and *American Literary History*. Baum's strongest scholarly footholds seem to be in the *Baum Bugle* and in the emerging scholarship on children's literature. The annual *Children's Literature*, begun in 1972, included articles on Baum in five of its first ten issues. And as I write the first draft of this chapter, the *Children's Literature Association Quarterly* has published an essay on *Oz*, book or movie, in three consecutive issues.

There's another factor at play in the popularity, high and low, of Baum's work, a factor that I have so far only alluded to—and that is the 1939 MGM movie. Some see the film as better than the book. Certainly the film is better known. When I surveyed fifty undergraduates in March 2000, I learned that all had seen the movie; only three had read the book.

If the adult fans of Baum have tended to be white men, the fans engendered by the MGM universe of *Oz* are a more diverse crew. They include white women and African Americans, perhaps especially those seeking access to the middle class and its culture: consider the all-black Broadway production of *The Wiz*, which in 1975 won seven Tony awards and a Grammy and later became a movie featuring Diana Ross and Michael Jackson. Fans also include gay men, friends of Dorothy, as they call themselves, for whom "Over the Rainbow" functions as an unofficial anthem at Gay Pride events;[86] a travel agency catering to gays can signal as much by calling itself Toto Tours ("We're not in Kansas anymore"). In part this popularity is due to Judy Garland's iconic status among gays. But perhaps also the family that the intrepid foursome socially constructs in *Oz*—creating "a new family romance on new terms"[87]—resonates as the true family. Perhaps the awarding of heart, brain, and courage, qualities that the Scarecrow, Tin Woodman, and Cowardly Lion already possess, functions as a kind of coming out. Perhaps the fact that Dorothy's three friends are so obviously humans, in nonhuman drag, gives play to the emphasis on performance that has been focal to gay culture, this minority that is visible only when it performs itself as gay. Dee Michel points to the lion "born to be a sissy," the wood-man "not gay, but certainly not a macho man," and another writer describes Oz as "fiercely tolerant of the outlandish."[88]

Oz has generated frequent allusions in the culture at large—likewise T-shirts, puzzles, games, and other memorabilia. Yet most of the *Oz* manifestations in popular culture refer to the 1939 movie rather than the 1900 book. There are games and toys, commemorative plates and ruby-slipper pendants, not to mention 1990 U.S. postage stamps. Recently I've come across advertisements for *Oz* thimbles, a "collector egg," a chess set, and plastic figures handed out with Burger King kids' meals—and the ruby slippers were one of the stars of the traveling Smithsonian exhibit of 1996. My college library has had trouble keeping the video of the movie on its shelf—the video is either in circulation or "lost"—because students want to test whether the Pink Floyd album *The Dark Side of the Moon* is coordinated with the film (one starts the CD on the third roar of the MGM lion). There's even a Dorothy Barbie. I suspect that there are more references of one sort or another to *Oz* in popular culture than to any of the other books I've focused on in this study.[89]

The movie may have been only sixth in the 1998 American Film Institute's rankings of the top hundred films of the previous century, but it would probably rank first in the sentimental sweepstakes. David Ansen begins the special issue of *Newsweek* that commemorates the rankings with a memory of *The Wizard of Oz*, "one of those officially beloved movies that grown-ups look back on with tender affection," to illustrate how "the movies have seized our dreams, co-opted our imaginations, snatched our bodies."[90]

The *Oz* movie is arguably "the most widely seen and most familiar film in history"—not least because of the frequency with which it has been shown on television, more than thirty times, often drawing more than half of the viewing audience.[91] Between 1956 and 1985, the film had been seen in 436 million homes.[92] For most people, Dorothy is not the little girl of W. W. Denslow's original illustrations but the corseted sixteen-year-old Judy Garland singing "Over the Rainbow."

And perhaps certain films are now positioned, with respect to audience, where certain works of children's literature were positioned in the nineteenth century. Douglas Street attempts to explain the broad appeal of the *Oz* film by claiming that it is for adults, whereas the book is for children: "Baum's simplistic, child-like innocence" in his "adventure fantasy for children" is transformed "into an adult cinema classic deserving of its long list of commercial, profes-

Not Judy
W. W. Denslow, *The Wonderful Wizard of Oz*, 1900; courtesy of the de Grummond
Children's Literature Collection, the University of Southern Mississippi, Hattiesburg

sional, and artistic accolades."[93] Yet such a claim ignores the ways in which many works of children's literature operate at multiple levels, only some of which may be accessible to most children: most children's literature has to target adults as well as children. I'm more inclined to agree with Salman Rushdie: "The world of books has become a severely categorized and demarcated affair, in which children's fiction is not only a kind of ghetto but one subdivided into writing for a number of different age groups. The cinema, however, has regularly risen above such categories. From Spielberg to Schwarzenegger, from Disney to Gilliam, it has come up with movies before which kids and adults sit side by side, united by what they are watching."[94] There may be some films more clearly targeted to children only, but the most popular films—of the likes of *Star Wars* and *Independence Day*, even *Titanic*, to judge by the prevalence of prepubescent crushes on Leonardo DiCaprio—seem to offer something to both audiences. Certainly the film of *The Wizard of Oz* does.

And it is partly because of the 1939 *Oz*, and the audience it helped to create, that the audience for film is now less subdivided than that for books. Baum himself, in his early ventures into staging and filming, was not altogether successful, because theaters feared to invest in films for children.[95] They didn't perceive a market there. As late as 1937 MGM rejected the idea of creating a cartoon series based on the Oz books because of a perceived lack of appeal to adults.[96] The popular and critical success of Disney's *Snow White and the Seven Dwarfs* later that year, however, "made fantasy and children's stories more palatable to producers than they had ever been before."[97] Even then, in mid-filming, MGM considered shutting down production of *Oz*, because "it's just for kids."[98]

Most of the film's reviewers refer to the dual audience. Occasionally they suggest that it is more appropriate for one audience than for the other, maybe too sophisticated for children, or maybe not sophisticated enough for adults. But usually the reviewers recommend the film for both the young and the young at heart, finding it suitable for "three generations," "a pushover for the children and family biz," "one of the few [films] to which grandfather can take grandchild and both of them find entertaining," to cite three different reviews.[99] And by the film's third release in 1955, the *Daily Variety* could report "the night trade topping the matinees"[100]—its greatest appeal by then was to adults.

Indeed, I suspect that MGM was largely responsible for guaranteeing Baum a place in the pantheon of children's literature. I suspect that the ongoing presence of the film in popular culture led critics to look closely at the original book.[101] This book that slipped into a critical black hole in the early twentieth century, while amassing a steady popularity, has now accrued a certain stature among academics. As with other works of children's literature, such as Alcott's, academics are now paying attention.

I hesitate, though, to argue that the reception of *The Wizard of Oz* is altogether paradigmatic of the reception of fantasy in the United States. It's tempting to claim that Americans have been more eager to treat as classics children's literature that could be considered realistic, that the intellectual elite has been happy to disparage or ignore fantasy. But such a claim falters, becomes more complicated, when confronted with the British imports I examine in the next chapter. The custodians of children's literature were a bit slow to welcome the American Oz series, early in the twentieth century, even as they idolized the British Alice books.

The Case of British Fantasy Imports

Alice and Harry in America

In 1928, when Alice Liddell Hargreaves put Lewis Carroll's 1864 manuscript of *Alice's Adventures Under Ground* up for auction, it was purchased by an American. When the manuscript was exhibited by the New York Public Library that year, more than twenty-three thousand people waited in line to see it during the first week of the exhibition alone.[1] When it was auctioned again in 1946, a group of Americans bought it and donated it to the British Museum—"an unsullied and innocent act in a distracted and sinful world . . . a pure act of generosity," as the Archbishop of Canterbury declared in accepting it.[2] Enthusiasm for Carroll readily crossed the Atlantic.

And here my exploration of responses to children's literature in the United States strays briefly from a focus on literature specifically by Americans. I've already discussed the anomalous position of fantasy in American literature, among both the custodians of literature for adults and those of literature for children. This anomalousness has, in fact, made it difficult to do a representative case study of works by a single author, as I was able to do for girls' books and boys' books. For the author whose works of fantasy have attracted the most attention from cultural gatekeepers in the United States, attention from academic and other elite critics, is British. As indeed is the author of the fastest-selling fantasies—arguably the most popular fantasy author—in U.S. history. The various twentieth-century lists of recommended reading that I draw on in this study name Twain and Alcott as a matter of course, and also Carroll; they do not name any American writer of fantasy with any consistency. So a study of American response needs to turn to British works: certain British fantasies have been able to circumvent the critical invisibility of most works of fantasy. I turn now to works that Americans have held in great critical esteem while still treating them as children's literature, and then to works that have sold more copies within three years of publication than any other books, for children or adults.

The contributors to the 1995 *Children's Literature: An Illustrated History* claim that the initial reception of *Wonderland* in the United States was lukewarm, that, in fact, "fantasy did not make such a strong appeal to American readers. When the *Nation* reviewed *Alice's Adventures in Wonderland* in December 1866, it was the humour, the puns, and word-play that were praised (qualities that had not been much noticed by English reviewers)."[3] Yet it's probably more apt to say, as Mary F. Thwaite has, that "fantasy, a theme less congenial to the temper of American letters than real life, was a popular importation from Britain."[4] The early American reviews of *Wonderland* were in fact quite positive, even more enthusiastically positive than the British ones on which critics have hitherto focused—though admittedly none of the American reviews appeared immediately upon the book's publication, and thus the reviewers benefited from whatever reputation *Wonderland* had accrued during the year following its first appearance.[5]

The reviewer for the *Catholic World* may lament the existence of fantasy—"One cannot help regretting that children should be entertained in this way instead of by some probable or possible adventures"[6]—but the reviewer for the *Overland Monthly*, writing in July 1869, is more typical. He or she opens thus: "To say that this little volume is the most originally entertaining and delightful child's story that ever grown reader enjoyed, may appear extravagant and not very comprehensive criticism. But we know no other way to describe the pleasure that we get from Alice's adventures." The reviewer goes on to praise "the remarkable skill with which . . . grown-up humor is made to appear entirely consistent with the odd fancies of a clever little girl" and finally acknowledges that the book "has been deservedly praised by the best critics in England and America."[7]

Even in what seems to be the earliest American review, in the *New York Times* on November 27, 1866, *Wonderland* is declared "the most attractive holiday book for juveniles which has been produced thus far this year."[8] (In 1871, when *Through the Looking-Glass* appeared, the enthusiastic *New York Times* reviewer referred to *Wonderland* as "renowned.")[9] In the first review in a journal, in the *Nation* in December 1866, *Wonderland* is declared "one of the best children's books we ever met with."[10] (In 1872 the *Nation*'s reviewer noted, "It is seldom that the appearance of a child's book attains the dignity of a literary 'event,' but this distinction the long-promised and long-delayed sequel to 'Alice's Adventures' may certainly lay claim to.")[11] When Carroll died in 1898, the *New York Times* declared that Alice's "wonderful adventures have probably delighted more children than any other book that was ever written."[12]

Certainly *Wonderland* was appearing on lists of recommended reading—the generation of which seems to have been a characteristically American pastime in the late nineteenth century—as early as 1880.[13] Dorothy Matthews claims that the Alice books appeared on almost all nineteenth-century American lists of works recommended for children. They appeared as a matter of course in librarian Caroline Hewins's influential *Books for the Young*, published in 1882. In 1892 they were described on another list as "already . . . a classic."[14] In 1893 Thomas Y. Crowell launched its Children's Favorite Classics series by reprinting the two Alice books. Late-nineteenth-century reviewers frequently treated the books as touchstones, on both sides of the Atlantic: Matthews finds that ninety-eight nineteenth-century works are explicitly compared to the Alice books, not including many other fleeting references.

During the twentieth century the Alice books continued to be highly popular. They have spawned innumerable posters, figurines, puzzles, paper dolls, wallpapers, and bars of soap, in both Britain and the United States. In 1965 there were at least 561 editions of the Alice books and other works by Carroll, as well as sound recordings and the like—not to mention the Jefferson Airplane singing about tripping with the White Rabbit.[15] In recent years, *Wonderland* has inspired a Rose Bowl float, a Macy's flower show display, and celebrations of Mad Hatter Day in Boulder, Colorado.[16] To quote the title of a 1990 essay in the *New York Times Book Review*, "That Girl Is Everywhere."[17]

Another index of Carroll's standing in the popular imagination is the frequency with which he is quoted. Some aficionados claim that, after Shakespeare, Carroll may be the world's most quoted author.[18] Innumerable American essayists do indeed allude to Carroll in both title and text, whether they relate, in

1908, how "Aunt Janet Meets the March Hare" or else, more recently, address "Alice's Adventure in Budgetland" or "Alice in Cyberspace" or in "Intensive-land" or take us "Through the Looking-Glass" to examine legal issues.[19] The range of those who quote Carroll is impressive as well: "President Wilson, Queen Victoria, *The Times* leader writer, the late Lord Salisbury," according to Virginia Woolf in 1939; and Edna Ferber, the president of the American Statistical Association, and writers for the *Christian Science Monitor, Cosmopolitan,* and the *Saturday Evening Post,* according to Lawrence J. Burpee in 1941.[20] Phyllis Greenacre is close to the mark when she states, "Perhaps no book except the Bible is quoted as often in unlikely places and by improbable people as *Alice.*"[21]

That said, it's difficult to gauge the popularity of the Alice books through the kinds of polls I've turned to in earlier chapters. Works whose primary target audience is younger than that for such books as *Tom Sawyer* or *Little Women* or even *Little Lord Fauntleroy* simply tend to figure less prominently. In an 1893 listing of the most circulated books in "important" public libraries—books circulated to adults as well as children—*Wonderland* ranked only 133d.[22] Yet if we are to judge by sales, it does much better: in 1947 Frank Luther Mott lists *Wonderland*—along with *Tom Sawyer* and *Little Women*—as one of the twenty-one all-time best-sellers in the United States.[23]

Wonderland tends not to appear at the top of U.S. polls of children's favorites either. But it's important to note the ages of those who are polled: children who are old enough to be addressed as respondents, say nine or twelve, may no longer be fully responsive to works they enjoyed as six-year-olds and may in fact be trying to distance themselves from what they conceive of as childish pleasures. When asked to list their favorites among the books they've read, they may be more likely to name works read recently, hence more vivid in their minds, than ones read six years earlier, and they may assume that they're not to list a book that was read to them. *Wonderland* nevertheless remains a presence in polls—maybe only eighth in a 1913 polling of the preferences of fourth graders in New York City, but still very much there.[24] In the most massive survey of the favored reading of schoolchildren conducted in the first half of the twentieth century, in 1924–25, *Wonderland* placed a respectable eighteenth, having been read by about 1 percent of the surveyed children during the previous year—compared to the 7 percent who had read the front-running *Adventures of Tom Sawyer.*[25]

In 1985 Gillian Adams reported that many college students have a hostile reaction to *Wonderland,* but in a context where they are trying to decide whether it's suitable for children and they incline more toward works with uplifting messages.[26] In informal surveys in my "Children's Literature" class during the past two decades, I have asked the mostly white, mostly middle-class, mostly female undergraduates to list their two or three favorite books from childhood: about 5 percent have listed *Wonderland*, well behind the front-running *Charlotte's Web*, at 17 percent, but ahead of *Tom Sawyer*, at 1 percent.[27]

More impressionistic accounts likewise suggest that *Wonderland* has figured importantly for American children. Among individuals born before the turn of the century, fans of Alice have included Alexander Woollcott, who claimed that his "own memories of childhood are inextricably interwoven with all the gay tapestry of *Alice in Wonderland*," as well as Edmund Wilson, Warren Weaver, James Cain, and Allen Tate.[28] Others who have listed *Wonderland* as a childhood favorite include Nat Hentoff, Ogden Nash, Richard Wilbur, Tennessee Williams, Maurice Sendak, Judith Krantz, Bette Midler, and Joyce Carol Oates.[29] Walt Disney called it "one of the masterpieces of all time, for both adults and children."[30]

As for me, a child of the midcentury, I can't remember not knowing *Wonderland*. When I was fifteen I wrote a puppet play called "Alice in Western Massachusetts Land," now fortunately lost. My own children too, despite their divergent personalities, have both taken to the book. I'd fully expected, given some reading about children's mixed responses to *Wonderland*, that my own might prefer *Charlotte's Web*. And my daughter did, but not my son. I couldn't get through more than a couple of chapters of *Charlotte's Web* with him; *Wonderland* was the first full-length book I was able to read to him in its entirety. The British may call Alice the "prime heroine of our nation,"[31] but Americans too have taken to Alice.

Another index to popular standing is the number of conscious imitations—and in this respect *Wonderland* fares well indeed. Close to half of the 115 books that Carolyn Sigler lists in her bibliography of Alice-inspired works were first published in the United States.[32] There have also been numerous stage, film, and musical adaptations, including Eva Le Gallienne's long-running Broadway show in the 1930s; Disney's 1951 feature-length cartoon; a 1969 soul musical called *But Never Jam Today*; a 1970 award-winning *Alice in Wonderland*, directed by André Gregory; a 1981 television musical *Alice at the Palace*, starring Meryl Streep; and a 1999 production on NBC television.

I find myself wanting to say that now, at the turn of the twenty-first century, every middle-class American child is likely to be familiar with some version of Alice, whether Carroll's or John Tenniel's or Disney's, not to mention every middle-class adult. But on reflection I hesitate. I think that middle-class children and adults may be familiar with Alice in the most generic sense, the sense that there was someone named Alice who went to a place called Wonderland or stepped through a looking glass. But I suspect that "curiouser and curiouser" or "we're all mad here" or "it was the *best* butter" do not resonate with as much of middlebrow America as they used to. In 1953 one of the contributors to an American history of children's literature could say that "when someone remarks 'I doubt it,' how hard it is not to add 'said the carpenter and shed a bitter tear.'"[33] For most Americans today, such a temptation is easy indeed to resist. When I see Alice memorabilia these days, it's more likely to be in bookstores or art museum gift shops than in the advertising inserts of Sunday papers. When I encounter Alice allusions beyond the most generic, they're in highbrow or scholarly venues. Alice now figures in the title of a treatise on the aesthetics of wine-tasting and not, as she once did, in advertising for beer.[34]

Some educators have suggested the popularity of the Alice books declined about midcentury with children, or at least with some children. Michael Hancher cites May Hill Arbuthnot's influential *Children and Books* (1947), in which she suggests that college students remember *Wonderland* either with hearty dislike or as one of their favorite books.[35] In another influential textbook, first published in 1961, Charlotte S. Huck simply states that "not all children enjoy *Alice's Adventures in Wonderland,* for many of them do not have the maturity or imagination required to appreciate this fantasy."[36] It's suggestive too that, as Carolyn Sigler notes, popular imitations of the Alice books started to decrease in the 1920s.[37]

About the middle of the century, *Wonderland* showed some tendency to drop off lists of recommended reading for children as well. In 1907 it had headed Hamilton Mabie's list of books for girls aged five to ten, published in the *Ladies' Home Journal,* and it still figured in "One Hundred Story Books for Children" in the New York *Bookman* in 1922, in the American Library Association's *Right Book for the Right Child* in 1933, and in Laura E. Richards's *What Shall the Children Read?* in 1939 (Richards was herself no mean writer of nonsense). Yet even in the 1933 ALA book we are told that Alice possesses "the most loyal lovers and decided haters of any juvenile heroine."[38] And the Alice books are not mentioned in the 1958 *Parent's Guide to Children's Reading* by Nancy Larrick, nor do they figure in Jim Trelease's 1985 edition of *The Read-Aloud Handbook.*

The Alice books seem to have been better known in the United States in the first half of the twentieth century than in the second, and a good deal of their current popularity—their current presence in the cultural ambience—stems from the 1951 Disney film. I don't remember watching it when I was growing up. But when rereading the book as an adult, I caught myself waiting for the White Rabbit to say, "I'm late, I'm late, for a very important date." He never does. For a child of the 1950s, Disney's *Alice in Wonderland* was very much a cultural presence.[39] Thanks to the video industry, it continues to be at least a modest presence in current children's culture.[40]

Whatever their current standing in popular culture, Carroll's *Wonderland* and *Through the Looking-Glass* started to receive accolades in elite venues soon after publication. I've already noted some of the early reviews. By the 1890s a writer for *Scribner's* could call *Wonderland* immortal and one for the *Atlantic* could call the Alice books classics.[41] In 1898 Carroll's obituary was the lead story in the weekly literary journal the *Dial*.[42] In the twentieth century, reminiscences of Carroll and appreciations of his nonsense appeared in such U.S. magazines as the *Nation, Saturday Review,* the *Atlantic,* and *Harper's Monthly.* The discovery in 1977 of *The Wasp in a Wig,* an episode omitted from *Through the Looking-Glass,* made the front page of both the *Times* of London and the *New York Times,* and the episode was reprinted in the *Smithsonian* magazine.

An intriguing sign of the esteem in which Carroll was held in midcentury appears in a 1936 report of a library reading survey. First the raw numbers, which speak more to popularity: of the 254 authors most popular with twenty thousand readers in the Chicago area, Carroll ranked 135th, compared to Alcott's 4th place and Twain's 9th, though if one tallies the number of readers per volume, Carroll's works ranked 16th. But more interesting for my purposes here is that the compiling librarian, infected by a then-common enthusiasm for elevating the reading sophistication of the masses, decided to place the books in six levels of quality, based on "reviews and standards of excellence that seemed most generally accepted."[43] Only ten immortals made it to the top tier of quality, including Austen, Joyce, Conrad, Woolf, Tolstoy. Carroll was placed in the second tier, the same level as Twain and, for instance, Hawthorne and Hemingway. That put him one tier above Dickens, two tiers above Alcott, three above Stowe.[44]

So it's no surprise that the librarian Alice M. Jordan wrote in the *Horn Book* in 1947, "Perhaps no other book for children is so generally called a classic as *Alice's Adventures in Wonderland.*"[45] The Alice books are the only works of literature for children—unless one counts Aesop's and La Fontaine's fables—among the thirty-two "great books" featured in CBS radio broadcasts hosted by Mark

Van Doren in 1941–42. Carroll's books are likewise the only works of literature for children admitted to Clifton Fadiman's 1960 pantheon of a hundred great works: "I do not include [Carroll] because he is a juvenile classic, for in that case we should also have Grimm and Andersen and Collodi and a dozen others. I include him because he continues to hold as much interest for grown-ups as for children."[46] In 1990 Carroll's "Jabberwocky," from *Through the Looking-Glass*, is listed as the eighteenth most anthologized British or American poem, the only work on the list of a hundred poems that was initially published for a child audience.[47]

Writing in the *New York Times* in 1932, G. K. Chesterton makes a strong claim for *Wonderland*'s status as a classic too, though in the guise of a lament: "Any educated Englishman and especially any educational Englishman (which is worse), will tell you with a certain gravity that *Alice in Wonderland* is a classic. Such is indeed the horrid truth"—for "the soap-bubble which poor old Dodgson blew from the pipe of poetry . . . has been robbed by educationists of much of the lightness of the bubble, and retained only the horrible healthiness of the soap."[48] Something peculiar is happening here, in Chesterton's construction of Carroll. He finds it regrettable that *Wonderland* should be considered a classic since that makes it too serious, removes it too far from the pleasures of childhood. Nevertheless, he states elsewhere, "Nonsense is a thing of Meredithian subtlety. It is not children who ought to read the words of Lewis Carroll; they are far better employed making mudpies."[49] Though, of course, Chesterton is being consciously paradoxical; he goes on to claim, "The child has no need of nonsense: to him the whole universe is nonsensical, in the noblest sense of that noble word."[50] Or, in a similar vein, he claims "that the very best of Lewis Carroll was not written by a man for children, but by a don for dons."[51] In short, educationists are blamed for taking Carroll's work too seriously, yet in making of it "a thing of Meredithian subtlety," something "by a don for dons," Chesterton takes it very seriously indeed. And in doing so he both proffers it to and withholds it from children. What strikes me is the way that the hypothetical age of the audience is given play in Chesterton's considerations of the work's subtlety—whether it's a classic, whether, in effect, it's good enough for adults.

Chesterton is hardly the only commentator for whom a key crux is the nature of the appropriate audience for Carroll. Critical response frequently reveals the critic's construction of childhood and adulthood, as when Martin Gardner claims that *Wonderland* is "no longer a children's book"[52]—as if indeed it had ever been purely a children's book.

True, an occasional early reviewer suggested that Carroll's work appeals more to children than to adults: "ten-year-old misses . . . have some key to unlock the nonsense of its text, which wiser hands have lost; but the pictures commend themselves alike to old and young."[53] Yet adults found themselves enthralled by *Wonderland* almost as soon as it was published. If in 1865 the reviewer for the British *Spectator* was simply claiming that "big folks who take it home to their little folks will find themselves reading more than they intended, and laughing more than they had any right to expect," by 1869 the reviewer for the same magazine was suggesting that "though grown people are better able than children to enter into that wonderful production, it is by no means thrown away upon children."[54] In the United States too one finds a throwaway reference in the *Nation* in 1869, in a note announcing the publication of a German translation, to "Mr. Lewis Carroll's most admirable book for children—only the children care little or nothing for it, and it is to grown people that it is so charming."[55] The following week, the pioneering children's librarian Caroline Hewins responded that *Wonderland* "is liked by many children," including those in her own family, the twenty or more children to whom she'd lent their copy, and also children in a school who "listened eagerly" and subsequently quoted from it frequently.[56] To which the *Nation* editor appended a response: "We probably generalized from too limited an experience." Certainly most reviewers and other critics were suggesting that the Alice books could be enjoyed by both young and old, could be enjoyed both by those who could revel in Alice's unharmed freefall ("After such a fall as this, I shall think nothing of tumbling down-stairs! How brave they'll all think me at home! Why, I wouldn't say anything about it, even if I fell off the top of the house!") and by those who could appreciate the narrator's ironic parenthetical commentary: "(Which was very likely true)."[57]

In fact, even when a nineteenth-century writer suggested that the Alice books might be more appreciated by adults than by children, he or she did not mean thereby to exclude children from the potential audience—as was the case for the 1869 *Spectator* reviewer, the one who thought "grown people" "better able" to enter into *Wonderland* than children, in this era when children's literature was less segregated from that for adults. In 1898 the *Dial* obituarist commends Carroll's Alice books and also *The Hunting of the Snark* (1876) as "classics of the nursery" that "have also won a place among the books with which every cultivated reader is expected to have some acquaintance."[58] Far from being mutually exclusive, appreciation by both adults and children was synergistic. As the obituarist concludes, works like Carroll's that could be "equally appreciated by

young and old (although of course in different ways) . . . make for a better understanding between the ages, because they create a new bond of sympathy, setting the child and the man for the time being upon a common ground of interest."[59] The two audiences may have been separating by the end of the century,
but a writer could envision Carroll's work as reuniting them.

Yet for a number of twentieth-century critics, such as Martin Gardner, the
existence of an adult audience seems to preclude one of children. Consider Virginia Woolf's comment that "the two Alices are not books for children; they are
the only books in which we become children"[60]—the "we" clearly being adults.
Or Bertrand Russell's claim—despite his own childhood fondness, his knowing
it "by heart from an early age"—that he no longer considers *Wonderland* "a
suitable book for the young."[61] He explains that the book "is much too difficult
for the young. It raises metaphysical points, very interesting logical points, that
are good for the older ponderer, but for the young produce only confusion"
(212). Mark Van Doren tries to respond, in this radio broadcast, that children
often "really enjoy most those books which they don't wholly understand" (213),
but Russell won't budge. Or consider philosopher Peter Heath's statement that
"of all those who read [the Alice books] it is children especially who have the
smallest chance of understanding what they are about."[62]

These claims are not uncontested. As Morton N. Cohen argued in 1990, it's
true that, "because of their sophistication, the books appeal to adults as much as
they do to children. But Carroll wrote them for children, not for adults. He
knew that falling through space, swimming in a pool, changing size and encountering all manner of birds and beasts, let alone authoritarian and arrogant
adults, are all part of life's real or imagined ordeals. But he does not use the ordeals to intimidate. Instead, he tells his young readers that he understands their
trials and he offers reassurances."[63] Anthony Quinton tellingly puts it thus:
"The under-tens . . . do not so much achieve books as have books thrust upon
them. But could parental insensitivity have withstood a response of really massive uninterestedness by the recipients?"[64]

It's clear that *Wonderland* offers some adult pleasures, perhaps especially to
philosophers and mathematicians, to the Bertrand Russells, Peter Heaths, and
Martin Gardners.[65] Maybe few physicists would agree with literary historian
John Macy that "Lewis Carroll discovered relativity before Einstein was born,"
but it is true, as Macy states, that even then, in 1931, "the physicists are using
Lewis Carroll to explain the mathematical universe to us."[66] And the philosophers use Carroll to explain the linguistic universe: witness Heath's annotated

Philosopher's Alice, not least for the appendix listing fifty works that allude to Alice, by thinkers ranging from J. L. Austin to Wittgenstein. In the first half of the twentieth century Carroll is featured in articles in such journals as the *Mathematical Gazette* and the *American Mathematical Monthly*; in the latter half, in such journals as *Scientific American* and *Mind*.[67] Martin Gardner goes so far as to claim, "It is only because adults—scientists and mathematicians in particular—continue to relish the ALICE books that they are assured of immortality."[68]

Yet I'm tempted to consider claims that *Wonderland* is not really for children as reflecting a tendency to consider anything that adults find valuable as really adult. As J. H. Dohm recognizes, such a claim "is a periodic cry made over almost anything really good offered to children."[69] Sometimes the commentators look back to a Golden Age when the books did appeal to children. Which is to say, a bit smugly, that they appealed to the writer himself as a child. Such writers are reluctant to acknowledge that any other children may have the sophistication to appreciate Carroll.[70]

Carroll has also offered adult pleasures to artists and critics. Carolyn Sigler notes that, starting in the 1920s, his work "was discovered and appropriated by high literary artists, critics, and theorists," even as the popular appropriations, the imitations, sharply declined.[71] It wasn't just the French surrealists who took to Carroll, naming him in the first surrealist manifesto in 1924 and frequently thereafter.[72] So did James Joyce (referring to "Dodgfather, Dodgson, and Coo"), so did such later figures as Vladimir Nabokov ("Lewis Carroll Carroll") and Joyce Carol Oates (author of her own *Wonderland*). In the words of the *New Yorker* columnist Adam Gopnik, "Huck and Alice, the hero and heroine of the two best children's books of the nineteenth century, have become models for heroes and heroines of grown-up books in the twentieth century. The modern novel, with a stream of consciousness as its only order, needed an idea of the wise reflecting innocent who experiences things without being transformed by them. Huck just moves on. Alice just wakes up."[73]

Among academic critics, after the *English Journal* published what could be considered its first scholarly piece on Carroll in 1921, a new scholarly journal followed suit more or less every decade until the early 1970s; since then, a new scholarly journal has done so more or less annually.[74] The MLA CD-ROM has now indexed 619 scholarly items for Carroll, placing him well behind James and Twain, ahead of Baum and Alcott, and well ahead of Burnett. The Norton Critical Editions, a textbook series that reprints authoritative texts of important literature and significant criticism thereof, has long included *Wonderland* in its stable—along with three volumes devoted to Twain, six to James, but none to Alcott (though one is in progress), Baum, or Burnett. In the words of science fiction and fantasy writer Ursula Le Guin—and it's noteworthy that her science fiction receives serious scholarly attention from leading mainstream critics while her fantasy, generally classified as for children, does not—"People to whom sophistication is a positive intellectual value shun anything 'written for children.' . . . With the agreed exception of *Alice in Wonderland*, books for children are to be mentioned only dismissively or jocosely by the adult male critic."[75]

Wonderland is the one work of children's literature to be held in great critical esteem—to have received "an unusual degree of reverent admiration in America"[76]—precisely *as* a work of children's literature. By which I mean to differentiate it from *Huckleberry Finn*, which has had great esteem to the extent that it has been closeted from children's literature, decreed not a work for children. *Wonderland* has, among critics, been important as a work for children, not least when enthusiasts protest, too loudly, that it is not really for children.

The first article to focus on children's literature in *PMLA*, aside from pieces on the ambiguously situated Twain, is Donald Rackin's, in 1966. It addresses Carroll. The second, James R. Kincaid's, published in 1973, and the third, William A. Madden's, published in 1986, likewise address Carroll. Only in 1991 does an essay appear that unabashedly includes the word *children* in its title. Sarah Gilead too addresses Carroll, among other figures. It may have taken eight decades for the flagship journal of the Modern Language Association to publish scholarly work on children's literature, but when it did, it published criticism of Carroll. Perhaps few critics would have agreed with Clifton Fadiman when he nominated *Wonderland* as probably the literary work in English most likely to be "universally alive" five hundred years hence—precisely because "the gods tend to grant immortality to those books which, in addition to being great, are loved by children."[77] But many would now agree with Donald Rackin's claim that *Wonderland* is "a book of major and permanent importance in the tradition of English fiction."[78]

Maybe it's permissible to attend to a work of children's literature if the author is not American and hence not entangled in Americans' twentieth- and twenty-first-century anxiety of immaturity, our attempts to free ourselves from associations of America with childhood. Attention to Carroll allows us instead to project childishness onto a representative of the mother country. Maybe it's permissible for the professoriate to engage fleetingly with Carroll if he too can be construed as simply a don on holiday.

Another author who allows us to project childishness onto a representative of the mother country—though not to construe her as a don on holiday—is J. K. Rowling. Hardly a don gliding idly down a river while spinning a spellbinding tale, the image of Rowling purveyed by the media has been that of a welfare mother who made good, someone who would wheel her infant daughter into a cafe and sip coffee while drafting the first of her Harry Potter books (not, alas, on a napkin, as some reporters have been eager to assert). It's harder to claim for her work what has been claimed for Carroll's—that it is major, of permanent importance, a classic. For one thing, the Harry Potter series is too recent: the first book, *Harry Potter and the Philosopher's Stone*, was published in 1997 in Britain (in 1998, as *Harry Potter and the Sorcerer's Stone*, in the United States).

But there's no doubt that Harry is wildly popular. For the fourth volume, *Harry Potter and the Goblet of Fire* (2000), Scholastic Press issued a first printing of 3.8 million, the largest in publishing history in the United States.[79] That number of copies amounts to well over 1 percent of the U.S. population, the benchmark used by Frank Luther Mott for determining the best-sellers of the nineteenth and early twentieth centuries—but he used each book's lifetime sales, not its sales upon publication.[80] *Goblet of Fire* has, in fact, been called "history's fastest-selling book."[81] In the words of children's novelist Tim Wynne-Jones, the book has "garnered a phenomenal amount of press, mostly of the Guinness kind: the biggest print-run ever, the highest one-day sales in history."[82] By the end of 2001, worldwide sales of the first four Harry Potter books had exceeded 130 million.[83]

Part of the popularity of the Harry Potter series, especially initially, results from word-of-mouth recommendations, child to child. Reviewers and other critics cite librarians who stress how avidly children take to it, how much it has done to encourage children to read. Jim Trelease, the author of *The Read-Aloud Handbook*, has claimed, "'Harry Potter' is the best thing to happen to children's books since the invention of the paperback."[84]

But adults are reading the Harry Potter books too. It would be hard otherwise to account for the eighty-two weeks that *Sorcerer's Stone* perched on the *New York Times* hardcover fiction best-seller list—before being editorially bumped to the newly inaugurated children's list. Many reviewers note this dual appeal: as Jonathan Levi says of the formula that the books are for readers "of all ages," "in this case hyperbole just might be understatement."[85] Bloomsbury, the British publisher, printed second editions of the books with grownup covers, and at least 150,000 adults have paid extra for the privilege of not being embarrassed about reading them in public.[86] One estimate is that 43 percent of the Harry Potter books sold in 1999, in Britain at least, were for people aged fifteen or older; another is that "30 percent of the first three Harry Potter books were purchased by and for a reader 35 or older"; another, based on a national survey conducted early in 2001, that "more than 60 percent of Americans between the ages of 6 and 17 had read at least one Harry Potter book, as had 14 percent of adults."[87]

Nevertheless, Harry Potter is too new a phenomenon to have had a great impact in the scholarly world. As of this writing, only ten items on Rowling are indexed in the MLA CD-ROM bibliography. Still, a number of public intellectuals have weighed in on her works' popularity and merits. In particular, they ask whether the books are classics—whether classics of children's literature or, simply, classics. Some reviewers readily apply the term *classic* to the Harry Potter books. This number includes the novelist and Cornell professor Alison Lurie, who calls them "brilliant," "the newest British children's classics."[88] But most of those who might be considered public intellectuals have been reluctant to do so. Many are simply cautious about declaring books of such recent vintage classics. Eden Ross Lipson, the editor of the children's book section for the *New York Times Book Review*, states that "time will tell if Harry Potter will achieve classic status. For the moment, it's a phenomenon. But hard work, luck and travails like those of Rowling may be the stuff of which a children's classic is made."[89]

If few public intellectuals have been unabashedly positive, several have been positively willing to bash. The three critics who have received the most publicity for their dismissive views are the newspaper columnist William Safire, the Shakespeare scholar Anthony Holden, and Yale professor Harold Bloom, all writing in the year 2000.

In February, Safire expresses relief that Seamus Heaney's translation of *Beowulf* managed to edge out the third Harry Potter book as winner of the Whitbread Book of the Year award in Britain. Not that Safire had actually read *Harry Potter and the Prisoner of Azkaban* (1999); he admits that *Sorcerer's Stone* is "the one I read." Rowling's books "are children's books," Safire asserts, not "books for adults." And "the trouble is that grown-ups are buying these books ostensibly to read to kids, but actually to read for themselves," contributing to "the infantilization of adult culture." Rowling deserved "the lesser award she received for best children's book."[90] Lana Whited rightly points out that "Safire displays a common prejudice toward children's books—that they are deserving of 'lesser' prizes."[91] Safire replays, yet again, the mid-twentieth-century prejudice among academics and other intellectuals against children's literature.

Holden was one of the judges of the Whitbread prize, an outspoken advocate of Heaney over Rowling. In June 2000 he calls the Harry Potter books "one-dimensional children's books, Disney cartoons written in words," and worries "what these books are doing to the literary taste of millions of potential young readers." Unlike Safire, he's careful not to condemn children's literature per se, though he does express himself with a metaphor that disparages juvenility: he is concerned "that Britain is a country that refuses to grow up and take itself seriously." Holden focuses his ire on mass entertainment—and echoes Safire in his concern for the "dumbing down of all our lives." Holden also makes the interesting observation that "the more popular (or bestselling) an adult book, . . . the less likely it is to be considered literature, while the popularity of a children's book sees big literary claims being made on its behalf."[92] There's something in that assertion. The only other children's book to spend more than a few weeks on the *New York Times* best-seller list was apparently E. B. White's *Charlotte's Web* (1952), a book whose literary merit is rarely questioned.[93] In general, many adults seem to assume that literature for children is necessarily of inferior quality. Certainly some of the adult Potter enthusiasts that I encounter are impressed by the quality of Rowling's books, surprised that children's literature could be so well written.

The following month, July 2000, Bloom compares Rowling's first book—the only one he, like Safire, has read—to "superior fare" such as Kenneth Grahame's *Wind in the Willows* (1908) and the Alice books and finds it sadly wanting. "One can reasonably doubt that 'Harry Potter and the Sorcerer's Stone,'" he adds, "is going to prove a classic of children's literature, but Rowling, whatever the aesthetic weakness of her work, is at least a millennial index to our popular culture."[94] The Harry Potter books are not, for him, classics of any sort.

Despite the common gender of the most prominent vituperative critics, the cleavage that has most come into play in connection with the Harry Potter phenomenon is not gender (as with the Oz books) but age (as with the Alice books). There are all those crossover readers, of course, those adults as well as children who are reading the books. Then there is the gerrymandering of the *New York Times* best-seller list, or lists, published weekly in the *New York Times Book Re-*

view, a must-read for intellectuals. On July 23, 2000, the *New York Times* created a separate best-seller list for children's literature, just in time to ward off *Goblet of Fire*, which was about to become Rowling's fourth book on the general hardcover list, taking up four of the fifteen precious slots. As Bloom notes of Rowling, "she has changed the policy of the policy-maker."[95] An early hint of the change—"(The Times is now considering creating a separate children's list)"—appeared in a news story on February 28: "For the first time, five children's novels elbowed aside the grown-up fare on the fiction best-seller list of The New York Times on Feb. 20."[96] In a June 24 account of the final decision, Dinitia Smith writes that the change is in response to pressure from publishers and booksellers. The publishers complained that "a cluster of popular children's books can keep deserving adult books off the lists." She quotes Charles McGrath, the editor of the *Book Review*, as saying, "The time has come when we need to clear some room." He adds that "being on the kids' best-seller list wouldn't ghettoize" a true crossover book.[97] Another news story reports McGrath as bluntly saying that "the most pressing reason for a children's list was 'to get Harry off the fiction list.'"[98]

My reaction to this change in policy is mixed—a contradictory mix elsewhere signaled by the juxtaposition of the title and the first line of a news story in the Cleveland *Plain Dealer*: "Harry Brings Victory to Children's Literature" and "Harry Potter finally got the boot."[99] It's wonderful that the *New York Times Book Review* is finally publishing a list of best-selling children's books; in the past such lists appeared only sporadically, the last one in 1994. Having a regular best-seller list for children's literature will enable more children's books to receive recognition—can focus "attention on new children's book writers who otherwise might never have had the chance to make a bestseller list."[100] Yet the impetus behind the move does indeed seem to be to ghettoize children's literature. Unless the Harry Potter books have effected a major change in how adults in general think about children's literature—not likely—adults are not apt to look down the page from the general fiction to the children's list for guidance in what to read.

As I've already indicated, part of what attracts Americans to Rowling's books is their Britishness, whether one is "a terminal Anglophiliac" or simply claims that "the best kids' books—particularly ones by British writers—pull their readers through adventures of the sort that seem to have vanished from serious adult fiction."[101] The books also draw on nostalgia for an idealized bygone era. Their present is a rather old-fashioned one: there are no drug problems, no sexual abuse, no teen pregnancies. Rowling has stated in an interview, "I feel it would be inappropriate—in *these* books—were Hermione to have an underage pregnancy or if one of them were to start taking drugs, because it's unfaithful to the tone of the books."[102] As with Carroll's books, the old-fashioned ambience of Rowling's may contribute in turn to a static, rather dated U.S. image of Britishness: Suzanne Moore asks, "What child do you know these days who eats rock cakes and talks about galoshes? No wonder they love it in the States."[103] In the words of Jonathan Myerson, "Rowling has gone out of her way—maybe not cynically, maybe by genuine heartfelt choice—to place Potter-land in the traditional English milieu, all green fields and mossy stone quads, something more English than anyone under 80 has ever known." The books create an exotic world elsewhere, whether that world is strictly fantasy or in some sense real. In an article that stresses how many features of Harry's school, Hogwarts, do indeed correspond to those of British public schools—cryptic instructions regarding what to purchase from dusty shops, special school trains, unique local sports in which perhaps no official goal has been scored since 1909, peculiar prohibitions, such as not to walk down a particular side of a particular street—Pico Iyer notes, "If you describe the features of one culture to another, radically different, they will seem as strange and wonderful as fairy tale."[104]

Antiquated or not, it's the world of Harry Potter that seems most to attract readers. As Harold Bloom states, Rowling's millions of readers (he calls them "reader non-readers") "want to join her world, imaginary or not."[105] The reviewer Kevin C. Stevens claims, "During my life, there have been two fantasy worlds that are so real, so vivid, that I would trade anything short of my wife to be a part of them."[106] The first was the world of *Star Wars;* the second, Harry Potter's. Other readers offer comparable testimony. "I'm 18 years old and wish I lived in Harry Potter's world," writes one reader.[107] "When you read it, the rest of your world, like reality, just goes blank," and "it's really fun reading books that take you into a different world," state others.[108] Rowling herself spent years planning Harry's world before writing the first of her projected seven books about him.

Given the power of the extraordinary world that Rowling creates, the Harry Potter books have in fact considerable affinity with those by Baum. Rowling doesn't enthrall the reader with Carrollian word and logic play but with her inventiveness with respect to the quotidian—the self-shuffling cards, the staircases that sometimes go to different places on Fridays, the ghost affectionately known as Nearly Headless Nick, who hadn't been fully decapitated and hence, much to his chagrin, isn't eligible for the annual Headless Hunt. These minutiae help to create a fascinating parallel world of wizards and witches. This world may interpenetrate Rowling's Britain, rather than exist entirely elsewhere, but it functions much like the world of Oz. Rowling invites the reader into the world—invites reader participation in the world. It's not coincidental that one of the merchandising guidelines for Harry Potter, in connection with the opening of the film of the first book, is "Take people into Harry's world, don't put Harry into our world": hence no ads with Harry eating at McDonald's or sipping Coke, even though Coca-Cola is the film's global promotional partner.[109] Rowling even, in effect, invites the reader to extend the world she has created. And indeed Harry Potter fans, like Oz fans, are active in creating zines, fan fictions that extend or continue Rowling's story, telling perhaps the adventures of an adult Harry or recounting the early lives of his mother and father. A quick web search reveals that a single site (http://fanfiction.net) offers, as of this writing, 31,850 items of fan fiction.

It's too soon to tell whether Harry Potter will, like his compatriot Alice, achieve the status of a classic in the United States. Given their phenomenal popularity and their reception so far, it seems unlikely that Rowling's books will need the embattled underground following that has sustained Baum's reputation or the less embattled but similarly underground following that has sustained Burnett's. And as Anthony Holden suggests, the relationship between popularity and critical esteem at the turn of the twenty-first century is complex for children's literature. If, in the nineteenth century, popularity and esteem could be synergistic, and in the twentieth century they were often seen as opposed, the latter is particularly true for literature for adults. Not for children's literature.

I've mentioned that so far there are only ten scholarly articles on Harry Potter in the MLA CD-ROM bibliography. Yet that dearth won't last long. Rare is the recent MLA or Children's Literature Association conference that doesn't include papers if not indeed full panels on Harry Potter.[110] Given the heightened attention to cultural studies in the academy, indeed the increasing attention to children's literature, I'm confident that Harry will receive considerable scholarly notice. I expect he'll contribute to at least some erosion of the twentieth-century boundary between literature for children and literature for adults.

Whatever their academic standing, though, it was inevitable that the Harry Potter books would be translated into film. Given their enormous popularity, and especially their popularity with both children and adults, the books are ideally suited for the family audience that movies can so readily accommodate. The movie of the first book, produced by Warner Brothers—a subsidiary of AOL

Time Warner, the media conglomerate that is even larger than Disney—came out in late 2001. It was the largest grossing film of the year, making an estimated $286.1 million.[111] And some of the merchandise has done well—the $90 Lego sets for building a replica of Hogwarts Castle, the Bertie Bott's Every Flavor Beans (choose from Berry Blue, Orange Sherbet, Toasted Marshmallow, Sardine, Black Pepper, Booger, . . .)—though a good many other items have been remaindered.[112]

Joel Chaston has argued that the Disney film of *Wonderland* was subject to "Ozification"—made to resemble the *Oz* film with its intensification of the Wonderland threats, its stripping of Alice's own power, and consequently its emphasis on the desire to return home.[113] The NBC production of *Wonderland* in 1999 even more obviously drew on the MGM *Oz* film, with its real-world frame of eccentric characters played by actors who go on to play fantasy exaggerations in the fantasy world. MGM's *Oz* thus helped to make Disney's *Wonderland* possible, and NBC's, and has in turn helped Carroll's *Wonderland* to live on. And perhaps it will abet Harry too. At the turn of the twenty-first century, the ongoing life of children's literature, whether British or American, seems intimately bound up with its translation to the big and little screens.

CHAPTER EIGHT

The Case of the Disney Version

How have Americans responded to children's literature during the last century and a half? How have we constructed childhood? These questions have guided my study of reception. The most revealing works were published before the middle of the twentieth century. More recent works have not usually generated the kind of history that strikingly illuminates the cultural construction of children's literature, nor do they register a remarkable shift in consciousness in our imagination of childhood. One exception is a set of works that we would not normally consider literature but that nonetheless has strong ties to children's literature.

For perhaps another shift in the cultural construction of childhood is now taking place. Perhaps what's occurring is a shift away from literature to more visual media, especially the mass media—as signaled by the fact that the *Oz* of most people's imaginations is not L. Frank Baum's but Victor Fleming's, not the "real" *Oz*, from the perspective of literary folk, but the one done with the celluloid wizardry of smoke and mirrors. I turn now to someone whose work has been highly contested, at least by the literati, in the second half of the twentieth century. Someone who wreaks havoc with the "original" words of a story, disrupts what some have seen as an original purity (yet thereby reminds us that a pure point of origin is illusory). Someone who disliked adapting *Wonderland*, he subsequently reflected, since he felt more constrained by Carroll's fixed words than by the more malleable versions of fairy tales. (Though he'd hankered after Alice, dallied with her, for decades: in the 1920s he produced a series of fifty-six *Alice* comedies; in 1933 he discussed an adaptation of *Wonderland* with Mary Pickford; in 1936 he produced a short cartoon called *Thru the Mirror*, inspired by *Through the Looking-Glass*; in 1945 he announced a film version of *Wonderland* featuring Ginger Rogers; in 1950 he called his television debut *One Hour in Wonderland*.)[1]

I mean, of course, Walt Disney.

It's a surprise for a baby boomer like me to realize the esteem in which Disney was held in the 1930s, so low has his esteem now fallen among intellectuals. It's not just that, as Eric Smoodin suggests, Disney's Mickey Mouse cartoon shorts were likely to be paired with serious, even classic, feature films in the 1930s— treated as if they too were classics.[2] Nor that Charlie Chaplin and Mary Pickford were fans of Mickey Mouse; FDR, of the *Three Little Pigs*; Mussolini, of Donald Duck.[3] Nor that "Mickey Mouse" was the password for Allied Supreme Headquarters in Europe on D Day.[4] But, as Leonard Maltin notes, Disney was both popular with millions and "the darling of America's intelligentsia."[5]

In the 1930s the philosopher Mortimer Adler, architect of the Great Books program, claimed that Disney's work "reaches greatness, a degree of perfection in its field which surpasses our best critical capacity to analyze."[6] H. G. Wells called Disney a genius, Mark Van Doren called him a "first rate artist," René Clair called his artistry sublime, Walter Benjamin admired its utopian potential, Sergei Eisenstein acclaimed Disney's work as "the greatest contribution of the American people to art," E. M. Forster whimsically found in it "a scandalous element . . . which I find most restful," and composer Jerome Kern, impressed by the way Disney treated film as language, declared his cartoons "the 20th century's only important contribution to music."[7] In 1942 artist David Low called Disney "the most significant figure in graphic art since Leonardo."[8] Other artists and critics compared him to Hogarth, Raphael, Michelangelo, Rembrandt.[9] Sergei Prokofiev was so impressed with *Fantasia* (1940) that he offered *Peter and the Wolf*, unsolicited, for Disney to use if he decided to make a sequel.[10]

Disney's 1930s cartoon shorts were praised in such journals as *McCall's*, *American Magazine*, and the *New Yorker*. The *New York Herald Tribune* called the Silly Symphonies Rabelaisian.[11] Smoodin points to a 1936 review in the *Washington Post* that opens by announcing that "a great picture and its equally

renowned sequel for the first time are being shown on the same bill at the Ri-
alto Theater."[12] The reviewer goes on to praise the reissue of *Morocco*, Marlene
Dietrich's first Hollywood film, but top critical billing has gone to reissues of
Disney's *Three Little Pigs* and *The Big Bad Wolf*. In fact, Disney's cartoons frequently garnered top billing on theater marquees in the 1930s.[13]

As for Disney's feature-length films, in 1938 the *New York Times* reviewer
called *Snow White and the Seven Dwarfs*, Disney's first such film, "a classic" ("if
you miss it, you'll be missing the ten best pictures of 1938"); the *New York Herald Tribune* reviewer claimed that it ranked "with the greatest motion pictures of
all time"; the *New Republic* reviewer announced, "To say of 'Snow White and the
Seven Dwarfs' that it is among the genuine artistic achievements of this country takes no great daring."[14] Three years later the *New York Times* reviewer called
Pinocchio "the best cartoon ever made"; the *Herald Tribune* reviewer, "a com-
pound of imagination and craftsmanship, of beauty and eloquence, which is to
be found only in great works of art."[15]

Or consider the response of film historian Lewis Jacobs, writing in 1939, in a
text that continued to be reprinted for at least four decades (I consulted a 1975
copy, a fifth printing of the third edition). Jacobs starts the chapter devoted to
Disney by declaring him "the most renowned and acclaimed" of current directors.[16] For he "has made the animated cartoon perhaps the finest expression of
motion picture art in contemporary America," consummating "the cinematic
contributions of Melies, Porter, Griffith, and the Europeans," becoming "the
first of the sight-sound-color film virtuosos" (496). Disney's willingness to incur
major financial risks in order to achieve desired effects is here construed not as
entrepreneurial savvy, building for long-term gains (as it has subsequently been
construed), but as artistic integrity. Disney is "the modern Aesop": "Today,
when the real world is full of ruthless conflict, it is significant that Disney's films
more than anyone else's (perhaps because he is the ablest of all) are full of ruthless conflict" (499). Jacobs goes on to discuss the skill with which the films are
structured—the impossibility of cutting a scene without destroying the flow—
and Disney's technical virtuosity: "Disney is unexcelled among directors in his
exploitation of the full resources of his tools. An unlimited technical range of effects marks his structure: his camera swoops, glides, shoots, zooms, rides,
bounces, and uses other movements that would be impossible in conventional
studio pictures and as with his camera, so with his sound" (500–501). In short,
thanks to his "technical dexterity and remarkable command of the medium" and
"his constant flow of fresh ideas and keen observation of contemporary foibles,"

he is "the most distinctive and advanced of directors since the adoption of sound"—"the virtuoso of the film medium" (453, 505).

If film is the distinctive art medium of the twentieth century, then animated film, which seems most fully to exploit the medium's potential, could be seen not just as "the perfection of the movie" but as the acme of twentieth-century art.[17] In the 1930s and 1940s, photography was still considered somewhat dubious— many art critics and historians were reluctant to call it art. Hence moving photography, motion pictures, had only a precarious claim to artistry. Cartoons, however—animated drawings and paintings—seemed to make a stronger claim: their ancestry could be traced to traditions of the fine arts in a way that the genealogy of live-action films could not. In the words of muralist Jean Charlot, Disney's work is not just the "classic flowering of the medium" but "the unexpected flowering of the cubist seed."[18]

Between 1932 and 1941 Disney won eleven Academy Awards, including eight for animated short subjects and a special award for creating Mickey Mouse. In 1937 a Mickey Mouse book was placed on the list of recommended reading for New York City elementary schools.[19] In 1938 Disney was granted honorary degrees by Harvard and Yale (the latter conferred by an aging William Lyon Phelps). In 1939 a scene from *Snow White and the Seven Dwarfs* was featured in the Metropolitan Museum of Art. As a writer for the *New York Times Magazine* noted in 1935, "university presidents praise him, the League of Nations recommends him, Who's Who and the Encyclopaedia Britannica give him paragraphs, learned academies hang medals on him, art galleries turn from Picasso and Epstein to hold exhibitions of his monkey-shines, and the King of England won't go to the movies unless Mickey is on the bill."[20]

In the 1940s and 1950s, Disney's reputation began to wane. James Agee, film critic for the *Nation* in the 1940s, acknowledged that "at his best," before World War II, Disney was "an inspired comic inventor and teller of fairy stories," but Agee became quite acerbic about some of the productions of the 1940s, finding "Disney's famous cuteness, however richly it may mirror national infantilism, . . . hard on my stomach" or finding "an obvious connection between the Disney artists' increasing insipidity and their increasing talent for fright, but I will leave it to accredited sado-masochists to make the official discovery."[21]

The decline in critical approbation seems in part related to Disney's decision to include human figures in his cartoons, beginning with *Snow White and the Seven Dwarfs*. Caricaturist Al Hirschfeld complained that Disney's treatment of Snow White, Prince Charming, and the Queen "belongs in the oopsy-woopsy

Drawn especially for THE AMERICAN SCHOLAR   Courtesy of the Disney Studios

Mickey holds the key—and takes the honors.
American Scholar, Summer 1939, 260; © Disney Enterprises, Inc.

school of art."[22] The eminent art historian Erwin Panofsky was also uneasy with Disney's portrayal of humans. He found in Disney's early films, "within their self-imposed limitations," and in some sequences in later ones, "a chemically pure distillation of cinematic possibilities."[23] But it was "a fall from grace when *Snow White* introduced the human figure," since "the very virtue of the animated cartoon is to animate, that is to say endow lifeless things with life, or living things with a different kind of life" (23, n. 1). Even the idolizing Jacobs admitted that in such an ambitious project as *Snow White and the Seven Dwarfs* there was bound to be some unevenness, something still for Disney to tackle in future feature-length films: he faulted Snow White and the Prince as "indifferently good drawings of the 'cute' school of art," who "move (because we associate them with real people) choppily."[24] Cuteness: the accusation would intensify over the decades, as Disney's artists increasingly stylized their big-eyed ingenues and infants of whatever species.

If many in the cultural elite, including Agee and Panofsky, appreciated Disney as a folk artist—for producing what Dorothy Grafly called "folk art of a sophisticated century"—then the 1941 strike at the Disney Studios may have undermined Disney's "populist authenticity."[25] As a contemporary critic wrote, "We want to love the creator of Mickey Mouse and not have the reluctant Disney be the oppressing plant owner."[26] Whether the shift in opinions on Disney occurred in 1941, or in connection with the experimentalism of the 1945 *Three Caballeros*, or in connection with the "embarrassing attempts at 'culture'" of the 1946 *Make Mine Music*, as Leonard Maltin claims,[27] the 1940s were pivotal. Eric Smoodin finds a tendency, in about 1945, for critics to see Disney as failing to bridge gaps—between art and commerce, between high and low art, between young and old—that he once seemed to surmount with ease.[28] Disney was financially strapped. He'd invested in an expensive new studio; his foreign markets dried up during World War II; *Pinocchio* (1940) and *Fantasia* were not, upon first release, the commercial successes he'd hoped they would be. He found it difficult to invest in another feature-length cartoon.

And when he returned to full-scale cartooning in the 1950s, his target audience had subtly shifted. In the 1930s, Disney's cartoons were for everyone, young and old, rich and poor—a "universal audience," "patrons of differing taste," in the words of a 1931 critic.[29] Cartoon shorts played as part of a film bill that included a newsreel, previews, a feature film, and perhaps an additional short subject: no matter how sophisticated the feature film, theater-goers expected to see a cartoon as part of the program. Those of us who were raised on Saturday morning cartoons may find it difficult to imagine that cartoons weren't always just for children. But in the 1930s and 1940s critics stressed that this vibrant new art form was for young and old: a writer for the *Atlantic* in 1940 praised the way Disney's cartoons elicited "the laughter of little children and very old men and women"; a film critic in 1939 noted the "unanimous praise from artists, intellectuals, children, workers, and everyday people the world over."[30] Reviewers of *Snow White and the Seven Dwarfs* may have recognized the primacy of the child audience, yet they also found the movie suitable for adults, happily transporting "the care-worn adult back to the happy days of his child-hood."[31] Or in the words of a movie critic for the *New York Times*, "Primarily, 'Snow White' is a fairy tale for adults—and don't look down your nose, now, be-cause most of the pictures you see during the year are merely fairy tales for ado-lescents. You can bring the children, of course."[32] David Forgacs points out that Disney's early feature films "were not targeted at a 'family audience' in the mod-ern sense of the term—adults accompanying children as the primary reason," even if eventually "they helped bring such an audience into being."[33] They tar-geted adults, and they targeted children, not the two in tandem.

Consider the response of merchandisers and retailers, those astute readers of popular taste. Barring the occasional T-shirt or wristwatch, we're likely nowa-days to think of Disney merchandise as targeting children. And it usually did, even in the early days. Richard deCordova has tellingly documented the way Mickey Mouse was marketed to children by way of toys and local Mickey Mouse Clubs in order, in part, to make films acceptable fare for children—at a time when children's attendance at movies had precipitously fallen off.[34] Yet in the 1930s there was also considerable Disney merchandising for adults: ladies' fancy garters, powder compacts, bread boxes, canister sets, ashtrays, and beer trays; not to mention, in the 1950s, Donald Duck Bread, Mayonnaise, Mustard, Rice, Grapefruit Juice, and Coffee.[35]

From the vantage of sixty years later, it's striking how little the merchandis-ing for *Snow White and the Seven Dwarfs*, in particular, was limited to a child au-dience. In addition to children's raincapes and underwear and party dresses there was also women's clothing, from a dwarf-inspired "chapeau," modeled in at least one newspaper advertisement by Lucille Ball, to dresses and night-gowns.[36] A woman could purchase matching culottes and boleros, sorority frocks, handbags, babushkas, housecoats, even negligees. For 1930s reporters, the crucial divide that Disney bridged, the one worth commenting on, the one that wasn't just assumed, was not age but class: a writer for *Women's Wear Daily* noted in 1938 that the merchandising for *Snow White and the Seven Dwarfs* was unusual in that it appealed to "all classes, wealthy and not wealthy alike."[37] There were costume-jewelry charm bracelets but also bracelets by Cartier. Bon-wit Teller sold dwarf-inspired hats. Lord and Taylor experienced a brisk trade in boys' ties with Snow White motifs. The Paris couturier Ardanse featured Snow White prints in its fall collection.[38] Saks Fifth Avenue created Snow White win-dow displays in which, amidst tastefully scattered jewelry and souvenir pro-grams, mannequins wore evening gowns and ermine coats.[39]

Not until perhaps the 1950s did cartoons come to be seen as primarily—or only—for children. That shift had a good deal to do with the advent of television.[40] Despite some rhetoric in the 1950s about TV fostering family togetherness[41]—and it did foster some togetherness, extended families gathering to watch a special program such as *Disneyland*—the net effect has been to increase family segmentation and niche marketing. Parents who wouldn't dream of letting their children go to the movies without an adult could happily park them in front of a television set while they themselves were engaged elsewhere in the house. Cartoons started disappearing from theatrical film bills and materializing on Saturday morning television.

Steven Watts points to ideological shifts in Disney's work from the 1930s to the 1950s, from a kind of instinctive, egalitarian populism to a Cold War paranoid populism, and from ambivalence about domesticity in the animated films, especially the short subjects, to a commitment to the nuclear family as central to American life.[42] Watts points to Disney's statements in the 1950s that emphasize pleasing "the family taste" and enhancing "all that is good for the family and our country."[43] What I would stress is Disney's increased targeting of children. His television specials, starting in 1950, reached a family audience, one that importantly included children; his televised *Mickey Mouse Club*, starting in 1955, more exclusively addressed children.

Watts also points to a shift in Disney's stance toward his subject matter, between the 1930s and 1950s, from productions that included "a charge of social criticism," probing the conventional, to a more preservationist stance.[44] This, too, is related to the shift in target audience, for there's a strong temptation, when one is consciously addressing children, not to be subversive but to be preservationist. (I'm reminded of an assignment for my course "Children's Literature" in which a self-avowed feminist, drafting a story for children, was stunned to find herself creating a stay-at-home mom in an apron and a dad returning with a briefcase—but she was simply the most self-conscious of scores of students who have found themselves shifting into high didacticism and preservationism when attempting stories for children.)

There was, in addition, a visual shift in Disney characterization between the 1930s and 1950s. Biologist Stephen Jay Gould has documented the progressive juvenilization of Mickey Mouse, visually, between the early 1930s and now—the larger head, relative to the size of the body, the larger eyes, the appearance of a larger cranium (the upper front of the head), even the appearance of thicker, pudgier legs and feet. Gould relates the changes to attempts to make this national symbol appear more cute and friendly.[45] Watts points to changes in Mickey in the mid-1930s that enabled animators to express a broader range of emotions—a pear-shaped body that allowed for more varied and expressive squashing and stretching than did a circular one, larger eyes to contain pupils and hence increase the expressivity of the face.[46] Yet the modifications to Mickey continued beyond the mid-1930s (note that the third Mickey in the accompanying illustration is from 1940's *Fantasia*, in which Mickey played the role of the Sorcerer's Apprentice, and the changes continue beyond him). I would suggest that the changes reflect, at least in part, an increasing urge to create a more childlike character for works increasingly targeting children.[47]

Certainly the juvenilization of Disney's audience gets metaphorical play in the criticism. Remember Agee's 1943 comment that Disney cuteness "may mirror national infantilism." The critic who gives the fullest scope to disparaging juvenility is Richard Schickel, in his controversial 1968 critique, *The Disney Version* (a title I couldn't resist borrowing for this chapter). Early in the book he claims, "In this most childlike of our mass communicators I see what is most childish and therefore most dangerous in all of us who were his fellow Americans."[48] Schickel continues by referring to Disney's "boyishly" scoffing, to his "childlike desire to make a little world all his own," to his becoming "as a child himself," to the "child's play" of his work, to his having an "immature . . . conscious vision of his own motives and achievements."[49] If Schickel concludes that "Disney was something more than a mere teller of childish stories, a mere maker of childish tricks,"[50] the claim is not so much an elevation of Disney as a sign of how very low children rank with Schickel.

In any case, by the 1950s critics were significantly less enthusiastic than they had been in the 1930s, and not just in academic venues. A *Time* reviewer found *Alice in Wonderland* (1951) "a dreadful mockery of the classic"; a *Herald Tribune* reviewer saw the foregrounding of "soft cuteness" in *Sleeping Beauty* (1959) as "Disney imitating Disney"; a *Time* reviewer called *Swiss Family Robinson* (1960) "good Disney and bad culture."[51] Responses were complicated too by the ways in which Disney's enterprises were diversifying, and distaste for his new ventures could easily attach to the rest of his work. Disney had begun creating non-cartoon films, usually not to great acclaim: a London *Times* reviewer asserted of *Rob Roy, the Highland Rogue* (1954), "To say that this is the best of what Disney calls his all-live action films is, I fear, not saying much, but one must do what small kindnesses one can."[52] Disney also launched Disneyland Park: a writer for the *Nation* lamented in 1958 that "the whole world, the universe, and all man's striv-

Mickey on parade: fifty years of the Mouse
Stephen Jay Gould, *The Panda's Thumb: Reflections in Natural History*, 1980; © Disney
Enterprises, Inc.

ing for dominion over self and nature, have been reduced to a sickening blend of cheap formulas packaged to sell" in Disneyland and Disney films, leaving him feeling an overwhelming "sadness for the empty lives which accept such tawdry substitutes."[53] With respect to the animated features in particular, a critic in the London *Observer* reminisced, "Even when we criticized, we felt that Disney had the root of the matter in him. Here was a splendid new way of telling fairy stories, which should grow even better as the years went on." Yet when reflecting on whether Disney's work has developed, this critic concluded, "So far as techniques are concerned, yes, undoubtedly. In all that affects the imagination, regrettably but definitely no."[54]

Among the conscious custodians of children's culture, the first widely heard salvo was fired in 1965, when the librarian Frances Clarke Sayers objected to Disney's reductions of classics, in films and books, making everything too obvious and "pretending that everything is so sweet, so saccharine, so without any conflict except the obvious conflict of violence."[55] Since then the critiques have been legion. In 1977 the noted children's author Jane Yolen complained that in mass-market book versions of such a tale as "Cinderella," especially after the 1950 Disney film, "the magic of the old tales has been falsified, the true meaning lost," the heroine denied "her birthright of shrewdness, inventiveness, and grace under pressure."[56] Typical nowadays is a passing reference in 1996 to Disney's *Alice in Wonderland*: a writer for the *New York Times Book Review* refers to its "reactionary politics, vigorous vulgarity, equal parts of sadism and sentimentality."[57] Or indeed Anthony Holden's description, quoted in the previous chapter, of J. K. Rowling's work as "one-dimensional children's books, Disney cartoons written in words."[58]

Consider the responses of E. B. White. Having made his name first in an adult arena, as an essayist, his reputation as a writer for children—most notably as the author of *Charlotte's Web* (1952)—seems only to have added to its luster.[59] He declined the Disney offer to animate *Charlotte's Web:* as he noted in 1969, "The Disney organization tried for years to beat me down. I didn't beat, and Disney is dead. But he's still trying from the grave."[60] White explained, "My feeling about animals is just the opposite of Disney's. He made them dance to his tune and came up with some great creations, like Donald Duck. I preferred to dance to their tune and came up with Charlotte and Wilbur."[61] When *Charlotte's Web* was finally made into an animated movie and White was not altogether pleased, he wrote of his displeasure thus: "The Blue Hill Fair . . . has become a Disney world, with 76 trombones."[62] It's tempting, though, to suggest that one reason for the vehemence of his response to Disney might be that in 1948, the year before White began writing *Charlotte's Web*—that story of a girl rescuing a pig and nurturing it, then watching it being nurtured by a spider, until finally it wins not first prize but a special award for attracting so many visitors to the county fair—Disney released *So Dear to My Heart.* In this live-action film a child rescues a black lamb from its mother and then rears it, determined to bring it to the county fair, having been inspired by the determination of Robert Bruce, who had in turn been inspired by a spider's persistence in spinning a web. Once at the fair, the lamb fails to win the Blue Ribbon but does win the Award of Special Merit, as an animal not distinctive in itself but loved and cared for and hence prized.[63] Even if the echo is not fully conscious, it could account for some of the strength of White's disavowal.

In the past decade certain intellectuals, especially film historians and cultural critics, have again focused attention on Disney, often finding him simply reinforcing corporate and patriarchal and imperialistic values—no longer the representative of the folk but of that which crushes the folk. The Walt Disney Company, with more than $25 billion in annual revenues, not only produces movies and operates theme parks and retail stores but owns television and radio networks, record companies, and publishing houses; indeed its CEO claimed in 2001 that "1.2 billion . . . consumers [worldwide] had used at least one Disney product over the preceding 12 months."[64] The corporation also claims to be "the world's largest publisher of children's books and magazines." So it's not surprising that many commentators complain about the commercialism of Disney enterprises, this "industry leader at using cross-selling and cross promotion to maximize revenues,"[65] luring consumers back for more and more: a video of Disney tunes set at Walt Disney World Resort lures one to the theme park, where one buys a cuddly Lion King, which then draws one to watch the film yet one more time—and so on. Beyond the explicit commercialism, many commentators point to, say, the stereotyping of African-American or Middle-Eastern characters, or the insipidity of the fairy-tale heroines, early and late, conforming to expected roles.

Yet some cultural critics find sites of contestation: Elizabeth Bell, for instance, notes that the use of classical dancers as models for the bodies of teenaged heroines/princesses has challenged some of that coding, giving the heroines backbone, giving them bodies that are "portraits of strength, discipline, and control."[66] And as Lori Kenschaft argues, not everyone experiences a movie as a totalizing narrative; not everyone experiences Disney's *Mary Poppins* (1964) as a movie simply about the consolidation of the nuclear family. Especially in the age of VCRs, children and other viewers may respond to isolated fragments and episodes. If these episodes focus on "the value of sociability and play" in the workplace and on people mingling "on the basis of shared interests and pleasures, not shared age and class," then "the movie's intermittent critiques of class, capitalism, and middle-class gender and family relations may stick."[67]

Like E. B. White, then, Disney first gained a name for himself by addressing adults. Yet unlike White, his turn to children seems to have tarnished perceptions of his entire oeuvre. Other factors affected these perceptions as well, but it's noteworthy that once Disney's work was firmly associated with a child audience, his critical reputation nose-dived. Despite the occasional demurrals of cultural critics, academics and other intellectuals are fond nowadays of castigating Disney because of his popularity and profitability. But it's worth pondering whether some of our disdain—a disdain we're likely to feel even if we're committed to revaluing childhood and children's literature—may have roots in twentieth-century intellectuals' eagerness to disparage anything juvenile.

Mickey Mouse and Donald Duck, not to mention the Teenage Mutant Ninja Turtles, Barney, the Teletubbies, Harry Potter—has their impact been significantly different from that of Fauntleroy a century ago? True, from the perspective of a parent dragged unwillingly through the aisles of Toys "R" Us by a child desperately in search of a Darth Maul action figure or a booster pack of Pokémon cards, the merchandise tie-ins seem chosen by children rather than imposed by doting adults. Though of course the children "choose" with a good deal of media and marketing encouragement: it's more a question of which adults are doing the imposing. Yet children are creative, not just imposed on.

They infuse their own meanings into stories and artifacts; they do things to Barbie that Mattel never dreamed of. (One of the Barbies in my household, tossed aside in a closet, is a multiple amputee; the other, replacing a less durable plastic figure, is now in Darth Vader drag.) Even turning to mass-marketed toys and artifacts may be, as Ellen Seiter avers, a way to "subvert the didactic norm of the approved stories and express a resistance to the middle-class culture of parenting—with its emphasis on achievement, on play as work, and on the incessant teaching of numbers and letters."[68]

Furthermore, despite the increasing attention to glitzy packaging and merchandising, the dumbing down of classics, the celebrity writers who figure that anyone can write a book for children, the hastily produced novelizations of popular movies, there is even now outstanding literature being written for children. The economic attractions of writing for children, including the continuing financial impact of the Newbery and Caldecott Medals, draw some brilliant writers and artists to the field: not just E. B. White but Maurice Sendak, Cynthia Rylant, Walter Dean Myers, Paul Fleischman, Virginia Hamilton, Julius Lester, Faith Ringgold, to name only a few. There may have been a few librarians who condemned Oz to the dustbins, early in the last century, but countless librarians, and also children themselves, have kept children's literature vibrantly alive.

My focus in this book has been on changes in how we adults perceive and think about childhood in the United States, and how those changes reflect and are reflected in the popular and especially the critical imaginations. The cultural elite of the nineteenth century, the editors of literary magazines such as the *Atlantic*, were much more willing to attend to children's literature than the twentieth-century cultural elite, the academics, have been. Nineteenth-century critics were less likely to ghettoize it. They did not treat *Huckleberry Finn* any more seriously than—did not treat it as more significant or greater than—*Tom Sawyer* or indeed *The Prince and the Pauper*. *Little Women* was often considered not just an important work of literature for children but an important work of literature. Some critics even considered Alcott's work more important than Twain's.

Among books for younger children, especially works of fantasy, the situation has been somewhat more complicated. Homegrown fantasies such as *Oz* have generally fallen off the critical radar screen, at least until recently (much as Burnett's work disappeared, though in her case the cause seems to have been distaste associated with one particular work, *Fauntleroy*). A couple of fantasy imports, however, defy the pattern associated with *Oz*. Whether being a British import simply lends a certain cachet, *Wonderland* has continued to have at least a small place in the twentieth-century academy. And the recent Harry Potter books, whether or not they find a place in the academy, have certainly had a popular impact—and suggest that books still can have an impact, that the shift to film as the most important medium for constructing childhood is not yet complete.

In any case, once Henry James and others started carving a niche for fiction for adults around the turn of the twentieth century, and once cultural gatekeeping professionalized—once its site became the academy instead of the literary journal—children's literature generally disappeared from the purview of the cultural elite. *Huckleberry Finn* had to be strenuously differentiated from *Tom Sawyer* and *The Prince and the Pauper* so that it would no longer be defined as for children. The rest of children's literature simply dropped from the canon.

So did literature by women and literature by men of color. In winnowing the canon, academics buttressed and policed boundaries associated with age, gender, race, and also class. A crisscrossing between age and gender has been particularly prominent in the reception of children's literature during the past century and a half. Sometimes the two are conflated, along with class, as in the response to Fauntleroy: early-twentieth-century critics denounced the boy's gendering as a way of policing not just gender but also class (the genteel) and age. And *Little Women* was pushed out of the precincts of high culture because of its associations with both women and children. Sometimes age and gender become interchangeable tokens, in competition, as in the turn-of-the-century response to *Huckleberry Finn:* this book, which would soon make its way into a redefined canon, could be rescued for women by banning children or rescued for boys by banning females. Or, more recently, race has become prominent, in critical discussions of *Huckleberry Finn,* in attempts once again to police age boundaries. Sometimes gender becomes pivotal in the history of a work's reception, as with *Oz,* whose adult male fans have been known to regard the prominence of girls in the reading audience with some unease and have wanted to blame the absence of the book from public libraries, early in the century, on lady librarians (ladies, of course, being not just female but also genteel). Sometimes age assumes prominence when books make a crossover appeal to adults, whether critics try to claim that the books aren't really for children, as with the Alice books, or editors create a separate best-seller list for children, as with Harry Potter. It's as if a book's being British makes it easier for Americans to give play to age in their responses, as if the cultural authority we're still likely to grant to Britain can withstand the potential taint of puerility.

And maybe, at the dawn of the twenty-first century, the positioning of children's literature is changing yet again. Some snapshots from the last decade of the twentieth century hint at both problems and possibilities. Consider two essays with suggestive titles, published not long ago in general-interest journals: "The Trashing of Children's Literature" and "Kiddie Litter."[69] In the first, Francelia Butler, the founding mother of the literary discipline, discusses the resistance that proponents of children's literature, mostly women, have experienced in the academy. She notes that the MLA did not offer a session on children's literature at its annual convention until 1969. She recounts the trials of starting the journal *Children's Literature* at the University of Connecticut, how in working on the journal she was "threatened for moonlighting"—she clearly wasn't advancing the cause of anything that could be called scholarship. She might almost be responding to John R. Dunlap, the author of the second article. He opens with a potted—and rather dated—history of children's literature. He closes with a peroration on the serpent lurking in the garden. In between, he praises books by William Armstrong and Mildred Taylor but dismisses the "wooden characters" in Robin McKinley's *Hero and the Crown* (1985) as "little more than backdrop for a feminist yawp" and claims that in Virginia Hamilton's *M. C. Higgins the Great* (1975), which I consider one of the most important children's books of the past four decades, "an episodic plot is dominated by a heavy-handed symbolism."[70] The problem with award-winning books in the late twentieth century, he makes quite clear, is that "the 'field' of children's books is disproportionately populated by maiden aunts and bluestockings."[71] Gender again; a bit of gentility perhaps too.

Yet there are nevertheless some promising signs of change. Two years after the brouhaha over the possibility that a Harry Potter book might defeat Seamus Heaney's translation of *Beowulf* as the Whitbread Book of the Year, a work of children's literature has, for the first time, won that honor: Philip Pullman's *Amber Spyglass*, the stunningly evocative third book in his fantasy trilogy (Harry Potter for the thinking child, as it were). This award may signal how, in the words of the London *Times*, "children's books are increasingly joining the mainstream."[72]

In the United States, in academia, the MLA may have been slow to grant divisional status to children's literature, doing so only in 1980, eight decades after the ALA created its Section for Children's Librarians, but at least it has now done so. In 1992 the MLA published Glenn Edward Sadler's *Teaching Children's Literature: Issues, Pedagogy, Resources*, and in 1997 the association sponsored its first forum on children's literature at an annual meeting.[73] Prestigious presses are now bringing out books by American children's literature critics—witness Oxford University Press's publication in 1992 of Jerry Griswold's *Audacious Kids: Coming of Age in America's Classic Children's Books* and in 1996 of Dianne Johnson-Feelings's *Best of the "Brownies' Book"*; Yale University Press's publication in 1994 of Lois R. Kuznets's *When Toys Come Alive: Narratives of Animation, Metamorphosis, and Development* and in 1995 of Lynne Vallone's *Disciplines of Virtue: Girls' Culture in the Eighteenth and Nineteenth Centuries*; and the Johns Hopkins University Press's publication in 1999 of the collection *Girls, Boys, Books, Toys: Gender in Children's Literature and Culture*, which I coedited with Margaret R. Higonnet.[74] Emblematic of the move into academic respectability is that Jacqueline Rose's pathbreaking *Case of Peter Pan*, first published by Macmillan in 1984, was reissued by the University of Pennsylvania Press in 1993. Furthermore, such "adultstream" journals as *Victorian Studies, Nineteenth-Century Literature, College English, American Literature, Signs, differences, New Literary History,* and indeed *PMLA* are now publishing the occasional article on children's literature.

It's true that the position of children and childhood is still somewhat precarious in the academy and in the broader culture. Calling someone puerile is still no compliment. Nor, usually, is calling children's literature kiddie lit. For many critics *Little Women* is still too little, *Harry Potter* too potted, *Oz* too far over the rainbow. *Huckleberry Finn* is too important for mere juveniles—and therefore, oddly, important as required reading for the young. Children want to grow up quickly because they too get the message: childhood is childish.

The best response is probably Walt Disney's: "What the hell's wrong with something being childish?"[75]

Notes

ONE: Kids and Kiddie Lit

Epigraphs: I am grateful to Kay Vandergrift, Wendy Betts, Perry Nodelman, and Stephen Roxburgh, and to Michael Joseph, owner of the Children's Literature: Theory and Criticism online list, for permission to quote from October and November 1997 interchanges.

1. *The World Almanac and Book of Facts 2002* (New York: World Almanac Books, 2002), 388. In the early 1970s children seemed to be about 25 percent overrepresented (see George E. Delury, ed., *The World Almanac and Book of Facts 1978* [New York: Newspaper Enterprise, 1977], 198); the rate was 50 percent or more in most of the 1990s. For a similar account of how we both worship and devalue the child in American culture at large, see James R. Kincaid, *Erotic Innocence: The Culture of Child Molesting* (Durham: Duke University Press, 1998). As Jacqueline Rose puts it, on the other side of the Atlantic, "Conservatism in Britain neglects provision for children in exact proportion as it elevates the principle of the good fairy . . . into a social law (one version of the child—'a little person'—doing service for another)," thereby showing "the extent to which sentimentality about childhood . . . is the other side of guilt" (*The Case of Peter Pan, or the Impossibility of Children's Fiction* [1984; reprint, Philadelphia: University of Pennsylvania Press, 1993], x).

2. The only such list I've found is that of the 1998 Radcliffe Publishing Course, created in response to the more highly publicized Modern Library list of the hundred best novels of the century. The Radcliffe Course ranked *Charlotte's Web* thirteenth ("Top 100 Novels of the 20th Century," www.radcliffe.edu/news/list.html, accessed 3 August 1998). The Modern Library listed no work of children's literature, unless one counts *The Catcher in the Rye*, which came in sixty-fourth (see David Gates and Ray Sawhill, "The Dated and the Dead," *Newsweek*, 3 August 1998, 65).

3. Jane Tompkins, *Sensational Designs: The Cultural Work of American Fiction, 1790–1860* (New York: Oxford University Press, 1985), xii.

4. Ibid., xi.

5. For a recent discussion of how to define children's literature—whether by its readership or by its implied readership, not to mention the vexed issues of what "children" are and what "literature" is—see Peter Hunt, *Criticism, Theory, and Children's Literature* (Oxford: Blackwell, 1991), 42–64.

6. Carol McPhee and Ann FitzGerald, *Feminist Quotations: Voices of Rebels, Reformers, and Visionaries* (New York: Crowell, 1979).

7. Fredric Jameson, *The Political Unconscious: Narrative as a Socially Symbolic Act* (Ithaca: Cornell University Press, 1981), 86.

8. Ibid., 103–4.

9. Sherry B. Ortner, "Is Female to Male as Nature Is to Culture?" in *Women, Culture, and Society*, ed. Michelle Zimbalist Rosaldo and Louise Lamphere (Stanford: Stanford University Press, 1974), 77–78.

10. Rose, 139.

11. Though often, if given the chance, children do make wise decisions—about medical treatments, for example, as my colleague Roz Ladd informs me. They can also engage in philosophical thought, as Gareth B. Matthews argues in, for instance, *Philosophy and the Young Child* (Cambridge: Harvard University Press, 1980).

12. Deborah Thacker suggests that "it is in the area of feminist theory that we come closest to a dialogue [regarding children's literature], yet there is very little evidence that, even here, children's literature is considered" ("Disdain or Ignorance? Literary Theory and the Absence of Children's Literature," *The Lion and the Unicorn* 24 [2000]: 6).

13. Lissa Paul, "Enigma Variations: What Feminist Theory Knows about Children's Literature," *Signal* 54 (1987): 187.

14. Perry Nodelman, "Children's Literature as Women's Writing," *Children's Literature Association Quarterly* 12 (Spring 1988): 33, 34.

15. Margaret Higonnet, "La politique dans la cours de récréation: la critique féministe et la littérature enfantine," in *Culture, texte et jeune lecteur*, ed. Jean Perrot (Nancy, France: Presse Universitaire de Nancy, 1993), 109–25.

16. Margaret Fuller, *Woman in the Nineteenth Century* (1844), excerpt reprinted in *The Heath Anthology of American Literature*, ed. Paul Lauter et al. (Lexington, Mass.: Heath, 1990), 1:1624.

17. Susan Faludi, *Backlash: The Undeclared War against American Women* (New York: Crown, 1991), 56.

18. Sandra M. Gilbert and Susan Gubar, *The Madwoman in the Attic: The Woman Writer and the Nineteenth-Century Literary Imagination* (New Haven: Yale University Press, 1979), 49.

19. C. S. Lewis, "On Three Ways of Writing for Children" (1952), reprinted in *Only Connect: Readings on Children's Literature*, ed. Sheila Egoff, G. T. Stubbs, and L. F. Ashley, 2d ed. (Toronto: Oxford University Press, 1980), 210.

20. Tillie Olsen, "One out of Twelve: Writers Who Are Women in Our Century" (1971), reprinted in her *Silences* (New York: Delta, 1978), 31–32.

21. Adrienne Rich, *Of Woman Born: Motherhood as Experience and Institution*, 10th anniv. ed. (New York: Norton, 1986), 16, 24, 37–38.

22. Susan Rubin Suleiman, "Writing and Motherhood," in *The (M)other Tongue: Essays in Feminist Psychoanalytic Interpretation*, ed. Shirley Nelson Garner et al. (Ithaca: Cornell University Press, 1985), 356.

23. Sara Ruddick, *Maternal Thinking: Toward a Politics of Peace* (New York: Ballantine, 1989), 37, 122.

24. E. Ann Kaplan, *Motherhood and Representation: The Mother in Popular Culture and Melodrama* (London: Routledge, 1992), 40, 5.

25. Marianne Hirsch, *The Mother/Daughter Plot: Narrative, Psychoanalysis, Feminism* (Bloomington: Indiana University Press, 1989), 12.

26. Ibid., 169.

27. Julia Kristeva, "A New Type of Intellectual: The Dissident" (1977), trans. Seán Hand, in *The Kristeva Reader*, ed. Toril Moi (New York: Columbia University Press, 1986), 300.

28. Ibid., 297.

29 Jane Flax, "Postmodernism and Gender Relations in Feminist Theory," *Signs* 12 (Summer 1987): 640.

30. Janice Radway, "Mail-Order Culture and Its Critics: The Book-of-the-Month Club, Commodification and Consumption, and the Problem of Cultural Authority," in *Cultural Studies*, ed. Lawrence Grossberg et al. (New York: Routledge, 1992), 513.

31. Susan Stanford Friedman, "Post/Poststructuralist Feminist Criticism: The Politics of Recuperation and Negotiation," *New Literary History* 22 (Spring 1991): 471.

32. Mitzi Myers, "Canonical 'Orphans,' Critical *Ennui:* Rereading Edgeworth's Cross-Writing," *Children's Literature* 25 (1997): 122.

33. Barbara Johnson, "Apostrophe, Animation, and Abortion," *Diacritics* 16 (1986), reprinted in *Feminisms: An Anthology of Literary Theory and Criticism*, ed. Robyn R. Warhol and Diane Price Herndl (New Brunswick, N.J.: Rutgers University Press, 1991), 642.

34. Avi, "The Child in Children's Lierature," *Horn Book*, January/February 1993, 45. Or as Peter Hollindale has said of those who write for children, "the adult children's author is always obsolete" (*Signs of Childness in Children's Literature* [Stroud, England: Thimble, 1997], 22).

35. Henry David Thoreau, "Resistance to Civil Government" (1849), reprinted in Lauter et al., 1:1974, 1976.

36. Audre Lorde, "An Open Letter to Mary Daly" (1979), reprinted in her *Sister Outsider: Essays and Speeches* (Freedom, Calif.: Crossing Press, 1984), 66–71; Barbara Smith, "Toward a Black Feminist Criticism," *Conditions: Two* (1977), revised and reprinted in *All the Women Are White, All the Blacks Are Men, but Some of Us Are Brave: Black Women's Studies*, ed. Gloria T. Hull et al. (Old Westbury, N.Y.: Feminist Press, 1982), 157–75; Alice Walker, "One Child of One's Own: A Meaningful Digression within the Work(s)" (1979), reprinted in her *In Search of Our Mothers' Gardens* (San Diego: Harcourt Brace, 1983), 361–83.

37. Walker, *In Search*, xi.

38. Gloria I. Joseph, "Black Mothers and Daughters: Their Roles and Functions in American Society," in *Common Differences: Conflicts in Black and White Feminist Perspectives*, by Gloria I. Joseph and Jill Lewis (Garden City, N.Y.: Anchor Doubleday, 1981), 90; see also Patricia Hill Collins, *Black Feminist Thought: Knowledge, Consciousness, and the Politics of Empowerment* (Boston: Unwin Hyman, 1990), 119–37.

39. bell hooks, *Feminist Theory: From Margin to Center* (Boston: South End, 1984), 133–34.

40. African-American women writers may portray vexed, even murderous, relationships between mother and child—Toni Morrison's *Beloved* springs to mind—but always there seems to be some sensitivity to the child's perspective, to possibilities for guilt and also renewal. Not, in short, cavalier dismissal or obliviousness of the child's perspective.

41. Walker, "One Child," 382.

42. Bruce A. Ronda, "An American Canon of Children's Literature," in *Teaching Children's Literature: Issues, Pedagogy, Resources*, ed. Glenn Edward Sadler (New York: Modern Language Association, 1992), 36–37.

43. Carol Gilligan, *In a Different Voice: Psychological Theory and Women's Development* (Cambridge: Harvard University Press, 1982), 18.

44. See Sigmund Freud, "Three Contributions to the Theory of Sex," in *The Basic Writings of Sigmund Freud*, trans. and ed. A. A. Brill (New York: Modern Library, 1938), 619.

45. Barrie Thorne, "Re-Visioning Women and Social Change: Where Are the Children?" *Gender and Society* 1 (March 1987): 98.

46. Ibid., 93.

47. Rose, 13.

48. Adam Phillips, *The Beast in the Nursery* (New York: Pantheon, 1998), 56.

49. Nina Baym, "The Feminist Teacher of Literature: Feminist or Teacher?" (1988), reprinted in *Gender in the Classroom: Power and Pedagogy*, ed. Susan L. Gabriel and Isaiah Smithson (Urbana: University of Illinois Press, 1990), 75. See also the other essays in Gabriel and Smithson; Margo Culley and Catherine Portuges, eds., *Gendered Subjects: The Dynamics of Feminist Teaching* (Boston: Routledge, 1985); Paula A. Treichler, "Teaching Feminist Theory," in *Theory in the Classroom*, ed. Cary Nelson (Urbana: University of Illinois Press, 1986), 57–128; and Beverly Lyon Clark et al., "Giving Voice to Feminist Criticism: A Conversation," in *Teaching Contemporary Theory to Undergraduates*, ed. Dianne F. Sadoff and William E. Cain (New York: Modern Language Association, 1994), 125–40.

50. Stephen M. North, "Writing in a Philosophy Class: Three Case Studies," *Research in the Teaching of English* 20 (1986): 255.

51. Ibid., 230. North does offer caveats in his use of Perry's developmental scheme: "Perry offers an abstracted description, not some sort of norm that describes how people ought to develop. Any use of the scheme needs to be governed accordingly" (232). Yet despite subsequent caution in phrasing, North basically uses Perry's categories as developmental stages, associating earlier stages with juvenility. In a sense, North simply underscores how any developmental scheme, however descriptively rather than prescriptively deployed, implicitly devalues children.

52. Ibid., 239, 240, 251, 242, 246, 254, 242. Perhaps even the choice of which exemplum to quote at length from the student's journal—not the one about the reggae singer, not the one about a person considered ugly, but the one about "a sort of generalized child derived from her reading on Locke" (242–43)—perhaps even this choice is guided by an underlying association of the student with the childish.

53. Ursula K. Le Guin, *Buffalo Gals and Other Animal Presences* (Santa Barbara, Calif.: Capra, 1987), 10.

54. Perry Nodelman, "Cott im Himmel," review of *Pipers at the Gates of Dawn: The Wisdom of Children's Literature*, by Jonathan Cott, *Children's Literature* 13 (1985): 208.

55. Margaret R. Higonnet, "Critical Apertures," *Children's Literature* 17 (1989): 143–44.

56. For a fuller treatment of what study of children's literature can offer, see U. C. Knoepflmacher, introduction, Sadler, 1–9.

T W O : What Fauntleroy Knew

1. W. D. Howells, *Criticism and Fiction* (New York: Harper, 1891), 149, 151.

2. Quoted in Ann Thwaite, *Waiting for the Party: The Life of Frances Hodgson Burnett, 1849–1924* (New York: Scribner's 1974), 55. I am greatly indebted to Thwaite for leads to early commentary on Burnett.

3. *Atlantic*, November 1877, 631. Subsequent reviews of Burnett's work in the *Atlantic*, most anonymously contributed by Horace Scudder, were more lukewarm; Scud-

der concluded his review of *Through One Administration* by saying, "The book, when all is said, is a brilliant book. It might have been a great one" (*Atlantic*, July 1883, 123).

4. Quoted in Edith Mary Jordan, "My Sister," *Good Housekeeping*, July 1925, 146.

5. "A Portrayer of Lovable Children," *Outlook*, 12 November 1924, 397.

6. R. H. Stoddard, "Frances Hodgson Burnett," *Critic*, 17 December 1881, 346.

7. Quoted in Thwaite, 98.

8. James Herbert Morse, "The Native Element in American Fiction: Since the War," *Century*, July 1883, 365.

9. *Quarterly Review*, January and April 1883, 209.

10. "A Hundred American Authors," *Critic*, 24 July 1886, 37.

11. Louisa May Alcott, review, *Book Buyer*, December 1886, 432.

12. "The Best American Books," *Critic*, 3 June 1893. Burnett was one of the thirty most cited authors, only ten of whom were still living; she and Harriet Beecher Stowe were the only living women on the list.

13. The other two books were *King Solomon's Mines* and *War and Peace*. See Frank Luther Mott, *Golden Multitudes: The Story of Best Sellers in the United States* (New York: Macmillan, 1947), 310.

14. Thwaite, 95. But see Hamilton W. Mabie, "The Most Popular Novels in America," *Forum*, December 1893, 508; he names *Fauntleroy* as the twelfth most popular book in terms of circulation. As for the play, it ran for 680 performances in London and four years on Broadway, not to mention performances by four hundred companies in the provinces (see Dorothy Kunhardt, "*Little Lord Fauntleroy*," *Life*, 5 December 1949, 71).

15. "What Children Like to Read," *Pall Mall Gazette*, 1 July 1898, 2. The other named American "work" was actually an author: Louisa May Alcott. And of course Burnett could be claimed as British as well, since she was born in England. *Little Lord Fauntleroy* and Alcott's *Little Women* are also the only two American works in the top ten "best" books for children as voted by almost a thousand readers of the British *Daily Mail* ("The Best Hundred Books for Children," *Eclectic Magazine*, June 1900, 800).

16. Jerry Griswold, *Audacious Kids: Coming of Age in America's Classic Children's Books* (New York: Oxford University Press, 1992), 103.

17. Quoted in Thwaite, 236, 107.

18. Quoted in Thwaite, 116.

19. Quoted in Thwaite, 94.

20. Thwaite, 116, 112–13.

21. William McHaig, "The Young Heart," *Good Housekeeping*, quoted in Thwaite, 93.

22. See, e.g., Phyllis Bixler, *Frances Hodgson Burnett* (Boston: Twayne, 1984), 55.

23. William Archer, London *World*, 23 May 1888, quoted in Thwaite, 112.

24. "Frances H. Burnett, Author, Dies at 74," *New York Times*, 30 October 1924, 19.

25. *Times* (London), 30 October 1924, 16.

26. Frances Hodgson Burnett to Richard Watson Gilder, quoted in Bixler, *Burnett*, 29; Bixler, *Burnett*, 14. Bixler dates the shift in critical opinion to 1896, when Burnett published *A Lady of Quality*.

27. *Atlantic*, August 1896, 275.

28. H. W. Boynton, "Books New and Old: 'For the Young,'" *Atlantic*, May 1903, 703.

29. "Inferior Work from Mrs. Burnett," *New York Times Saturday Review of Books and Art*, 20 November 1897, 8.

30. "What Was Hid in a Garden," *New York Times Review of Books*, 3 September 1911, 526.

31. "The Literary Spotlight: XIII: Frances Hodgson Burnett," *Bookman* (New York), October 1922, 158, 160.

32. H. W. Boynton, *Independent*, 2 September 1922, quoted in Thwaite, 240.

33. See Francis J. Molson, "Frances Hodgson Burnett (1848–1924)," *American Literary Realism* 8 (Winter 1975): 36, 41. And it was the wrong kind of romance to be championing, not the imperialistic adventure kind—see Nancy Glazener, "Romances for 'Big and Little Boys': The U.S. Romantic Revival of the 1890s and James's *The Turn of the Screw*," in *Cultural Institutions of the Novel*, ed. Deidre Lynch and William B. Warner (Durham: Duke University Press, 1996), 369–98.

34. Susan R. Gannon provides an illuminating discussion of Burnett's conscious address of an adult audience and the book's initial reception by both children and adults, in "'The Best Magazine for Children of All Ages': Cross-Editing *St. Nicholas Magazine* (1873–1905)," *Children's Literature* 25 (1997): 153–80.

35. "Little Lord Fauntleroy on the Stage," *Literary News*, February 1889, 54.

36. Ibid.

37. For a fuller discussion of these competing versions of masculinity, see my *Regendering the School Story: Sassy Sissies and Tattling Tomboys* (New York: Garland, 1996), esp. 200–201, 221–22. My working out of possible types has been informed by Mark C. Carnes and Clyde Griffen, eds., *Meanings for Manhood: Constructions of Masculinity in Victorian America* (Chicago: University of Chicago Press, 1990); James V. Catano, "The Rhetoric of Masculinity: Origins, Institutions, and the Myth of the Self-Made Man," *College English* 52 (1990): 421–36; R. Gordon Kelly, *Mother Was a Lady: Self and Society in Selected American Children's Periodicals, 1865–1890* (Westport, Conn.: Greenwood, 1974); Michael Kimmel, *Manhood in America: A Cultural History* (New York: Free Press, 1996); E. Anthony Rotundo, *American Manhood: Transformations in Masculinity from the Revolution to the Modern Era* (New York: Basic, 1993).

38. See, e.g., Ann Douglas, *The Feminization of American Culture* (1977; reprint, New York: Avon, 1978).

39. Alan Richardson argues that *Fauntleroy* inscribes feminine values while ultimately reasserting the patriarchal ("Reluctant Lords and Lame Princes: Engendering the Male Child in Nineteenth-Century Juvenile Fiction," *Children's Literature* 21 [1993]: 3–19). Anna Wilson suggests that the book—and the Fauntleroy image—functioned for women as "an attempt to inscribe feminine values in the public sphere" ("Little Lord Fauntleroy: The Darling of Mothers and the Abomination of a Generation," *American Literary History* 8 [Summer 1996]: 236).

40. Perhaps, in part, the Christian component of Christian gentility fostered certain reversals, the Christ child having been able to lead his elders, children in nineteenth-century evangelical fiction (and in earlier works as well) being able to educate and inspire others.

41. E. L. Godkin, "Chromo-Civilization," in his *Reflections and Comments, 1865–1895* (Westminster, England: Constable, 1896), 202, my emphasis.

42. George H. Calvert, *The Gentleman*, rev. ed. (Boston: Dutton, 1866), 110–11.

43. Godkin, 203.

44. Frances Hodgson Burnett, *Little Lord Fauntleroy* (New York: Knopf, 1995), 101.

45. The grocer, Mr. Hobbs, that other representative of the emerging bourgeoisie, is

the other character to show the greatest discomfort with femininity: he says of being ruled by a queen, "If the womenfolks can sit up on their thrones . . . ; who's to know what's happening to him [Cedric] this very minute" (Burnett, *Fauntleroy*, 199).

46. Anne Scott MacLeod, *American Childhood: Essays on Children's Literature of the Nineteenth and Twentieth Centuries* (Athens: University of Georgia Press, 1994), 83.

47. Robert Lee White, "Little Lord Fauntleroy as Hero," in *Challenges in American Culture*, ed. Ray B. Browne et al. (Bowling Green, Ohio: Bowling Green University Popular Press, 1970), 211; "What Was Hid," 526.

48. See "Fauntleroy," *New York Times*, 31 October 1924, 18; Charles Willis Thompson, "A Defense of the Mid-Victorians," letter to the editor, *New York Times*, 14 November 1924, 18; "Boy of Today Is Not a Fauntleroy," *New York Times Magazine*, 16 November 1924, 9–10.

49. Jordan, 146.

50. White, 210–11.

51. Quoted in Thwaite, 118.

52. John Nicholas Beffel, "The Fauntleroy Plague," *Bookman* (New York), April 1927, 135.

53. F. J. Harvey Darton, *Children's Books in England: Five Centuries of Social Life*, 3d ed., rev. Brian Alderson (Cambridge: Cambridge University Press, 1982), 233.

54. Molson, 39.

55. Marghanita Laski, *Mrs. Ewing, Mrs. Molesworth, and Mrs. Hodgson Burnett* (New York: Oxford University Press, 1951), 80.

56. Quoted in Thwaite, ix.

57. Laski, 83.

58. Mark Spilka, "Victorian Keys to the Early Hemingway: Part II—*Fauntleroy* and *Finn*," *Journal of Modern Literature* 10 (March 1983): 296, 297.

59. It's worth noting that Fauntleroy wasn't the only target—so were other attempts to trick out boys in finery. In Booth Tarkington's *Penrod* (1914), for instance, Penrod's mother and sister dress the boy for the role of the Child Sir Lancelot, with a ruff here, a couple of rosettes there, some faded silk stockings, a discarded bodice, and red flannel underwear. Nevertheless Fauntleroy did provide a convenient target for concerns about gentility and sartorial style—nor did the style associated with him altogether die out after the 1930s. Fauntleroy-style clothes may have functioned as a bizarre marker of skewed elitism in the 1960s television series *The Addams Family*, yet even now one can purchase a black velvet knicker-and-jacket set, more a laceless Eton jacket perhaps than a Fauntleroy one, from couturiers such as the Wooden Soldier (see p. 5 of its Fall/Holiday 1999 catalog).

60. See Anne Higonnet, *Pictures of Innocence: The History and Crisis of Ideal Childhood* (London: Thames, 1998), 46–47.

61. I have found only regrets by art historians that the image had become so debased, so sentimentalized, by frequent reproduction—"on playing cards, candy-box covers, cocktail napkins, porcelain plates, highball glasses, and ash trays," not to mention needlepoint pictures and clothiers' advertisements (Robert R. Wark, *Ten British Pictures, 1740–1840* [San Marino, Calif.: Huntington Library, 1971], 29).

62. "One Hundred Story Books for Children," *Bookman* (New York), November 1922, 366.

63. *The Secret Garden* did, however, appear in the 1976 edition of *Children's Classics*.

Phyllis Bixler charts a similar absence through the 1950s (*The Secret Garden: Nature's Magic* [New York: Twayne, 1996], 9–10).

64. Irving Harlem Hart, "The Phenomena of Popularity in Fiction," *Library Journal*, 15 April 1923, 357. Burnett is tied for fifty-first in a listing of eighty-four authors of popular works published before 1920 (358). The results must be weighed carefully, as Hart notes, since the survey relies on the variable impressions of responding librarians—as is generally the case with early library surveys.

65. Cited in Esther Jane Carrier, *Fiction in the Public Libraries, 1900–1950* (Littleton, Colo.: Libraries Unlimited, 1985), 206–11.

66. In a 1923 survey of children visiting the San Antonio library, Burnett was the seventh most popular author (see Carrier, 290). In a survey of the reading of 36,750 children, published in 1926, *The Secret Garden* ranks fifteenth, *Little Lord Fauntleroy* twenty-eighth (Carleton Washburne and Mabel Vogel, *Winnetka Graded Book List* [Chicago: American Library Association, 1926]). In a readers' survey conducted by *Youth's Companion*, reported on the following year, *The Secret Garden* ranks twelfth among girls' favorites and *Fauntleroy* does not appear at all in the top fifteen favorites for boys and girls (Louise Seaman Bechtel, "The Giant in Children," *Atlantic*, 1927, reprinted in *Books in Search of Children* [1940; reprint, n.p.: Macmillan, 1969], 146). In a 1931 survey of New York children, *The Secret Garden* was listed as the fifteenth most popular choice among girls aged twelve and thirteen (see Carrier, 291).

67. See Carrier, 289.

68. "What Was Hid," 526. The reviewer also suggests that Burnett is one of the rare authors able to please both young and old—thereby revealing the extent to which the reading of young and old has indeed bifurcated, even if an occasional author can still bridge the chasm.

69. "Frances H. Burnett," *New York Times*, 30 October 1924, 19; "Death of Mrs. Frances Hodgson Burnett," *Times* (London), 30 October 1924, 16; Hildegarde Hawthorne, "Frances Hodgson Burnett," *St. Nicholas*, January 1925, 306–8; William Fayal Clarke, "The Beloved Author of 'Little Lord Fauntleroy,'" *St. Nicholas*, January 1925, 308–10. In a brief editorial in the *New York Times* the following day, a piece mentioning the immortality of the child character Fauntleroy, the title of the later novel is misremembered as *The Secret Orchard* (*New York Times*, 31 October 1924, 18)—as Bixler also notes (*Secret Garden: Nature's Magic*, 9). Fred Lewis Pattee's comment is from *Dictionary of American Biography* (New York: Scribner's, 1929).

70. Isabella M. Cooper, ed., *A.L.A. Catalog* (Chicago: American Library Association, 1926), 904. In the 1904 *A.L.A. Catalog* (ed. Melvil Dewey [Washington: Government Printing Office, 1904]), which predates *The Secret Garden*, the only Burnett juvenile that is recommended is *Fauntleroy*. It was no longer being recommended in the 1920s.

71. Louise Seaman Bechtel, "A Rightful Heritage" (1953), reprinted in *Books in Search of Children*, 29.

72. Robert Nathan, in *Attacks of Taste*, ed. Evelyn B. Byrne and Otto M. Penzler (New York: Gotham Book Mart, 1971), 32.

73. Bernice Cullinan and M. Jerry Weiss, eds., *Books I Read When I Was Young: The Favorite Books of Famous People* (New York: Avon, 1980).

74. "Frances H. Burnett," *New York Times*, 30 October 1924, 19.

75. Rumer Godden, "The Secret Garden Revisited," *New York Times Book Review*, 15 May 1961, part II, 36.

76. See Phyllis Bixler, "*The Secret Garden* 'Misread': The Broadway Musical as Creative Interpretation," *Children's Literature* 22 (1994): 101.

77. "All-Time Bestselling Hardcover Children's Books," *Publishers Weekly*, 27 October 1989, 28; "All-Time Bestselling Paperback Children's Books," *Publishers Weekly*, 27 October 1989, 29. Curiously, the volume does not appear on a longer 1995 listing by *Publishers Weekly* (www.bookwire.com/pw/articles/childrens/, accessed 4 January 1999): perhaps the publisher did not respond to the journal's inquiry; perhaps this edition was out of print; perhaps it was in the public domain (although the lists claim to consist of "all-time" best-sellers, they omit most works in the public domain).

78. "Children's Best Sellers," *New York Times Book Review*, 22 May 1994, 26. Since no nineteenth-century works appear on the list, it's not clear whether *The Secret Garden* outsells *Little Women* and *Tom Sawyer*. One should also bear in mind that the survey was conducted soon after the release of a movie of *The Secret Garden*, and film versions often lead to heightened sales of books. *The Secret Garden* has not, in any case, appeared on the weekly lists of children's best-sellers now being published (since July 2000) in the *New York Times Book Review*.

79. Celia McGee, "Gambling on a 'Garden': Can a Children's Classic Become a Broadway Hit?" *New York*, 22 April 1991, 64.

80. Laski, 88; MacLeod, 119.

81. Alison Lurie, *Don't Tell the Grown-ups: Subversive Children's Literature* (Boston: Little, Brown, 1990), 143.

82. Laski, 88. See also Godden, 36.

83. Frances Hodgson Burnett, *The Secret Garden* (New York: Dell, 1979), 39.

84. Ibid., 16.

85. Bixler, "*Secret Garden*: Nature's Magic," 119–20. See also Judith Plotz, "Secret Garden II; or *Lady Chatterley's Lover* as Palimpsest," *Children's Literature Association Quarterly* 19 (Spring 1994): 15–19.

86. Jerry Phillips, "The Mem Sahib, the Worthy, the Rajah, and His Minions: Some Reflections on the Class Politics of *The Secret Garden*," *The Lion and the Unicorn* 17 (1993): 168–94.

87. Heather Murray, "Frances Hodgson Burnett's *The Secret Garden*: The Organ(ic)ized World," in *Touchstones: Reflections on the Best in Children's Literature*, ed. Perry Nodelman (West Lafayette, Ind.: Children's Literature Association, 1985), 1:39. Other recent critics who have pointed to Mary's receding importance include Elizabeth Lennox Keyser, "'Quite Contrary': Frances Hodgson Burnett's *The Secret Garden*," *Children's Literature* 11 (1983): 8–9; U. C. Knoepflmacher, "Little Girls without Their Curls: Female Aggression in Victorian Children's Literature," *Children's Literature* 11 (1983): 24–25; Lissa Paul, "Enigma Variations: What Feminist Theory Knows about Children's Literature," *Signal* 54 (1987): 196–97.

   In her provocative essay, Murray suggests that the most remembered myth of the story, of the place that heals, is intertwined with a second myth, "the real story of the patriarchal order—generationally coherent, socially hierarchic, reassuringly benevolent—whose restoration heals the hurts and calms the crises in the narrative" (39–40); this story of "escape to the natural, the apolitical, the imaginary" (41), erases both the feminine and the lower class. Her claims shake my confidence in some of what I say in the ensuing paragraph. (Am I capitulating to the patriarchal or finding moments of release? Does *The Secret Garden* merely indulge a sneaking American fondness for the aristocratic somewhat more subtly than does *Fauntleroy?*) But not entirely. For a contrasting view of the sexual politics of the story, see Adrian Gunther, *"The Secret Garden* Revisited," *Children's Literature in Education* 25 (1994): 159–68.

88. Phyllis Bixler Koppes, "Tradition and the Individual Talent of Frances Hodgson Burnett: A Generic Analysis of *Little Lord Fauntleroy, A Little Princess,* and *The Secret Garden," Children's Literature* 7 (1978): 191–207.

89. [Henry James], "A Poor Play Well Acted," *Pall Mall Gazette,* 24 October 1883, reprinted in *The Scenic Art: Notes on Acting and the Drama: 1872–1901,* ed. Allan Wade (New Brunswick, N.J.: Rutgers University Press, 1948), 195.

90. Or to translate the differences between James and Burnett into matters of class: Laski describes one of Burnett's novels for adults as a "poor man's James" (quoted in Thwaite, 198).

91. Quoted in Thwaite, 155.

92. Henry James to Frances Hodgson Burnett [undated], in *Selected Letters of Henry James,* ed. Leon Edel (London: Hart-Davis, 1956), 240.

93. [James], "Poor Play," 195.

94. Henry James to Frederick Macmillan, 30 December [1881], *The Correspondence of Henry James and the House of Macmillan, 1877–1914,* ed. Rayburn S. Moore (Baton Rouge: Louisiana State University Press, 1993), 68.

95. Henry James to Mrs. Hugh Bell, 7 January 1892, in *Letters,* ed. Leon Edel, vol. 3, 1883–95 (Cambridge: Belknap, Harvard University Press, 1980), 370; Henry James to Mrs. W. D. Howells, 24 February 1907, in *Letters,* ed. Leon Edel, vol. 4, 1895–1916 (Cambridge: Belknap, Harvard University Press, 1984), 440. (Mrs. E.D.E.N. Southworth was the author of sixty or so novels, including the best-selling *Hidden Hand.*)

96. Review of *Louisiana, Quarterly Review,* January and April 1883, 223.

97. Ibid., 213.

98. Felicity A. Hughes, "Children's Literature: Theory and Practice," *ELH* 45 (1978): 542–61.

99. "Henry James Dead at His London Home," *New York Times,* 29 February 1916, 11.

100. Vernon Louis Parrington, *The Beginnings of Critical Realism in America, 1860–1920, Completed to 1900 Only,* vol. 3 of *Main Currents in American Thought: An Interpretation of American Literature from the Beginnings to 1920* (New York: Harcourt, Brace, 1930), 240.

101. Richard A. Hocks, "Recanonizing the Multiple Canons of Henry James," in *American Realism and the Canon,* ed. Tom Quirk and Gary Scharnhorst (Newark: University of Delaware Press, 1994), 155.

102. Cynthia Ozick, "What Henry James Knew," *New Criterion,* January 1993, 17.

103. Robert E. Spiller, "Henry James," in *Eight American Authors: A Review of Research and Criticism,* ed. Floyd Stovall (New York: Norton, 1963), 378.

104. Quoted in "British Tribute to James," *New York Times,* 29 February 1916, 11.

105. Martin Kreisworth, "Henry James," in *The Johns Hopkins Guide to Literary Theory and Criticism,* ed. Michael Groden and Martin Kreisworth (Baltimore: Johns Hopkins University Press), www.press.jhu.edu/books/hopkins_guide_to_literary_theory, accessed February 1999.

106. Michael Anesko, *"Friction with the Market": Henry James and the Profession of Authorship* (New York: Oxford University Press, 1986); Mabie, 508–10; Hart, 356–57.

107. Since Mott's lists in *Golden Multitudes* record total sales to 1945, and hence may

overrepresent books that sold poorly when first published but then gained esteem (with sales as assigned reading in courses augmenting their numbers, perhaps), it's striking that James is entirely omitted. For additional accounts of popular polls and sales lists on which James makes a weak showing, see Jay B. Hubbell, *Who Are the Major American Writers?* (Durham: Duke University Press, 1972), 81, 84.

108. "A Hundred American Authors," *Critic*, 24 July 1886, 37; "Best American Books," *Critic*, 3 June 1893, 357.

109. Quoted in Muriel G. Shine, *The Fictional Children of Henry James* (Chapel Hill: University of North Carolina Press, 1969), 25.

110. Henry James, "The Belton Estate," *Nation*, 4 January 1866, reprinted in *Theory of Fiction: Henry James*, ed. James E. Miller, Jr. (Lincoln: University of Nebraska Press, 1972), 294.

111. Henry James, "Nana," *Parisian* (Paris), 26 February 1880, reprinted in Miller, 135.

112. Henry James, "Matilde Serao," *North American Review* 172 (March 1901), reprinted in Miller, 147.

113. Henry James, "The Future of the Novel," in *The International Library of Famous Literature*, ed. Richard Garnett (1899), reprinted in Miller, 337.

114. Henry James, "Robert Louis Stevenson" (1887), reprinted in *Partial Portraits* (London: Macmillan, 1894), 168, 171.

115. James, "Future of the Novel," 336–37.

116. This contrast is also noted by Lois R. Kuznets in "Henry James and the Storyteller: The Development of a Central Consciousness in Realistic Fiction for Children," in *The Voice of the Narrator in Children's Literature: Insights from Writers and Critics*, ed. Charlotte F. Otten and Gary D. Schmidt (New York: Greenwood, 1989), 188.

117. Marcia Jacobson views both Burnett's autobiography *The One I Knew the Best of All* and James's *What Maisie Knew* as participating in a phenomenon of the 1890s: the child novel, a work that features children, usually (though not in *Maisie*) to indulge in nostalgia (*Henry James and the Mass Market* [Tuscaloosa: University of Alabama Press, 1983], 100–120). Jacobson finds strong echoes of Burnett's autobiography in *Maisie* (117–18).

118. Henry James, "The Pupil," in *Great Short Works of Henry James*, introd. Dean Flower (New York: Harper, 1966), 326.

119. W. C. Brownell, "Henry James," *Atlantic*, April 1905, reprinted in *Henry James: The Critical Heritage*, ed. Roger Gard (London: Routledge, 1968), 401.

120. Henry James, *What Maisie Knew* (1909; reprint, Harmondsworth, England: Penguin, 1973), 8. *Maisie* was initially published in 1897 and then revised for the 1909 New York edition of James's works. Subsequent references to this reprinted edition are cited as *Maisie*; references to James's preface to this edition are cited as *preface*.

121. Dan McCall, "What Maisie Saw," *Henry James Review* 16 (1995): 50.

122. Juliet Mitchell, "*What Maisie Knew*: Portrait of the Artist as a Young Girl," in *The Air of Reality: New Essays on Henry James*, ed. John Goode (London: Methuen, 1972), 181. Or one might see a "'delicate homosexuality' often confused with . . . homosociality in Victorian culture" (John Carlos Rowe, *The Other Henry James* [Durham: Duke University Press, 1998], 129).

123. Another way in which Maisie defies age categories is that it's difficult to assign a final age to her by the end of the novel. Have a couple of years passed? Several? A decade? As Barbara Everett notes, James "invents his own chronologies," Maisie growing from six

to perhaps sixteen psychologically, whatever she grows chronologically ("Henry James's Children," in *Children and Their Books: A Celebration of the Work of Iona and Peter Opie*, ed. Gillian Avery and Julia Briggs [Oxford: Clarendon Press, 1989], 332). Or as James himself noted, "I must handle freely and handsomely the years—treat my *intervals* with art and courage; master the little secrets in regard to the expression of duration—be superior I mean, on the question of time" (22 December 1895, *The Complete Notebooks of Henry James*, ed. Leon Edel and Lyall H. Powers [New York: Oxford University Press, 1987], 149).

124. Though, of course, whether Maisie's choice is indeed the right one has been grist for critical debate, especially in the mid twentieth century. Could her offer to go off alone with Sir Claude be in fact a sexual proposition? Is Maisie innocent or not? See, e.g., Harris W. Wilson, "What *Did* Maisie Know?" *College English* 17 (February 1956): 279–82; Edward Wasiolek, "Maisie: Pure or Corrupt?" *College English* 22 (December 1960): 167–72.

125. Henry James, review, *North American Review*, July 1865, reprinted in *Critical Essays on Louisa May Alcott*, ed. Madeleine B. Stern (Boston: Hall, 1984), 69–70.

126. Henry James to T. S. Perry, 24 January 1881, in *Letters*, ed. Leon Edel, vol. 2, 1875–83 (Cambridge: Belknap, Harvard University Press, 1975), 335.

127. Everett, 318, 324.

128. M. A. Williams, "The Drama of Maisie's Vision," *Henry James Review* 2 (Fall 1980): 48.

129. Shine, 124.

130. Julie Rivkin, "Resisting Readers and Reading Effects: Some Speculations on Reading and Gender," *Papers in Comparative Studies* 5 (1987): 19. Rivkin goes on, however, to emphasize Maisie's resistances.

131. Sara Blair, "In the House of Fiction: Henry James and the Engendering of Literary Mastery," in *Henry James's New York Edition: The Construction of Authorship*, ed. David McWhirter (Stanford: Stanford University Press, 1995), 70.

132. Henry James, preface, *The Ambassador* (1909; reprint, Boston: Houghton Mifflin, 1960), 3.

133. Review of *What Maisie Knew*, *Academy* (fiction suppl.), October 1897, reprinted in Gard, 269; review of *The Awkward Age*, *Critic*, August 1899, reprinted in Gard, 296.

134. *Providence Sunday Journal*, 31 October 1897, reprinted in Linda J. Taylor, *Henry James, 1866–1916: A Reference Guide* (Boston: Hall, 1982), 254.

135. *Spectator*, October 1897, reprinted in Gard, 270; *Literary World*, December 1897, reprinted in Gard, 273.

136. Consider, for example, the following: "To him [James] she [Maisie] is merely the *raison d'être* of a curiously complicated situation, which he can twist and untwist for purposes of fiction" (*Literary World*, in Gard, 272).

137. *Spectator*, in Gard, 270–71.

138. *Literary World*, in Gard, 272.

139. *Critic*, 8 January 1898, reprinted in *Henry James: The Contemporary Reviews*, ed. Kevin J. Hayes (Cambridge: Cambridge University Press, 1996), 296. For Stephen Spender in 1934, "There is something particularly obscene about *What Maisie Knew*, in which a small girl is, in a rather admiring way, exhibited as prying into the sexual lives of her very promiscuous elders. For what else does the subject amount to, unless we are entirely absorbed by the beautiful surface of James's art?" ("The School of Experience in the Early Novels," *Hound and Horn*, April/May 1934, 432).

140. H. G. Dwight, "Henry James—'In His Own Country,'" *Putnam's*, May and July 1907, reprinted in Gard, 435.

141. Edmund Wilson, "The Ambiguity of Henry James," *Hound and Horn*, April/May 1934, revised and reprinted in his *The Triple Thinkers* (1938), reprinted in *The Question of Henry James*, ed. F. W. Dupee (London: Wingate, 1947), 192.

142. Marius Bewley, "Appearance and Reality in Henry James," *Scrutiny* 17 (Spring 1950): 113.

143. Henry James to Mme Paul Bourget, cited in Ward S. Worden, "Henry James's *What Maisie Knew*: A Comparison with the Plans in *The Notebooks*," *PMLA* 68 (April 1953): 383.

144. Ruth Bernard Yeazell, "Henry James," in *Columbia Literary History of the United States*, ed. Emory Elliot et al. (New York: Columbia University Press, 1988), 685.

145. Everett, 325, 321.

146. Alfred Habegger, *Henry James and the "Woman Business"* (Cambridge: Cambridge University Press, 1989), 234.

147. Lynn Wardley, "Henry James in the Nineties," *New England Quarterly* 67 (March 1994): 142.

148. Hocks, 159.

149. Rowe, 23.

150. Brownell, 421.

151. H. G. Wells, *Boon, the Mind of the Race* (1915), excerpt reprinted in Gard, 519.

152. E. Wilson, 194, 191.

153. Brownell, 414.

154. Van Wyck Brooks, "Two Phases of Henry James," in his *The Pilgrimage of Henry James* (1925), reprinted in Dupee, 139.

155. Max Beerbohm, *A Christmas Garland*, reprinted in Dupee, 61.

156. In psychoanalytic terms, what James does is *"use* the feminine orphan provisionally to help him escape dysfunction" (William Veeder, "The Feminine Orphan and the Emergent Master: Self-Realization in Henry James," *Henry James Review* 21 [1991]: 49).

157. Everett, 325; E. Wilson, 194; Everett, 333.

THREE: Kiddie Lit in the Academy

1. Henry Steele Commager, "When Majors Wrote for Minors," *Saturday Review*, 10 May 1952, 10, 11.

2. Jerry Griswold, *Audacious Kids: Coming of Age in America's Classic Children's Books* (New York: Oxford University Press, 1992), vii.

3. Henry James's work appears on none of the lists of best-sellers (works that had total sales equaling 1 percent of the population) or better-sellers (works that almost did) compiled by Frank Luther Mott for books sold in the United States before 1945 (*Golden Multitudes: The Story of Best Sellers in the United States* [New York: Macmillan, 1947]). *Moby-Dick* did eventually achieve best-seller status, but only because of its twentieth-century sales; it was "a very poor seller indeed when it first appeared" (131).

4. See David L. Greene, "*The Youth's Companion*," in *Children's Periodicals of the United States*, ed. R. Gordon Kelly (Westport, Conn.: Greenwood, 1984), 511.

5. Lovell Thompson, ed., *Youth's Companion* (Boston: Houghton Mifflin, 1954). For

comparable lists of contributors to the children's periodicals *Our Young Folks* and *St. Nicholas*, see, respectively, Gillian Avery, *Behold the Child: American Children and Their Books, 1621–1922* (Baltimore: Johns Hopkins University Press, 1994), 146; and Griswold, *Audacious Kids*, 188.

6. See Frank Luther Mott, *A History of American Magazines, 1865–1885*, vol. 3 of *A History of American Magazines* (Cambridge: Harvard University Press, 1938), 457–58.

7. Quoted in Frank Luther Mott, *A History of American Magazines, 1850–1865*, vol. 2 of *History of American Magazines*, 401.

8. Richard L. Darling, *The Rise of Children's Book Reviewing in America, 1865–1881* (New York: Bowker, 1968), 250. For discussion of reviewing in the United States and England during the last two decades of the nineteenth century, a study that similarly notes the overlap between literature for adults and that for children, see Anne H. Lundin, "Victorian Horizons: The Reception of Children's Books in England and America, 1880–1900," *Library Quarterly* 64 (January 1994): 30–59.

9. Mary Harris Veeder, "Journalistic Reviewing and Children's Books: A Personal and Professional Perspective," *The Lion and the Unicorn* 16 (1992): 84. As Marc Aronson notes, "The daily papers, the Sunday review sections, and the weekly or monthly magazines pay halfhearted, impossibly delayed, or summary attention to the field," the *New York Times Book Review* often offering capsule reviews of award-winning books months after the books were first published ("Not a Necessary Purchase: The Journals Judged," *Horn Book*, July/August 1997, 427–28).

10. For a different view of the relationship between children's literature and canonicity, one that focuses not on the academy but on a popular canon, a canon of sentiment rather than of significance, see Deborah Stevenson, "Sentiment and Significance: The Impossibility of Recovery in the Children's Literature Canon or, the Drowning of *The Water-Babies*," *The Lion and the Unicorn*, 21 (1997): 112–30.

11. Julian Hawthorne, "Man-Books," *America*, 27 September 1888, 11.

12. Nathaniel Hawthorne to William D. Ticknor, 19 January 1855, in *The Letters, 1853–1856*, ed. Thomas Woodson et al., vol. 17 of *The Centenary Edition of the Works of Nathaniel Hawthorne* ([Columbus]: Ohio State University Press, 1987), 304; Boyesen quoted in Robert E. Spiller, Willard Thorp, Thomas H. Johnson, and Henry Seidel Canby, eds.; Howard Mumford Jones, Dixon Wecter, and Stanley T. Williams, assoc. eds., *Literary History of the United States* (New York: Macmillan, 1948), 3 vols., 1:518; J. Hawthorne, 12.

13. Nina Baym, *Novels, Readers, and Reviewers: Responses to Fiction in Antebellum America* (Ithaca: Cornell University Press, 1984), 28, 50. Cathy N. Davidson documents that the audience for American novels before 1820 was similarly mixed: "they were often targeted specifically for children, women, or a new and relatively untutored readership, not for the intellectual elite" (*Revolution and the Word: The Rise of the Novel in America* [New York: Oxford University Press, 1986], 70).

14. Review of *White-Jacket*, by Herman Melville, *Spirit of the Times*, 6 April 1850, reprinted in *Herman Melville: The Contemporary Reviews*, ed. Brian Higgins and Hershel Parker (Cambridge: Cambridge University Press, 1995), 330.

15. J. Hawthorne, 11.

16. See review of *Typee*, *Albion*, 4 April 1846, quoted in Hugh W. Hetherington, *Melville's Reviewers: British and American, 1846–1891* (Chapel Hill: University of North Carolina Press, 1961), 53; William Charvat, *The Profession of Authorship in America*,

1800–1870, ed. Matthew J. Bruccoli ([Columbus]: Ohio State University Press, 1968), 212.

17. *Douglas Jerrold's Shilling Magazine*, April 1846, reprinted in Higgins and Parker, 30.

18. Review of *Omoo*, *Columbian Magazine*, June 1847, reprinted in Higgins and Parker, 124.

19. [Evert Duyckinck], review of *Redburn*, *Literary World*, 17 November 1849, reprinted in Higgins and Parker, 277; review of *Mardi*, New York *Evening Mirror*, 13 April 1849, reprinted in Higgins and Parker, 207; and "A Trio of American Sailor-Authors," reprinted in *The Recognition of Herman Melville: Selected Criticism Since 1846*, ed. Hershel Parker (Ann Arbor: University of Michigan Press, 1967), 81.

20. *Boston Post*, 2 October 1891, reprinted in *Moby-Dick as Doubloon: Essays and Extracts (1851–1970)*, ed. Hershel Parker and Harrison Hayford (New York: Norton, 1970), 111. Paul Lauter traces the continuing characterization of Melville's audience as youthful to the eve of the Melville revival in 1919, adding that the shift in reputation at this time had everything to do with "the validation of boys' tastes in men['s] criticism" ("Melville Climbs the Canon," *American Literature* 66 [March 1994]: 16–17).

21. *Athenaeum*, 26 July 1856, reprinted in Higgins and Parker, 481; Hetherington, 150, 285. Hetherington's contemporary William Charvat, an early scholar of the history of the book, is more measured when he notes in passing that a Cleveland bookseller advertised *Typee* and *Omoo* as "Books for Little Folks," though Charvat also refers to the then "unstratified literary market" as a problem (262, 265).

22. Quoted in Jack Salzman, "Literature for the Populace," in *Columbia Literary History of the United States*, ed. Emory Elliott et al. (New York: Columbia University Press, 1988), 552.

23. Barbara Sicherman, "Sense and Sensibility: A Case Study of Women's Reading in Late-Victorian America," in *Reading in America: Literature and Social History*, ed. Cathy N. Davidson (Baltimore: Johns Hopkins University Press, 1989), 208, 222 n. 41.

24. Horace E. Scudder, *Childhood in Literature and Art, with Some Observations on Literature for Children: A Study* (Boston: Houghton, Mifflin, 1895), 178.

25. Clarence Gohdes, "The *Atlantic* Celebrates its Hundredth Birthday," *South Atlantic Quarterly* 57 (Spring 1958): 163.

26. Ellen B. Ballou, "Horace Elisha Scudder and the *Riverside Magazine*," *Harvard Library Bulletin* 14 (Autumn 1960): 429.

27. See Nancy Glazener, *Reading for Realism: The History of a U.S. Literary Institution, 1850–1910* (Durham: Duke University Press, 1997), esp. 43.

28. Jerry Griswold, "Children's Literature in the USA: A Historical Overview," in *International Companion Encyclopedia of Children's Literature*, ed. Peter Hunt (London: Routledge, 1996), 874. As for the late nineteenth century, "What could be better suited for the Americanizing of the young immigrant, some argued, than a literature authored by native-born Americans—preferably of several generations' descent—composed in English, expressing American values and representing American themes and events? What more likely to deflect the (usually foreign-born) poor from their desire to have a substantial piece of the country's settled wealth than exposure to an idealism from whose lofty perspective the materialist struggle would seem unworthy?" (Nina Baym, "Early Histories of American Literature: A Chapter in the Institution of New England," *American Literary History* 1 [Fall 1989]: 462).

29. "Mr. Scudder and the Atlantic," *Atlantic*, March 1902, 433.

30. Horace E. Scudder, diary, 17 June 1890, quoted in Ellery Sedgwick, *The Atlantic Monthly, 1857–1909: Yankee Humanism at High Tide and Ebb* (Amherst: University of Massachusetts Press, 1994), 206.

31. Scudder, *Childhood*, 180.

32. Alexander V. G. Allen, "Horace E. Scudder: An Appreciation," *Atlantic*, April 1903, 556.

33. Ibid., 555.

34. Quoted in Ellen B. Ballou, *The Building of the House: Houghton Mifflin's Formative Years* (Boston: Houghton Mifflin, 1970), 262.

35. Scudder, *Childhood*, 220.

36. H. L. Mencken, "The Dean," *Smart Set*, January 1917, revised and reprinted in his *A Mencken Chrestomathy* (New York: Knopf, 1949), 490.

37. W. D. Howells, *Criticism and Fiction* (New York: Harper, 1891), 160; letter to Brander Matthews (1880), quoted in E. Sedgwick, 151.

38. [William Dean Howells], review of *The Story of a Bad Boy*, by Thomas Bailey Aldrich, *Atlantic*, January 1870, 124.

39. Ibid.

40. [William Dean Howells], review of *Adventures of Tom Sawyer*, by Mark Twain, *Atlantic*, May 1876, 621.

41. [William Dean Howells], review of *Being a Boy*, by Charles Dudley Warner, *Atlantic*, December 1877, 764.

42. Horace E. Scudder, "Literature in the Public Schools," *Atlantic*, August 1888, 226. See also his "Nursery Classics in School," *Atlantic*, June 1887, 800–803; and "American Classics in School," *Atlantic*, July 1887, 85–91.

43. Charles Dudley Warner, *Critic*, 16 January 1897, 48. See also Lundin, 40–42.

44. Hamilton W. Mabie, "Reading for Children," *Outlook*, 17 April 1897, 1026.

45. Everett T. Tomlinson, "Reading for Boys and Girls," *Atlantic*, November 1900, 693, 694.

46. Ibid., 698.

47. Bliss Perry, *And Gladly Teach* (Boston: Houghton Mifflin, 1935), 182.

48. Bliss Perry, "The Centenary of Longfellow," *Atlantic*, March 1907, 387, 388. The prevalence of this way of thinking about Longfellow, in the early twentieth century, is underscored by the title of a ten-volume collection of literature for children published by Houghton Mifflin in the same year: the collection is called *The Children's Hour*.

49. E. Sedgwick, 300.

50. Perry, *Gladly Teach*, 166.

51. Paul Lauter, "Race and Gender in the Shaping of the American Literary Canon: A Case Study from the Twenties," *Feminist Studies* 9 (1983), reprinted in his *Canons and Contexts* (New York: Oxford University Press, 1991), 22–47.

52. Richard H. Brodhead, *The School of Hawthorne* (New York: Oxford University Press, 1986), 210.

53. Elizabeth Renker, "Resistance and Change: The Rise of American Literature Studies," *American Literature* 64 (1992): 358. Sometimes, paradoxically, proponents of the field use the metaphor of rebirth—of renaissance—to mark its new stature (see Charlene Avallone, "What American Renaissance? The Gendered Genealogy of a Critical Discourse," *PMLA* 112 [October 1997]: 1102–20).

54. See Griswold, *Audacious Kids*, 13–15. For a parallel argument, focused on British literary traditions and addressing the emergence of the "serious" novel as it dissociated itself from children and women around the turn of the century, see Felicity A. Hughes, "Children's Literature: Theory and Practice," *ELH* 45 (1978): 542–61.

55. Marian Wright Edelman, introduction, *The Best of the "Brownies' Book,"* ed. Dianne Johnson-Feelings (New York: Oxford University Press, 1996), 10–11. Du Bois later looked back on the short-lived magazine as one of two efforts in which he found "infinite satisfaction" (quoted in Johnson-Feelings, afterword, *Best*, 346).

56. Melville, of course, was read by children, as I've already suggested. He also apparently promised Scudder something for the *Riverside Magazine for Young People*, but nothing ever came of that promise (see Ballou, "Scudder," 437).

57. For useful accounts of this professionalization and of the positioning of American literature in the academy, see Gerald Graff, *Professing Literature: An Institutional History* (Chicago: University of Chicago Press, 1987); David R. Shumway, *Creating American Civilization: A Genealogy of American Literature as an Academic Discipline* (Minneapolis: University of Minnesota Press, 1994); and Kermit Vanderbilt, *American Literature and the Academy: The Roots, Growth, and Maturity of a Profession* (Philadelphia: University of Pennsylvania Press, 1986).

58. As Jacqueline Rose has stated in another context, in *The Case of Peter Pan, or the Impossibility of Children's Fiction* (1984; reprint, Philadelphia: University of Pennsylvania Press, 1993), 8.

59. Ronald S. Crane, "The Vogue of *Guy of Warwick* from the Close of the Middle Ages to the Romantic Revival," *PMLA* 30 (1915): 194.

60. A fourth compendium is currently in progress: four of the eight volumes of a new *Cambridge History of American Literature* have so far appeared—not enough yet to be able to draw clear conclusions.

61. William Peterfield Trent, John Erskine, Stuart P. Sherman, and Carl Van Doren, eds., *The Cambridge History of American Literature* (1917–21; reprint, New York: Macmillan, 1958), 4 vols., preface, 1:iii.

62. Spiller et al., 1:xiv.

63. E.g., Tremaine McDowell, addressing another fireside poet, William Cullen Bryant, finds much to praise in him for his Americanness, even, as it were, his "New Englandness": in Bryant's poetry "New England found its authentic voice," and "his nationalism was more consistent than that of Catharine Sedgwick or John Neal and more solidly grounded than that of any contemporary New Englander except Channing" (in Spiller et al., 1:284, 304). So much for Sedgwick and Neal.

64. Spiller et al., 1:595.

65. Nina Baym, "Melodramas of Beset Manhood: How Theories of American Fiction Exclude Women Authors," *American Quarterly* 33 (1981), reprinted in *The New Feminist Criticism: Essays on Women, Literature, and Theory*, ed. Elaine Showalter (New York: Pantheon, 1985), 63–80.

66. Emory Elliott, ed.; Martha Banta, Terence Martin, David Minter, Marjorie Perloff, and Daniel B. Shea, assoc. eds.; Houston A. Baker, Nina Baym, Sacvan Bercovitch, and Louis D. Rubin, Jr., advisory eds., *Columbia Literary History of the United States* (New York: Columbia University Press, 1988), preface, xiii.

67. See Robert D. Leigh, *The Public Library in the United States* (New York: Columbia University Press, 1950), 99.

68. For historical background on U.S. library service to children, see, e.g., Harriet G. Long, *Public Library Service to Children: Foundation and Development* (Metuchen, N.J.: Scarecrow, 1969); Elizabeth Nesbitt, "Major Steps Forward," in *A Critical History of Children's Literature: A Survey of Children's Books in English*, rev. ed., ed. Cornelia Meigs (London: Macmillan, 1969), 384–90.

69. Dee Garrison, *Apostles of Culture: The Public Librarian and American Society, 1876–1920* (New York: Free Press, 1979), 180.

70. For another account of how "children's and adult literature had begun to diverge" by 1910, one that sees "the professionalization of children's literature" as having "a gradual but profound effect on children's reading"—and hence gives it a more directly causal role than I do—see Anne Scott MacLeod, *American Childhood: Essays on Children's Literature of the Nineteenth and Twentieth Centuries* (Athens: University of Georgia Press, 1994), 124. MacLeod substantiates the existence of a shared culture of adult-and-child reading around the turn of the century, but she claims that it existed for only a couple of decades, following and followed by periods of greater segregation.

71. Leonard S. Marcus, *Margaret Wise Brown: Awakened by the Moon* (Boston: Beacon, 1992), 54; Barbara Bader, *"Only* the Best: The Hits and Misses of Anne Carroll Moore," *Horn Book* 73 (September/October 1997): 520; Frances Clarke Sayers, *Anne Carroll Moore* (New York: Atheneum, 1972), 258; Margaret K. McElderry, "Remarkable Women: Remembering Anne Carroll Moore and Company," *School Library Journal* 38 (March 1992): 160.

72. Marcus, 55.

73. See Sayers, 89, 215.

74. Anne Carroll Moore to Herbert Jenkins, 6 February 1936, quoted in Julie Cummins, "'Let Her Sound Her Trumpet': NYPL Children's Librarians and Their Impact on the World of Publishing," *Biblion* 4 (Fall 1995): 98. The files of the New York Public Library contain letters to Moore from more than 350 editors, publishers, authors, and educators (Cummins, 95).

75. George Dutton to Anne Carroll Moore, 28 August 1913, quoted in Cummins, 90.

76. Anne Carroll Moore to Virginie Fowler, 13 July 1956, quoted in Cummins, 107.

77. Letter of 11 April 1938, quoted in Karen Nelson Hoyle, *Wanda Gág* (New York: Twayne, 1994), 75.

78. Letter of 27 April 1938, quoted in Hoyle, 76.

79. Ernestine Evans to Anne Carroll Moore, 16 March 1929, quoted in Cummins, 98. Evans was contemplating an illustrated and abridged *Uncle Tom's Cabin*.

80. "A Publisher's Perspective," *Horn Book* 65 (May/June 1987): 372.

81. Quoted in Marcus, *Brown*, 102.

82. Anne Carroll Moore to E. B. White, 20 June 1945, quoted in Sayers, 244.

83. Leonore St. John Power, "Recollections of Anne Carroll Moore," *Bulletin of the New York Public Library* 60 (November/December 1956): 626.

84. Leonard S. Marcus, "An Interview with Susan Hirschman: Part II," *Horn Book* 72 (May/June 1996): 282, ellipsis in original.

85. Bader, 528.

86. Anne Carroll Moore, *Roads to Childhood: Views and Reviews of Children's Books* (New York: Doran, 1920), 23; Anne Carroll Moore, *New Roads to Childhood* (New York: Doran, 1923), ix.

87. Kay E. Vandergrift, "Female Advocacy and Harmonious Voices: A History of

Public Library Services and Publishing for Children in the United States," *Library Trends* 44 (Spring 1996): 695. More recently, a 1964 survey revealed that the most important single influence on a book editor's decision to publish a children's book was "librarians' requests or comments," and in 1978 a children's publisher stated, "Librarians are very important to us because they are the ones who bring books to children" (quoted in Joseph Turow, *Getting Books to Children: An Exploration of Publisher-Market Relations* [Chicago: American Library Association, 1978], 9, 21).

88. Margaret McElderry, "The Best of Times, the Worst of Times," *Horn Book* 50 (October 1974): 87.

89. Moore, *Roads*, 75.

90. Moore's words, in *Roads*, 72.

91. "Books for the Young," *Dial*, 1 December 1901, 449. Moore herself, underscoring the differences in publishing in 1920 and four decades earlier, remarked, "With a few notable exceptions novels of the twentieth century are being written for a sophisticated middle-aged audience" (*Roads*, 175).

92. See M. P. Dunleavey, "The Crest of the Wave?" *Publishers Weekly*, 19 July 1993, 31; Kera Bolonik, "A List of Their Own," *Salon*, 16 August 2000, 3, www.salon.com/mwt/feature/2000/08/16/bestseller/index.html, accessed 22 January 2001; Turow, 8.

93. E. J. Graff pegs the sales value of the Newbery at a hundred thousand ("A Gold Star for Tedium: Do the Newbery Medal-Winning Children's Books Really Have to Be So Dreary?" *Salon*, 25 January 2001, www.salon.com/books/feature/2001/01/25/newbery/print.html, accessed 28 January 2001.

94. See Donnarae MacCann, "Effie Lee Newsome: African American Poet of the 1920s," *Children's Literature Association Quarterly* 13 (1988): 64–65.

95. E.g., Donnarae MacCann and Gloria Woodard, eds., *The Black American in Books for Children: Readings in Racism*, 2d ed. (Metuchen, N.J.: Scarecrow, 1985); Donnarae MacCann and Gloria Woodard, eds., *Cultural Conformity in Books for Children: Further Readings in Racism* (Metuchen, N.J.: Scarecrow, 1977); Betty Bacon, ed., *How Much Truth Do We Tell the Children? The Politics of Children's Literature* (Minneapolis: MEP, 1988); Arlene B. Hirschfelder, ed., *American Indian Stereotypes in the World of Children: A Reader and Bibliography* (Metuchen, N.J.: Scarecrow, 1982).

96. Renker, 358.

97. Garrison, 173, 26.

98. Not that librarians haven't in fact written "real"—and "good"—"literary criticism." The best book-length overview of nineteenth-century U.S. children's literature, at least until Griswold's, is probably librarian Alice M. Jordan's *From Rollo to Tom Sawyer*, published in 1948.

99. In 1998 the MLA screened *Bookbird, The Journal of Youth Services in Libraries, Horn Book Magazine, Language Arts, New Advocate, Five Owls, Voice of Youth Advocates,* and *Signal;* it seems to have continued screening only *Bookbird, Language Arts,* and *Signal.*

FOUR: The Case of the Boys' Book

1. T. S. Eliot, introduction, *The Adventures of Huckleberry Finn* (London: Cresset, 1950), reprinted in *Adventures of Huckleberry Finn: An Authoritative Text, Backgrounds and Sources, Criticism,* ed. Sculley Bradley, Richmond Croom Beatty, E. Hudson Long, and Thomas Cooley, 2d ed. (New York: Norton, 1977), 328. Like most other influential

pieces of Twain criticism, this essay has been reprinted more than once in the scores of collections of Twainiana and Twain criticism.

For most items of criticism that I cite in this chapter, I will list both the original source and one of the subsequent reprintings (if there is one); the latter is often more generally accessible—and the cumulative effect of such listings hints at the extent of the current Twain industry. I might add as well that in most cases I'm simply citing representative critics from the scores available.

2. Charles Johnston, "The Essence of American Humor," *Atlantic*, February 1901, 199. For additional accounts of mergings, see Louis J. Budd, "The Recomposition of *Adventures of Huckleberry Finn*," *Missouri Review* 10 (1987), reprinted in *The Critical Response to Mark Twain's "Huckleberry Finn,"* ed. Laurie Champion (New York: Greenwood, 1991), 199.

3. Frank Luther Mott, *Golden Multitudes: The Story of Best Sellers in the United States* (New York: Macmillan, 1947), 157; John C. Gerber, "Introduction: The Continuing Adventures of *Huckleberry Finn*," in *One Hundred Years of "Huckleberry Finn": The Boy, His Book, and American Culture*, ed. Robert Sattelmeyer and J. Donald Crowley (Columbia: University of Missouri Press, 1985), 2.

4. Irving Harlem Hart, "The Phenomena of Popularity in Fiction," *Library Journal*, 15 April 1923, 356. The top circulators were *The Three Musketeers, Treasure Island*, and *Les Misérables*.

5. Charles H. Compton, "Who Reads Mark Twain?" *American Mercury*, April 1934, 465; the second study is cited in Esther Jane Carrier, *Fiction in the Public Libraries, 1900–1950* (Littleton, Colo.: Libraries Unlimited, 1985), 206.

6. Carleton Washburne and Mabel Vogel, *Winnetka Graded Book List* (Chicago: American Library Association, 1926). *Tom Sawyer* is marked with an asterisk in the listing, to indicate its "unusually high literary value"; *Huckleberry Finn* is not.

7. For the second- and ninth-place finishes in 1927, see Louise Seaman Bechtel, "The Giant in Children," *Atlantic* (1927), reprinted in her *Books in Search of Children* (1940; reprint, n.p.: Macmillan, 1969), 146. The rest of the surveys are cited in Carrier, 288–90, 284–86, 287, 284–86, 246, 284–86, 291–92, 284–86, 284–86.

8. See Bernice Cullinan and M. Jerry Weiss, eds., *Books I Read When I Was Young: The Favorite Books of Famous People* (New York: Avon, 1980); "Uncle Wiggily's Karma and Other Childhood Memories," *New York Times Book Review*, 7 December 1986, 46–47.

9. For useful accounts of Twain's hold on the popular imagination, see Louis J. Budd, "Mark Twain as an American Icon," in *The Cambridge Companion to Mark Twain*, ed. Forrest G. Robinson (Cambridge: Cambridge University Press, 1995), 1–26; Shelley Fisher Fishkin, *Lighting out for the Territory: Reflections on Mark Twain and American Culture* (New York: Oxford University Press, 1997), 127–81.

10. Mark Twain to William Dean Howells, 21 June 1875, *Mark Twain–Howells Letters: The Correspondence of Samuel L. Clemens and William D. Howells, 1872–1910*, ed. Henry Nash Smith and William M. Gibson, with the assistance of Frederick Anderson (Cambridge: Belknap, Harvard University Press, 1960), 2 vols., 1:87–88. Subsequent references to letters are given parenthetically in the text.

11. Complicating Howells's position is his role as editor of the *Atlantic*: his early urging of an adult focus seems connected to the possibility that the book might appear serially in the *Atlantic*. When that was no longer likely—Twain feared that serial publication would detract from book sales—Howells was more ready to consider *Tom Sawyer* a book

for boys, because he considered works addressed to children either inferior or simply not suitable for the *Atlantic*. The editors of the Iowa Center/University of California edition of *Tom Sawyer* point out that neither the British nor the American publishers chose specifically to target children as an audience (John C. Gerber, introduction, *The Adventures of Tom Sawyer; Tom Sawyer Abroad; Tom Sawyer, Detective*, ed. John C. Gerber, Paul Baender, and Terry Firkins, vol. 4 of *The Works of Mark Twain*, Iowa Center for Textual Studies [Berkeley: University of California Press, 1980], 19, 25 n. 53).

12. Mark Twain, preface, *The Adventures of Tom Sawyer* (1876; reprint, New York: Airmont, 1962), 6. For an illuminating discussion of Twain's use of contrasting constructions of childhood in *Tom Sawyer*, see Gillian Brown, "Child's Play," *differences* 11 (1999): 76–106, esp. 94–101.

13. See Leslie A. Fiedler, *No! In Thunder: Essays on Myth and Literature*, 2d ed. (1971; reprint, New York: Stein, 1972), 271.

14. These representative excuses are set forth by Lionel Trilling, in his introduction to an edition of the *Adventures of Huckleberry Finn* (New York: Holt, 1948), reprinted in Bradley et al., 319. The uneasiness of his dismissal of Twain's claim for *Tom Sawyer*, in particular, is underscored by the shifts Trilling must go on to make: Twain's statement is simply a "way of asserting, with a discernible touch of irritation, the degree of truth he had achieved" in the book, though of course Twain's usual view is not that adults have a greater affinity for truth than boys do, but quite the opposite—even if boys can be "profound liars in their own defense."

15. Gary Scharnhorst, introduction, *Critical Essays on "The Adventures of Tom Sawyer,"* ed. Gary Scharnhorst (New York: Hall, 1993), 4; Mark Twain, 7 July 1902, quoted in Albert E. Stone, Jr., *The Innocent Eye: Childhood in Mark Twain's Imagination* (New Haven: Yale University Press, 1961), 60.

16. Stone, 60.

17. Louis J. Budd, ed., *Mark Twain: The Contemporary Reviews* (Cambridge: Cambridge University Press, 1999).

18. *New York Times*, 13 January 1877, reprinted in Scharnhorst, *Critical Essays*, 57.

19. W. D. Howells, *Criticism and Fiction* (New York: Harper, 1891), 83, 98–99.

20. Moncure D. Conway, *Examiner* (London), 17 June 1876, reprinted in Scharnhorst, *Critical Essays*, 25. Another reviewer, anticipating critical maneuvers in the late twentieth century, is almost willing to dismiss children in favor of an adult readership: the book "is said to be written for boys. It is a masterly reproduction of boy's life and feeling, but, at the same time, it is written above boys: that is, the best part of it—the wit, the humor, the genius of it will fly miles above every boy's head in the country" (*Hartford Daily Courant*, 27 December 1876, reprinted in Scharnhorst, *Critical Essays*, 50). The review appeared in Twain's hometown newspaper; Scharnhorst lists Twain's friend Charles Dudley Warner as the probable author.

21. At this point it quietly dropped off. See Marion E. Potter, assisted by Bertha Tannehill and Emma L. Teich, *The Children's Catalog: A Guide to the Best Reading for Young People Based on Twenty-Four Selected Library Lists* (Minneapolis: Wilson, 1909); "One Hundred Story Books for Children," *Bookman* (New York), November 1922, 367; American Library Association, *The Right Book for the Right Child: A Graded Buying List of Children's Books* (New York: Day, 1933); and Laura E. Richards, *What Shall the Children Read?* (New York: Appleton-Century, 1939), 49—all of which recommend *Tom Sawyer* and

Huckleberry Finn as well. In 1960, however, J. Sherwood Weber, in *Good Reading*, rev. ed. (New York: Mentor, 1960), 121–22, sponsored by the College English Association, recommends only *Tom Sawyer, Huckleberry Finn, A Connecticut Yankee in King Arthur's Court,* and *Pudd'nhead Wilson.* Perhaps it's significant that in the various early-twentieth-century polls of children's favorites, where *Tom Sawyer* and *Huckleberry Finn* fare so well, *The Prince and the Pauper* figures much less prominently.

22. The reviewer for the *Atlantic,* for instance, proclaims that the book "is by no means a tale exclusively for children" ([H. H. Boyesen], *Atlantic,* December 1881, reprinted in Budd, *Contemporary Reviews,* 200). The reviewer for the *British Quarterly Review,* nervous whether "this sort of writing"—quasi-historical, both satirical and matter-of-fact—"in ordinary hands would be advisable for the young of any age," concludes that this work proves to be "an exception" and attests to its accessibility to the young, "having tried it on some youngsters" (*British Quarterly Review,* January [and April] 1882, reprinted in Budd, *Contemporary Reviews,* 209). A decade later William Peterfield Trent, who would subsequently coedit the *Cambridge History of American Literature,* refers to *The Prince and the Pauper* as a "juvenile classic, which has charmed many an older reader" (review of *Personal Recollections of Joan of Arc,* by Mark Twain, *Bookman* (New York), May 1896, reprinted in Frederick Anderson, ed., with the assistance of Kenneth M. Sanderson, *Mark Twain: The Critical Heritage* [New York: Barnes, 1971], 187).

23. *Critic,* 31 December 1881, reprinted in Budd, *Contemporary Reviews,* 208.

24. Howells, *Criticism,* 128.

25. [Edwin Pond Parker], *Hartford Courant,* 28 December 1881, reprinted in Budd, *Contemporary Reviews,* 205; Mary Mason Fairbanks to Mark Twain, 4 January 1882, quoted in Lin Salamo, introduction, *The Prince and the Pauper,* ed. Victor Fischer and Lin Salamo, with the assistance of Mary Jane Jones, vol. 6 of *Works of Mark Twain,* (1979), 13; [Boyesen], 201; [Joel Chandler Harris], *Atlanta Constitution,* 25 December 1881, reprinted in Budd, *Contemporary Reviews,* 204.

26. Mark Twain to Mary Mason Fairbanks, 5 February 1878, quoted in Salamo, 4.

27. Arthur Lawrence Vogelback, "*The Prince and the Pauper*: A Study in Critical Standards," *American Literature* 14 (March 1942): 53–54.

28. One critic assumes in passing that *Huckleberry Finn* will delight boys "of any age"; another states, "It will hugely please the boys, and also interest people of more mature years"; a third claims, "It is meant for boys; but there are few men (we should hope) who, once they take it up, will not delight in it" (Laurence Hutton, *Harper's Monthly,* September 1896, quoted in Victor Fischer, "Huck Finn Reviewed: The Reception of *Huckleberry Finn* in the United States, 1885–1897," *American Literary Realism* 16 [Spring 1983]: 38; *Hartford Times,* 9 March 1885, reprinted in Budd, *Contemporary Reviews,* 267; *Athenaeum,* 27 December 1885, reprinted in Budd, *Contemporary Reviews,* 259). But see Franklin B. Sanborn, who recommends the book more for the "mature in mind" (*Springfield Republican,* 27 April 1885, reprinted in Budd, *Contemporary Reviews,* 276). Fischer provides an excellent brief overview of *Huckleberry Finn'*s early reception.

29. Walter Besant, "My Favorite Novelist and His Best Book," *Munsey's Magazine,* February 1898, reprinted in Anderson, 138.

30. N.H.M., *Cleveland Leader and Herald,* 19 April 1885, quoted in Fischer, 31. A reviewer in the *San Francisco Bulletin* displays the two tendencies I've been sketching side by side. He or she is positive when assuming an audience of children and adults: Twain "rarely fails when he sets out to tickle the ribs of young or old." But when focusing on the

young the reviewer is more dubious: "Whether young people who read this volume will be the better for it will be an open question" since Huck provides a model that "is not altogether desirable" (*San Francisco Bulletin*, 14 March 1885, reprinted in Budd, *Contemporary Reviews*, 269–70).

31. Cited, e.g., by Michael Patrick Hearn, introduction, *The Annotated Huckleberry Finn*, ed. Michael Patrick Hearn (New York: Potter, 1981), 21.

32. See my "Man-Books, Kiddie Lit, and Critical Distemper," *Signal* 87 (September 1998): 199–200.

33. *Boston Transcript*, March 1885, reprinted in Bradley et al., 285.

34. *Boston Commonwealth*, 21 March 1885, 3; *Packard's Short-hand Reporter and Amanuensis*, April 1885—quoted in Fischer, 20, 32.

35. Budd, "Recomposition," 198. Nor do early critics always distinguish these two books from others by Twain, such as *The Prince and the Pauper* or *Roughing It*.

36. Brander Matthews, *Saturday Review*, 31 January 1885, reprinted in Bradley et al., 291–92. In 1901 a writer for *Book Buyer* cautiously refers to *Tom Sawyer* and *Huckleberry Finn* as "what may be considered, with the possible exception of the *Prince and Pauper*, and the *Connecticut Yankee at the Court of King Arthur* [*sic*], the best Mark Twain has done in the way of fiction" (R. E. Phillips, "Mark Twain: More Than Humorist," *Book Buyer*, April 1901, reprinted in Anderson, 238). For more examples of the ready coupling, see, e.g., Anderson, 179, 205, 244.

37. David Masters, "Mark Twain's Place in Literature," *Chautauquan*, September 1897, reprinted in Anderson, 202. Consider too that in 1898 a Twain enthusiast seems to place *Tom Sawyer* and *The Prince and the Pauper* at the head of Twain's productions; he suggests that *Huckleberry Finn* "lacks artistic unity . . . because it is a poor sequel and the connective tissue is flabby" (Theodore de Laguna, "Mark Twain as a Prospective Classic," *Overland Monthly*, April 1898, reprinted in Anderson, 220, 219). In 1907 a writer for the *Spectator* singles out, "as typical of his best work," Twain's *Tom Sawyer*, *The Prince and the Pauper* and—not *Huckleberry Finn* but *A Tramp Abroad* ("Mark Twain," *Spectator*, 25 May 1907, reprinted in Anderson, 260).

38. Elmer J. Bailey, "The Essayists and the Humourists," in *A Manual of American Literature*, ed. Theodore Stanton (New York: Putnam's, 1909), quoted in Anderson, 313.

39. Robert M. Gay, "The Two Mark Twains," *Atlantic*, December 1940, reprinted in *Critics on Mark Twain*, ed. David B. Kesterson (Coral Gables: University of Miami Press, 1973), 52.

40. Andrew Lang, *Illustrated London News*, 14 February 1891, reprinted in *Critical Essays on Mark Twain, 1867–1910*, ed. Louis J. Budd (Boston: Hall, 1982), 89.

41. This was at a time, admittedly, when fairy tales and folklore had their own independent stature for critics and scholars—or, rather, a time when fairy tales still had the stature of folklore.

42. Quoted in Fischer, 23. Subsequent quotations in this paragraph are from p. 24.

43. E. L. Pearson, "The Children's Librarian *versus* Huckleberry Finn: A Brief for the Defence," *Library Journal* 32 (July 1907): 312. Men were still caricaturing lady librarians for censoring the likes of *Huckleberry Finn* half a century later: see William Corbin McGraw, "Pollyanna Rides Again," *Saturday Review*, 22 March 1958, 37–38. Yet as Evelyn Geller notes in her study of censorship in American libraries, "Females were never in the vanguard of censorship, and they hardly trailed in its dissolution" (*Forbidden Books in American Public Libraries, 1876–1939* [Westport, Conn.: Greenwood, 1984], 132). See also

Christine Jenkins, "'Since So Many of Today's Librarians Are Women . . .': Women and Intellectual Freedom in U.S. Librarianship, 1890–1990," in *Reclaiming the American Library Past: Writing the Women In*, ed. Suzanne Hildenbrand (Norwood, N.J.: Ablex, 1996), 221–49. Linton Weeks has recently noted that "despite the meek, shush-shushing stereotype, librarians are largely a freedom-upholding, risk-taking group. In the name of the First Amendment and anti-censorship, they have championed the causes of provocative writers and spoken out against banned and challenged books" ("Books That May Make Parents Blush: Fiction Aimed at Teens Features Grown-up Themes," *Washington Post*, 11 March 2001, A1, www.washingtonpost.com/wp-dyn/articles/A52148-2001Mar10.html, accessed 26 June 2001.

44.   See *Boston Transcript*, in Bradley et al., 285; "Huck Finn Tabooed by Denver Library," *Harper's Weekly*, 6 September 1902, 1253; Asa Don Dickinson, "Huckleberry Finn is Fifty Years Old—Yes; But Is He Respectable?" *Wilson Bulletin for Librarians* 10 (November 1935), reprinted in Champion, 31–35. In addition, Justin Kaplan refers to early incidents of banning or the threat thereof in connection with the New York State Reformatory and the Omaha Public Library (*Born to Trouble: One Hundred Years of "Huckleberry Finn"* [Washington: Library of Congress, 1985], 14).

45.   And they ranked lower than such gems as E. P. Roe's *Barriers Burned Away*, Francis Marion Crawford's *Mr. Isaacs*, and Ik Marvel's *Reveries of a Bachelor* (Hamilton W. Mabie, "The Most Popular Novels in America," *Forum*, December 1893, 508–16).

46.   Daniel A. Wells notes that Twain is mentioned in the *Atlantic Monthly* at least ninety-five times before 1910 and in *Harper's Monthly* at least fifty-five times before 1900 ("Mark Twain in the *Atlantic Monthly* to 1910: An Annotated List of Allusions," *Mark Twain Journal* 23 [Spring 1985]: 21–28; "An Annotated Checklist of Twain Allusions in *Harper's Monthly*, 1850–1900," *American Literary Realism, 1870–1910* 17 [Spring 1984]: 116–23). I might add that in 1885 alone the *Critic* referred to Twain eighteen times.

47.   "Huck Finn Tabooed," 1253.

48.   C. M. Hewins, *Books for the Young: A Guide for Parents and Children* (New York: Leypoldt, 1882).

49.   Hamilton Mabie, "Mr. Mabie on Books for Young People," *Ladies' Home Journal*, October 1907, 24. One other venue where Twain makes a surprisingly poor showing was edited by a man: in the 1904 *A.L.A. Catalog*, ed. Melvil Dewey (Washington: Government Printing Office, 1904), which recommends eight thousand volumes for popular libraries, the only work by Twain is *Joan of Arc*.

50.   For a more sophisticated invocation of gender, divorcing it from biological sex— disavowing the feminine while yet admitting the female—in a piece published the same year as that in the *San Francisco Chronicle*, see Matthews, who exults in the reading matter now available for "the boy of to-day" and goes on to say that "only he or she who has been a boy"—as opposed to "old maids of either sex"—will "truly enjoy" *Huckleberry Finn* (292).

51.   H. W. Boynton, "For the Young," *Atlantic*, May 1903, 703. Subsequent quotations in this paragraph are from this page.

52.   Algernon Tassin, "Books for Children," in *The Cambridge History of American Literature*, ed. William Peterfield Trent, John Erskine, Stuart P. Sherman, and Carl Van Doren (New York: Putnam's, 1918), 2:405–6. Budd also comments on the two discussions in the *Cambridge History*, in "Recomposition," 199.

53.   Stuart P. Sherman, "Mark Twain," in Trent et al., *Cambridge History* (1921), 3:16.

54. Ibid., 15, 16.

55. Children's librarians, however, continued to recommend *Huckleberry Finn* for children along with *Tom Sawyer*. And one can, of course, find earlier adumbrations of the enthusiastic, separatist view. In 1913, for instance, H. L. Mencken announced his credo: "I believe that *Huckleberry Finn* is one of the great masterpieces of the world, that it is the full equal of *Don Quixote* and *Robinson Crusoe*, that it is vastly better than *Gil Blas, Tristram Shandy, Nicholas Nickleby* or *Tom Jones*" ("The Burden of Humor," *Smart Set*, February 1913, reprinted in Anderson, 329). And when Mencken mentions other important works by Twain he lists *Life on the Mississippi, Captain Stormfield's Visit to Heaven,* and *A Connecticut Yankee*—not, significantly, either *Tom Sawyer* or *The Prince and the Pauper.*

In 1913 also, John Macy calls *Tom Sawyer* a boys' book, while declaring *Huckleberry Finn* "more than a boy's book or a book about boys" but instead "the greatest piece of American fiction" (*The Spirit of American Literature* [New York: Doubleday, 1913], excerpt reprinted in Anderson, 319, 314). Yet he does not entirely banish children from the audience for *Huckleberry Finn:* he notes that both it and *The Prince and the Pauper* are "read with delight by children" (320). And his age metaphors do not so much dissociate Twain from juvenility as signal a tug of war between youth and age. Twain is revalued by adults who pride themselves simultaneously on their maturity and on their youthfulness. On the one hand, Macy dismisses the thinking of the American public as childish and adds, "Imagination is wasted on a people who hug Mark Twain's jokes as a child hugs a jumping-jack" (318). On the other hand, he compares Twain to Robert Louis Stevenson, "that other wise man with the heart of a boy," and approves of the boys' book: "The adult novel in America is not yet adult, but four men of letters, Aldrich, Warner, Mr. Howells and Mark Twain, have limned us immortally as we all were in the golden age" (319). The boys' book may be mature, but the adult novel is not—in a usage that metaphorically lauds maturity and yet substantively undermines adulthood.

56. Bernard DeVoto, *Mark Twain's America* (Boston: Little, Brown, 1932), 272. Aidan Chambers has rightly stated, "Even a critic of such notable sensibility as T. S. Eliot can only allow himself to call *Huckleberry Finn* a masterpiece . . . by telling us at the same time that it 'does not fall into the category of juvenile fiction'" ("All of a Tremble to See His Danger," in *The Arbuthnot Lectures, 1980–1989,* Association for Library Service to Children [Chicago: American Library Association, 1990], 86).

57. Budd, "Recomposition," 201.

58. Carl Van Doren, *The American Novel* (New York: Macmillan, 1921), 174.

59. Ibid., 175.

60. William Lyon Phelps, "Makers of American Literature: Mark Twain—the American Humorist," *Ladies' Home Journal,* May 1923, 210. See his "Mark Twain," *North American Review* 185 (5 July 1907): 540–48 (also reprinted in Anderson, 262–70).

61. DeVoto, 320.

62. Ernest Hemingway, *Green Hills of Africa* (New York: Scribner's, 1935), 22.

63. Van Wyck Brooks, *The Ordeal of Mark Twain,* rev. ed. (New York: Dutton, 1933), 156, 238, 29.

64. Van Wyck Brooks, foreword, in "Letters to Van Wyck Brooks," *Story* 19 (September/October 1941), cited in Gerber, "Introduction: Continuing Adventures," 7.

65. Brooks, *Ordeal.*

66. Gamaliel Bradford, "Mark Twain," *Atlantic,* April 1920, 469; Phelps, "Makers," 211; Mark Van Doren, "A Century of Mark Twain," *Nation,* 23 October 1935, 472; L. H.

Robbins, "Mark Twain's Fame Goes Marching On," *New York Times Magazine*, 21 April 1935, 4.

67. Fred Lewis Pattee, "On the Rating of Mark Twain," *American Mercury*, June 1928, 183.

68. DeVoto, 320; Pattee quotes from Albert Bigelow Paine, *Mark Twain, A Biography: The Personal and Literary Life of Samuel Langhorne Clemens* (New York: Harper, 1912).

69. DeVoto, 318.

70. Eliot, 334.

71. "The Best American Books," *Critic*, 3 June 1893, 357. Twain did nonetheless appear fourteenth, right after James, in an earlier readers' poll nominating hypothetical members of an American Academy (eligible candidates were male and living), in "Our 'Forty Immortals,'" *Critic*, 12 April 1884, 109.

72. T. W. Higginson et al., "The Most American Books," *Outlook*, 6 December 1902, 776–88.

73. Henry W. Lanier, "'Million' Books and 'Best' Books: A Glance Towards the Top of the Fiction America Has Produced in Three Hundred Years," *Golden Book Magazine*, September 1926, cited in Jay B. Hubbell, *Who Are the Major American Writers?* (Durham: Duke University Press, 1972), 289–90.

74. "An American Canon," *Saturday Review of Literature*, 15 October 1927, 191.

75. Cited in Hubbell, 300–302.

76. Eliot, 328; Trilling, 319.

77. Dixon Wecter, "Mark Twain," in *Literary History of the United States*, ed. Robert E. Spiller, Willard Thorp, Thomas H. Johnson, and Henry Seidel Canby (New York: Macmillan, 1948), 2:931.

78. Jane Smiley, "Say It Ain't So, Huck: Second Thoughts on Mark Twain's Masterpiece," *Harper's*, January 1996, 61.

79. Kenneth S. Lynn, "Welcome Back from the Raft, Huck Honey!" *American Scholar* 46 (Summer 1977): 346; see also Hamlin Hill, "*Huck Finn*'s Humor Today," in Sattelmeyer and Crowley, 297–307.

80. Terry Teachout, "Salinger Then and Now," *Commentary*, September 1987, 62.

81. George Steiner, "The Salinger Industry," *Nation*, 14 November 1959, 362.

82. *Modern Fiction Studies* and *Wisconsin Studies in Contemporary Literature* published special issues. Jack Salzman provides a good overview of the critical reception in his introduction to *New Essays on "The Catcher in the Rye,"* ed. Jack Salzman (Cambridge: Cambridge University Press, 1991), 1–22.

83. William Van O'Connor, "Why *Huckleberry Finn* Is Not the Great American Novel," *College English* 17 (October 1955): 10.

84. Adam Moss, "Catcher Comes of Age," *Esquire*, December 1981, 57; Arthur N. Applebee, "Stability and Change in the High-School Canon," *English Journal* 81 (September 1992): 28.

85. Teachout, 61.

86. James R. Kincaid, *Child-Loving: The Erotic Child and Victorian Culture* (New York: Routledge, 1992), 309.

87. See Budd, "Recomposition," 202; Applebee, 28.

88. This claim draws on to *Readers' Guide* listings since 1983 and listings for twenty-five major newspapers since 1989. See also John C. Gerber, who charts about fifty articles on *Huckleberry Finn* before 1920, about eighty between 1920 and 1949, and more than

five hundred between 1950 and 1985 ("Introduction: Continuing Adventures," Sattelmeyer and Crowley, 6–8). Even if one acknowledges that all criticism increased greatly during this time, the increase in attention to *Huckleberry Finn* is impressive.

89. Jonathan Arac, *"Huckleberry Finn" as Idol and Target: The Functions of Criticism in Our Time* (Madison: University of Wisconsin Press, 1997), 133.

90. See, e.g., Richard P. Adams, "The Unity and Coherence of *Huckleberry Finn*," *Tulane Studies in English* 6 (1956): 89–103; James M. Cox, *Mark Twain: The Fate of Humor* (Princeton: Princeton University Press, 1966).

91. Leo Marx was the first critic to explore the problem in detail, in "Mr. Eliot, Mr. Trilling, and *Huckleberry Finn*," *American Scholar* 22 (Autumn 1953), reprinted in Bradley et al., 336–49. More recently critics point to, say, the rhetorical power of the closing chapters, which forces readers to interrogate the issues, to continue participating in rhetorical judgments about the book's performances (see Steven Mailloux, *Rhetorical Power* [Ithaca: Cornell University Press, 1989], 97).

92. Other genres that have been posited include picaresque fiction and political allegory (the ending functioning as a commentary on the breakdown of Reconstruction).

93. The best formal discussion of the boy book is Anne Trensky's "The Bad Boy in Nineteenth-Century American Fiction," *Georgia Review* 27 (1973): 503–17.

94. Edwin H. Cady, "*Huckleberry Finn* by Common Day," in his *The Light of Common Day: Realism in American Fiction* (Bloomington: Indiana University Press, 1971), excerpt reprinted in Bradley et al., 398.

95. Ibid., 386. Cady is echoed by Marcia Jacobson, in her generally insightful *Being a Boy Again: Autobiography and the American Boy Book* (Tuscaloosa: University of Alabama Press, 1994). Jacobson claims that the boy book is really for adults and cites Howells in support—without noticing that in the passage she cites Howells implies that such books are for both boys and men (2–3).

96. Chambers, 86.

97. Justin Kaplan, "Born to Trouble: One Hundred Years of *Huckleberry Finn*," lecture, 11 September 1984, in Graff and Phelan, 355.

98. Wecter, 932–33.

99. Phelps, "Mark Twain," 547.

100. DeVoto, 37.

101. Ralph Ellison, "Change the Joke and Slip the Yoke," *Partisan Review* 25 (Spring 1958), excerpt reprinted in Bradley et al., 422.

102. For a useful recapitulation of the history of the controversy, see Peaches Henry, "The Struggle for Tolerance: Race and Censorship in *Huckleberry Finn*," in *Satire or Evasion? Black Perspectives on "Huckleberry Finn*," ed. James S. Leonard, Thomas A. Tenney, and Thadious M. Davis (Durham: Duke University Press, 1992), 25–47. The volume as a whole explores the many issues surrounding the treatment of race in *Huckleberry Finn*; so do several essays in Robinson, *Cambridge Companion*; and Jocelyn Chadwick-Joshua, *The Jim Dilemma: Reading Race in "Huckleberry Finn"* (Jackson: University Press of Mississippi, 1998).

For recent censorship statistics, see People for the American Way, "Attacks on the Freedom to Learn," www.pfaw.org/attacks/96APPEN2.HTM, accessed June 1999; People for the American Way, "Attacks on the Freedom to Learn '96 96append.htm," www.pfaw.org/attacks/96APPEND.HTM, accessed June 1999; American Library Association, "Banned Books Week: 'Free People Read Freely,'" 10 September 1999, www.ala.org/bbooks/challeng.html, accessed 7 October 1999; American Library Association, "Harry Potter Series Tops List of Most Challenged Books of 1999," 13 March 2000, www.ala.org/news/archives/v5n12/99bookchallenges.html, accessed 18 August 2000; American Library Association, "The 100 Most Frequently Challenged Books of 1990–1999," 14 August 2000, www.ala.org/alaorg/oif/top100bannedbooks.html, accessed 18 August 2000. *Huckleberry Finn* was the fifth most frequently challenged book in the 1990s.

103. Arac, 137 ff.

104. Anderson, 205, 99, 244, 269. Arac notes, "I have never seen so much use of the term 'quintessentially' as in the claims for the Americanness of *Huckleberry Finn*" (18).

105. See, e.g., Leonard, 274. At times Wallace shifts into a nineteenth-century-style protective stance: "No one would want his children to emulate this pair," he says of Jim and of thieving, lying, sacrilegious Huck ("The Case Against Huck Finn," in Leonard et al., 20).

106. Julius Lester, "Morality and *Adventures of Huckleberry Finn*," *Mark Twain Journal* 22 (Fall 1984), reprinted in Leonard, 200.

107. Henry, 38; Richard K. Barksdale, "History, Slavery, and Thematic Irony in *Huckleberry Finn*," *Mark Twain Journal* 22 (Fall 1984), reprinted in Leonard et al., 55; Arnold Rampersad, "*Adventures of Huckleberry Finn* and Afro-American Literature," *Mark Twain Journal* 22 (Fall 1984), reprinted in Leonard et al., 217.

108. Cited by Peter Smagorinsky, *Standards in Practice Grades 9–12* (1996), quoted in Arac, 86.

109. Fishkin, *Lighting*, 122.

110. Toni Morrison, introduction, *Adventures of Huckleberry Finn* (New York: Oxford University Press, 1996), xxxvii.

111. For African Americans have "had to work in concert for survival" (Gloria I. Joseph, "Black Mothers and Daughters: Their Roles and Functions in American Society," in *Common Differences: Conflicts in Black and White Feminist Perspectives*, by Gloria I. Joseph and Jill Lewis [Garden City, N.Y.: Anchor Doubleday, 1981], 90). Whether or not they have explicitly sought racial uplift, the adults have often attended with particular intensity to the needs of African-American children.

112. Mailloux, 57–129.

F I V E : The Case of the Girls' Book

1. Louisa May Alcott, *The Journals of Louisa May Alcott*, ed. Joel Myerson and Daniel Shealy, assoc. ed. Madeleine B. Stern (Boston: Little, Brown, 1989), 109.

2. "Miss Louisa M. Alcott," *New York Times*, 28 April 1880, 2.

3. Louisa May Alcott to Thomas Bailey Aldrich, 23 October 1883; see Yale Collection of American Literature, Beinecke Rare Book and Manuscript Library. I am grateful to Betsey Shirley for sharing her transcription with me.

4. Quoted in Thomas Beer, *The Mauve Decade: American Life at the End of the Nineteenth Century* (1926; reprint, New York: Knopf, 1937), 18. This story, like the other one I've traced to Beer—Alcott's stating that "if Mr. Clemens cannot think of something better to tell our pure-minded lads and lasses, he had best stop writing for them" (25)—may well be apocryphal.

5. Janet Maslin, "The Gold Standard for Girlhood across America," *New York Times*,

21 December 1994, C13, C18. For more details about Alcott's popular reception, see Janice M. Alberghene and Beverly Lyon Clark, introduction, *"Little Women" and the Feminist Imagination*, ed. Janice M. Alberghene and Beverly Lyon Clark (New York: Garland, 1999), xvi–liv; and Susan R. Gannon, "Getting Cozy with a Classic: Visualizing *Little Women* (1868–1995)," in Alberghene and Clark, 103–38.

6. Stephen King, "Blood and Thunder in Concord," *New York Times Book Review*, 10 September 1995, 17–20.

7. Barbara Sicherman, "Reading *Little Women*: The Many Lives of a Text," in *U.S. History as Women's History: New Feminist Essays*, ed. Linda K. Kerber et al. (Chapel Hill: University of North Carolina Press, 1995), 256–60.

8. See Elaine Showalter, *Sister's Choice: Tradition and Change in American Women's Writing* (Oxford: Clarendon, 1991), 40; Ursula K. Le Guin, *Dancing at the Edge of the World: Thoughts on Words, Women, Places* (New York: Grove, 1989), 213; Tanya Barrientos, "'Little Women': Big Influence," *Providence Journal-Bulletin*, 27 December 1994, E2. See also Sue Standing, "In Jo's Garret: *Little Women* and the Space of Imagination," in Alberghene and Clark, 173–83.

Little Women has also been claimed as a childhood favorite by such other diverse figures as Susan Sontag, Judith Krantz, Ann Petry, Gloria Steinem, and two of the three women state governors in 1989. For Sontag and Krantz, see "Uncle Wiggily's Karma and Other Childhood Memories," *New York Times Book Review*, 7 December 1986, 46, 47; for the rest, see Bernice Cullinan and M. Jerry Weiss, eds., *Books I Read When I Was Young: The Favorite Books of Famous People* (New York: Avon, 1980), 138; "When I Was Very Young: Celebrities Tell Us Their Favorite Childhood Books," *Ladies' Home Journal*, April 1991, 84; "Governors Recall Books of Their Youth," *New York Times*, 15 November 1989, cited in Showalter, 42.

9. See Sicherman, 262–64; Sarah Crichton, "What We Read as Youngsters: Top Editors Recall Their Favorite Childhood Books," *Publishers Weekly*, 26 February 1982, 121; Leo Lerman, "*Little Women*: Who's in Love with Miss Louisa May Alcott? I Am," *Mademoiselle*, December 1973, reprinted in *Critical Essays on Louisa May Alcott*, ed. Madeleine B. Stern (New York: Hall, 1984), 113–14.

10. Paglia is quoted in Barrientos, E2; Manners (Judith Martin) is quoted in "Uncle Wiggily's Karma," 47.

11. See Joel Myerson and Daniel Shealy, "The Sales of Louisa May Alcott's Books," *Harvard Library Bulletin*, n.s., 1 (Spring 1990): 69–73.

12. Frank Luther Mott, *Golden Multitudes: The Story of Best Sellers in the United States* (New York: Macmillan, 1947), 8.

13. Review of *Little Men*, *New York Times*, 17 June 1871, 2.

14. Caroline H. Dall, review of *Eight Cousins*, *Independent*, 7 October 1875, 9.

15. H. R. Hudson, "Concord Books," *Harper's Monthly*, June 1875, 27.

16. See Albert E. Stone, Jr., *The Innocent Eye: Childhood in Mark Twain's Imagination* (New Haven: Yale University Press, 1961), 4.

17. Frank Preston Stearns, *Sketches from Concord and Appledore* (New York: Putnam's, 1895), 82.

18. Louisa May Alcott, *Little Women* (1868; reprint, New York: Modern Library, 1983), 440. This edition, unlike most modern ones, reprints the original 1868 edition. All quotations from *Little Women* in the text, denoted *LW*, are from this edition.

19. Van Wyck Brooks, *New England: Indian Summer, 1865–1915* (New York: Dutton,

1940), 65; review of *Miss Alcott of Concord*, by Marjorie Worthington, *New Yorker*, 18 October 1958, 194.

20. "Louisa M. Alcott," *Victoria Magazine*, July 1880, 7; editorial, *Godey's Lady's Book*, September 1871, 279; review cited in Janet S. Zehr, "The Response of Nineteenth-Century Audiences to Louisa May Alcott's Fiction," *American Transcendental Quarterly*, n.s., 1 (December 1987): 325.

21. Mary Cantwell, "Concord, Revisited," *New York Times*, 25 December 1994, sec. 4, 8.

22. Shrewd marketing by Alcott's publishers also played a role. See Sicherman, 255; Margery Fisher, "March Girls," in her *Who's Who in Children's Books: A Treasury of the Familiar Characters of Childhood* (New York: Holt, 1975), 198.

23. "Why Miss Alcott Still Lives," *New York Times Saturday Review of Books and Art*, 18 January 1902, 40. That Alcott did indeed cull anecdotes from children does not validate the writer's larger argument that she simply copied from life.

24. "Little Men," *Scribner's*, August 1871, 446. Even this reviewer adds, though, that Alcott's works thus far "are only simple 'studies,' and of very narrow range." The reviewer is not immune to the sense that portrayals of family life are limited—a perspective that recent feminist critics have done much to debunk.

25. Hamilton W. Mabie, "The Most Popular Novels in America," *Forum*, December 1893, 510.

26. Algernon Tassin, "Books for Children," in *The Cambridge History of American Literature*, ed. William Peterfield Trent, John Erskine, Stuart P. Sherman, and Carl Van Doren (New York: Putnam's, 1918), 2:402.

27. Jno. R. G. Hassard, "The New York Mercantile Library," *Scribner's* 1 (February 1871): 363; W. B. Shaw, "The Traveling Library—A Boon for American Country Readers," *Review of Reviews*, reprinted as "Wisconsin Traveling Libraries," *Littell's Living Age* 216 (12 February 1898): suppl. 481.

28. See Caroline Maria Hewins, "Reading of the Young" (1896), reprinted in *Library Work with Children*, ed. Alice I. Hazeltine (White Plains, N.Y.: Wilson, 1917), 43; Dorothea Lawrance Mann, "When the Alcott Books Were New," *Publishers Weekly*, 28 September 1929, excerpt reprinted in Stern, *Critical Essays*, 85.

29. *Des Moines News*, 6 October 1913 (clipping, in the Louisa May Alcott papers, bMS Am 800.23), quoted by permission of the Houghton Library, Harvard University.

30. "*Little Women* Leads Poll: Novel Rated ahead of Bible for Influence on High School Pupils," *New York Times*, 22 March 1927, reprinted in Stern, *Critical Essays*, 84.

31. See Louise Seaman Bechtel, "The Giant in Children," *Atlantic* (1927), reprinted in her *Books in Search of Children* (1940; reprint, n.p.: Macmillan, 1969), 146; Carleton Washburne and Mabel Vogel, *Winnetka Graded Book List* (Chicago: American Library Association, 1926).

32. See Esther Jane Carrier, *Fiction in the Public Libraries, 1900–1950* (Littleton, Colo.: Libraries Unlimited, 1985), esp. 288–92, 55, 206–12.

33. William E. Sage, "Suffragettes Rejoice. 'Tis a Fine Week for the 'Weaker Sex' at the Local Playhouses," *Cleveland Leader*, 12 October 1912; "Popularity of *Little Women*," *Albany Daily Press and Knickerbocker*, 22 December 1912 (clippings, bMS Am 800.23), quoted by permission of the Houghton Library, Harvard University.

34. Harriet Prescott Spofford, "Louisa May Alcott," *Chautauquan*, December 1988, 161; Spofford's spelling.

35. Mary Wilkinson et al., *The Right Book for the Right Child: A Graded Buying List of Children's Books* (New York: Day, 1933), 132.

36. Madelon Bell, introduction, *Little Women* (New York: Modern Library, 1983), ix.

37. Lavinia Russ, "Not to Be Read on Sunday," *Horn Book*, October 1968, reprinted in Stern, *Critical Essays*, 100.

38. Barbara Auchincloss, "Women Who Helped Mold America," *New York Times Magazine*, 20 July 1941, 14.

39. Milton Esterow, "TV Put in a Dither by *Little Women*," *New York Times*, 31 August 1958, 44.

40. The other book was *The Diary of Anne Frank*. See Russ, 99.

41. Richard H. Brodhead locates this precarious moment more in the 1910s than the 1920s (*The School of Hawthorne* [New York: Oxford University Press, 1986], 208–9). In a 1922 *Vanity Fair* poll of ten up-and-coming critics, Hawthorne achieves a score of only 5.9 out of a possible 25 (on a scale from −25 to +25), compared with 8.8 for Emerson, 10.7 for Henry Adams, 13.3 for Henry James, 15.8 for Walt Whitman—and 22.4 for Shakespeare ("The New Order of Critical Values," *Vanity Fair*, April 1922, 40–41).

42. "To Preserve Alcott Home," *New York Times*, 3 August 1928, 20; "Cobbler, 86, Recalls Emerson, Hawthorne," *New York Times*, 22 December 1935, 14.

43. Review of *Aunt Jo's Scrap-Bag* and *Proverb Stories*, *Critic*, 2 December 1882, 326; *Critic*, 25 October 1890, 202.

44. Alcott, November 1858, *Journals*, 92.

45. Louisa May Alcott to James Redpath, [early September 1863], *The Selected Letters of Louisa May Alcott*, ed. Joel Myerson and Daniel Shealy, assoc. ed. Madeleine B. Stern (Boston: Little, Brown, 1987), 91.

46. Alcott, November 1859, *Journals*, 95.

47. Richard H. Brodhead, *Cultures of Letters: Scenes of Reading and Writing in Nineteenth Century America* (Chicago: University of Chicago Press, 1993), 69–106.

48. John Habberton, "Author and Woman," *Cosmopolitan*, December 1889, 254.

49. Sheryl A. Englund, "Reading the Author in *Little Women*: A Biography of a Book," *ATQ*, n.s., 12 (September 1998): 211. On the gender segmenting of children's literature, see, e.g., Sarah A. Wadsworth, "Louisa May Alcott, William T. Adams, and the Rise of Gender-Specific Series Books," *The Lion and the Unicorn* 25 (2001): 17–46. Anne H. Lundin suggests that reviewers didn't fully differentiate between girls' and boys' books till the 1890s ("Victorian Horizons: The Reception of Children's Books in England and America, 1880–1900," *Library Quarterly* 64 [January 1994]: 43).

50. Editorial, *Godey's Lady's Book*, November 1870, 472.

51. C. M. Hewins, *Books for the Young: A Guide for Parents and Children* (New York: Leypoldt, 1882); John Tebbel, *The Expansion of an Industry, 1865–1919*, vol. 2 of *A History of Book Publishing in the United States* (New York: Bowker, 1975), 600–601.

52. Melvil Dewey, ed., *A.L.A. Catalog* (Washington: Government Printing Office, 1904), 184–85. The titles listed as juveniles are *Aunt Jo's Scrap-Bag, Eight Cousins, Jack and Jill, Jo's Boys, Little Men, Little Women, An Old-Fashioned Girl, Spinning-Wheel Stories*, and *Under the Lilacs*. The 1893 *Catalogue of "A.L.A." Library* (Washington: Government Printing Office, 1893) partly anticipates the 1904 catalogue but excludes *Work* (and hence has only one "adult" title), *Aunt Jo's Scrap-Bag, Jo's Boys*, and *Spinning-Wheel Stories*.

53. Review of vol. 3 of *Aunt Jo's Scrap-Bag, Godey's Lady's Book*, February 1874, reprinted in Stern, *Critical Essays*, 178. Writers for *Godey's* seemed especially willing to en-

vision overlapping child and adult audiences: see its review of *An Old-Fashioned Girl,* June 1870, 576; editorial, November 1870, 472; editorial, September 1871, 279; and review of vol. 1 of *Aunt Jo's Scrap-Bag,* March 1872, 290.

54. *National Anti-Slavery Standard,* 18 September 1869, reprinted in Stern, *Critical Essays,* 26.

55. [H. E. Scudder], review of *Jack and Jill, Atlantic,* January 1881, reprinted in Stern, *Critical Essays,* 171. Reviews that drew similar lines appeared in such magazines as the *Nation* and *Literary World* and in the British journals the *Athenaeum* and the *Saturday Review.*

56. Katharine Fullerton Gerould, "Miss Alcott's New England," *Atlantic,* August 1911, 181.

57. [Lyman Abbott], review of *Little Men, Harper's Monthly,* August 1871, reprinted in Stern, *Critical Essays,* 157–58; [Lyman Abbott], review of *Little Women,* part 2, *Harper's Monthly,* August 1869, reprinted in Stern, *Critical Essays,* 83.

58. Review of *An Old-Fashioned Girl, Atlantic,* June 1870, 752.

59. Henry James, review of *Eight Cousins, Nation,* 14 October 1875, reprinted in Stern, *Critical Essays,* 165–66.

60. "Children's Literature" (clippings, bMS Am 800.23), quoted by permission of the Houghton Library, Harvard University.

61. *Nation,* 14 July 1870, reprinted in Stern, *Critical Essays,* 155; *Nation,* 31 July 1873, 73; *Nation,* 21 November 1889, 416.

62. Review of *An Old-Fashioned Girl, Atlantic,* 752; [Scudder], review of *Jack and Jill,* 171.

63. [G. P. Lathrop], *Atlantic,* July 1877, reprinted in Stern, *Critical Essays,* 203, 204.

64. "Two New England Women," *Atlantic,* March 1890, 421.

65. Even a female reviewer for the *Independent,* in the midst of enthusing over Alcott herself and Alcott's "perfect success," admits that "we women turn to our light reading for faith and cheer" (Dall, 9). Alcott may, for this reviewer, be addressing adult women as well as children, but her work constitutes only light reading.

66. Review of *Jack and Jill, New York Times,* 17 October 1880, 4.

67. Theodore Roosevelt, *An Autobiography* (New York: Macmillan, 1913), 20.

68. "Playhouse—*Little Women,*" *Westfield Leader,* 16 October 1912 (clippings, bMS Am 800.23), quoted by permission of the Houghton Library, Harvard University.

69. *Godey's Lady's Book,* September 1871, 279; *Godey's Lady's Book,* November 1870, 472. See also Alice A. Chadwick, who laments Alcott's language and asserts, "I know the children love Miss Alcott; and I am sorry to be sorry that they do" ("Reading for Children," *Outlook,* 11 September 1897, 121); she preferred the "sweet idealism" of *Little Lord Fauntleroy* (122).

70. Thomas Wentworth Higginson, *Short Studies of American Authors,* enlarged ed. (Boston: Lee, 1888), 66–67.

71. "Two Books for Children," *Scribner's,* April 1876, 897.

72. Nina Baym, *Woman's Fiction: A Guide to Novels by and about Women in America, 1820–1870* (Ithaca: Cornell University Press, 1978), 23.

73. Peck reprints the identical Alcott excerpts, yet registers the shift from a cultural elite composed of men of letters, such as Warner, to one that requires academic credentials. Peck feels the need to string "A.M., Ph.D., L.H.D." after his name. And the verbiage on Peck's title page—the full title is *The International Library of Masterpieces, Literature, Art, and Rare Manuscripts; History, Biography, Science, Philosophy, Poetry, the Drama, Travel, Adventure, Fiction, and Rare and Little-Known Literature from the Archives of the*

Great Libraries of the World—suggests some cultural anxiety. Is Peck seeking to make cultural masterpieces readily available to a general audience? Or is he displaying the scholar's interest in cultural arcana, "rare and little-known literature"? Alcott is just as fully represented in the 1917 edition of Warner's *Library*—then labeled the "University edition."

74. Alcott is now represented, however, in such middlebrow "great books" collections as *The World's Hundred Greatest Books Audio Cassette Collection*—in capsule form, so you can "learn in a few weeks what would normally take a lifetime of study."

75. Barrett Wendell, *A Literary History of America* (1900; reprint, New York: Scribner's, 1909), 337.

76. The pieces that come closest to being exceptions are a journalistic essay on Alcott's funeral in *Sewanee Review* in 1928, a brief mention in an article in the *Journal of Negro History* in 1929, and the 1932 issue of the *Elementary English Review*, a journal that most of the professoriate would consider pedagogical rather than scholarly.

77. The situation is rather different in the popular media. In the *Reader's Guide to Periodical Literature*, Louisa has always outpaced Bronson: between 1890 and 1940, by about three to one; between 1941 and now, by about six to one. Yet in the fifty years between 1940 and 1990, compared to the previous fifty years, only half as many items address Louisa in the popular media (only a quarter as many address Bronson). While Louisa may have continued to be popular in the early twentieth century, by the mid-1930s, certainly by 1940, the popular media response paralleled the earlier academic lack of interest.

78. Cited in Richard Ohmann, "The Shaping of a Canon: U.S. Fiction, 1960–1975," *Critical Inquiry* 10 (September 1983): 204–5. Ohmann acknowledges that the *New York Review of Books* would seem, since its founding in 1963, to be even more influential.

79. *New York Times Book Review*, 25 July 1915, 265.

80. Brigid Brophy, "Sentimentality and Louisa M. Alcott," *Sunday Times Magazine* (London), December 1964, reprinted as "A Masterpiece, and Dreadful," *New York Times Book Review*, 17 January 1965, 1, 44.

81. Allan MacDonald, "A Boy's Spirit under Her Bib," *New York Times Book Review*, 28 May 1950, 10. Stern makes a similar point in her reply, 2 July 1950, 13.

82. Robert E. Spiller, Willard Thorp, Thomas H. Johnson, and Henry Seidel Canby, eds., *Literary History of the United States* (New York: Macmillan, 1948), 2:1383.

83. Edward Wagenknecht, *Cavalcade of the American Novel from the Birth of the Nation to the Middle of the Twentieth Century* (New York: Holt, 1952), 88.

84. Alice M. Jordan, "Children's Classics," *Horn Book*, February 1947, reprinted in her *Children's Classics*, 5th ed. (Boston: Horn Book, 1976), 8.

85. Clifton Fadiman, "Books for Children," *Holiday Magazine*, revised and reprinted in his *Party of One* (Cleveland: World, 1955), 385. He also listed *Huckleberry Finn* and *Alice's Adventures in Wonderland*—and suggested, noncensoriously, that their being read by juveniles helped a work's longevity.

86. Odell Shepard, "Mother of *Little Women*," *North American Review* 245 (Summer 1938): 392. Subsequent quotations in this paragraph are from p. 393.

87. "Sentimental Journal," *TLS*, 31 May 1957, vii. Subsequent quotations in this paragraph are from this page.

88. Nina Baym, "Melodramas of Beset Manhood: How Theories of American Fiction Exclude Women Authors," *American Quarterly* 33 (1981), reprinted in *The New Feminist Criticism: Essays on Women, Literature, and Theory*, ed. Elaine Showalter (New York: Pantheon), 63–80.

89. Ann Douglas, introduction, *Little Women* (New York: Signet, 1983), xii–xiii. For an account of *Little Women* as a "narrative of national recovery" from the Civil War, see Elizabeth Young, "A Wound of One's Own: Louisa May Alcott's Civil War Fiction," *American Quarterly* 48 (September 1996): 463.

90. Janice M. Alberghene, "Autobiography and the Boundaries of Interpretation: On Reading *Little Women* and *The Living Is Easy*," in Alberghene and Clark, 352.

91. My use of the term *national narrative* differs from Jonathan Arac's when he contrasts the fiction of James Fenimore Cooper and the history of George Bancroft with the "literary narratives" emerging in the middle of the nineteenth century in the work of Nathaniel Hawthorne and Herman Melville ("Narrative Forms," in *The Cambridge History of American Literature*, ed. Sacvan Bercovitch, assoc. ed. Cyrus R. K. Patell [Cambridge: Cambridge University Press, 1995], 2:605–777). For Alcott engages with national themes obliquely and imagistically, the way a "literary narrative" might.

92. Leona Rostenberg, "Some Anonymous and Pseudonymous Thrillers of Louisa M. Alcott," *Bibliographical Society of America Papers* 37 (2d Quarter 1943), reprinted in Stern, *Critical Essays*, 43–50.

93. In 1950, for instance, Stern published her biography of Alcott. In 1954 she published work by and about Alcott in the flagship journal of the American Literature Group of the Modern Language Association, *American Literature*. In the 1970s Stern began publishing Alcott's forgotten thrillers, starting with *Behind a Mask* (New York: Morrow, 1975).

94. Brophy, 1.

95. See Karen Lindsay, "Louisa May Alcott: The Author of 'Little Women' as Feminist," *Women: A Journal of Liberation* 2 (Fall 1970): 35–37; Carolyn Forrey, "The New Woman Revisited," *Women's Studies* 2 (1972): 37–56.

96. Patricia Meyer Spacks, "Taking Care: Some Women Novelists," *Novel* 6 (Fall 1972), reprinted in her *The Female Imagination* (1975; reprint, New York: Avon, 1976), 121. Spacks reveals her overall condescension toward children when she says she "hesitates" to call *Little Women* a novel "since the narrative complexity is on the level of a child's story" (121).

97. Baym, *Woman's Fiction*, 296. More recently Baym has written sensitively about Alcott—though necessarily briefly—in "The Rise of the Woman Author," in *Columbia Literary History of the United States*, ed. Emory Elliot et al. (New York: Columbia University Press, 1988), 303–4.

98. Sandra M. Gilbert and Susan Gubar, *The Madwoman in the Attic: The Woman Writer and the Nineteenth-Century Literary Imagination* (New Haven: Yale University Press, 1979), 64. When scholars in the 1970s were more appreciative, their discussions appeared in more marginal contexts, not in a volume published by an Ivy League press. As late as 1982, an appreciation by noted scholar Carolyn G. Heilbrun strains to accommodate itself to a collection called *Women, the Arts, and the 1920s in Paris and New York*. Alcott died in 1888, and she never lived in New York or Paris.

99. Nina Auerbach, "Austen and Alcott on Matriarchy: New Women or New Wives?" *Novel* 10 (Fall 1976), revised and reprinted in her *Communities of Women: An Idea in Fiction* (Cambridge: Harvard University Press, 1978), 55–73.

100. See Judith Fetterley, "*Little Women*: Alcott's Civil War," *Feminist Studies* 5 (Summer 1979): 369–83.

101. Alcott to Samuel Joseph May, 22 January [1869], *Letters*, 121–22; Alcott to Elizabeth Powell, 20 March [1869], *Letters*, 125. Alcott's italicized misspelling makes an allusion to Dickens.

102. Sicherman, 251.

103. See Susan S. Lanser, "Feminist Criticism, 'The Yellow Wallpaper,' and the Politics of Color in America," *Feminist Studies* 15 (1989): 415–41.

104. Catharine R. Stimpson, "Reading for Love: Canons, Paracanons, and Whistling Jo March," *New Literary History* 21 (Autumn 1990): 957–76.

105. Anna Quindlen, introduction, *Little Women* (Boston: Little, Brown, 1994), [vi].

SIX: The Case of American Fantasy

1. Selma G. Lanes, *Down the Rabbit Hole: Adventures and Misadventures in the Realm of Children's Literature* (New York: Atheneum, 1976), 111, 91, 94–95. Most theorists of fantasy literature would not use the term *fairy tale* as broadly as Lanes does; most would restrict it to tales that are of oral origin or close thereto. In any case, I am concerned in this chapter not with the history of the on-again, off-again reception of fairy tales in the United States but with the response to novel-length works whose worlds violate everyday physical rules. And since my focus is on academic reception, I'm not primarily interested in works that were highly popular but received little critical acclaim, such as comic strips. I've also chosen not to address picture books, since preliminary investigation of their reception has not revealed particularly striking patterns.

2. Gillian Avery, *Behold the Child: American Children and Their Books, 1621–1922* (Baltimore: Johns Hopkins University Press, 1994), 131 ff.; Mark I. West, *Before Oz: Juvenile Fantasy Stories from Nineteenth-Century America* (Hamden, Conn.: Archon, 1989). Avery acknowledges that these early fantasy works are little known, that it was only in 1900 "that an American fantasy became part of the national consciousness"—when *The Wonderful Wizard of Oz* was published (134).

3. Eric S. Rabkin, *The Fantastic in Literature* (Princeton: Princeton University Press, 1977), 8 ff.

4. Brian Attebery, *Strategies of Fantasy* (Bloomington: Indiana University Press, 1992), 14–16.

5. Felicity A. Hughes, "Children's Literature: Theory and Practice," *ELH* 45 (1978): 542–61.

6. Edward Wagenknecht, *Utopia Americana* (1929), excerpt reprinted in *The Wizard of Oz*, by L. Frank Baum, ed. Michael Patrick Hearn (New York: Schocken, 1983), 147. Hereafter this book is referred to in notes as Hearn, ed., *Wizard of Oz*.

7. David Dempsey, "The Wizard of Baum," *New York Times Book Review*, 13 May 1956, 30.

8. John Goldthwaite, *The Natural History of Make-Believe: A Guide to the Principal Works of Britain, Europe, and America* (New York: Oxford University Press, 1996), 211.

9. Brian Attebery, *The Fantasy Tradition in American Literature: From Irving to Le Guin* (Bloomington: Indiana University Press, 1980), 185.

10. L. Frank Baum, "Modern Fairy Tales," *Advance*, 19 August 1909, reprinted in Hearn, ed., *Wizard of Oz*, 138.

11. *The Bookseller and Latest Literature*, July 1900, quoted in Michael Patrick Hearn, introduction, *The Annotated Wizard of Oz*, ed. Michael Patrick Hearn (New York: Potter, 1973), 33; *New York Times Saturday Review of Books*, 10 September 1904, 604. A comic strip called *The Wonderland of Oz* ran in U.S. newspapers in 1931–32.

12. Martin Gardner, cited in Roger Sale, *Fairy Tales and After: From Snow White to E.*

B. White (1978; reprint, Cambridge: Harvard University Press, 1979), 226; Vernon H. Jones, "The Oz Parade," *New Orleans Review* 3 (1973): 375.

13. Shirley Jackson, "The Lost Kingdom of Oz," *Reporter*, 10 December 1959, 42; Martin Gardner, "The Librarians in Oz," *Saturday Review*, 11 April 1959, 19. Gardner's source would seem to be "These Books We Loved When We Were Still Quite Young," *New York Times Book Review*, 18 November 1956, part II, 6. The article gives no details as to how the excerpted student papers were gathered; one possibility is the annual Police Athletic League essay contest, which in 1963 garnered a record 570 entries (see Lewis Nichols, "In and Out of Books," *New York Times Book Review*, 12 May 1963, part II, 8). When the 1939 film of *The Wizard of Oz* was shown on television in 1956, it captured two-thirds of the viewing audience (see "How *The Wizard* Rates . . . ," *Baum Bugle* 29 [Spring 1985]: 21).

14. This estimate is by William F. Brown, cited in "Following the Yellow Brick Road from 'The Wonderful Wizard of Oz' to 'The Wiz,'" *American Cinematographer*, November 1978, 1090.

15. Frank Joslyn Baum and Russell P. MacFall, *To Please a Child: A Biography of L. Frank Baum, Royal Historian of Oz* (Chicago: Reilly, 1961), 139. Their list includes translations and coloring-book versions, however, and also a premium booklet for Cocomalt powdered drink. The number of copies sold in trade editions was apparently 610,396.

16. Dempsey, 30.

17. Frank Luther Mott, *Golden Multitudes: The Story of Best Sellers in the United States* (New York: Macmillan, 1947), 8.

18. Ibid., 224, 312–13. *Oz* is nevertheless listed as one of the "better sellers" (324).

19. Carleton Washburne and Mabel Vogel, *Winnetka Graded Book List* (Chicago: American Library Association, 1926). In a smaller-scale, 1923 survey of children visiting the San Antonio library and asked to vote for their favorite book, Baum's work came in fourteenth; he was the fourth most popular author with children under ten (cited in Esther Jane Carrier, *Fiction in Public Libraries, 1900–1950* [Littleton, Colo.: Libraries Unlimited, 1985], 290).

20. Deidre Johnson, "Re Book Awards," Children's Literature: Criticism and Theory e-mail list, 14 November 1995; Deidre Johnson, personal communication, 27 August 1997.

21. George W. Norvell, *What Boys and Girls Like to Read* (Morristown, N.J.: Silver Burdett, 1958), esp. 193–95. Norvell does not indicate when he gathered the data or whether he attempted any controls to guarantee that the children were responding to the book and not the film versions; nor does his measure of "interest" factor in—or control for—the number of children who had in fact encountered a particular work. In general, among the surveys I cite, the older a survey is the less likely it is to conform to latter-day standards of reliability and validity; the most valid and reliable of the pre-1950 surveys is probably Washburne and Vogel's Winnetka study. Among post-1950 surveys, Norvell's strikes me as having some problems with validity—with whether it measures what it purports to measure.

22. "A New Book for Children," *New York Times Saturday Review of Books and Art*, 8 September 1900, 605.

23. Quoted in Hearn, introduction, *Annotated Wizard of Oz*, 34.

24. Review of *The Marvelous Land of Oz*, *New York Times Saturday Review of Books*, 10 September 1904, 604.

25. "L. Frank Baum Dead," *New York Times*, 8 May 1919, 17. In the length-of-obituary-in-the-*New-York-Times* sweepstakes, Baum comes in last among the authors on whom I focus in this study.

26. Martin Gardner, "Why Librarians Dislike Oz," *American Book Collector*, special number (December 1962), reprinted in Hearn, ed., *Wizard of Oz*, 188.

27. See, e.g., Michael Patrick Hearn, preface, Hearn, ed., *Wizard of Oz*, xi. By the eighth edition of Arbuthnot's book, revised by Zena Sutherland, the Oz books are simply listed as an example of "books that stir controversy," remaining "favorites of many children despite the fact that many authorities in the field of children's literature feel that the style is flat and dull, and that the inventiveness of the first book was followed by mediocrity and repetition in subsequent volumes" (May Hill Arbuthnot, *Children and Books*, 8th ed., rev. Zena Sutherland [New York: HarperCollins, 1991], 279).

28. Charlotte S. Huck, *Children's Literature in the Elementary School*, 3d ed., updated (New York: Holt, 1979), 257. Huck finds Oz lacking in "wonder and awe" because Dorothy is so practical and matter-of-fact—though Alice's being matter-of-fact and "always the proper Victorian young lady" apparently enhances rather than diminishes her book's power (256).

29. See Gardner, "Librarians in Oz," 18; Michael Patrick Hearn, "'Toto, I've a Feeling We're Not in Kansas City Anymore . . . or Detroit . . . Or Washington, DC!'" *Horn Book*, January/February 2001, 21, 24, 26, 29. In 1938 Stewart Robb found a single copy of *Oz* listed in the holdings of the New York Public Library ("The Red Wizard of Oz," *New Masses*, 4 October 1938, 8); in 1975 Alix Kates Shulman found that the New York Public Library carried only the original *Oz* and none of the subsequent volumes ("Ozomania under the Rainbow," *Village Voice*, 3 March 1975, reprinted in Hearn, ed., *Wizard of Oz*, 256). Ann E. Prentice reports that in the 1950s the children's room of the New York Public Library carried only *Oz*, though Baum's other titles were in the main reading room and the rare book collection ("Have You Been to See the Wizard?" *Top of the News*, November 1970, 40). Prentice also reports on its absence from a Chicago library in the 1930s and from unspecified libraries in New York State in 1969, and on its absence from such a list of recommended titles as the 1967 *Subject Index to Books for Primary Grades* (40–42).

30. Hamilton W. Mabie, "Mr. Mabie on Books for Young People," *Ladies' Home Journal*, October 1907, 24; "One Hundred Story Books for Children," *Bookman* (New York), November 1922, 366–67. As I've noted earlier, Mabie's list is somewhat quirky for the time: he includes nothing by Twain, nor does he list *Fauntleroy*. The *Bookman* list, prepared in consultation with eight prominent teachers, librarians, and professors, appears more representative of then-current thinking by the experts.

31. Irving Harlem Hart, "The Phenomena of Popularity in Fiction," *Library Journal*, 15 April 1923, 355–58; see Carrier, 206–11.

32. Cited in Carrier, 239.

33. Marion E. Potter, comp., assisted by Bertha Tannehill and Emma L. Teich, *The Children's Catalog: A Guide to the Best Reading for Young People Based on Twenty-Four Selected Library Lists* (Minneapolis: Wilson, 1909).

34. Nancy Larrick, *A Parent's Guide to Children's Reading* (1958; reprint, New York: Pocket, 1959), 64. Burnett is again omitted. Larrick, former president of the International Reading Association, lists consultants from organizations that range from the American Library Association to the Boy Scouts to the National Council of Teachers of English.

35. Cited in "10 Best American Children's Books in 200 Years Listed," *Publishers Weekly*, 23 February 1976, 64. The *Touchstones* list includes, in addition to picture books and folk tales, twenty-eight novels or series. According to the editor of the volumes, one fault of the list is that it "implies that there is no possibility for excellence outside the confines of linguistic distinction, and so eliminates innovative and popular but stylistically undistinguished authors like . . . Baum" (Perry Nodelman, "Introduction: Matthew Arnold, a Teddy Bear, and a List of Touchstones," in *Touchstones: Reflections on the Best in Children's Literature*, ed. Perry Nodelman [West Lafayette, Ind.: Children's Literature Association, 1985], 1:8).

36. Alison Lurie, *Don't Tell the Grown-ups: Subversive Children's Literature* (Boston: Little, Brown, 1990), x.

37. Lois Belfield Watt, "L. Frank Baum: The Widening World of Oz," *Imprint of the Stanford Libraries Associates*, October 1979, 17. Watt adds that at the time she was writing, Oz was available in the Palo Alto and Santa Clara County libraries.

38. Bernard M. Golumb, "A Defense of the Oz Books," *Library Journal*, 15 October 1957, reprinted in Hearn, ed., *Wizard of Oz*, 186.

39. Richard Paul Smyers, "A Librarian Looks at Oz," *Library Occurrent*, December 1964, 191, 192.

40. "Oz and the Fifth Criterion," *Baum Bugle*, Christmas 1971, reprinted in Hearn, ed., *Wizard of Oz*, 195. See also Paul Gallico, "This Man's World: *The Wonderful Wizard of Oz*," *Esquire*, February 1957, reprinted in Hearn, ed., *Wizard of Oz*, 183; Andre Norton, in *Books I Read When I Was Young: The Favorite Books of Famous People*, ed. Bernice Cullinan and M. Jerry Weiss (New York: Avon, 1980), 130.

41. Hearn, "'Toto,'" 19.

42. Osmond Beckwith, "The Oddness of Oz," *Children's Literature* 5 (1976), reprinted in Hearn, ed., *Wizard of Oz*, 233.

43. Gardner, "Why Librarians Dislike Oz," 191.

44. Hollister, 194.

45. Evelyn Geller, *Forbidden Books in American Public Libraries, 1876–1939* (Westport, Conn.: Greenwood, 1984), 143.

46. Gardner, "Why Librarians Dislike Oz," 190.

47. Sale, 224.

48. See, e.g., Hearn, introduction, *Annotated Wizard of Oz*, 29. *The Wonderful Wizard of Oz* was published by George M. Hill in Chicago; subsequent Oz books, indeed most of Baum's subsequent books, were published by the successor firm, Reilly and Britton, which later became Reilly and Lee.

49. See Deidre Johnson, *Edward Stratemeyer and the Stratemeyer Syndicate* (New York: Twayne, 1993), 6, 15.

50. Franklin K. Mathiews, "Blowing out the Boy's Brains," *Outlook*, 18 November 1914, 652–54. Mathiews was Chief Scout Librarian of the Boy Scouts.

51. Michael Patrick Hearn, "L. Frank Baum," in *American Writers for Children, 1900–1960*, ed. John Cech, vol. 22 of *Dictionary of Literary Biography* (Detroit: Gale, 1983), 21.

52. See Stuart Culver, "What Manikins Want: *The Wonderful Wizard of Oz* and *The Art of Decorating Dry Goods Windows*," *Representations*, no. 21 (Winter 1988): 97–116; William Leach, "Strategists of Display and the Production of Desire," in *Consuming Visions: Accumulation and Display of Goods in America, 1880–1920*, ed. Simon J. Bronner (New

York: Norton, 1989), 107–10; Stuart Culver, "Growing up in Oz," *American Literary History* 4 (Winter 1992): 607–28.

53. Susan Wolstenholme, introduction, *The Wonderful Wizard of Oz*, The World's Classics (Oxford: Oxford University Press, 1997), xvi. For a discussion of how Baum problematizes intellectual property boundaries as well, see M. David Westbrook, "Readers of Oz: Young and Old, Old and New Historicist," *Children's Literature Association Quarterly* 21 (Fall 1996): 116. For a counterargument that the Wizard is alien and Oz a socialist paradise, see Jack Zipes, *When Dreams Came True: Classical Fairy Tales and Their Tradition* (New York: Routledge, 1999), 159–82.

54. Wolstenholme, xx–xxii; David L. Greene and Dick Martin, *The Oz Scrapbook* (New York: Random House, 1977), 154. There was in fact a "Land of Oz" theme park in North Carolina between 1969 and 1980 (see John Fricke, Jay Scarfone, and William Stillman, *The Wizard of Oz: The Official Fiftieth Anniversary Pictorial History* [New York: Warner, 1989], 234); another was scheduled to open in Kansas in 2000 but has run into delays (see Martha Barnette, "Field Report: The 'Oz' Convention," *Salon*, 27 July 2000, www.salon.com/people/feature/2000/07/27/ozcon/index1.html, accessed 16 July 2001; Grace Hobson, "JoCo Commission Deadlocked Again on Oz Theme Park," *Kansas City Star*, 15 March 2001, www.kcstar.com/item/pages/home.pat,local/377534a2.315. html, accessed 16 July 2001).

55. Hearne, "Researching Oz," 59; Michael O. Riley, *Oz and Beyond: The Fantasy World of L. Frank Baum* (Lawrence: University Press of Kansas, 1997), 99.

56. Hearn, "L. Frank Baum," 27.

57. For Tate and Williams, see Evelyn B. Byrne and Otto M. Penzler, eds., *Attacks of Taste* (New York: Gotham Book Mart, 1971), 43, 48; for Krantz, see "Uncle Wiggily's Karma and Other Childhood Memories," *New York Times Book Review*, 7 December 1986, 47. Gardner adds Dylan Thomas, James Thurber, Phyllis McGinley, Philip Wylie, Ray Bradbury, Ellery Queen, and John Dickson Carr ("Librarians in Oz," 19).

58. Norton, 130.

59. Quoted in Amy Wallace and Jerry Griswold, "What Famous People Read," *Parade Magazine*, 13 March 1983, 25.

60. Hearn cites Elizabeth Fuller and John Rowe Townsend ("'Toto,'" 33).

61. Goldthwaite, 212.

62. Thwaite, 238.

63. Avery, *Behold the Child*, 145, 144.

64. Ibid., 145.

65. Gillian Avery et al., "Children's Literature in America, 1870–1945," in *Children's Literature: An Illustrated History*, ed. Peter Hunt et al. (Oxford: Oxford University Press, 1995), 241.

66. See, e.g., Paul Nathanson, *"The Wizard of Oz" as a Secular Myth of America* (Albany: State University of New York Press, 1991); Michael J. Murphy, "The Wizard of Oz as Cultural Narrative and Conceptual Model for Psychotherapy," *Psychotherapy* 33 (Winter 1996): 531–38; Henry M. Littlefield, "The Wizard of Oz: Parable on Populism," *American Culture* (1968), reprinted in Hearn, ed., *Wizard of Oz*, 221–33; Hugh Rockoff, "The 'Wizard of Oz' as a Monetary Allegory," *Journal of Political Economy* 98 (August 1990): 739–60; Francis MacDonnell, "'The Emerald City was the New Deal': E. Y. Harburg and *The Wonderful Wizard of Oz*," *Journal of American Culture* 13 (Winter 1990): 71–75.

67. See Hearn, "L. Frank Baum," 26.

68. See Beckwith, 234.

69. Edward Wagenknecht, "Utopia Americana: A Generation Afterwards," *American Book Collector,* December 1962, reprinted Hearn, ed., *Wizard of Oz,* 158.

70. Hearn, preface, in Hearn, ed., *Wizard of Oz,* xiv.

71. See Fricke, Scarfone, and Stillman, 15. For a checklist of seventy-two "published" book-length narratives about Oz—beyond the initial forty—see Stephen J. Teller, "A Checklist of Published Apocrypha," *Baum Bugle* 34 (Fall 1990): 14–21. Joel Chaston refers to an online list of 150 Oz novels ("Baum, Bakhtin, and Broadway: A Centennial Look at the Carnival of Oz," *The Lion and the Unicorn* 25 [2001]: 128); the list no longer seems to be online.

72. See Greene and Martin, 78.

73. Ruth Plumly Thompson was also young when she assumed the mantle of Royal Historian in 1919: part of the Oz mythology is that she was only twenty; she was in fact twenty-eight.

74. See Riley, 204.

75. Riley points to an early published manifestation of this urge, a 1926 story in the magazine *Child's Garden for Cheerful and Happy Homes,* by nine- and thirteen-year-old siblings (239).

76. Richard Flynn, "The Imitation Oz: The Sequel as Commodity," *The Lion and the Unicorn* 20 (1996): 123.

77. Certainly Holmes and Watson are memorable. Though as for Star Trek, the three later generations, each a series in its own right, do not replicate the original cast of characters. Worf may figure in more than one series, and two generations may mingle in the occasional Star Trek movie, but such carryover is largely confined to cameo appearances. Maybe what's significant in the Trekkie phenomenon is the memorability of species rather than individual characters—the Vulcans, the Klingons, the Borg.

78. Katy Lau, "An Ozzy 'Aloha' from a Hawaiian Fan," *Oz Gazette* 8 (Winter 1996), cited in Suzanne Rahn, *The Wizard of Oz: Shaping an Imaginary World* (New York: Twayne, 1998), 79. For the pioneering work that suggests that fantasy is driven not by fixed identifications but by "the shifting place of the subject and desubjectification"—by the possibility of identifying with an entire scene—see Jean Laplanche and J.-B. Pontalis, "Fantasy and the Origins of Sexuality," *International Journal of Psycho-Analysis* 49 (1968): 1–18. Perhaps also Baum's notorious casualness with respect to style has made him less intimidating to imitate. In any case, I am grateful for July 1995 discussions on the Children's Literature: Criticism and Theory e-mail list, particularly contributions from Monica Edinger and Marya DeVoto, for insights that I've played with in this paragraph. For a good discussion of participatory fan culture—though it does not address the Oz phenomenon—see Henry Jenkins, *Textual Poachers: Television Fans and Participatory Culture* (New York: Routledge, 1992).

79. Yet participatory fan cultures—and that's one way in which Thompson's work could be defined—have often been particularly inviting to women (see Constance Penley, "Feminism, Psychoanalysis, and the Study of Popular Culture," in *Cultural Studies,* ed. Lawrence Grossberg, Carey Nelson, and Paula A. Treichler [New York: Routledge, 1992], 479–500). At least 20 percent of the authors of "apocrypha" listed by Teller are women.

80. Ray Bradbury, "Two Baumy Promenades along the Yellow Brick Road," *Los An-*

geles Times Book Review, 9 October 1977, 1. Subsequent quotations in this and the next paragraph are from p. 3.

81. Baum, in Hearn, *Annotated Wizard of Oz*, 125.

82. Bradbury, "Two Baumy Promenades," 3.

83. Wolstenholme, xxxiv.

84. Douglas J. McReynolds and Barbara J. Lips, "A Girl in the Game: *The Wizard of Oz* as Analog for the Female Experience in America," *North Dakota Quarterly* 54 (Spring 1986): 88. See also Katharine Rogers, "Liberation for Little Girls," *Saturday Review*, 17 June 1972, 72, 75.

85. See Linda Rohrer Paige, "Wearing the Red Shoes," *Journal of Popular Film and Television* 23 (1996): 146–53; Bonnie Friedman, "Relinquishing Oz: Every Girl's Anti-Adventure Story," *Michigan Quarterly Review* 35 (Winter 1996): 9–28. Or, for the argument that Baum's Dorothy is more independent than MGM's, see, e.g., Mark I. West, "The Dorothys of Oz: A Heroine's Unmaking," in *Stories and Society: Children's Literature in its Social Context*, ed. Dennis Butts (New York: St. Martin's, 1992), 125–31.

86. For a Jungian analysis of the gay following, see Robert H. Hopcke, "Dorothy and her Friends: Symbols of Gay Male Individuation in *The Wizard of Oz*," *Quadrant* 22 (1989): 65–77.

87. Eve Kosofsky Sedgwick, quoted in Kim Michasiw, "Camp, Masculinity, Masquerade," in *Feminism Meets Queer Theory*, ed. Elizabeth Weed and Naomi Schor (Bloomington: Indiana University Press, 1997), 164.

88. Quoted in Barnette. See also Richard Smith, "Daring to Dream," *Gay Times* (London), April 1996, 60–61.

89. Chaston would concur (129). For a listing of 1980s allusions, see Nathanson, 302–5. See also issues of the *Baum Bugle;* a 2000 issue lists more than a hundred media allusions in that year alone ("Oz in the News," *Baum Bugle*, Autumn 2000, 37–43). As Fricke and his coauthors note, "By the mid-1980s, it would be a rare week of TV viewing that did not provide several direct or indirect references drawn from MGM's *Oz*" (238).

90. David Ansen, "Our Movies, Ourselves," *Newsweek Extra*, Summer 1998, 10. In particular, it's Margaret Hamilton's Wicked Witch who seized his imagination: "As far as I'm concerned, every witch since then has been an impostor, a fraud, a mere shadow of the ur-witch."

91. Fricke, Scarfone, and Stillman, 241; see also 216, 220, 222.

92. Aljean Harmetz, "After 46 Years, Hollywood Revisits Oz," *New York Times*, 16 June 1985, sec. 2, 1, 10. See also "How *The Wizard* Rates," 19–23.

93. Douglas Street, "The Wonderful Wiz That Was: The Curious Transformation of *The Wizard of Oz*," *Kansas Quarterly* 16 (Summer 1984): 95, 97.

94. Salman Rushdie, *The Wizard of Oz* (1992; reprint, London: British Film Institute, 1993), 18.

95. See Allen Eyles, *The World of Oz* (Tucson: HP Books, 1985), 50, citing a statement by Baum's son.

96. Fricke, Scarfone, and Stillman, 16.

97. Ibid., 18.

98. Producer Mervyn LeRoy, quoted in ibid., 85. The studio decided to delay news about the filming until just before the film's release out of fear that "indiscriminate art" might give the impression that the film was just "a child's fantasy" (*Daily Variety*, 8 May 1939, quoted in ibid., 124).

99. Jack Moffat, *Kansas City Star; Variety*, 16 August 1939; *Hollywood Spectator*, 2 September 1939—quoted in Fricke, Scarfone, and Stillman, 186, 183, 174.

100. Quoted in Fricke, Scarfone, and Stillman, 212.

101. Karla Walters has made a similar suggestion, in "Golden Press," Children's Literature: Criticism and Theory e-mail list, 4 July 1995.

SEVEN: The Case of British Fantasy Imports

1. R. W. G. Vail, *Alice in Wonderland: The Manuscript and Its Story* (New York: New York Public Library, 1928), 8.

2. Quoted in Luther H. Evans, "The Return of *Alice's Adventures under Ground*," *Columbia Library Columns* 15 (November 1965): 29–35. See also Selwyn H. Goodacre, "The 'Alice' Manuscript—From 1928," *Jabberwocky* 7 (Autumn 1978): 85–88.

3. Gillian Avery et al., "Children's Literature in America, 1870–1945," in *Children's Literature: An Illustrated History*, ed. Peter Hunt et al. (Oxford: Oxford University Press, 1995), 227.

4. Mary F. Thwaite, *From Primer to Pleasure in Reading*, rev. ed. (Boston: Horn Book, 1972), 238.

5. There were also fewer American reviews, not uncommon for works first published in England. But there were nevertheless some American reviews, even if most accounts of the early reception of Carroll's work ignore them. For exceptions to this trend of omission, see Richard L. Darling, *The Rise of Children's Book Reviewing in America, 1865–1881* (New York: Bowker, 1968), esp. 237–41; and Dorothy Otterman Matthews's immensely useful "The Literary Reputation of Lewis Carroll in England and America in the Nineteenth Century" (diss., Western Reserve University, 1962). I am indebted to Matthews's painstaking combing of nineteenth-century periodicals for leads to pieces that are referred to nowhere else in Carroll criticism.

6. *Catholic World*, June 1869, 469.

7. *Overland Monthly*, July 1869, 102. Another sign of American interest is that *Wonderland* was immediately pirated, at this time when there was no international copyright law, in the January and February 1867 issues of *Merryman's Monthly*, in *Haney's Journal* in 1869, and in two separately bound volumes, *Fun for All* and vol. 1 of *The Children's Library* (see Selwyn Goodacre, "The Nineteenth-Century American *Alice*," in *Proceedings of the Second International Lewis Carroll Conference*, ed. Charlie Lovett [n.p.: Lewis Carroll Society of North America, 1994], 69).

8. *New York Times*, 27 November 1866, 2.

9. *New York Times*, 25 December 1871, quoted in Matthews, 105.

10. "Some Holiday Books," *Nation*, 13 December 1866, 468.

11. *Nation*, 8 February 1872, 95.

12. "The Rev. C. L. Dodgson Dead," *New York Times*, 16 January 1898, 7.

13. The earliest such listing located by Matthews (145), and one of the first published listings of books recommended for children, is James Smart, *Books and Reading for the Young* (Indianapolis, Ind.: Carlon, 1880). See also Matthews, 166–67, 227, 232, 270.

14. Quoted in Matthews, 232.

15. "A Century of Alice," *Newsweek*, 12 July 1965, 86.

16. See *Knight Letter*, Spring 1996, [12]; Summer 1995, [5]. For documentation of the proliferation of Alice images in the United States, see Byron W. Sewell, *Lewis Carroll in*

the Popular Culture: A Continuing List (New York: Lewis Carroll Society of North America, 1976).

17. Vicki Weissman, "That Girl Is Everywhere," *New York Times Book Review*, 11 November 1990, 55.

18. See Robert Phillips, foreword, *Aspects of Alice: Lewis Carroll's Dreamchild as Seen through the Critics' Looking-Glasses, 1865–1971*, ed. Robert Phillips (New York: Vanguard, 1971), xix. Such a claim may not be entirely borne out by dictionaries of quotations: the 1953 *Shorter Bartlett's Familiar Quotations* lists only 16 entries for Carroll, compared with 20 for Twain, 102 for Tennyson, and 805 for Shakespeare. Still, the *Shorter Bartlett's* omits such Carrollian favorites as "curiouser and curiouser," and of course the number of items listed in a dictionary of quotations is not the surest gauge of frequency of citation: a single phrase may be quoted repeatedly.

19. *Woman's Home Companion*, March 1908, 28 (see also June 1910, 30); *Time*, 23 June 1975, cited in Sewell, K17; *Colorado Business Magazine*, cited in *Knight Letter*, Spring 1996, [11]; *Chest* 108 (October 1995): 1129–39; *University of Texas Law Review*, 27 October 1973, cited in Sewell, K30. See also Sewell, K10, K14–16, K19, K22, K25, K27, K29.

20. Virginia Woolf, "Lewis Carroll" (1939), in *The Moment and Other Essays* (1948), reprinted in her *Collected Essays* (1966; reprint, New York: Harcourt, Brace, 1967), 1:255; Lawrence J. Burpee, "Alice Joins the Immortals," *Dalhousie Review* 21 (1941): 194–201.

21. Phyllis Greenacre, *Swift and Carroll: A Psychoanalytic Study of Two Lives* (New York: International Universities Press, 1955), excerpt reprinted in Phillips, 331.

22. Hamilton W. Mabie, "The Most Popular Novels in America," *Forum*, December 1893, 509.

23. Frank Luther Mott, *Golden Multitudes: The Story of Best Sellers in the United States* (New York: Macmillan, 1947), 8. Like other works in the public domain, *Wonderland* has not been included on subsequent lists of best-sellers, even when such lists lay claim in their titles to naming "all-time bestsellers."

24. Cited in Esther Jane Carrier, *Fiction in Public Libraries, 1900–1950* (Littleton, Colo.: Libraries Unlimited, 1985), 289.

25. Carleton Washburne and Mabel Vogel, *Winnetka Graded Book List* (Chicago: American Library Association, 1926).

26. Gillian Adams, "Student Response to *Alice in Wonderland* and *At the Back of the North Wind*," *Children's Literature Association Quarterly* 10 (Spring 1985): 8–9.

27. The total population surveyed is almost twelve hundred students. *Wonderland* is the eleventh most frequently cited work.

28. Alexander Woollcott, introduction, *The Complete Works of Lewis Carroll* (1936; reprint, New York: Vintage, 1976), 9; Edmund Wilson, "C. L. Dodgson: The Poet Logician," reprinted in Phillips, esp. 202; Warren Weaver, "In Pursuit of Lewis Carroll," *Library Chronicle of the University of Texas at Austin*, n.s., 2 (November 1970), reprinted in *Lewis Carroll at Texas*, comp. Robert N. Taylor et al. (Austin: Harry Ransom Humanities Research Center, University of Texas, 1985), 9; James Cain and Allen Tate quoted in *Attacks of Taste*, ed. Evelyn B. Byrne and Otto M. Penzler (New York: Gotham Book Mart, 1971), 9–10, 43.

29. Hentoff in "Looking Backwards—and Ahead—with 'Alice,'" *Wilson Library Bulletin* 45 (October 1970): 170; Nash, Wilbur, and Williams in Byrne and Penzler, 32, 48, 48; Sendak in Bernice Cullinan and M. Jerry Weiss, eds., *Books I Read When I Was Young: The Favorite Books of Famous People* (New York: Avon, 1980), 152; Krantz in "Uncle Wig-

gily's Karma and Other Childhood Memories," *New York Times Book Review,* 7 December 1986, 47; Midler in "When I Was Very Young," *Ladies' Home Journal,* April 1991, 84; Oates in her "First Loves: From 'Jabberwocky' to 'After Apple-Picking,'" *American Poetry Review,* November/December 1999, 9.

30. Walt Disney, "How I Cartooned 'Alice': Its Logical Nonsense Needed a Logical Sequence," *Films in Review* 11 (May 1951): 9.

31. Robert Graves, "Alice" (1925), reprinted in Phillips, 114.

32. Carolyn Sigler, *Alternative Alices: Visions and Revisions of Lewis Carroll's "Alice" Books* (Lexington: University Press of Kentucky, 1997), 387–91.

33. Anne Eaton, "Widening Horizons, 1840–1890," in *A Critical History of Children's Literature,* ed. Cornelia Meigs (New York: Macmillan, 1953), 210.

34. See Kevin W. Sweeney, "Alice's Discriminating Palate," *Philosophy and Literature* 23 (1999): 17–31.

35. Michael Hancher, "Alice's Audiences," in *Romanticism and Children's Literature in Nineteenth-Century England,* ed. James Holt McGavran, Jr. (Athens: University of Georgia Press, 1991), 198. In the eighth edition of Arbuthnot's textbook, revised by Zena Sutherland, these comments are framed by the acknowledgment that some children dislike fantasy (May Hill Arbuthnot, *Children and Books,* 8th ed., rev. Zena Sutherland [New York: HarperCollins, 1991], 257).

36. Charlotte S. Huck, *Children's Literature in the Elementary School,* 3d ed., updated (New York: Holt, 1979), 256.

37. Sigler, xvi.

38. Mary Wilkinson et al., *The Right Book for the Right Child: A Graded Buying List of Children's Books* (New York: Day, 1933), 56.

39. The film was a relative failure, both financially and critically, when it first appeared. Disney later said he did not much like it, having felt trapped by the book's literary reputation, though it's also the case that he didn't attend as closely to the details of production as he had for earlier films, engrossed as he was with creating Disneyland. A Disney animator has pointed to the presence of too many directors: "Here was a case of five directors each trying to top the other guys and make his sequences the biggest and craziest in the show. This had a self-cancelling effect on the final product" (quoted in Leonard Maltin, *The Disney Films* [New York: Crown, 1973], 103).

Richard Schickel suggests that the inflexible realism of what had become the studio style prevented the Disney artists from capturing "the free, fantastical parody of conventional logic which is the reason for *Alice*'s existence and which makes it a work of art" (*The Disney Version: The Life, Times, Art, and Commerce of Walt Disney* [New York: Simon, 1968], 296). Disney himself felt "it was imperative that we create a plot structure," for "when you look at a moving picture you do not have a chance to ponder over the meaning, or to re-read" ("How I Cartooned 'Alice,'" 8, 9).

40. The video has "been consistently at the top of the family programming charts for 17 years," according to a report of Daniel Singer's talk "Disney's *Alice* in Theme Parks and Beyond," presented at the fall 1998 meeting of the Lewis Carroll Society of North America ("Fall in Angeles," *Knight Letter,* Winter 1999, 2).

41. "The Point of View," *Scribner's,* April 1896, 519; cited in Matthews, 268.

42. "Lewis Carroll," *Dial,* 1 February 1898, 65–66.

43. *Library Quarterly* (1936), quoted in Carrier, 212.

44. See Carrier, 213–16.

45. Alice M. Jordan, "Children's Classics," *Horn Book*, February 1947, reprinted in her *Children's Classics*, 5th ed. (Boston: Horn Book, 1976), 3. She continued, "It delights us when we are young, it is cherished, reread and quoted for its philosophy and humor when we are old."

46. Clifton Fadiman, *The Lifetime Reading Plan*, rev. ed. (New York: Crowell, 1978), 72. Carroll appears in both the 1960 and the revised 1978 editions. Fadiman also includes the more ambiguously situated *Adventures of Huckleberry Finn*.

47. William Harmon, ed., *The Concise Columbia Book of Poetry* (1990), reprinted as *The Classic Hundred: All-Time Favorite Poems* (New York: Columbia University Press, n.d.), 36. The rankings are based on the ninth edition of *The Columbia Granger's Index to Poetry*.

48. G. K. Chesterton, *New York Times* (1932), reprinted in *A Handful of Authors: Essays on Books and Writers*, ed. Dorothy Collins (1953; reprint, New York: Kraus, 1969), 113.

49. G. K. Chesterton, "The Library of the Nursery," *Daily News* (1901), reprinted in *Lunacy and Literacy*, ed. Dorothy Collins (New York: Sheed, 1958), 26.

50. Ibid., 27.

51. G. K. Chesterton, *The Spice of Life and Other Essays*, ed. Dorothy Collins (Beaconsfield, England: Finlayson, 1964), 68.

52. Martin Gardner, "A Child's Garden of Bewilderment," *Saturday Review*, 17 July 1965, reprinted in *Only Connect: Readings on Children's Literature*, ed. Sheila Egoff, T. T. Stubbs, and L. F. Ashley, 2d ed. (Toronto: Oxford University Press, 1980), 151.

53. *Putnam's*, July 1869, 124. Reviewers of the 1860s often gave greater praise to the better-known Tenniel's illustrations than to Carroll's text.

54. *Spectator*, 23 December 1865, 1441; *Spectator*, 4 December 1869, 1431.

55. *Nation*, 8 April 1869, 276.

56. C. M. H[ewins], letter, *Nation*, 15 April 1869, 295.

57. Lewis Carroll, *Alice's Adventures in Wonderland*, in *Alice in Wonderland: Authoritative Texts of "Alice's Adventures in Wonderland," "Through the Looking-Glass," "The Hunting of the Snark,"* ed. Donald J. Gray (New York: Norton, 1971), 8. For a good discussion of the double audience that Carroll necessarily addressed, see U. C. Knoepflmacher, "The Balancing of Child and Adult: An Approach to Victorian Fantasies for Children," *Nineteenth-Century Fiction* 37 (1983): 497–530.

58. "Lewis Carroll," *Dial*, 1 February 1898, 66.

59. Ibid.

60. Woolf, 255.

61. Katherine Anne Porter, Bertrand Russell, and Mark Van Doren, "Lewis Carroll: *Alice in Wonderland*," transcript of radio broadcast, in *The New Invitation to Learning*, ed. Mark Van Doren (New York: Random House, 1942), 209, 210.

62. Peter Heath, introduction, *The Philosopher's Alice: "Alice's Adventures in Wonderland" and "Through the Looking-Glass*, illus. John Tenniel (New York: St. Martin's, 1974), 3.

63. Morton N. Cohen, "Curiouser and Curiouser! The Endurance of Little Alice," *New York Times Book Review*, 11 November 1990, 54.

64. Anthony Quinton, "Humpty-Dumpty for Eggheads," *TLS*, 20 December 1974, 1436.

65. In the middle of the century *Wonderland* seemed to offer a good deal of pleasure to psychoanalysts as well. In a 1936 address to the American Psychoanalytical Society, Paul Schilder claimed that Carroll was guilty of portraying "oral sadistic trends of canni-

balism," among other things ("'Alice in Wonderland' a Sadistic Fantasy, Bad for Children, Psychiatrist Declares," *New York Times,* 30 December 1936, 10). For a useful overview of psychoanalytic criticism, see Paula Johnson, "Alice among the Analysts," *Hartford Studies in Literature* 4 (1972): 114–22.

66. John Macy, "Her Majesty's Jesters," *Bookman* (New York), April 1931, 155.

67. See Calvin R. Petersen, "Time and Stress: Alice in Wonderland," *Journal of the History of Ideas* 44 (1985): 427–28.

68. Martin Gardner, introduction, *The Annotated Alice: "Alice's Adventures in Wonderland" and "Through the Looking-Glass,"* illus. John Tenniel ([New York]: Potter, 1960), 8.

69. J. H. Dohm, "Alice in America," *Junior Bookshelf* 5 (October 1965): 265.

70. Or writers are reluctant to appreciate the way that Carroll gives play to naive and sophisticated readings within child readers, not just directing the naive to children and the sophisticated to adults; see Alan Richardson, "Nineteenth-Century Children's Satire and the Ambivalent Reader," *Children's Literature Association Quarterly* 15 (Fall 1990): 125.

71. Sigler, xvi.

72. See Michael Holquist, "What is a Boojum? Nonsense and Modernism," *Yale French Studies* 43 (1969): 145–64.

73. Adam Gopnik, "Wonderland," *New Yorker,* 9 October 1995, 90. For the fullest account of Carroll's influence on (primarily British) modernists, see Juliet Dusinberre, *Alice to the Lighthouse: Children's Books and Radical Experiments in Art* (New York: St. Martin's, 1987).

74. I am indebted to the amplitude of Rachel Fordyce's bibliography, *Lewis Carroll: A Reference Guide* (Boston: Hall, 1988). Also striking, as James R. Kincaid notes of the commentary, is "its wild variety (the variety less striking than the wildness)" (preface, *Alice's Adventures in Wonderland,* illus. Barry Moser [Berkeley: University of California Press, 1982], 7). Was Carroll the real author, some commentators speculate, or was it Queen Victoria, as evidenced by a word-frequency study of italicized words in the Alice books and the Queen's diaries? Or perhaps Mark Twain? Or was Carroll really Jack the Ripper? Is *Looking-Glass* an allegory of Judaism, given that when one reads "Jabber" and "wocky" backwards one almost gets Rabbi Yacov? Or do the two books refer to religious controversies at Oxford at the time, or does the "Pig and Pepper" chapter refer to Queen Elizabeth rescuing her natural son Bacon from murder? And that's not counting the drug-trip and pornographic versions. For the fullest compendium of "wild" interpretations, see Phillips's collection.

75. Ursula K. Le Guin, *Buffalo Gals and Other Animal Presences* (Santa Barbara, Calif.: Capra, 1987), 10.

76. Avery, *Behold the Child,* 142.

77. Clifton Fadiman, "Books for Children," *Holiday Magazine,* revised and reprinted in his *Party of One: The Selected Writings* (Cleveland: World, 1955), 385. At the same time he was a bit bemused by twentieth-century Carrollatry (Fadiman, "The Maze in the Snow," in his *Party of One,* 404–10).

78. Donald Rackin, "Alice's Journey to the End of Night," *PMLA* 81 (1966): 313.

79. See Michael Pakenham, "The $1 Billion Potter Payoff," *Baltimore Sun,* 17 July 2000, F1, http://web.lexis-nexis.com, accessed 3 August 2000.

80. Mott, 7.

81. Elizabeth Mehren, "Upward and Onward toward Book Seven—Her Way," *Los Angeles Times,* 25 October 2000, E1, http://web.lexis-nexis.com, accessed 18 January 2001. Within two and a half years of publication, *Harry Potter and the Sorcerer's Stone* had

sold 15.9 million copies, equal to almost 6 percent of the U.S. population in 2000. See "Wild about Harry," *New York Times*, 1 March 2001, C1, http://web.lexis-nexis.com, accessed 5 June 2001.

82. Tim Wynne-Jones, "Harry Potter and the Blaze of Publicity: On the Whole, the Junior Wizard Deserves It All," *Ottawa Citizen*, 16 July 2000, C16, http://web. lexis-nexis.com, accessed 3 August 2000.

83. See Brian MacArthur, "Rowling Books Unique Place in History," *Times* (London), 21 December 2001, http://web.lexis-nexis.com, accessed 4 February 2002.

84. Quoted in Barbara F. Meltz, "Child Caring: Harry Has Special Powers—Over Us," *Boston Globe*, 13 July 2000, 3d ed., E1, http://web.lexis-nexis.com, accessed 3 August 2000. Children's books that are this popular are also likely to attract would-be censors, and indeed the Harry Potter books have: the series topped the ALA list of the most challenged books of 1999 (see www.ala.org/news/archives/v5n12/99bookchallenges.html). The objections come from conservative Christians concerned about the positive portrayal of witchcraft; for a thoughtful account of why some conservative Christians object, see Kimbra Wilder Gish, "Hunting down Harry Potter: An Exploration of Religious Concerns about Children's Literature," *Horn Book*, May/June 2000, 262–71.

85. Jonathan Levi, "Pottermania," *Los Angeles Times*, 16 July 2000, Book Review, 1, http://web.lexis-nexis.com, accessed 3 August 2000.

86. Anthony Holden, "Why Harry Potter Doesn't Cast a Spell over Me," *Observer*, 25 June 2000, www.observer.co.uk/review/story/0,6903,335923,00.html, accessed 25 June 2000.

87. The 43 percent statistic from Sandy Naiman, "Not Just for Kids; Like Other Literary Classics, Harry Potter Casts a Spell on Readers of All Ages," *Toronto Sun*, 22 November 2001, 75, http://web.lexis-nexis.com, accessed 11 January 2002; the 30 percent estimate from Rowling's U.S. publisher, as cited in Kera Bolonik, "A List of Their Own," *Salon*, 16 August 2000, 1, www.salon.com/mwt/feature/2000/08/16/bestseller/index.html, accessed 22 January 2001; the 60 percent estimate from Seth Schiesel, "Young Viewers Like Screen Translation," *New York Times*, 19 November 2001, E1, http://web. lexis-nexis.com, accessed 11 January 2002.

88. Alison Lurie, "Not for Muggles," *New York Review of Books*, 16 December 1999, 6.

89. Eden Ross Lipson, "Bookmarks: The Downside of Kiddie Classics," *Minneapolis Star Tribune*, 23 July 2000, F16, http://web.lexis-nexis.com, accessed 3 August 2000.

90. William Safire, "Besotted with Potter," *New York Times*, 27 January 2000, A27. Safire quotes "the infantilization of adult culture" from Philip Hensher in the *Independent*. A more recent writer in the *Independent*, Jonathan Myerson, echoes Safire's condescension: "There is no such psychological understanding ["understanding of complex human psychologies"] in children's novels" ("Harry Potter and the Sad Grown-ups," *Independent*, 14 November 2001, http://enjoyment.independent.co.uk/books/news/story.jsp?story=105103, accessed 24 November 2001).

91. Lana Whited, "Could Harry Potter Rescue the Eminent Columnist?" 12 February 2000, www.roanoke.com/magazine/whited/, accessed 16 February 2000.

92. Holden, "Why Harry Potter."

93. See Chris Reidy, "Publishing's New Adventure," *Boston Globe*, 8 September 1999, D4.

94. Harold Bloom, "Can 35 Million Book Buyers Be Wrong? Yes," *Wall Street Journal*, 11 July 2000, A26.

95. Ibid.

96. Doreen Carvajal, "Booksellers Grab a Young Wizard's Cloaktails," *New York Times*, A16. See also Elizabeth Gleich and Andrea Sachs on some publishers pressuring the *New York Times* to exclude children's literature from the best-seller list ("Wild about Harry," *Time*, 20 September 1999, 67–68); and Philip Nel's thorough account of Rowling's reception through the end of 1999, noting, for instance, that the London *Times* already had a policy of excluding children's literature from its main best-seller list ("The Harry Potter Phenomenon," in *Dictionary of Literary Biography Yearbook: 1999*, ed. Matthew J. Bruccoli [Detroit: Gale, 2000], 173–79).

97. Dinitia Smith, "The Times Plans a Children's Best-Seller List," *New York Times*, 24 June 2000, B12, http://web.lexis-nexis.com, accessed 3 August 2000.

98. Karen Sandstrom, "Harry Brings Victory to Children's Literature," Cleveland *Plain Dealer*, 25 July 2000, E5, http://web.lexis-nexis.com, accessed 3 August 2000.

99. Sandstrom, E5. She goes on to say that "the change is a victory for authors and publishers of adult fiction."

100. Bolonik, 2.

101. Margaret Weir, "Of Magic and Single Motherhood," *Salon*, 31 March 1999, www.salon.com/mwt/feature/1999/03/cov_31featureb.html, accessed 6 March 2000; Polly Shulman, "Not for Children Only," *Slate*, 23 August 1999, http//:slate.msn.com/id/2000111/entry/1003466, accessed 21 March 2003.

102. Malcolm Jones, "The Return of Harry Potter!" *Newsweek*, 10 July 2000, 59.

103. Quoted in Holden.

104. Myerson, "Harry Potter"; Pico Iyer, "The Playing Fields of Hogwarts," *New York Times Book Review*, 10 October 1999, 39.

105. Bloom, "Can 35 Million?" A26.

106. Kevin C. Stephens, "'Goblet of Fire' Sets Magical Scene, but Leaves You Wanting More," *Buffalo News*, 12 July 2000, D1, http://web.lexis-nexis.com, accessed 3 August 2000.

107. Lisa Bruce, letter to the editor, *Newsweek*, 7 August 2000, 16.

108. Brian Heigel, age ten, and Megan Campanelle, age eleven, quoted in Jodi Wilgoren, "Don't Give Us Little Wizards, the Anti-Potter Parents Cry," *New York Times*, 1 November 1999, A21. For a sampling of statements suggesting the importance of Harry Potter's world, see Sharon Moore, ed., *We Love Harry Potter! We'll Tell You Why* (New York: St. Martin's Griffin, 1999), 6, 10; Bill Adler, ed., *Kids' Letters to Harry Potter from around the World* (New York: Carroll, 2001), 7, 29, 71, 99; Ruth Nicola, "Returning to Reading with Harry Potter," *Journal of Adolescent and Adult Literacy* 44 (May 2001): 746.

109. Cited in Rick Lyman, "Coming Soon: Harry Potter and Hollywood's Cash Cow," *New York Times*, 4 November 2001, 1A1, http://web.lexis-nexis.com, accessed 11 January 2002.

110. The media have been quick to pounce on papers and panels at scholarly conferences ranging from the meetings of the American Educational Research Association to those of the International Congress on Medieval Studies. See Michelle Nichols, "Harry Potter: Victim of the PC-Brigade," *Scotsman*, 5 May 2001, 5, http://web.lexis-nexis.com, accessed 5 June 2001; Stephen Kinzer, "An Improbable Sequel: Harry Potter and the Ivory Tower," *New York Times*, 12 May 2001, B13, http://web.lexis-nexis.com, accessed 5 June 2001; and, for a redaction of a paper presented at an MLA meeting, see June Cum-

mins, "Read between the Lines for a Lesson in Consumer Coercion," *Times Higher Education Supplement*, 21 December 2001, 20, http://web.lexis-nexis.com, accessed 11 January 2002.

111. Rick Lyman, "Box Office Was Busy, and Potter Was King," *New York Times*, 31 December 2001, E5, http://web.lexis-nexis.com, accessed 4 February 2002.

112. Since Rowling doesn't like action figures, Mattel took to calling its Harry Potter and Professor Snape dolls "collectible characters." See Julian E. Barnes, "The Media Business: Advertising; Dragons and Flying Brooms," *New York Times*, 1 March 2001, C1, http://web.lexis-nexis.com, accessed 5 June 2001.

113. Joel Chaston, "The 'Ozification' of American Children's Fantasy Films: *The Blue Bird, Alice in Wonderland,* and *Jumanji,*" *Children's Literature Association Quarterly* 22 (Spring 1997): 16.

E I G H T : The Case of the Disney Version

1. See Leonard Maltin, *The Disney Films* (New York: Crown, 1973), 101. At some point Disney also toyed with making a short film based on Carroll's "Jabberwocky" (see Charles Solomon, *The Disney That Never Was: The Stories and Art from Five Decades of Unproduced Animation* [New York: Hyperion, 1995], 66).

2. Eric Smoodin, *Animating Culture: Hollywood Cartoons from the Sound Era* (New Brunswick, N.J.: Rutgers University Press, 1993), 66–67.

3. See Leonard Mosley, *Disney's World* (New York: Stein, 1985), 135, 149, 151.

4. See "Walt Disney, 65, Dies on Coast; Founded an Empire on a Mouse," *New York Times*, 16 December 1966, 40.

5. Maltin, 11.

6. Quoted in Richard Schickel, *The Disney Version: The Life, Times, Art, and Commerce of Walt Disney* (New York: Simon & Schuster, 1968), 223.

7. Wells, Clair, and Kern quoted in Christopher Finch, *The Art of Walt Disney: From Mickey Mouse to the Magic Kingdoms,* rev. ed. (Burbank, Calif.: Disney, 1988), 54–55; Mark Van Doren, "Fairy Tale in Five Acts," *Nation*, 22 January 1938, 109; Benjamin quoted in Miriam Hansen, "Of Mice and Ducks: Benjamin and Adorno on Disney," *South Atlantic Quarterly* 92 (Winter 1993): 27–61; Eisenstein quoted in Steven Watts, *The Magic Kingdom: Walt Disney and the American Way of Life* (Boston: Houghton Mifflin, 1997), 128; E. M. Forster, "Mickey and Minnie," *Spectator*, 19 January 1934, 81.

8. David Low, "Leonardo da Disney," *New Republic*, 5 January 1942, 18.

9. See Watts, 101, 121.

10. See Mosley, 209; also, personal communication from a Disney archivist, May 2002.

11. Cited in Watts, 38.

12. Smoodin, 55.

13. See Arthur Mann, "Mickey Mouse's Financial Career," *Harper's*, May 1934, 721.

14. Frank S. Nugent, *New York Times*, 13 January 1938, 21; *Herald Tribune* quoted in Schickel, *Disney Version*, 222; Otis Ferguson, "Walt Disney's Grimm Reality," *New Republic*, 26 January 1938, 339.

15. Both quoted in Schickel, *Disney Version*, 235.

16. Lewis Jacobs, *The Rise of the American Film: A Critical History,* 3d ed. (1967; reprint, New York: Teachers College Press, 1975), 496.

17. Gilbert Seldes, quoted in Watts, 129.

18. Jean Charlot, "But Is It Art? A Disney Disquisition," *American Scholar* 8 (Summer 1939): 267, 269. For another account of how cartoons seemed to embody the essence of the film medium, see Gregory A. Waller, "Mickey, Walt, and Film Criticism from *Steamboat Willie* to *Bambi*," in *The American Animated Cartoon: A Critical Anthology*, ed. Danny Peary and Gerald Peary (New York: Dutton, 1980), 51–52.

19. "Mickey Mouse Gets Schools' Backing," *New York Times*, 16 July 1937, 21.

20. L. H. Robbins, "Mickey Mouse Emerges as Economist," *New York Times Magazine*, 10 March 1935, 8.

21. James Agee, *Agee on Film* (New York: McDowell, 1958), 18, 29, 307.

22. Quoted in Maltin, 14.

23. Erwin Panofsky, "Style and Medium in the Motion Pictures" (1934), revised and reprinted in *Critique* (1947), reprinted in *Film: An Anthology*, ed. Daniel Talbot (New York: Simon & Schuster, 1959), 23.

24. Jacobs, 504.

25. Dorothy Grafly, "America's Youngest Art," *American Magazine of Art*, July 1933, quoted in Watts, 121; Richard Schickel, "Walt Disney," *Time*, 7 December 1998, 124. Schickel suggests that "liberal intellectuals . . . found this demonstration of their idol's political views at surprising variance with the folkish merits of his films" (*Disney Version*, 260). But see Waller, 55.

26. Philip T. Hartung, "The Screen: Stars, Strikes, and Dragons," *Commonweal*, 8 August 1941, quoted in Watts, 213.

27. See Watts, 248; Maltin, 72.

28. Smoodin, 100–104.

29. James William Fitzpatrick, "Catering to the American Amusement Diet," *Motion Picture Herald*, 4 March 1931, quoted in Watts, 33.

30. Paul Hollister, "Walt Disney," *Atlantic*, December 1940, 695; Jacobs, 496.

31. M. F. L., "Walt Disney Scores Again," *Wall Street Journal*, 14 January 1938, quoted in Watts, 161.

32. Frank S. Nugent, "One Touch of Disney," *New York Times*, 23 January 1938, sec. 11, 5.

33. David Forgacs, "Disney Animation and the Business of Childhood," *Screen* 33 (Winter 1992): 366.

34. Richard deCordova, "The Mickey in Macy's Window: Childhood, Consumerism, and Disney Animation," in *Disney Discourse: Producing the Magic Kingdom*, ed. Eric Smoodin (New York: Routledge, 1994), 203–13; Richard deCordova, "Tracing the Child Audience: The Case of Disney, 1929–1933," in *Prima dei Codici 2: Alle porte di Hays*, XLVII Mostra Internazionale d'Arte Cinematografica (Venice: Fabbri Editori, 1991), 217–21.

35. See Cecil Munsey, *Disneyana: Walt Disney Collectibles* (New York: Hawthorne, 1974), 246, 81; Robert Heide and John Gilman, *Disneyana: Classic Collectibles, 1928–1958* (New York: Hyperion, 1994), 100, 70, 135, 130.

36. See Watts, 161.

37. Edward Atkins, " 'Snow White' Is Here to Stay," *Women's Wear Daily*, 9 February 1938, sec. 2, 2. *Snow White* was also unusual in that its apparel merchandising did not primarily target boys, with sweatshirts and the like (4).

38. See Green, 8.

39. "'Snow White' Theme Clothed in Ermine Too," *Women's Wear Daily*, 9 February 1938, sec. 2, 17.

40. See, e.g., Smoodin, 112–15.

41. See, e.g., Ellen Seiter, *Sold Separately: Children and Parents in Consumer Culture* (New Brunswick, N.J.: Rutgers University Press, 1993), 26–30.

42. See, e.g., Watts, 70, 239, 326. But for some indication that Disney was interested in a family audience even in the 1930s, see Walt Disney, "The Cartoon's Contribution to Children," *Overland Monthly* 91 (October 1933): 138; and J. B. Kaufman, "Good Mouse-keeping: Family-Oriented Publicity in Disney's Golden Age," *Animation Journal* 3 (Spring 1995): 78–85.

43. Watts, 327.

44. Ibid., xvi.

45. Stephen Jay Gould, "A Biological Homage to Mickey Mouse," in his *The Panda's Thumb: More Reflections in Natural History* (1980; reprint, New York: Norton, 1982), 96–100. Heide and Gilman, however, point out that Mickey's external trappings— long pants, suit and tie—often showed him as aging during the 1940s, 1950s, and 1960s (12).

46. Watts, 135.

47. For documentation of the studio's increasing emphasis on achieving "cuteness," in in-house discussions of its characters, see Forgacs, 364–65. Disney admits that, say, his Alice has features that "are somewhat more youthful than those of" Tenniel's Alice ("How I Cartooned 'Alice': Its Logical Nonsense Needed a Logical Sequence," *Films in Review* 11 [May 1951]: 10).

48. Schickel, *Disney Version*, 12.

49. Ibid., 86, 192, 247, 290, 361.

50. Ibid., 360.

51. Quoted in Maltin, 103; Schickel, *Disney Version*, 297; Maltin, 179. Individual reviewers continued to praise Disney productions, but the balance had tipped to the negative.

52. Dilys Powell, quoted in Maltin, 116–17.

53. Julian Halevy, "Disneyland and Las Vegas," *Nation*, 7 June 1958, 511; for a counter-response, see Ray Bradbury, letter, *Nation*, 28 June 1958, 572. The one group of professionals who have seemed inclined to laud Disney, in the 1960s and beyond, have been urban planners and perhaps architects, on the basis of his material innovations in Disneyland Park and Walt Disney World Resort (see especially Paul Goldberger, "Mickey Mouse Teaches the Architects," *New York Times Magazine*, 22 October 1972, 40–41, 92–99; Arata Isozaki, "Theme Park," *South Atlantic Quarterly* 92 [Winter 1993]: 175–82; and The Project on Disney, *Inside the Mouse: Work and Play at Disney World* [Durham: Duke University Press, 1995], 199–229).

54. C. A. LeJeune, quoted in Maltin, 156, 157.

55. Frances Clarke Sayers and Charles M. Weisenberg, "Walt Disney Accused," *Horn Book* 40 (December 1965), reprinted in *Children and Literature: Views and Reviews*, ed. Virginia Haviland (Glenview, Ill.: Scott, 1973), 124. Sayers's earliest response was a 1965 letter in the *Los Angeles Times*. Her comments may have been the first widely heard salvo, but other librarians, such as her predecessor at the New York Public Library, Anne Carroll Moore, had been expressing concern about Disney, especially the books based on the films, since 1938: see Moore's "The Three Owls' Notebook," *Horn Book* 14 (January/February 1938): 32.

56. Jane Yolen, "America's Cinderella," *Children's Literature in Education* 8 (1977), reprinted in *Cinderella: A Casebook*, ed. Alan Dundes (1982; reprint, Madison: University of Wisconsin Press, 1988), 303, 298.

57. Sean Kelly, "The Wonderful World of Dahl," *New York Times Book Review*, 19 May 1996, 33.

58. Anthony Holden, "Why Harry Potter Doesn't Cast a Spell over Me," *Observer*, 25 June 2000, www.observer.co.uk/review/story/0,6903,335923,00.html, accessed 25 June 2000.

59. *Charlotte's Web* is one of the two American works that bid fairest to become children's classics, among works published in the second half of the twentieth century; the other is Maurice Sendak's *Where the Wild Things Are* (1963). For information on popularity and sales, see, e.g., "All-Time Bestselling Hardcover Children's Books" and "All-Time Bestselling Paperback Children's Books," *Publishers Weekly*, 27 October 1989, 28, 29; "All-Time Bestselling Children's Books," *PW Online Edition*, 1996, www.bookwire.com/pw/articles/childrens/, accessed 4 January 1999; "Children's Best Sellers," *New York Times Book Review*, 22 May 1994, 26. The two books rank respectively first and second—a childhood favorite with 17 percent and 11 percent—in informal surveys in my "Children's Literature" class, though *Wild Things* has recently been outpacing *Charlotte's Web*.

As for esteem, a Children's Literature Association poll is representative: *Charlotte's Web* and *Wild Things* top this account of "10 Best American Children's Books in 200 Years Listed" (*Publishers Weekly*, 23 February 1976, 64). As for the relationship between White's reputation and his children's books, see Jason Epstein: "His success with his children's books served to enhance his reputation—and, into the bargain, to authenticate his sensitivity. You cannot, after all, fool children about these things, can you?" ("E. B. White," *Commentary* [1986], reprinted in his *Partial Payments: Essays on Writers and Their Lives* [New York: Norton, 1989], 298).

60. E. B. White to Ursula Nordstrom, 28 October 1969, *Letters of E. B. White*, ed. Dorothy Lobrano Guth (New York: Harper, 1976), 585.

61. White to Gene Deitch, 12 January [1971], *Letters*, 614.

62. White to Susanna Waterman, 26 March 1973, *Letters*, 646.

63. I draw on Maltin, 85–87, for this summary.

64. Michael Eisner to Shareholders, The Walt Disney Company Annual Report 2001, http://disney.go.com/corporate/investors/financials/annual.html, accessed 20 February 2002.

65. Robert W. McChesney, "The Global Media Giants," *Extra!* November/December 1997, www.fair.org/extra/9711/gmg.html#disney, accessed 20 February 2002.

66. Elizabeth Bell, "Somatexts at the Disney Shop: Constructing the Pentimentos of Women's Animated Bodies," in *From Mouse to Mermaid: The Politics of Film, Gender, and Culture*, ed. Elizabeth Bell, Lynda Haas, and Laura Sells (Bloomington: Indiana University Press, 1995), 112.

67. Lori Kenschaft, "Just a Spoonful of Sugar? Anxieties of Gender and Class in 'Mary Poppins,'" in *Girls, Boys, Books, Toys: Gender in Children's Literature and Culture*, ed. Beverly Lyon Clark and Margaret R. Higonnet (Baltimore: Johns Hopkins University Press, 1999), 241, 242.

68. Seiter, 232.

69. Francelia Butler, "The Trashing of Children's Literature," *Ms.*, September/Octo-

ber 1992, 61; John R. Dunlap, "Kiddie Litter," *American Spectator*, December 1989, 19–21.

70. Dunlap, 20.

71. Ibid.

72. Erica Wagner, "Courageous and Dangerous: A Writer for All Ages," *Times* (London), 23 January 2002, http://web.lexis-nexis.com, accessed 18 March 2002.

73. For papers from the forum, see *Signal* 87 (September 1998).

74. British critics have been active too: witness various works by Peter Hunt, beginning with the collection *Children's Literature: The Development of Criticism* (London: Routledge, 1990).

75. Walt Disney, interview (1956), quoted in Watts, 401.

Essay on Sources

This bibliographical essay is not intended to be a comprehensive guide to criticism of children's literature but simply lists the secondary sources I have found most helpful. It concentrates on sources that address critical response and that place works of children's literature in cultural contexts. I should stress that even within these parameters the bibliography is not complete; interested readers may want to track down additional references in the notes for each chapter.

I won't list the scores of exciting works of criticism addressing children's literature that have appeared in the last two decades, except to note that the fullest single compendium of approaches is Peter Hunt, ed., *International Companion Encyclopedia of Children's Literature* (London: Routledge, 1996).

Among recent works that address the positioning of children in the English-speaking world—providing background for Chapter 1—the ones I found especially helpful are Anne Higonnet, *Pictures of Innocence: The History and Crisis of Ideal Childhood* (London: Thames, 1998); Henry Jenkins, ed., *The Children's Culture Reader* (New York: New York University Press, 1998); James R. Kincaid, *Erotic Innocence: The Culture of Child Molesting* (Durham: Duke University Press, 1998); Adam Phillips, *The Beast in the Nursery* (New York: Pantheon, 1998); Jacqueline Rose, *The Case of Peter Pan, or the Impossibility of Children's Fiction* (1984; reprint, Philadelphia: University of Pennsylvania Press, 1993); Ellen Seiter, *Sold Separately: Children and Parents in Consumer Culture* (New Brunswick, N.J.: Rutgers University Press, 1993); Cary Bazalgette and David Buckingham, eds., *In Front of the Children: Screen Entertainment and Young Audiences* (London: British Film Institute, 1995); and Beverly Lyon Clark and Margaret R. Higonnet, eds., *Girls, Boys, Books, Toys: Gender in Children's Literature and Culture* (Baltimore: Johns Hopkins University Press, 1999).

One way of gauging esteem for a literary work is to look at lists of recommended reading. The lists of recommended juvenile reading on which I have drawn most frequently are, in chronological order, C. M. Hewins, *Books for the Young: A Guide for Parents and Children* (New York: Leypoldt, 1882); Marion E. Potter et al., *The Children's Catalog: A Guide to the Best Reading for Young People Based on Twenty-Four Selected Library Lists* (Minneapolis: Wilson, 1909); "One Hundred Story Books for Children," *Bookman* (New York), November 1922, 367; Mary Wilkinson et al., *The Right Book for the Right Child: A Graded Buying List of Children's Books* (New York: Day, 1933); Laura E. Richards, *What Shall the Children Read?* (New York: Appleton-Century, 1939); Alice M. Jordan, *Children's Classics* (Boston: Horn Book, 1947); Nancy Larrick, *A Parent's Guide to Children's Reading*, sponsored by the National Book Committee (1958; reprint, New York: Pocket, 1959); and Betsy Hearne, *Choosing Books for Children: A Commonsense Guide*, rev. ed. (New York:

Delacorte, 1990). Lists of more general recommendations, not limited to juvenile reading, include Melvil Dewey et al., eds., *A.L.A. Catalog: Eight Thousand Volumes for a Popular Library, with Notes: 1904* (Washington: Government Printing Office, 1904); Isabella M. Cooper, ed., *A.L.A. Catalog, 1926: An Annotated Basic List of Ten Thousand Books* (Chicago: American Library Association, 1926); and J. Sherwood Weber, *Good Reading*, rev. ed., sponsored by the College English Association (New York: Mentor, 1960).

Other sources for gauging esteem include a Children's Literature Association poll cited in "10 Best American Children's Books in 200 Years Listed," *Publishers Weekly*, 23 February 1976, 64; and the three volumes in the Children's Literature Touchstones series, the first of which is Perry Nodelman, ed., *Touchstones: Reflections on the Best in Children's Literature* (West Lafayette, Ind.: Children's Literature Association, 1985).

For the fullest survey of children's own reading preferences in the early twentieth century, see Carleton Washburne and Mabel Vogel, *Winnetka Graded Book List* (Chicago: American Library Association, 1926). Other lists and surveys can be found in Esther Jane Carrier, *Fiction in Public Libraries, 1900–1950* (Littleton, Colo.: Libraries Unlimited, 1985); and Jay B. Hubbell, *Who Are the Major American Writers?* (Durham: Duke University Press, 1972).

Two book-length compilations of the favorite books of famous people are Evelyn B. Byrne and Otto M. Penzler, eds., *Attacks of Taste* (New York: Gotham Book Mart, 1971); and Bernice Cullinan and M. Jerry Weiss, eds., *Books I Read When I Was Young: The Favorite Books of Famous People* (New York: Avon, 1980). Shorter lists, such as "Uncle Wiggily's Karma and Other Childhood Memories," *New York Times Book Review*, 7 December 1986, 46–47, have appeared from time to time in various magazines.

For information on the sales of nineteenth-century and early-twentieth-century works, Frank Luther Mott's *Golden Multitudes: The Story of Best Sellers in the United States* (New York: Macmillan, 1947) has been indispensable. For information on the sales of late-twentieth-century children's literature, I've turned to "All-Time Bestselling Hardcover Children's Books" and "All-Time Bestselling Paperback Children's Books," *Publishers Weekly*, 27 October 1989, 28, 29; "All-Time Bestselling Children's Books," *PW Online Edition*, 1996, www.bookwire.com/pw/articles/childrens/, accessed 4 January 1999; and "Children's Best Sellers," *New York Times Book Review*, 22 May 1994, 26–27. Since July 2000 there have been weekly lists of children's best-sellers in the *New York Times Book Review*.

For current censorship statistics, see the American Library Association website. The listings change yearly, but recent ones include "Harry Potter Series Tops List of Most Challenged Books of 1999," 13 March 2000, www.ala.org/news/archives/v5n12/99bookchallenges.html, accessed 18 August 2000; and "The 100 Most Frequently Challenged Books of 1990–1999," 14 August 2000, www.ala.org/alaorg/oif/top100bannedbooks.html, accessed 18 August 2000.

Useful accounts of professionalization and of the positioning of American literature in the academy include Gerald Graff, *Professing Literature: An Institutional History* (Chicago: University of Chicago Press, 1987); Paul Lauter, "Race and Gender in the Shaping of the American Literary Canon: A Case Study from the Twenties," *Feminist Studies* 9 (1983), reprinted in his *Canons and Contexts* (New York: Oxford University Press, 1991), 22–47; Richard Ruland, *The Rediscovery of American Literature: Premises of Critical Taste, 1900–1940* (Cambridge: Harvard University Press, 1967); David R. Shumway, *Creating American Civilization: A Genealogy of American Literature as an Academic Discipline* (Minneapolis: University of Minnesota Press, 1994); and Kermit Vanderbilt, *American Litera-*

ture and the Academy: The Roots, Growth, and Maturity of a Profession (Philadelphia: University of Pennsylvania Press, 1986).

The three twentieth-century histories of U.S. literature that I have used as touchstones are William Peterfield Trent et al., eds., *The Cambridge History of American Literature* (1917–1921; reprint, New York: Macmillan, 1958), 3 vols.; Robert E. Spiller et al., eds., *Literary History of the United States* (New York: Macmillan, 1948), 3 vols.; and Emory Elliott et al., eds., *Columbia Literary History of the United States* (New York: Columbia University Press, 1988). A fourth comparable compendium is currently in progress: Sacvan Bercovitch et al., eds., *The Cambridge History of American Literature* (Cambridge: Cambridge University Press, 1994–); four of the eight volumes have so far appeared.

Useful accounts of readers' responses to American literature in general include Nina Baym, *Woman's Fiction: A Guide to Novels by and about Women in America, 1820–1870* (Ithaca: Cornell University Press, 1978); Nina Baym, *Novels, Readers, and Reviewers: Responses to Fiction in Antebellum America* (Ithaca: Cornell University Press, 1984); Cathy N. Davidson, ed., *Reading in America: Literature and Social History* (Baltimore: Johns Hopkins University Press, 1989); and James L. Machor, ed., *Readers in History: Nineteenth-Century American Literature and the Contexts of Response* (Baltimore: Johns Hopkins University Press, 1993).

Accounts of children's literature in the United States include Gillian Avery, *Behold the Child: American Children and Their Books, 1621–1922* (Baltimore: Johns Hopkins University Press, 1994); Anne Scott MacLeod, "Children's Literature in America from the Puritan Beginnings to 1870," and Gillian Avery et al., "Children's Literature in America, 1870–1945," in *Children's Literature: An Illustrated History*, ed. Peter Hunt (Oxford: Oxford University Press, 1995), 102–29, 225–51; Jerry Griswold, *Audacious Kids: Coming of Age in America's Classic Children's Books* (New York: Oxford University Press, 1992); Alice M. Jordan, *From Rollo to Tom Sawyer* (Boston: Horn Book, 1948); and Anne Scott MacLeod, *American Childhood: Essays on Children's Literature of the Nineteenth and Twentieth Centuries* (Athens: University of Georgia Press, 1994). Richard L. Darling provides an account of published response to children's literature during a couple of decades in the nineteenth century in *The Rise of Children's Book Reviewing in America, 1865–1881* (New York: Bowker, 1968); Anne H. Lundin addresses the subsequent two decades in "Victorian Horizons: The Reception of Children's Books in England and America, 1880–1900," *Library Quarterly* 64 (January 1994): 30–59.

Useful histories of libraries and librarians include Sidney Ditzion, *Arsenals of a Democratic Culture: A Social History of the American Public Library Movement in New England and the Middle States from 1850 to 1900* (Chicago: American Library Association, 1947); Dee Garrison, *Apostles of Culture: The Public Librarian and American Society, 1876–1920* (New York: Free Press, 1979); Evelyn Geller, *Forbidden Books in American Public Libraries, 1876–1939: A Study in Cultural Change* (Westport, Conn.: Greenwood, 1984); Suzanne Hildenbrand, ed., *Reclaiming the American Library Past: Writing the Women In* (Norwood, N.J.: Ablex, 1996); and Jesse Shera, *Foundations of the Public Library: The Origins of the Public Library Movement in New England, 1629–1855* (1949; reprint, n.p.: Shoe String, 1965). For historical background on U.S. library service to children, see Harriet G. Long, *Public Library Service to Children: Foundation and Development* (Metuchen, N.J.: Scarecrow, 1969); Elizabeth Nesbitt, "Major Steps Forward," in *A Critical History of Children's Literature: A Survey of Children's Books in English*, ed. Cornelia Meigs, rev. ed. (London: Macmillan, 1969), 384–90; and the Spring 1996 issue of *Library Trends* (vol. 44), which includes such essays as Christine A. Jenkins, "Women of ALA Youth Services and Professional Jurisdiction: Of Nightingales, Newberies, Realism and the Right Books, 1937–1945," 813–40, and Kay E. Vandergrift, "Female Advocacy and Harmonious Voices: A History of Public Library Services and Publishing for Children in the United States," 683–719.

The sources on the librarian Anne Carroll Moore that I have found most informative are Barbara Bader, "*Only* the Best: The Hits and Misses of Anne Carroll Moore," *Horn Book* 73 (September/October 1997): 520–29; Julie Cummins, "'Let Her Sound Her Trumpet': NYPL Children's Librarians and Their Impact on the World of Publishing," *Biblion* 4 (Fall 1995): 83–114; and Frances Clarke Sayers, *Anne Carroll Moore* (New York: Atheneum, 1972).

Informative sources on the editor and writer Horace Scudder include Alexander V. G. Allen, "Horace E. Scudder: An Appreciation," *Atlantic Monthly* 91 (April 1903): 549–60; Ellen B. Ballou, "Horace Elisha Scudder and the *Riverside Magazine*," *Harvard Library Bulletin* 14 (Autumn 1960): 426–52; and Ellery Sedgwick, "Horace Elisha Scudder (1890–1898): Missionary of Yankee Culture," in his *The Atlantic Monthly, 1857–1909: Yankee Humanism at High Tide and Ebb* (Amherst: University of Massachusetts Press, 1994), 200–243.

In the realm of twentieth-century publishing for children, especially useful are Leonard S. Marcus's *Margaret Wise Brown: Awakened by the Moon* (Boston: Beacon, 1992) and his collection *Dear Genius: The Letters of Ursula Nordstrom* (New York: HarperCollins, 1998); and Joseph Turow, *Getting Books to Children: An Exploration of Publisher-Market Relations* (Chicago: American Library Association, 1978). Barbara Bader has also been publishing a series of essays in the *Horn Book Magazine* on twentieth-century publishing, including "Macmillan Children's Books, 1919–1995" (September/October 1995): 548–62.

As for individual authors on whom I've focused, the leading Burnett critic is Phyllis Bixler, whose work has appeared in, for instance, *Frances Hodgson Burnett* (Boston: Twayne, 1984) and *The Secret Garden: Nature's Magic* (New York: Twayne, 1996). Ann Thwaite's biography of Burnett, *Waiting for the Party: The Life of Frances Hodgson Burnett, 1849–1924* (New York: Scribner's, 1974), provides much useful information on reception.

For most authors I will highlight collections of criticism, since such collections generally reprint the most influential and provocative essays. But because there has been no anthology of Burnett criticism, I here provide an extended list of shorter works that I have found stimulating: Elisabeth Rose Gruner, "Cinderella, Marie Antoinette, and Sara: Roles and Role Models in *A Little Princess*," *The Lion and the Unicorn* 22 (1998): 163–87; Elizabeth Lennox Keyser, "'Quite Contrary': Frances Hodgson Burnett's *The Secret Garden*," *Children's Literature* 11 (1983): 1–13; U. C. Knoepflmacher, "Little Girls without Their Curls: Female Aggression in Victorian Children's Literature," *Children's Literature* 11 (1983): 14–31; Marghanita Laski, "Mrs. Hodgson Burnett," in her *Mrs. Ewing, Mrs. Molesworth, and Mrs. Hodgson Burnett* (New York: Oxford University Press, 1951), 73–91; Claudia Marquis, "The Power of Speech: Life in *The Secret Garden*," *AUMLA* 68 (November 1987): 163–87; Francis J. Molson, "Frances Hodgson Burnett (1848–1924)," *American Literary Realism* 8 (Winter 1975): 35–41; Heather Murray, "Frances Hodgson Burnett's *The Secret Garden*: The Organ(ic)ized World," in *Touchstones: Reflections on the Best in Children's Literature*, ed. Perry Nodelman (West Lafayette, Ind.: Children's Literature Association, 1985), 1:30–43; Jerry Phillips, "The Mem Sahib, the Worthy, the Rajah, and His Minions: Some Reflections on the Class Politics of *The Secret Garden*,"

The Lion and the Unicorn 17 (1993): 168–94; Judith Plotz, "Secret Garden II; or *Lady Chatterley's Lover* as Palimpsest," *Children's Literature Association Quarterly* 19 (Spring 1994): 15–19; Alan Richardson, "Reluctant Lords and Lame Princes: Engendering the Male Child in Nineteenth-Century Juvenile Fiction," *Children's Literature* 21 (1993): 3–19; Robert Lee White, "Little Lord Fauntleroy as Hero," in *Challenges in American Culture*, ed. Ray B. Browne et al. (Bowling Green, Ohio: Bowling Green University Popular Press, 1970), 209–22; and Anna Wilson, "Little Lord Fauntleroy: The Darling of Mothers and the Abomination of a Generation," *American Literary History* 8 (Summer 1996): 232–58.

The collections of James criticism I have found most helpful are Neil Cornwell and Maggie Malone, eds., *"The Turn of the Screw" and "What Maisie Knew"* (New York: St. Martin's, 1998); Daniel Mark Fogel, ed., *A Companion to Henry James Studies* (Westport, Conn.: Greenwood, 1993); Jonathan Freedman, ed., *The Cambridge Companion to Henry James* (Cambridge: Cambridge University Press, 1998); Roger Gard, ed., *Henry James: The Critical Heritage* (London: Routledge, 1968); Kevin J. Hayes, ed., *Henry James: The Contemporary Reviews* (Cambridge: Cambridge University Press, 1996); and David McWhirter, ed., *Henry James's New York Edition: The Construction of Authorship* (Stanford: Stanford University Press, 1995). Linda J. Taylor provides an annotated bibliography of reviews and other secondary sources in *Henry James, 1866–1916: A Reference Guide* (Boston: Hall, 1982). Two insightful studies of childhood in the work of James are Barbara Everett, "Henry James's Children," in *Children and Their Books: A Celebration of the Work of Iona and Peter Opie*, ed. Gillian Avery and Julia Briggs (Oxford: Clarendon, 1989), 317–35; and Muriel G. Shine, *The Fictional Children of Henry James* (Chapel Hill: University of North Carolina Press, 1968). Other recent stimulating studies include Michael Anesko, *"Friction with the Market": Henry James and the Profession of Authorship* (New York: Oxford University Press, 1986); Richard A. Hocks, "The Several Canons of Henry James," *American Literary Realism* 23 (Spring 1991): 68–81; and John Carlos Rowe, *The Other Henry James* (Durham: Duke University Press, 1998). The *Henry James Review* publishes current scholarship.

The collections of Twain criticism I have found most useful are Frederick Anderson, ed., with the assistance of Kenneth M. Sanderson, *Mark Twain: The Critical Heritage* (New York: Barnes, 1971); Sculley Bradley et al., eds., *Adventures of Huckleberry Finn: An Authoritative Text, Backgrounds and Sources, Criticism*, 2d ed. (New York: Norton, 1977); Louis J. Budd, ed., *Mark Twain: The Contemporary Reviews* (Cambridge: Cambridge University Press, 1999); Gerald Graff and James Phelan, eds., *Adventures of Huckleberry Finn: A Case Study in Critical Controversy* (Boston: Bedford, 1995); James S. Leonard, Thomas A. Tenney, and Thadious M. Davis, eds., *Satire or Evasion? Black Perspectives on "Huckleberry Finn"* (Durham: Duke University Press, 1992); Forrest G. Robinson, ed., *The Cambridge Companion to Mark Twain* (Cambridge: Cambridge University Press, 1995); and Gary Scharnhorst, ed., *Critical Essays on "The Adventures of Tom Sawyer"* (New York: Hall, 1993). Victor Fischer provides an excellent brief overview of *Huckleberry Finn's* early reception in "Huck Finn Reviewed: The Reception of *Huckleberry Finn* in the United States, 1885–1897," *American Literary Realism* 16 (Spring 1983): 1–57. Other book-length studies that have prodded my thinking include Jonathan Arac, *"Huckleberry Finn" as Idol and Target: The Functions of Criticism in Our Time* (Madison: University of Wisconsin Press, 1997); Louis J. Budd, *Our Mark Twain: The Making of His Public Personality* (Philadelphia: University of Pennsylvania Press, 1983); Jocelyn Chadwick-Joshua, *The Jim Dilemma: Reading Race in "Huckleberry Finn"* (Jackson: University Press of Mississippi, 1998); Shelley Fisher Fishkin, *Lighting out for the Territory: Reflections on Mark Twain and American Culture* (New York: Oxford University Press, 1997); and Albert E. Stone, Jr., *The Innocent Eye: Childhood in Mark Twain's Imagination* (New Haven: Yale University Press, 1961). Current Twain scholarship appears in the *Mark Twain Journal*.

Marcia Jacobson, *Being a Boy Again: Autobiography and the American Boy Book* (Tuscaloosa: University of Alabama Press, 1994), provides a good full-length discussion of the boys' book. The best formal discussion of the boys' book is probably Anne Trensky, "The Bad Boy in Nineteenth-Century American Fiction," *Georgia Review* 27 (1973): 503–17; also particularly helpful are Alan Gribben, "Manipulating a Genre: *Huckleberry Finn* as Boy Book," *South Central Review* 5 (1988): 15–21; and Steven Mailloux, "Rhetorical Production and Ideological Performance" and "Cultural Reception and Social Practices" in his *Rhetorical Power* (Ithaca: Cornell University Press, 1989), 57–129.

Two useful collections of Alcott criticism are Janice M. Alberghene and Beverly Lyon Clark, eds., *"Little Women" and the Feminist Imagination* (New York: Garland, 1999); and Madeleine B. Stern, ed., *Critical Essays on Louisa May Alcott* (New York: Hall, 1984). Also valuable is Gregory Eiselein and Anne K. Phillips, eds., *The Louisa May Alcott Encyclopedia* (Westport, Conn.: Greenwood, 2001). Janet S. Zehr, "The Response of Nineteenth-Century Audiences to Louisa May Alcott's Fiction," *American Transcendental Quarterly*, n.s., 1 (December 1987): 323–42, provides an account of nineteenth-century reviews; my *Louisa May Alcott: Contemporary Reviews* is forthcoming from Cambridge University Press. Other studies that have sharpened my thinking include Richard H. Brodhead, "Starting Out in the 1860s: Alcott, Authorship, and the Postbellum Literary Field," in his *Cultures of Letters: Scenes of Reading and Writing in Nineteenth Century America* (Chicago: University of Chicago Press, 1993), 69–106; Christine Doyle, *Louisa May Alcott and Charlotte Brontë: Transatlantic Translations* (Knoxville: University of Tennessee Press, 2000); Elizabeth Lennox Keyser, *Whispers in the Dark: The Fiction of Louisa May Alcott* (Knoxville: University of Tennessee Press, 1993); and Barbara Sicherman, "Reading *Little Women*: The Many Lives of a Text," in *U.S. History as Women's History: New Feminist Essays*, ed. Linda K. Kerber et al. (Chapel Hill: University of North Carolina Press, 1995), 256–60.

Felicity A. Hughes has written about the relationship between fantasy and children's literature in twentieth-century thought in "Children's Literature: Theory and Practice," *ELH* 45 (1978): 542–61. Other studies more sharply focused on fantasy include Brian Attebery, *The Fantasy Tradition in American Literature: From Irving to Le Guin* (Bloomington: Indiana University Press, 1980); Brian Attebery, *Strategies of Fantasy* (Bloomington: Indiana University Press, 1992); W. R. Irwin, *The Game of the Impossible: A Rhetoric of Fantasy* (Urbana: University of Illinois Press, 1976); Rosemary Jackson, *Fantasy: The Literature of Subversion* (London: Methuen, 1981); Jean Laplanche and J.-B. Pontalis, "Fantasy and the Origins of Sexuality," *International Journal of Psycho-Analysis* 49 (1968): 1–18; Eric S. Rabkin, *The Fantastic in Literature* (Princeton: Princeton University Press, 1976); and Tzvetan Todorov, *The Fantastic: A Structural Approach to a Literary Genre*, trans. Richard Howard (Ithaca: Cornell University Press, 1975).

The fullest collection of Baum criticism appears in Michael Patrick Hearn, ed., *The Wizard of Oz*, by L. Frank Baum (New York: Schocken, 1983). Book-length scholarly studies include Neil Earle, *"The Wonderful Wizard of Oz" in American Popular Culture: Uneasy in Eden* (Lewiston, Maine: Mellen, 1993); Raylyn Moore, *Wonderful Wizard, Marvelous Land* (Bowling Green, Ohio: Bowling Green University Popular Press, 1974); Paul Nathanson, *Over the Rainbow: "The Wizard of Oz" as a Secular Myth of America* (Albany:

State University of New York Press, 1991); Suzanne Rahn, *The Wizard of Oz: Shaping an Imaginary World* (New York: Twayne, 1998); Michael O. Riley, *Oz and Beyond: The Fantasy World of L. Frank Baum* (Lawrence: University Press of Kansas, 1997); and Mark Evan Swartz, *Oz before the Rainbow: L. Frank Baum's "The Wonderful Wizard of Oz" on Stage and Screen to 1939* (Baltimore: Johns Hopkins University Press, 2000).

Insightful accounts of response to Baum include Michael Patrick Hearn, "'Toto, I've a Feeling We're Not in Kansas City Anymore . . . or Detroit . . . Or Washington, DC!'" *Horn Book*, January/February 2001, 16–34; and Ann E. Prentice, "Have You Been to See the Wizard?" *Top of the News*, November 1970, 32–44. Hearn is also the editor of *The Annotated Wizard of Oz: Centennial Edition* (New York: Norton, 2000). Provocative pieces that take a cultural studies or new historicist approach include Stuart Culver, "What Manikins Want: *The Wonderful Wizard of Oz* and *The Art of Decorating Dry Goods Windows*," *Representations* 21 (Winter 1988): 97–11; Stuart Culver, "Growing Up in *Oz*," *American Literary History* 4 (Winter 1992): 607–28; Richard Flynn, "Imitation Oz: The Sequel as Commodity," *The Lion and the Unicorn* 20 (1996): 121–31; William Leach, "Strategists of Display and the Production of Desire," in *Consuming Visions: Accumulation and Display of Goods in America, 1880–1920*, ed. Simon J. Bronner (New York: Norton, 1989), 99–132; Susan Wolstenholme, introduction, in *The Wonderful Wizard of Oz*, by L. Frank Baum, World's Classics ed. (Oxford: Oxford University Press, 1997), ix–xliii; and Jack Zipes, "L. Frank Baum and the Utopian Spirit of Oz," an introduction to *Oz* reprinted in his *When Dreams Came True: Classical Fairy Tales and Their Tradition* (New York: Routledge, 1999), 159–82. Salman Rushdie provides an insightful reading of the MGM film in *The Wizard of Oz* (1992; reprint, London: British Film Institute, 1993). *The Baum Bugle* publishes Baum scholarship and Oziana.

The most historically diverse collection of Carroll criticism is Robert Phillips, ed., *Aspects of Alice: Lewis Carroll's Dreamchild as Seen through the Critics' Looking-Glasses, 1865–1971* (New York: Vanguard, 1971); also useful is Donald J. Gray, ed., *Alice in Wonderland: Authoritative Texts of "Alice's Adventures in Wonderland," "Through the Looking-Glass," "The Hunting of the Snark"* (New York: Norton, 1971). Dorothy Otterman Matthews provides the fullest account of nineteenth-century response to Carroll in her dissertation, "The Literary Reputation of Lewis Carroll in England and America in the Nineteenth Century" (Western Reserve University, 1962). Other accounts of response include Michael Hancher, "Alice's Audiences," in *Romanticism and Children's Literature in Nineteenth-Century England*, ed. James Holt McGavran, Jr. (Athens: University of Georgia Press, 1991); and Carolyn Sigler, *Alternative Alices: Visions and Revisions of Lewis Carroll's "Alice" Books* (Lexington: University Press of Kentucky, 1997). And other useful sources include Rachel Fordyce's bibliography, *Lewis Carroll: A Reference Guide* (Boston: Hall, 1988); Martin Gardner, ed., *The Annotated Alice*, rev. ed. (New York: Norton, 2000); and Peter Heath, *The Philosopher's Alice: "Alice's Adventures in Wonderland" and "Through the Looking-Glass"* (New York: St. Martin's, 1974). The journal *Jabberwocky* publishes scholarly work on Carroll.

Of the discussions of Rowling that have so far appeared, the ones in scholarly venues that I have found most useful include Roni Natov, "Harry Potter and the Extraordinariness of the Ordinary," *The Lion and the Unicorn* 25 (2001): 310–27; Philip Nel, "The Harry Potter Phenomenon," in *Dictionary of Literary Biography Yearbook: 1999*, ed. Matthew J. Bruccoli (Detroit: Gale, 2000), 173–79; John Pennington, "From Elfland to Hogwarts, or the Aesthetic Trouble with Harry Potter," *The Lion and the Unicorn* 26 (2002): 78–97;

Judith P. Robertson, "What Happens to Our Wishes: Magical Thinking in Harry Potter," *Children's Literature Association Quarterly* 26 (Winter 2001–2002): 198–211; Lucy Rollin, "Among School Children: The Harry Potter Books and the School Story Tradition," *South Carolina Review* 34 (Fall 2001): 198–208; Nicholas Tucker, "The Rise and Rise of Harry Potter," *Children's Literature in Education* 30 (December 1999): 221–34; and Jack Zipes, "The Phenomenon of Harry Potter, or Why All the Talk?" in his *Sticks and Stones: The Troublesome Success of Children's Literature from Slovenly Peter to Harry Potter* (New York: Routledge, 2001), 170–89. Book-length responses include Elizabeth E. Heilman, ed., *Harry Potter's World: Multidisciplinary Critical Perspectives* (New York: RoutledgeFalmer, 2002); and Philip Nel, *J. K. Rowling's Harry Potter Novels: A Reader's Guide* (New York: Continuum, 2002). Insightful and provocative pieces that have appeared in other venues include Kera Bolonik, "A List of Their Own," *Salon*, 16 August 2000, www.salon.com /mwt/feature/2000/08/16/bestseller/index.html, accessed 22 January 2001; Kimbra Wilder Gish, "Hunting down Harry Potter: An Exploration of Religious Concerns about Children's Literature," *Horn Book*, May/June 2000, 262–71; Paul Gray, "Wild about Harry," *Time*, 20 September 1999, 67–72; Malcolm Jones, "Why Harry's Hot," *Newsweek*, 17 July 2000, 52–56; and Polly Shulman and A. O. Scott, "Not for Children Only," *Slate*, 23 August 1999, http://slate.msn.com/code/BookClub/BookClub.asp?Show= . . . / 99&idMessage=3472&idBio=11, accessed 14 July 2000. The three provocative essays by public intellectuals on which I've focused in Chapter 7 are Harold Bloom, "Can 35 Million Book Buyers Be Wrong? Yes," *Wall Street Journal*, 11 July 2000, A26; Anthony Holden, "Why Harry Potter Doesn't Cast a Spell over Me," *Observer*, 25 June 2000, www.observer.co.uk/review/story/0,6903,335923,00.html, accessed 25 June 2000; and William Safire, "Besotted with Potter," *New York Times*, 27 January 2000, A27.

Collections that address Disney and his place in American culture include Elizabeth Bell, Lynda Haas, and Laura Sells, eds., *From Mouse to Mermaid: The Politics of Film, Gender, and Culture* (Bloomington: Indiana University Press, 1995); The Project on Disney, *Inside the Mouse: Work and Play at Disney World* (Durham: Duke University Press, 1995); and Eric Smoodin, ed., *Disney Discourse: Producing the Magic Kingdom* (New York: Routledge, 1994). Other useful book-length studies are Leonard Maltin, *The Disney Films* (New York: Crown, 1973); Eric Smoodin, *Animating Culture: Hollywood Cartoons from the Sound Era* (New Brunswick, N.J.: Rutgers University Press, 1993); Richard Schickel, *The Disney Version: The Life, Times, Art and Commerce of Walt Disney* (New York: Simon and Schuster, 1968); and Steven Watts, *The Magic Kingdom: Walt Disney and the American Way of Life* (Boston: Houghton Mifflin, 1997). Provocative shorter studies include Ariel Dorfman, "Of Elephants and Ducks," in his *The Empire's Old Clothes: What the Lone Ranger, Babar, and Other Innocent Heroes Do to Our Minds* (New York: Pantheon, 1983), 15–64; and David Forgacs, "Disney Animation and the Business of Childhood," *Screen* 33 (Winter 1992): 361–74.

Index